The Arab State
and
Neo-Liberal
Globalization

The Restructuring of State
Power in the Middle East

The Arab State and Neo-Liberal Globalization

The Restructuring of State Power in the Middle East

Edited by
Laura Guazzone and Daniela Pioppi

THE ARAB STATE AND NEO-LIBERAL GLOBALIZATION
The Restructuring of State Power in the Middle East

Published by
Ithaca Press
8 Southern Court
South Street
Reading
RG1 4QS
UK

www.ithacapress.co.uk
www.twitter.com/Garnetpub
www.facebook.com/Garnetpub
blog.ithacapress.co.uk

Ithaca Press is an imprint of Garnet Publishing Limited.

Copyright © Laura Guazzone and Daniela Pioppi
for the Istituto Affari Internazionali, 2009, 2012

All rights reserved.
No part of this book may be reproduced in any form or by any electronic or mechanical means, including information storage and retrieval systems, without permission in writing from the publisher, except by a reviewer who may quote brief passages in a review.

First Paperback Edition, 2012

ISBN: 9780863723896

British Library Cataloguing-in-Publication Data
A catalogue record for this book is available from the British Library

Typeset by Samantha Barden
Jacket design by Garnet Publishing

Printed and bound in Lebanon by International Press:
interpress@int-press.com

Contents

	List of Figures	vi
	Preface to the Paperback Edition	vii
	Preface and Acknowledgements	xv
	List of Contributors	xvii
1	Interpreting Change in the Arab World *Laura Guazzone and Daniela Pioppi*	1

PART I
CHANGING PATTERNS OF POLITICAL MOBILIZATION

2	Neo-liberal Structural Adjustment, Political Demobilization, and Neo-authoritarianism in Egypt *Joel Beinin*	19
3	An Analysis of Political Change in Lebanon in the Light of Recent Mobilization Cycles *Karam Karam*	47
4	Saudi Arabia's Political Demobilization in Regional Comparison: Monarchical Tortoise and Republican Hares *Steffen Hertog*	73

PART II
CHANGING PATTERNS OF WEALTH ACCUMULATION AND DISTRIBUTION

5	The Political Economy of Authoritarianism in Egypt: Insufficient Structural Reforms, Limited Outcomes and a Lack of New Actors *Ulrich G. Wurzel*	97
6	The Lebanese Socio-economic System, 1985–2005 *Charbel Nahas*	125

7	Globalization and the Saudi Economy: Gains and Losses *Tim Niblock*	159
8	Morocco's Political Economy: Ambiguous Privatization and the Emerging Social Question *Myriam Catusse*	185

PART III
CHANGING PATTERNS OF GLOBALIZED SECURITY

9	The Security Sector in Egypt: Management, Coercion and External Alliance under the Dynamics of Change *Philippe Droz-Vincent*	219
10	The Virtual Sovereignty of the Lebanese State: From Deviant Case to Ideal-type *Elizabeth Picard*	247
11	The Saudi Security Environment: *Plus Ça Change . . .* *Paul Aarts and Joris van Duijne*	275
12	Security Policy and Democratic Reform in Morocco: Between Public Discourse and Reality *Issandr el Amrani*	299
13	The Arab State and Neo-liberal Globalization *Karen Aggestam, Laura Guazzone, Helena Lindholm Schulz, M. Cristina Paciello, Daniela Pioppi*	325

Bibliography	351
Index	381

LIST OF FIGURES

4.1	Composition of the Saudi GDP in the 1960s	78
6.1	Age and unemployment rate	131
6.2	Cumulative migration rate	131

Preface to the Paperback Edition

The wave of anti-authoritarian protests in 2010–12 in several countries of North Africa and the Middle East, which came to be known as the Arab Spring, has deeply affected the Arab state(s) and the Arab world. After the fall of dictators in Tunisia and Egypt, elation about people's power and democratization prevailed in debates about the causes, meanings and possible outcomes of this epochal wave of popular mobilization. These debates turned to disenchantment and pessimism when Libya and Syria's uprisings transformed into ugly civil wars (with NATO intervention in the Libyan case), revolts in Yemen and Bahrain dragged on with much outside meddling and Tunisia and Egypt saw the Islamists sweep the first free elections in their countries' history.

This book provides a different approach to these debates. First published in 2009, it does not deal with the Arab Spring events. Instead it offers a structural analysis of the features of the Arab state in its general evolution in the last three decades and of a cluster of case studies (Morocco, Egypt, Lebanon and Saudi Arabia) deemed representative of the diversity existing within that evolution. This approach has the advantage of providing the current debate about the Arab Spring with much needed keys of analysis and historical depth.

Overall, the analyses presented in this book offer a detailed picture of the situation prevailing just before the outbreak of the Arab Spring. For reasons explained in chapter 1, these analyses consider the political, economic and security sectors as distinct although interconnected sectors of the state's system of power in each of the countries considered. On the basis of this sectorial, country-by-country analysis, the introductory and concluding chapters of the book outline a number of hypotheses and conclusions about the nature of the Arab states' systems of power on the eve of the uprisings. We believe that most of the considerations outlined in this book are still useful, not only for a sound understanding of the root causes of the Arab Spring but also for singling out the structural constrains of present and prospective developments, which will take years to fully unfold and consolidate.

THE ARAB STATE AND NEO-LIBERAL GLOBALIZATION

One of the main findings of the collective research published in this book is that the evolution of the Arab states in last three decades is not exceptional but, on the contrary, is fully in line with trends of change engendered by neo-liberal globalization, and often typifies such changes. Seen in this light the Arab Spring is not (or not only) the final eruption of popular needs long repressed by exceptionally authoritarian and corrupt regimes; it is the local-specific outburst of a global crisis. In fact, the results of three decades of neo-liberalism – i.e. the prevalence of finance over production, the concentration of wealth in the hands of restricted elites dominating pauperized middle and lower groups, the crisis of mass political participation – are found in Western post-democracies as well as in Arab states. The similarity of these problems is mirrored by similarity in people's reactions to them and, namely, of the slogans and the styles of mobilization of the "protesting citizen" (*Time* man of the year, 2011) in both Western and non-Western countries: from the US "Occupy Wall Street" to the Spanish *indignados* and from the Arab youth of Tahrir square to the Indian and Chinese anti-corruption movements. Obviously it is easier to spot these similarities, wide open to media scrutiny, than to catch sight of other parallels, for instance in the restructuring of the labour market in the same countries. The analyses in this book do just this kind of in-depth comparison for the Arab world, taking Morocco, Lebanon, Egypt and Saudi Arabia as examples.

Another major finding of the research published in this book is that it is the social question, and not the level of repression or of internal and external conflict, that is the major single problem affecting the stability of the Arab regimes. In fact, the analyses developed by the book's contributors show how the most destabilizing result of the last three decades' neo-authoritarian and neo-liberal rule is a devastating social question created by the increased inequality and growing marginalization of large part of the Arab population, as exemplified by rising unemployment rates, the rising concentration of former state-owned assets to only a limited number of well-connected and privileged groups, and the declining role of the state in providing social welfare. The worsening of people's standard of living and the termination of the old social contract had already begun, before the Arab Spring's eruption, to meet with resistance (as illustrated in Egypt by the massive strikes of 2006–7) and to fast erode the legitimacy of regimes everywhere (with the partial exception of oil rich countries), triggering the emergence of new forms of opposition.

The countries considered in this book, however, showed a different risk of instability depending not so much on the severity of the social question (as measured for instance by rates of unemployment), but on the country-specific modalities of the prevailing neo-authoritarian neo-liberal Arab state model described in chapters 1 and 13. In this light, Egypt emerged as the most unstable country among the cases considered, with Lebanon, Morocco, and Saudi Arabia being less unstable cases (in descending order) according to the ability of their power structure to cope with their respective social questions. From their different perspectives, the book's chapters on Egypt all argue how the cumulating processes of change had reached a critical mass, a sort of point of no return for the Egyptian regime: the 18 days uprising in 2011 that toppled Mubarak proved this judgement right. At the same time, the chapters on Saudi Arabia explain why the Saudi regime is able to sail relatively safely through the blowing winds of the Arab Spring and even to reap from it an enhanced regional influence; as Aarts and van Duijne noted for this introduction: "Though not immune to the many changes in the region, the Al Saud at present do not seem too shaken by current events".

A review of the present socio-economic situation in Egypt and Tunisia, the countries more advanced in the post-uprisings transformation of the state system, shows that the social question remains unresolved and has actually worsened as a consequence of the instability of the revolutionary period. A more worrying fact, however, is that there is no sign of a strategic rethinking of the economic policies that have contributed to the social question. This lack of change at the very heart of the state power structure is the consequence of the structural conditions underlined in this book: on the one hand the "post-revolutionary" Arab countries are labouring over their transformations in the context of an international environment that, in spite of a devastating global economic and social crisis, continues to be governed, politically and ideologically, by neo-liberal dogmas. On the other hand, despite being labelled as revolutions, the uprisings and wars in Tunisia, Egypt, Libya and Yemen have only succeeded in toppling the head of their regimes, and have not changed much in the composition of their ruling elites. It is true that the political power embodied by representative institutions has changed through elections, and that street protests have earned the people a right of interpellation that no political force can disregard (at least for some time), however the elites that supported the previous regimes have not disappeared and continue to hold considerable power, especially in the economic and security sector. With the exception of the most known figures, pre-uprisings elites can easily adjust to the new circumstances, as shown by their not negligible presence in the newly elected bodies in Tunisia and Egypt side by side with the Islamists, the apparent political winners of the first stage of transformation of the state system.

In effect, to actually monitor the ongoing changes in the structure of power of "post-revolutionary" countries, one should look beyond formal representative institutions and consider that the largely neo-patrimonial and clientelist system of governance typical of the neo-authoritarian neo-liberal Arab state model described in this volume essentially created a fragmentation of the elites (i.e. different segments of business sector, state bureaucracy, security services, ethnic and confessional communities and so on). This pre-uprisings picture of the elites' configuration provides important pieces of information for the analysis of current transitions, whose erratic path (in Egypt and elsewhere) can also be understood to be the result of intra-elite fighting.

Certainly, intra-elite fighting could provide the opportunity for an enlargement of political and economic participation but the recent Arab history analyzed in this volume proves that, without organized social pressures from below, elites will not form the vanguard of democratic change as they did in other historical contexts (e.g. Eastern Europe in the 1990s). Also, the contributions in this book show how – as a consequence of the neo-liberal age – Arab countries are sharing with other regions of the world an acute crisis of political participation exemplified by the decline of political ideologies and mass-based political organizations such as parties and trade-unions in favour of a purported purely technical economic discourse and a revival of religious-ethnic identities.

In Tunisia, Egypt and Yemen the forces that drove out the presidents were spontaneous combinations of many different small groups plus thousands of individuals engaging in political activism for the first time. The largely incoherent nature of the Arab opposition movements in organizational and ideological terms has made it hard for them to translate their initial political success into a sustained, focused vision for change that can successfully pressure elites towards change.

Preface to the Paperback Edition

Compared to the spontaneous and loosely structured nature of 2011–12 Arab social movements, Islamists appeared once again as extremely efficient and deep-rooted organizations, as demonstrated by their historical electoral victory both in Tunisia and Egypt, despite their late and secondary role in the popular uprisings. While the world anxiously watches the first moves of these new majority parties (Ennahda in Tunisia and the Muslim Brotherhood's Freedom and Justice Party in Egypt), the question is whether they truly represent an alternative force to the pre-uprisings system of power: are Islamists willing and capable of providing ideology and structure for organized popular mobilization towards a more equal and sustainable distribution of economic and political resources? The findings of this book suggest – for instance in the case of Egypt, Morocco and Lebanon – that mainstream Islamism is probably closer to the interests of a sub-elite which is wary of popular demands for a radical alteration of the status-quo and, at the end, more in line with the tenets of the (neo-authoritarian) neo-liberal governance.

With regards the security sphere we note in chapter 1 that since "the monopoly of the legitimate use of force is the quintessence of state power ... it is no surprise that any restructuring of the system of power of any given state is intimately linked to the restructuring of its conception of security and of the means to achieve it": the restructuring engendered by the Arab Spring is no exception to this rule. Armies played a central, although diverse, role in the demise of the dictatorships in Tunisia, Egypt and Yemen and they continue to play a key role in overseeing the ensuing transformation of the political system. The changes realized by the uprisings in the security sector are substantive but have not still brought about a complete overhaul of the previous structures of power in this field. The analysis of the Egyptian case presented in this book confirms this judgement. As Droz-Vincent noted for this introduction, under Mubarak the Egyptian security system was based on a model of a "strong state" with the military as rear-back pillar, the alliance with the US as the external pillar and repression as the day-to-day pillar of state–society relations. Every constitutive element of this system is now under challenge but not yet radically transformed. The military is eager to go back to its key behind-the-scene role after obtaining a central position in the future Egyptian system from the new civilian powers, but it has no clear roadmap for achieving this, apart from keeping an iron fist when it feels threatened. The role of the US in Egyptian security remains basically unchanged, even though it has had to absorb into its practical working the need for more public accountability. Finally the routine use of the security apparatus for the repression of public demands is less accepted after the uprising broke the wall of fear in people's mind. However, this novelty in the state–society relationship would require a thorough reform of the police and of the security services, something that the army and the remnants of the old elite are not yet ready to concede. The permanence, although with different modalities, of most of the structural conditions identified in this book for the security sphere of the neo-authoritarian neo-liberal Arab state seems true even when looking at the broader regional and international picture. Here a modest shift in the balance of power between the US and the other international powers (China, the EU and Russia) has surfaced in the management of the crises in Libya, Yemen and Syria. However the US remains the main provider of external security for most Arab countries and it is only the relative disengagement from the Greater Middle East decided by the Obama administration that has left some room open for an increased role of regional powers (such as Turkey, Iran, Saudi Arabia and, with nuances, Israel). Somehow this recreates the regional security situation prevailing before the '90s, which seems fully compatible with the political changes brought about by the uprisings, such as the need to conduct more national foreign and security policies, and does not alter the role that external alliances play in backing the neo-authoritarian neo-liberal regimes.

More generally, the distinction between the various functional areas (politics, economics and security) of state power adopted in this book can provide a rough yardstick for "measuring" changes and continuities in the post-uprisings Arab states.

A final point of introduction to the reading of this book into the post-Arab Spring context, is that the analyses presented here argue that the neo-authoritarian neo-liberal Arab state model has produced, *inter alia*, a fragmented and atomized society, unable to organize politically and kept together by authoritarianism and clientelism. In the absence of a global context conducive to real changes in the economic and security structures it seems plausible not only that more uprisings will erupt because of the enduring social question, but also that post-revolutionary countries will remain unstable for some time. The development of true participative democracies and the reversal of the neo-authoritarian neo-liberal Arab state model is still a possibility, at least for some countries and under certain circumstances; however we must stress that these fragmented societies may also find stability in a renewed kind of neo-authoritarian neo-liberal Arab state, one based on populism, sectarianism and on the "plurality of dictatorial parties", for which today's Iraq may provide an extreme but plausible example.

To conclude, we can say that it is too early to draw any firm conclusion about processes of change which are still unfolding at a global level as well as in the Arab world. Nevertheless the comparison between current events and the analysis of the neo-authoritarian neo-liberal Arab state model presented in this book provides a good guide to understand the roots of change and the structural constrains to its evolution.

Laura Guazzone and Daniela Pioppi
Rome, 15 April 2012

Preface and Acknowledgements

The drive to write this book originated in our growing frustration with the failure of current social sciences' explanatory paradigms to foresee and explain political change in the Arab world. Between 2000 and 2003, we were both involved in a collective research project on the prospects for democratization in the Arab region and we came to the conclusion that, not only was the Arab world not democratizing, but the democratization discourse in its international and regional dimensions was configuring and legitimating a re-structuring of the power system which was in many respects reinforcing the authoritarian and patrimonial nature of the regimes.[1] We also realized that the Arab world was not "exceptional" in its neo-authoritarian trajectory and that the dynamics observable in the region could be taken as local examples of more general, "global" trends. In this respect, the Arab world could profitably enter the realm of comparative politics, but new empirical data and analytical insights were needed as to how the current Arab neo-authoritarian adjustments interact with change at the global level: *What are the effects of the Arab regimes' growing participation, in a subordinate position, in a renewed globalized order? In what ways are current Arab neo-authoritarian regimes different from their post-independence predecessors in terms of social bases and ruling coalitions, distribution of resources, modes of governing, political discourses?*

To answer these and similar questions, in 2005 we launched a research project by the Istituto Affari Internazionali (IAI) of Rome and the Swedish Institute of International Affairs (SIIA) of Stockholm. The project, concluded in 2008, was funded by a generous grant from the Swedish Riksbankens Jubileumsfond (RJ) and the Italian Fondazione della Compagnia di San Paolo. In a first stage of the project, we worked out the overarching rationale of the research on the basis of which a core group from the two participating institutes developed three sectorial papers as the conceptual background to the research. We developed the political concept paper; Maria Cristina Paciello, attached to the IAI for this project, wrote the economic concept paper; while Karin Agge am and Helena Lindholm Schulz, attached to the SIIA for this project, wrote the security concept paper. In a second stage, the core group selected four country case studies (i.e. Morocco, Egypt, Lebanon and Saudi Arabia) and invited an enlarged research group made up of 12 international scholars, three for each chosen country, to develop the project.[2] This enlarged research group met in Rome at the IAI in February 2007 to discuss both the concept papers and the outline of their country research in an informal two-day workshop. The project was concluded in September 2008 with an international conference organized by Gunilla Herolf (SIIA) in Stockholm to discuss the research results with a wider public.

This book would not have seen the light without the help of many people and institutions. First of all, we would like to thank the authors of the country studies for their highly qualified contributions and their stimulating and friendly cooperation for the entire duration of the project. We are also very grateful to Maria Cristina Paciello for her valuable intellectual and technical help. David Ashton efficiently language edited or translated most chapters, while Gabriele Tonne (IAI in-house language editor) did the rest of the language revisions. Last, but not least, we are of course indebted to the two foundations, RJ and Compagnia di San Paolo, whose financial support made the endeavour possible.

Finally, a brief note on transliteration. No diacritical marks have been used in the text. The letter *'ayn* is represented by an opening quotation mark and the *hamza* by a closing quotation mark.

Laura Guazzone and Daniela Pioppi
Istituto Affari Internazionali (IAI) of Rome
November 2008

Notes

1 Bicchi *et al.* 2004.
2 Unfortunately, the selected author for the political case study for Morocco defaulted at the last minute. As a consequence, one of the chapters originally envisaged is missing from the book.

LIST OF CONTRIBUTORS

Paul Aarts is Senior Lecturer in International Relations at the Department of Political Science, University of Amsterdam. He has published widely on Middle East politics and economics. His most recent publications are "Saudi Arabia walks the tightrope", *The International Spectator* 42 (4), December 2007; and (together with Joris van Duijne and Roos Meertens), "Kingdom with borders: the political economy of Saudi-European relations", in Madawi Al-Rasheed (ed.), *Kingdom without Borders: Saudi Political, Religious and Media Frontiers,* Hurst & Co, 2008.

Karin Aggestam is Associate Professor in Political Science and Director of Peace and Conflict Studies at Lund University, Sweden. She is the coordinator of a research project within the EU's 7th Framework Programme on just and durable peace in the Middle East and Western Balkans. Aggestam has published widely in the field of negotiation, diplomacy, conflict resolution and the Middle East peace process.

Issandr el Amrani is the Egypt and North Africa analyst for the International Crisis Group. He is a former editor of the *Cairo Times* and has contributed reports and analyses on Egypt, North Africa and the Middle East to a range of publications, including *The Economist, The Guardian, Middle East Research Information Project*, the *Arab Reform Bulletin*.

Joel Beinin is Professor of Middle East History at Stanford University and was Director of Middle East Studies at the American University in Cairo from 2006 to 2008. His latest books are *The Struggle for Sovereignty: Palestine and Israel, 1993–2005* (co-edited with Rebecca L. Stein), Stanford University Press, 2006; and *Workers and Peasants in the Modern Middle* East, Cambridge University Press, 2001. In 2001/2 he was president of the Middle East Studies Association of North America.

Myriam Catusse is Research Fellow at the Centre National de la Recherche Scientifique and at the French Institute for Middle Eastern Studies (IFPO, Beirut). She holds a PhD in Political Science and is the author of *Le Temps des entrepreneurs: Politique et transformations du capitalisme au Maroc*, Maisonneuve et Larose, 2008. At the IFPO, she leads a research group on "Development: the Making of Public Action in MENA".

Philippe Droz-Vincent is Assistant Professor of Political Science at the Institut d'Etudes Politiques of Paris and Toulouse. He is the author of *Moyen-Orient: pouvoirs autoritaires, sociétés bloquées*, Presses Universitaires de France, 2004; *Vertiges de la puissance, le moment américain au Moyen-Orient*, La Découverte, 2007 and, forthcoming, *Moyen-Orient, 16 idées reçues*, Le Cavalier Bleu, January 2009.

Laura Guazzone is Professor of History of the Contemporary Arab World at the Faculty of Oriental Studies of "La Sapienza", University of Rome and Senior Research Fellow at the Institute of International Affairs (IAI, Rome). Her main interests are the comparative politics and international relations of North African and Middle Eastern countries. She is the author and editor of various books including: *The Islamist Dilemma*, Ithaca, 1995; *The Middle East in Global Change*, Macmillan, 1997; *The Question of Democracy in the Arab World* (in Italian, co-edited with Federica Bicchi and Daniela Pioppi), Polimetrica, 2004.

Steffen Hertog is Kuwait Professor at the Mediterranean Chair at Sciences Politiques in Paris. He has published in a variety of area studies and comparative politics journals, including *Review of International Political Economy*, *International Journal of Middle East Studies*, *Middle East Policy* and *Business History*. His book on Saudi state-building is forthcoming with Cornell University Press.

Karam Karam is Director of Research at the Lebanese Center for Policy Studies (LCPS) in Beirut, an independent non-profit research organization concerned with issues of political, social and economic development, and lecturer at the Université Libanaise. He is the author of *Le movement civil au Liban*, Karthala, 2006.

Helena Lindholm Schulz is Professor in Peace and Development Research, Gothenburg University. Her research focuses on the Palestinian–Israeli conflict, identity politics in relation to security and conflict, diaspora and refugee issues, globalization and new wars as well as on the reconstruction of war-torn societies.

Charbel Nahas has a PhD in Social Anthropology. He conducts research and consultancy work in urban planning and spatial economy, fiscal and financial issues, and social and economic development. Among his recent works are *Un programme socio-economique pour le Liban* (in French and Arabic), Lebanese Centre for Policy Studies, March 2006, and *Exploring Lebanon's Growth Prospects*, The World Bank, August 2007.

Tim Niblock is Emeritus Professor of Middle East Politics at the University of Exeter, having previously been Director of the University's Institute of Arab and Islamic Studies. He taught previously at the Universities of Durham, Khartoum and Reading. Among his recent works are *Saudi Arabia: Power, Legitimacy and Survival*, Routledge, 2006; and *The Political Economy of Saudi Arabia*, Routledge, 2007.

Maria Cristina Paciello is a socio-economist with research experience in the Middle East and North Africa region. She holds a PhD in Development Economics from the University of Florence. Currently, she is lecturer in Economic and Political Geography of Developing Countries at the Faculty of Oriental Studies of "La Sapienza", University of Rome. Her main research interests include inequality and poverty issues, as well as the social implications of economic policies. Among her recent publications are "Income Distribution in the Middle East and North Africa, 1960–2000", in K.S. Jomo, J. Baudot (eds), *Flat World, Big Gaps: Economic Liberalization, Globalization, Poverty and Inequality*, Zed Books, 2007.

Elizabeth Picard is senior researcher at the Institut de Recherches et d'Études sur le Monde Arabe et Musulman (IREMAM), Centre National de la Recherche Scientifique, Aix-en-Provence, where she teaches Middle East politics. She directed the French research centre in Beirut and Amman from 1997 to 2000. She has written extensively on security and identity politics in the Middle East. Among her recent works are *La Politique dans le Monde Arabe*, Armand Colin, 2006; and *Liban, une guerre de 33 jours*, La Découverte, 2007.

Daniela Pioppi is Senior Research Fellow in the Mediterranean and Middle East Programme of the International Affairs Institute (IAI, Rome) and lecturer in the Contemporary History of Egypt at the Faculty of Oriental Studies of "La Sapienza", University of Rome. She holds a PhD from the Department of Political Science, University of Pisa. Among her recent publications are "The Privatization of Social Services as a Regime Strategy: Islamic Endowments (Awqaf) in Egypt", in Oliver Schlumberger (ed.), *Debating Arab Authoritarianism*, Stanford University Press, 2007; and *The Question of Democracy in the Arab World* (in Italian, co-edited with Federica Bicchi and Laura Guazzone), Polimetrica, 2004.

Joris van Duijne holds an MA in International Relations from the University of Amsterdam. He has studied the Gulf region extensively and has spent several months in Riyadh. His publications include (together with Paul Aarts), *Saudi–Iranian Ties: Stocktaking and Look into the Future*, SGIARWPO8-4, August 2008 and (together with Paul Aarts and Ross Meertens), "Kingdom with borders: the political economy of Saudi–European relations" in Madawi Al-Rasheed (ed.), *Kingdom without Borders: Saudi Arabia's Political, Religious and Media Frontiers*, Hurst & Co., 2008.

Ulrich G. Wurzel is a political economist and currently Professor of Economics at the Fachhochschule für Technik und Wirtschaft (FHTW, University for Applied Sciences), Berlin. He is also active as a policy consultant for, among others, German and foreign ministries and the EU Commission.

1
INTERPRETING CHANGE IN THE ARAB WORLD

Laura Guazzone and Daniela Pioppi

Over the last three decades Arab regimes have had to face a number of new or renewed internal and external challenges, ranging from fiscal deficits to legitimacy crises and military interventions. These challenges have been the main driver of a complex process of transformation affecting all aspects of political life, a process which has been analysed by a vast body of literature. Today, a significant number of analysts agree that this transformation neither represents a process of democratization nor is preliminary to such a process, and that, on the contrary, it has actually configured and legitimated a restructuring of the power system that has left unchanged the authoritarian and patrimonial nature of the Arab regimes.[1] Yet, in spite of the growing academic consensus on the neo-authoritarian character of the ongoing political change in the Arab world, its inner and international dynamics and effects have remained in many senses obscure.

For this reason, the research presented in this book aims at clarifying the nature of the political change which has occurred in recent decades in the Arab world by adopting an analytical approach that focuses on the state, understood as a system of power, and on the way it has been restructured worldwide by the dynamics of globalization as they have unfolded under the aegis of neo-liberal policies. As applied here, this approach represents an alternative to analyses of political change and globalization in the Arab world which are predicated – critically or not – on normative paradigms which use the "question of democratization" or the "question of cultural exceptionalism" as the fundamental explanatory variable.

Our assumption is, in fact, that, far from representing an exceptional case of resilience against global trends, change in the Arab world is fully in line with trends of change engendered by neo-liberal globalization elsewhere in the world and may even, in some respects, be seen as typifying the effects of such change.

The first two sections of this introduction set out the rationale for the adoption of an analytical approach centred on the concept of "state restructuring", while the third introduces the starting assumptions behind, and the key issues in, the research, whose findings are presented in the rest of the book and summarized in the final chapter.

1. Interpreting Change in the Arab World: The Limits of the Transition Paradigm

For the last three decades, the study of change in developing countries has been dominated by a framework of analysis – so dominant as to become a paradigm – largely inspired by theories of transition from authoritarianism towards democracy.[2] The so-called democratization theory can be viewed as a particularly fortunate offspring of the modernization theory that, since the late 1950s, has provided the most popular framework of analysis of the developing world in Western social sciences.[3]

Formulated on the basis of the Latin American experiences of the 1970s, the theories of transition postulate the possibility of linear transitions from authoritarianism to liberal democracy whose evolution depends on the existence of structural preconditions, rational choice on the part of the elites and free market reforms.[4] This approach was reinforced at the end of the Cold War by the experiences of transition from communism of Eastern European and former USSR countries, whose early political trajectory added emphasis on the liberalization of the economic environment and active international support as key preconditions for successful transition to democracy. In the same period, political science transition theories merged with – and/or become confused with – a much broader ideological discourse about "the end of history", or more precisely the heralded arrival at "the end point of mankind's ideological evolution and the universalization of Western liberal democracy as the final form of human government" made possible by "an unabashed victory of economic and political liberalism".[5] Since the early 1990s, the analyses and policies based on this ideological discourse proactively considered the transition to liberal democracy and the free market economy as the inescapable result, for the entire world, of the acceleration of globalization due to the revolution in information technologies and the end of the Cold War.

However, by the beginning of the new century, the faith in this "new world order" had disappeared in most circles, and many studies began to criticize the so-called democratization paradigm for its prescriptive and normative bias. More precisely, they questioned the idea that political change can be analysed and measured on the basis of a rigid and universal path going from authoritarianism to democracy through a set of pre-given sequences, thus determining a sort of teleological search for democracy, even where empirical evidence is very weak (to say the least).[6] According to the critics of the democratization "paradigm", the prescriptive and volontaristic bias of transition theory had the consequence of granting a primary importance to the institutional and formal aspect of politics to the disadvantage of an analysis of power relations and variables in both their national and international dimensions.

The Arab world was no exception to this general trend and from the mid-1990s onwards was widely examined through the democratization analytical prism, although "transitologists" have always considered the Arab countries as latecomers and/or exceptional with respect to the much more advanced transitions taking place in most other parts of the world.[7]

In the case of the Arab world, the debate has been further obscured by the interlocking of the "democratization paradigm" with the "cultural exceptionalism" paradigm[8] that posits the historical or essential inability of Islamic society and culture to accept, let alone implement, democracy as understood in the West. Although there have been many variations and evolutions in this debate, its very existence has strongly contributed to the notion of the exceptionality of Arab political culture, namely the exceptional resilience of its political regimes to the "third wave of democracy".

2. Interpreting Change in the Arab World: Globalization and the Changing Structure of State Power

The approach adopted in this book aims precisely at overcoming the limits of the explanatory paradigms considered above by approaching the analysis of the ongoing restructuring of the power system in the Arab world from a different and more comprehensive perspective that, as was said at the beginning of this introduction, interprets change as the effect of the interactions between domestic and international factors in the context of neo-liberal globalization.

We use the expression "neo-liberal globalization" to refer to the specific forms that globalization has taken since the early 1980s, when its dynamics have been intertwined with the spread of neo-liberal policies of privatization, liberalization and deregulation. Moreover, we use the expression "neo-liberal globalization" to indicate a clear distinction between neo-liberalism and globalization: the former is a policy approach, while the latter is a new human condition.[9]

More precisely, globalization is a new context of social relations characterized by the acceleration of interconnections between places and people to an extent which is qualitatively and quantitatively different from any previous historical episode of increased global interaction, such as the period of the great geographical discoveries of the fifteenth and sixteenth centuries or that of the spread of new communication and transport technologies, such as the telegraph and the train in the nineteenth century. In this sense, the real novelty of globalization resides in the global simultaneity of the manifestations it produces in the different spheres of social relations: culturally (in the "village" of global information), economically (in the global financial market), ideationally (in global consciousness), physically (in global climate change) and so on.

While the nature and effects of today's globalization remain subject to debate, there is no doubt that in the last three decades the accelerated growth of global relations has been dominated by and oriented towards a dominant neo-liberal worldview. Neo-liberalism is a policy approach first adopted in the US and the UK in the Reagan and Thatcher years which interpreted and constructed globalization as an unstoppable economically driven process that could only be accompanied by a policy framework based on market economics and more specifically privatization, liberalization and deregulation.

Powerfully sponsored by the leading Western powers and by an emerging global managerial class, the neo-liberal policy framework has derived its strength from the simultaneous pursuit of the policies of privatization, liberalization and deregulation worldwide and across multiple levels and channels of governance including international institutions, supra-state agencies, national governments, local governments and private institutions. This simultaneity has created a global swing from statist to decentralized regulation for all sort of social interactions, not only in the principal fields of economics such as trade, finance and production. This swing towards decentralized regulation has been widely seen as the phasing-out of the state as the overarching structure of social organization and the "retreat of the state" in the face of the unstoppable forces unleashed by globalization, such as civil society, market forces and transnational actors.[10]

Recent studies on Arab countries, however, have effectively demonstrated that neo-liberal political and economic reforms do not necessarily result in a loosening of the state's control over society and, hence, the emergence of independent actors.[11] In countries like Morocco and Egypt, for example, privatization processes have represented a chance for ruling elites to reorganize or, better, shift patronage networks towards the private sector without undermining the power of the state as the ultimate source of rent. On the contrary, they have provided the state with new sources of wealth and new opportunities for accumulation and distribution. In fact, the emerging private sector in Arab countries remains dependent upon state connections for its own survival and can thus be easily coopted by the regimes.

At the political level, the introduction of limited or formal institutional reform and multiparty systems allows, in the best scenario, for a system of controlled and limited representation of the social groups that have benefited from economic reform. Such a system temporarily eases internal tensions and bolsters the international legitimacy of the regime while most of the population remains excluded from significant political processes, as demonstrated by the lack of social constituencies of most opposition parties and groups. In a similar fashion, the restructuring of the state in the security sector has not diminished the resort to internal and external violence, but quite to the contrary has in many cases increased the regime's "securitization" of public policies and enhanced the role of physical intimidation and repression as the state's central device for the management of the increasingly diversified demands of international partners, competing elites and popular movements.

These empirical findings question the state retreat/expanding society approach that characterizes much transition literature. In fact, they all indicate that the state is still the main source of authority and control, although it might delegate some of its functions to private actors and use more indirect and sometime informal modes of government.[12]

The empirical observation of the endurance of state power in the Arab world has produced a wide-ranging debate on the Arab states' exceptional "resistance" to global trends.[13] In general, this "post-democratization" literature emphasizes the successful survival strategies of the incumbent Arab elites that have allowed them exceptionally to maintain state power despite externally imposed political and economic reforms.

However, the existence of a coherent global trend towards a reduction of state power to which the Arab world is supposed to be "resistant" is far from being proved. At closer inspection, in fact, not only does the state not seem to be in question globally, but it also significantly remains the main internationally recognized framework for political action and the main mediation structure between the global and the local.[14] Local ruling elites in the Arab world derive their power and their patronage networks precisely from their control of a globally recognized state, just as political and economic elites in core industrialized countries utilize state power to expand and protect their interests.

In fact, the idea of a global trend of state "retreat" and, we add consequently, the opposite but symmetrical thesis of the Arab state's exceptional resilience to this trend[15] are based on a substantialist and normative definition of the state as artificially separated from the social group holding power within it and from society at large. Instead, considering the state as a system of power which can extend its control well beyond its formal institutions leads to a more useful approach for the study of the dynamics of change engendered by globalization in the Arab world, as elsewhere. Taking this approach, we see that the state can "retreat" from certain functions (such as providing social services to the population) as a consequence of privatization and/or liberalization, but can still maintain its control over the economy and the accumulation and distribution of wealth through its informal patronage networks. In addition, the appearance of extra-state actors, apparently in opposition to or competition with the state itself, can be interpreted as a redeployment of the state, using new strategies that demonstrate a growing reliance on private intermediaries such as the informal association of state officials with private entrepreneurs in most Arab countries (this can be seen also in the US or Italy), with smugglers in Morocco or with private providers of social services – including NGOs and Islamists – in Egypt and Morocco.[16]

Hence, what is at issue at the global level (and in the Arab world) is not the relevance of the state as a system of power, but the forms and points of state intervention and the nature of the values and norms that the state reproduces. In fact, the role, functions and formal boundaries of the state have constantly been reformulated according to the results of the struggle for the management and distribution of political and economic resources. This constant reformulation has produced historically and geographically different definitions of what pertains to the private sphere and what to the public; what distributional role the state should have; what is the sacred realm of national sovereignty and what is the sphere of international competence. In this perspective, the epoch we live in does not necessarily represent a radical divide from the past, but it does definitely correspond to a significant alteration of the distribution of political and economic resources both within states and between them. Globalization in the context of neo-liberal policies could therefore be seen as just one specific phase of the continuous historical process of state restructuring, both for industrialized core countries and for peripheral weak states.

As varied as they may be, reforms adopted in pursuit of neo-liberal policies have several common characteristics: they all find approval in (neo-)liberal ideological discourse, they all make increasing use of private means of governing and they all alter not only the forms of economic regulation but also those of political regulation and sovereignty. In other words, they all displace, relativize and redraw the borders between the "public" and the "private".[17]

However, the effects, arrangements and responses to this global process of restructuring of the state towards an increased use of private and indirect modes of government vary greatly from context to context, for instance between Western democracies and authoritarian Arab regimes, depending *inter alia* on the local historical configuration of power, so that some global trends (for example the change in the distributional role of the state reflecting changes in the power relation between labour and capital in favour of the latter) result in very different local or national arrangements or responses.

As the case studies in this book will show, the restructuring of Arab states in response to neo-liberal globalization is characterized by the emergence and gradual consolidation of a new model of authoritarian political regime, in which the state increasingly represents the sum of the private interests of the members of the regime and is less and less accountable to its own citizens (i.e. privatization of the state). This development is characterized by a fragmentation of the power structure and by an increase in informal modes of government (such as neo-patrimonialism and corruption), with a parallel political and economic marginalization of large social sectors.

3. Interpreting Change in the Arab World: Key Issues and Case Studies

The ideas outlined above represent the starting-point and common conceptual framework for the empirical research presented in the following chapters. The design of the research was organized to test the validity of our starting hypotheses and its scheme is quite simple. We selected four Arab countries as case studies – Morocco, Egypt, Lebanon and Saudi Arabia – and asked a group of international scholars of the Middle East to analyse the changes that have taken place in each of these four countries since the 1980s in the three main sectors of traditional state power: politics, economics and security. The three parts into which this book is divided mirror this division. In choosing to focus the research on these three sectors we were aware of the fact that from many points of view the three sectors are not equivalent, mostly because the "security" sector does not correspond to any distinct fundamental structure of social interactions as politics and economics do. Nevertheless we decided to consider security as a distinct sector of the power system not just because it is commonly accepted as a distinct field of research, but because we considered it particularly relevant to the object of our research: not only is the monopoly of the legitimate use of force the quintessence of state power, but also the military and the security apparatus have had a central role in the history of the formation of the postcolonial Arab states and regimes.

The selection of the national cases was based on the principles of representation and most different comparison. First, the four countries selected are representative of the different sub-types of political, economic and security conditions that have existed in the Arab world since independence. At the same time, these countries are oriented toward different sub-complexes of the Arab world and, to a certain extent, are representative of the conditions prevailing in their respective sub-regions: the Maghreb for Morocco; the Mashreq for Lebanon; the Gulf for Saudi Arabia; and the entire Arab world for Egypt.

For each of the three sectors of traditional state power – politics, economics and security – we singled out a number of research issues that we deemed representative of the ways in which the restructuring of state power as a result of neo-liberal globalization has taken place. The list of key indicators of state restructuring in the political, economic and security sectors was thoroughly discussed with the scholars involved in the project and, at the end of the discussion process, some issues were dropped, some were refined and/or framed in different terms and others were considered relevant only for certain of the countries considered.

Following this design, our research project has "produced" a total of 11 case studies – the chapters of this book – whose findings can be read and compared along three main axes:

(a) a *sectoral* axis that reveals the differences and similarities between the processes of change in the economic, security and political sectors;
(b) a *country-system* axis that highlights the specificities of different national trajectories within the general patterns of the restructuring of the (Arab) state as a result of neo-liberal globalization;
(c) a *regional* axis that looks at the features of a model of the "new" Arab state and its modalities of participation in the new globalized international order.

In the following paragraphs we will briefly present our starting hypotheses as regards the key indicators of the change that has taken place both globally and in the Arab states in the three fundamental sectors of traditional state power under consideration. In the concluding chapter of the book the issues and hypotheses introduced here will be reconsidered in the light of the findings of the various case studies presented in the intervening chapters.

3.1 Key research issues in the political sector: changing patterns of participation and mobilization

Globally, as well as in the Arab world, the general direction of change in the political arena is, above and beyond the different political contexts, towards a strong elitism in and privatization of political decisions. Decisions are increasingly taken by restricted circles and technocrats, often through private or semi-private institutions and without democratic oversight, where such oversight exists. In addition, one can observe a marked decline in political ideologies and mass-based political organizations in favour of a purported purely technical economic discourse and a revival of globalizing religious-ethnic identities.

In the Arab countries, new patterns of political participation and mobilization have emerged as the result of domestic and international pressure for political reform. Accordingly, the change which has occurred in the political sector is the result of the interaction between, firstly, the changing political strategies of globalizing Arab regimes; secondly, the changing elites, their internal competition and external relations; and, finally, the depoliticization and demobilization of the middle and lower social strata.

As far as the strategies of the regimes are concerned, renewed participatory mechanisms for compliant elites have been combined with repressive policies towards political actors that are potentially autonomous or that simply have a grassroots base (e.g. the Islamists). Top-down political liberalization has been accompanied by a marked decline in nationalist ideology (where, as in Egypt, it constituted a pillar of regime legitimacy), the diffusion of a pervasive pro-reform "technical" discourse and a parallel reinforcement of informal (neo-patrimonialism, private–public symbiosis) and communitarian (tribal, ethnic, religious) affiliation or cooptation.[18] One result of this process is increased elite variety and increased competition between different elite factions.[19] The new and old elites blur the lines between opposition and regime more and more and have a primary interest in building their own constituencies but no interest in politicizing social conflict for fear of undermining the status quo and hence losing their privileged status. This is why the main liberal, nationalist or leftist parties in the Arab countries evidently lack a popular basis and do not offer alternative political programmes. They are more tools for client-seeking than channels for the expression of competing social interests.

The only partial exception to this trend is the Islamist movements with a reformist political wing (e.g. the Justice and Development Party in Morocco, the Muslim Brotherhood in Egypt or the Islamic Action Front in Jordan). However, in countries such as Egypt and Jordan, the religious-conservative bourgeoisie – which benefited from the oil boom and economic reform – has also used its Islamist popular constituencies to bargain for a greater role within the ruling coalition. An apparent counter-tendency in all countries of the region is the Islamic and non-Islamic associational sector (non-governmental organizations etc.). Many of the opposition reform movements of recent years have been organized and led by associations or platforms of associations (for example *Kifaya* in Egypt, the Movement for the Reform of the *Mudawana* in Morocco or the *Qornet Shehwan* Gathering for the Syrian withdrawal in Lebanon). However, associations can hardly replace the role of political parties and trade unions in the long run in terms of mass representation, and they often indeed contribute to the fragmentation of the political landscape.

3.2 Key research issues in the economic sector: changing patterns of the accumulation and distribution of wealth[20]

Neo-liberal globalization has been at work first and foremost in the economic realm, where its main trends are well known. The privatization of the processes of production and exchange has not only taken the form of the sale of property from the public to the private sector, but also of the outsourcing of former public services (including education, transport and health) that often involves the creation of hybrid public–private partnerships with little democratic accountability. Liberalization has brought the elimination of restrictions on freedom of action, but only in sectors and areas of major interest to the strongest states, corporations and individuals; thus foreign investment and exchange has been liberalized, but, for example, migration and trade in textiles products have not. The Arab world has been no exception to these policies and their effects.

Economic liberalization measures have been used mainly by incumbent elites as a strategic tool for restructuring external relations (e.g. negotiating external rents or reorienting international trade) and redistributing internal resources (e.g. coopting new social groups and excluding others). For instance, privatization policies in Morocco, Egypt and Jordan – just to name a few – have resulted in a shift in patronage networks and the formation of new crony capitalists, rather than in the creation of competitive markets. At the same time, the reduction in state budgets and the decline of social services have resulted in the growing marginalization of a large part of the population.[21]

With the structural adjustment programmes of the 1980s and 90s, Arab governments, with the exception of Algeria, did not cut social spending as drastically as other countries. However, there is evidence that the social policies of the past have been challenged by declining incomes and the neo-liberal agenda.[22] Countries are increasingly unable to finance or sustain their previous levels of health, educational and welfare services. In this context, the state reorganizes itself by increasingly delegating its social welfare functions to private and informal actors. The emergence of various private/semi-public institutions established by key political figures to channel aid provided by private sources to the needy is an example of state restructuring increasingly based on indirect/private modes of government, but not of a decline in the capacity of the state understood as a system of power.

Structural adjustment policies were unable to create sufficient jobs to keep pace with the steady increase in the workforce. The obligation to liberalize trade and reduce customs duties as a result of joining the World Trade Organization (WTO) and the Euro-Mediterranean Partnership Agreements also exposed local industries to unequal competition, resulting in increased rates of closure of many industrial units or in the further informalization of the labour market. Moreover, under the competitive pressures associated with globalization, Arab governments started to implement measures in favour of capital at the expense of labour. This tendency appears clearly in the Arab countries' attempts to create free-trade zones providing tax exemptions and other incentives to foreign companies.

Most Arab countries also began to revise their labour laws to introduce greater labour market flexibility in the second half of the 1990s: Algeria, Jordan and Tunisia amended their labour laws in 1996, while Egypt and Morocco adopted a new labour code in 2003.[23] Yet, in order to minimize social conflict at a time when unemployment and social tensions are on the increase, Arab states are also reconfiguring labour relations, with the result that trade unions are losing ground everywhere in the region.

3.3 Key research issues in the security sector: changing patterns of global (in)security

The monopoly of the legitimate use of force is the quintessence of state power and hence it is no surprise that any restructuring of the system of power of any given state is intimately linked to the restructuring of its conception of security and of the means to achieve it; the process of state restructuring under neo-liberal globalization is not an exception to this rule. Since the late 1980s, a number of developments linked to globalization, such as the so-called revolution in military affairs and the emergence of global terrorism, have profoundly modified security perception and policies. However, it is not the emergence of new global threats and forms of conflict that has changed the nature of international security, but, conversely, it is the restructuring of the state due to globalization and, in some extreme cases, the disintegration of the state (the failed state) that has brought about the present reconfiguration of international security conditions.[24] Globally and in the Arab world, the main features of this reconfiguration have been the emergence of the so called "post-modern" or "new" wars, and a strong securitization of public policies. New wars can be described as a mixture of war, organized crime and massive violations of human rights, supported by an informal criminalized economy and waged for particularistic political goals by actors who are both global and local and public and private.[25] "Securitization" can be defined as the construction of a policy subject – e.g. migration – as essential for the survival of the state or of society in order to legitimize the use of extraordinary means to solve the perceived problem.[26]

The effects of this reconfiguration of international security have been particularly evident and pervasive, although not unique or exceptional, in the Arab world, and especially in the Arab Middle East, to such an extent that the conflicts presently raging in the Middle East in and about Iraq, Lebanon and Palestine are among the most glaring examples of new wars. More broadly, the Arab world – for the reasons analysed below – can be seen as typifying the effects of neo-liberal globalization in the security sector as well.

Firstly, there is a strong link between the "new" global conflicts and regional conflict formation.[27] The new patterns of international security have come to be perceived as a global phenomenon, namely with regard to *al-Qa'ida*-style global terrorism, through conflicts which have originated in the Arab Middle East, such as the Egyptian–Saudi roots of Sunni jihadism in Afghanistan, the revival of the Israeli–Palestinian conflict since 2000 and Iraqi insurgency since 2004.

Secondly, there is an enduring history of strong foreign involvement in the Arab region. Indeed, the unique concentration of European and US security concerns in the region, as represented by energy resources, Israel's survival, migration flows to the EU, and the sanctuaries of global jihadism, has translated into different kinds of repeated political and military intervention over the last three decades.

Thirdly, the restructuring of state power in the political and economic sectors, as described above, has increasingly fragmented states and societies in the Arab world, thus facilitating (and often encouraging) the permanence and/or re-emergence of sub-state ethnic and confessional identities, particularly through the increasing privatization and/or communitarization of the provision of public goods, including security. In this context, the relationship between sovereign territoriality and the redistribution of resources is particularly relevant,[28] and the enhanced capacity of non-state actors to take control of and distribute resources has reinforced their claims to political authority, as in the case for example of *Hezbollah* in Lebanon.

Finally, change in the relations between the political regime and the state's security institutions (the armed forces, the police and the intelligence services) represents a crucial, although less visible, facet of the restructuring of the power system in the political as well as the security sector. In the weak Arab states, such as Lebanon, Yemen or Sudan or the failed Arab states, such as Iraq, Palestine or Somalia, all new patterns of globalized security are fully evident. They can be seen in the high level of direct outside military intervention, in the inability to provide basic security goods (territorial integrity, physical survival) at a purely national level and the consequent limited sovereignty of security institutions and regimes, and, finally, in the key role that non-state actors, such as ethnic or confessional communities, transnational "terrorist" networks, humanitarian NGOs or private contractors, have acquired in security affairs. In the "stronger" Arab states, such as Morocco, Egypt or Saudi Arabia, the most prominent changes in the security sector are the increasing securitization of public policies and the ensuing banalization of violence (routine torture and physical intimidation of opponents). In turn, all aspects of the reconfiguration of international security have a influence on changes in relations between the political regime and the state's security institutions, and translate not only into different patterns of civilianization of the regime and institutionalization of the armed forces, but also into an increasingly patrimonial management of law and order and military institutions linked to the increased role in business of security institutions and personnel.[29]

NOTES

1. Cf., for instance, Brumberg 2002; Diamond 2002; Albrecht *et al.* 2004; or Bicchi *et al.* 2004.
2. O'Donnell *et al.* 1986; Huntington 1991.
3. For an appraisal of the modernization theory, cf. Gilman 2007; for its early application to the questions of democracy and of the Middle East, cf. Lipset 1959 and Lerner 1958 respectively.
4. Different authors have prioritized these components differently; hence our reference to "theories" of transition.
5. Quotes from Fukuyama 1989.
6. Carothers 2002.
7. Norton 1996; Salamé 1994; Brynen *et al.* 1998.
8. For an analysis of the interlocking use of these two paradigms, see Guazzone 2004.
9. This distinction and the ensuing analysis follows Scholte 2005a and 2005b.
10. Cf., for instance, World Bank 1997.
11. Hakimian *et al.* 2001.
12. Hibou 2004, pp. 1–46.
13. Henry *et al.* 2001.
14. Bayart 2004; Hibou 2004, pp. 1–46.
15. Cf., for instance, Henry *et al.* 2001.
16. Hibou 2004, pp. 1–46; but also Mitchell 1991.
17. Hibou 2004, p. viii.
18. Cf., for instance, Albrecht *et al.* 2004; Pripstein Posusney *et al.* 2005; or Bicchi *et al.* 2004 and the literature cited therein.
19. Perthes 2004.
20. Many of the ideas elaborated in this section are taken from the background concept paper for the economic sector of the research (Paciello 2006).
21. Cf., for example, Karshenas *et al.* 2006.
22. Ibid.
23. International Labour Organization (n.d.).
24. Clark 1999, pp. 107–26; Barkawi *et al.* 1999; Kaldor 2006.
25. Kaldor 2006, pp. 1–14.
26. Buzan *et al.* 1997.
27. Leenders 2007a and 2007b; cf. also Ehteshami 2007.
28. Bayart 1993, pp. 74–5; Duffield 2001, pp. 136–40.
29. Bellin 2005, pp. 21–41.

Part I

Changing Patterns of Political Mobilization

2

NEO-LIBERAL STRUCTURAL ADJUSTMENT, POLITICAL DEMOBILIZATION AND NEO-AUTHORITARIANISM IN EGYPT[1]

Joel Beinin

Introduction

When Egypt was the centre of gravity of the Arab world in the 1950s and 60s, President Gamal Abd al-Nasser could mobilize hundreds of thousands to support a vaguely defined pan-Arab nationalism and Arab socialism. The defeat in the 1967 Arab–Israeli war destabilized the entire Arab system. The rise of Arab petro-power following the 1973 Arab–Israeli war began a still incomplete remaking of the entire Arab region. Because Nasser championed secular Arab nationalism and Arab socialism and his successor, Anwar al-Sadat, demonstratively articulated an alternative orientation, the transformations prompted by the 1967–73 conjuncture were perhaps most dramatic in Egypt. Political community and political culture were reimagined; various forms of Islamism replaced secular Arab nationalism as the dominant populist discourse; authoritarian populism gave way to bureaucratic authoritarianism; Egypt and the broader region began to be reintegrated into the transnational political economy on a subordinate basis regulated by a new mode of neo-liberal capital accumulation. While the official opposition parties have become ineffectual, a diverse Islamist movement, an extra-parliamentary protest movement and a workers' movement have emerged to challenge the status quo.

The public face of the regime has changed, or perhaps merely aged, under President Hosni Mubarak. A putatively "reform" wing within the ruling National Democratic Party (NDP) is manoeuvring to contain opposition to neo-liberal economic development and secure the succession of first son Gamal Mubarak to the presidency. Economic and political changes since the mid-1970s, while significant, have neither unequivocally reshaped the economy nor undermined the regime's grip on power. Consequently, the contest for Egypt's future remains undecided.

The conjuncture of 1967–73 had global, regional and local features, all of which informed the possibilities for collective action and political mobilization in post-1973 Egypt. Globally, the Fordist-Keynesian regime of capital accumulation, which prevailed from the Bretton Woods Agreement of 1944 until the delinking of the dollar from gold and the establishment of floating exchange rates in 1971–3, came to an end. The transition to a neo-liberal regime of flexible accumulation and stabilization and structural adjustment programmes promoted by the United States (US) and British governments, the International Monetary Fund (IMF), and the World Bank followed the global recession of 1973–5 and the subsequent decade of stagflation. Politically, the United States was defeated in Vietnam and its dominance challenged in Central America, Portugal's African empire collapsed, and Britain withdrew from "East of Suez" in 1971. The US assumed primary responsibility for guarding the oil resources of the Persian Gulf, enhancing the likelihood of its armed intervention in the region.

Regionally, the Arab defeat of 1967 was accompanied by a retreat from economic nationalism exemplified by Egypt's 1974 "open door" (*infitah*) policy and the imposition of neo-liberal economic policies through stabilization and structural adjustment agreements between the international financial institutions and Egypt, Jordan, Morocco and Tunisia during the 1980s and 90s.[2] The oil boom of 1974–86 altered the circulation patterns of labour and capital and infused cash into local Islamist projects as well as the anti-Soviet *jihad* in Afghanistan (1979–92), which cycled back into the Arab world, most violently to Egypt and Algeria. These economic changes reshaped the possibilities for collective action and political mobilization, although not in a direct and mechanical way.

In Egypt, this conjuncture is indelibly marked by the country having been the first Arab state to sign a peace treaty with Israel and its foreign policy realignment with the United States. As a reward for signing the 1979 Camp David accords and the 1982 Egyptian–Israeli treaty, Egypt has received over USD 60 billion in US economic and military aid since 1979, the second highest total after Israel.[3] This foreign policy reorientation became an easy target for both secular and Islamist forces seeking to mobilize opposition to the regime.

1. The Mubarak Regime: From Relative Tolerance to Neo-authoritarianism

The regime of Hosni Mubarak, who came to power after Sadat's assassination in 1981, can be divided into two periods. In the first decade, Mubarak lightened the hand of the repressive state apparatus on the regime's opponents. He released the 1,300 political prisoners Sadat arrested a month before his assassination. Opposition press and political parties were given more leeway. Members of the still nominally illegal Society of Muslim Brothers were allowed to run, as individuals, in an alliance with the *Wafd* as candidates in the 1984 election for the People's Assembly and again in a more ideologically compatible Muslim Brothers–Labour Party "Islamic Alliance" in the 1987 election. But, like his predecessors, Mubarak never contemplated a democratic rotation of power.

Applying Guillermo O'Donnell's terminology, the Nasser regime was authoritarian-populist, while the Sadat regime and the first decade of Mubarak's rule were bureaucratic-authoritarian. The oil boom accelerated the circulation and investment of oil wealth, enhanced the political capacities of Islamist forces, and allowed Sadat to delay implementing neo-liberal policies after a first effort to cut food subsidies sharply ignited widespread popular rioting in January 1977. The oil bust prompted somewhat less dilatory implementation of the neo-liberal agenda symbolized by the 1991 Economic Reform and Structural Adjustment Programme (ERSAP) agreements with the IMF and World Bank. Since then, deepening authoritarian rule masked by limited and reversible political liberalization, political demobilization enforced by varying degrees of naked coercion and, since 2004, more vigorous implementation of neo-liberal policies have marked the emergence of neo-authoritarianism.[4] The Mubarak regime excused its neo-authoritarianism and obtained sanction for it from its Western patrons because of Islamist violence, the successes of non-violent Islamism, the 1986 riot of the Central Security Forces, and popular opposition to the emerging neo-liberal order.

Muslim Brothers occupied 38 of the 60 seats won by the Islamic Alliance in 1987, a strong signal that despite the constraints of Egypt's autocratic political system they had become a powerful force. These electoral successes led Abd al-Munim Abu al-Futuh, head of the Cairo University Student Union from 1974 to 1977, and other younger Muslim

Brothers leaders to develop a plan to contest the leadership of Egypt's professional associations. Under the banner of the "Islamic Trend" or the "Islamic Voice", they and their allies ran for positions on the executive boards of professional associations enrolling some two million engineers, doctors, dentists, pharmacists, lawyers, journalists, teachers, commercial employees, agronomists, and others. By 1992, most of the associations and university faculty clubs were in their hands.

The Islamic Trend's message of equity, social justice, moral renewal, and criticism of official corruption and neglect of the common welfare provided a cogent explanation for the social experiences and blocked ambitions of students and recent graduates and was an important factor in their professional association victories. Wickham offers this social movement theory explanation for the Islamist successes:

> Graduates became Islamists not because of the intrinsic appeal of the *da'wa* but because the networks of its transmission were deeply embedded in urban, lower-middle-class communities; its social carriers were familiar and respected; and its content resonated with the life experience and belief system of potential recruits.[5]

The Muslim Brothers focused on building institutions and social networks, which eventually made them the leading Islamist organization and the strongest opposition to the regime. In contrast, several smaller groups adopted *jihad*. In June 1985, Islamist radicals attempted to assassinate Hosni Mubarak during his trip to Addis Ababa. This was followed by a rash of fire bombings of video rental stores by the *Najun min al-Nar* ("Saved from Hellfire") group, attacks on Christians in several provinces in 1986 and 1987, and three attempted assassinations of prominent pro-regime personalities in 1987. The Islamic Group (*al-Jama'a al-Islamiyya*) launched an armed offensive signalled by the assassination of secularist journalist, Faraj Fuda, in June 1992. Its targets included the tourist industry, culminating in a massacre of 58 foreigners and 4 Egyptians in Luxor on 17 November 1997. The combination of repression and loss of credibility due to this incident ended the viability of the *jihad* option in Egypt. But the regime did not end the state of emergency in effect since 1981 or restore civil and human rights.

The Mubarak regime's relationship to the Islamists has been complex. It largely succeeded in annihilating the armed Islamist opposition by military measures, indefinite detentions without charges, trials in security courts without appeal, systematic torture, and extra-judicial executions.[6] Simultaneously, it sought to outflank and coopt the Islamists by promoting a state-sponsored Islam. Until 1991, it also allowed Egyptians to join the anti-Soviet *jihad* in Afghanistan.

Although the Muslim Brothers have been tolerated most of the time, the extent of toleration depends on the whims of the regime. It is useful to the regime that the Brothers appear to be the only alternative to its "secularism". However, they cannot be allowed to become strong enough to alter the status quo. The Brothers, in turn, do not seek to threaten the regime because doing so would endanger the network of social services and other institutions which form the social base of their political power.

The collapse of the oil boom in 1985–6 increased pressure on Egypt from the international financial institutions to adopt neo-liberal Washington consensus policies resulting in price increases, falling real wages, and fewer opportunities for labour migration.[7] In response, there was a sharp rise of workers' collective actions in 1984–9; some 50 to 75 collective actions a year were reported in the Egyptian press during these years, surely not a comprehensive tally.[8] Some elements of the workers' movement began to assume an insurgent political character linked to both the legal and underground left. Local workers newspapers and organizations were established in the industrial centres of Helwan, Mahalla al-Kubra and Shubra al-Khayma.[9]

Most working-class collective actions of this period involved public sector workers. In the first three post-open-door policy decades, the capacity for collective action of private sector employees was generally low. Many private enterprises are located in the new cities on the periphery of Cairo where the social fabric creating mutual obligations is still weak. Therefore strikes of workers in these enterprises have never won broad support from the surrounding population, as regularly happens in the established textile centres of Kafr al-Dawwar or Mahalla al-Kubra. There are few trade unions in the private sector. About 1,300 private enterprises are located in Tenth of Ramadan City, but only about 25 trade union committees; Sixth of October City hosts 1,000 private establishments with only about a dozen trade union committees.[10] Consequently, even the minimal organization and representation afforded by the Egyptian Trade Union Federation (ETUF) is absent. As part of the drive to encourage private investment, in 1996 the ETUF increased the minimum number of workers required to form an enterprise-level union committee from 50 to 250, making the formation of such committees more difficult in small and medium enterprises, which the United States Agency for International Development (USAID) has been promoting.

Despite the insurgent character of some of the collective actions of 1984–9, most of them, as in the 1970s and early 80s, were framed by a moral economy consciousness.[11] They aimed primarily to restore the standard of living and working conditions that public sector industrial workers enjoyed in the Nasser era or to establish parity between private and public sector workers. This partly explains the relatively meagre long-term organizational and political results of the strike wave of 1984–9.

Another factor is the policy of the *Tajammu'* (The National Progressive Unionist Party), a multi-tendency left party. Its popular base radically diminished during the 1990s because it decided to support the Mubarak regime against the Islamist insurgency and the Muslim Brothers alike.[12] *Tajammu'* chief Rifat Said convinced both the *Tajammu'* and the Communist Party to adopt this strategy, hoping to create more space for the secular left to manoeuvre on the margin of an authoritarian political structure that showed no signs of weakening. However, this ultimately became a local expression of the global retreat of left and workers' movements in the 1990s and their incapacity for sustained mobilization opposing the neo-liberal agenda.

Two sit-in strikes at the Iron and Steel Co. in Helwan in July and August 1989 were the fiercest confrontations between workers and the state in the 1980s and resulted in the most important exception to the failure to establish long-term institutions and an alternative political vision in the years 1984–9.[13] Kamal Abbas, a leader in these strikes, was fired for participating in an "illegal" strike. In 1990 he and veteran communist militant Yusuf Darwish established the Center for Trade Union and Workers' Services (CTUWS). The CTUWS subsequently established branches in Shubra al-Khayma and Mahalla al-Kubra, which served primarily the textile workers in these areas and in the upper Egyptian city of Naja Hammadi, the site of the large, modern public sector aluminium mill. In the 1990s Abbas joined Darwish and another veteran communist, Nabil al-Hilali, in the leadership of the underground People's Socialist Party, a small group that left the Communist Party of Egypt objecting to its strategy of supporting the Mubarak regime against the Islamists. After this early association with illegal Marxist politics,

Abbas and the CTUWS abandoned overt political demands to focus on bread-and-butter issues.

The 1986 riot of the Central Security Forces and the Islamist insurrection of the 1990s provided the pretexts for ratcheting up the regime's repression of its opponents.[14] The entrenchment of anti-democratic and extra-legal procedures as standard practice, the demonstrative Islamization of public culture, and an amalgam of intimidation and cooptation resulted in the fragmentation and corruption of nearly all forms of secular opposition, the end of the more tolerant period of Mubarak's rule, and the consolidation of a neo-authoritarian national security regime.

Political life became ossified. The party of the regime, the NDP, heir of the Nasserist Arab Socialist Union, had already been successfully demobilized in the 1970s by Sadat. The NDP is not a political party as the term is commonly understood. Its ideology is malleable and serves to justify the regime's policies, whatever they may be; it has little or no local political organization; it does not have a transparent mechanism for selecting candidates for office. It is a machine for distributing patronage and an arm of the regime which would have no coherence without access to state power.

Some of the legal opposition parties had elements of a popular base in the 1970s and 80s. But in the 1990s secular opposition parties – left, Nasserist, or liberal – lost all efficacy and credibility. In contrast to the NDP, they may have an ideology, although this often consists of little more than clichéd slogans. But they have little organization or popular support, especially outside Cairo.

The parliamentary elections of 1987, 1990 and 1995 are widely considered less democratic than those of 1984. Judicial supervision made the 2000 elections cleaner than those of 1995, which were particularly violent and fraudulent. There were declines in the secular vote, the rate of participation of registered voters, and the number of voters as a percentage of those eligible to vote from 1987 to 2000 despite an upward tick in 1995, possibly due to ballot box stuffing.[15] The Supreme Constitutional Court ruled that the electoral procedures of 1987, 1990 and 2000 were illegal. There was significant fraud and violence in the 2005 elections as well.[16]

Egyptian electoral politics cannot be considered a form of political mobilization; rather, it is a form of demobilization. Parliamentary political life has been in decline since the first post-monarchy election in 1956.

After the dismal record of the last half-century, it should be no surprise that most Egyptians scorn elections and see them, at best, as an opportunity to secure much-needed services from aspirants for public office. Participation in the 2005 parliamentary elections varied inversely with education and income.[17] Except for supporters of the Muslim Brothers, the educated middle class was least likely to participate in parliamentary elections. The constituencies with the highest proportion of turnout were the poorest regions in Egypt, where clientalism, money, or other electoral gifts motivate participation.[18]

The 2005 elections also revealed the weakness of the NDP. Only 33.8 per cent of its official nominees were elected. In contrast, despite considerable violence and fraud in the third round, the Muslim Brothers won a stunning 88 seats, 19.3 per cent of the members in the People's Assembly, and elected 54.6 per cent of their candidates.[19] The 7 secular opposition parties performed dismally, winning only 14 out of 444 elected parliamentary seats altogether.

In the current stage of neo-authoritarianism, the main political actors, in addition to the intelligence services and armed forces are: (1) the extra-parliamentary opposition; (2) business-oriented elements within the NDP who promote "reforms" which in no way threaten the regime's reliance on the coercive state apparatuses as its principal social base or weaken its grip on power; (3) the Islamist opposition, of which the largest component by far is the Muslim Brothers; and (4) a working-class social movement involving over 1,300 strikes and collective actions from mid-2004 to mid-2008.

2. The Extra-parliamentary Opposition

Since the 1980s, dozens of secular, liberal, and left-oriented non-governmental organizations rooted among the oppositional intelligentsia have emerged alongside the tens of thousands of community development and Islamist welfare organizations.[20] Some receive foreign funding (a matter of sharp contention), and are influenced by the global feminist or human rights movements. They do not have the capacity or mission to mobilize popular opposition to the regime. Nonetheless, to the extent that they are independent of its control system, the regime is very suspicious of such organizations. They operate under constant supervision of the state security authorities. The Arab Women's Solidarity Association (AWSA) (established in 1982), the New Woman Foundation (NWF) (established in 1984 as the New Woman Research Center), the Egyptian Organization for Human Rights (EOHR) (established in 1985), and The Ibn Khaldun Center for Development Studies (established in 1988) exemplify NGOs with a feminist or human rights agenda and the likely fate of such organizations.[21] AWSA was dissolved by an administrative decree after it criticized the regime's support for the US-led coalition in the 1991 Gulf War. The EOHR and the NWF were denied registration by the Ministry of Social Affairs. The EOHR was eventually registered. But the ministry has still not implemented a 2003 court order directing that the NWF be duly registered.[22] The Ibn Khaldun Center and its director, Professor of Sociology at the American University in Cairo Saad Eddin Ibrahim, were the target of exceptional hostility. Between 2000 and 2003 Ibrahim was imprisoned on spurious charges. In 2007 renewed legal actions forced him into indefinite exile.

The NGO phenomenon inspired a wave of academic studies, which celebrated them along with other expressions of what was imagined to be a resurgent "civil society" and claimed that they would promote democratization.[23] Nothing of the sort has happened in Egypt. While NGOs may perform excellent and even essential work, as Langohr argues, such organizations typically promote technocratic expertise over political ideology, weaken parties, and may actually inhibit political mobilization and democratization.[24]

Extra-parliamentary protests have had more of an impact on public culture. But they are dominated by the same urban upper-middle-class intelligentsia that operates most advocacy NGOs. Therefore, their capacity to strike popular roots is limited.

In the autumn of 2000, twenty NGOs and Nasserist and leftist intellectuals organized a Popular Committee in Solidarity with the Palestinian *intifada*. In early 2001 the committee held the first legal street demonstrations not sponsored by the regime in half a century.[25] Demonstrations of anti-globalization, pro-democracy, Palestine and Iraq solidarity groups subsequently became a regular phenomenon. But they are hardly an unfettered expression of freedom of speech. There is no certainty that any given demonstration will be permitted. The regime has found it useful to allow intellectuals to let off steam on foreign policy questions that arouse considerable emotion but are unlikely to become the basis for a sustained opposition movement. Demonstrations advocating democracy or targeting economic issues have usually been less well tolerated. Permitting some demonstrations has allowed the regime to identify and intimidate political activists by periodically allowing hired thugs to beat or sexually harass them during demonstrations or the police to jail and torture them. Demonstrators are typically surrounded by thousands of security forces who block them from the view of passers-by and prevent those who have not arrived on the scene well before the scheduled start of a demonstration from joining.

Greater room to manoeuvre on the street was accompanied by enhanced, but still limited, freedom of the press. One of the most explosive new topics was expressing opposition to the succession of Gamal Mubarak to the presidency. In the fall of 2002 Nasserist icon Muhammad Hasanayn Haykal became the first prominent personality to break this taboo publicly.[26] He was followed by the Nasserist weekly, *al-'Arabi*, which, while full of stale slogans and conspiracy theories, began regularly criticizing the Mubaraks by name.[27] Two years later its editor, Abd al-Halim Qandil, was kidnapped and told by thugs who beat him and left him naked on the Cairo–Suez road, "This will teach you to talk about your masters ('*asyadak*')".[28] *Al-Misri al-Yawm*, a liberal Arabic daily established in May 2004, has transgressed many red lines, usually on a higher journalistic level than *al-'Arabi*. Its animating figure and founding editor was Hisham Qasim, a leading member of the liberal *al-Ghad* ("Tomorrow") Party. After a long delay in obtaining its licence, in 2007 *al-Badil* was launched. It aims to present a more consistent left alternative to the regime than the *Tajammu'* weekly, *al-Ahali*. However, *al-Badil*'s editorial policies rarely deviate from the nationalist consensus and are at times distant from the values of the international left.

There are now some two dozen independent dailies and weeklies, some with barely distinguishable editorial positions. New liberal and leftist dailies are in the planning stage. While this proliferation has many positive aspects, it is also a symptom of the inability of the intelligentsia to unite in opposition to the regime.

Personally criticizing the President and his family broke a taboo in Egyptian politics. That achievement was consolidated by *Kifaya* ("Enough") – The Egyptian Movement for Change, whose first public appearance was in the autumn of 2004.[29] *Kifaya* had a broader political base than the committees in solidarity with Palestinians and against the US war on Iraq, or the Popular Campaign for Change, which grew out of these committees (the Muslim Brothers were founding members of the Popular Campaign, but never fully participated in its activities). Like them, *Kifaya*'s constituency was primarily intellectuals. Its main demand, endorsed by nearly 2,000 public figures, was for direct and competitive presidential elections. This is both an impressive and a pathetic number in a country of nearly 80 million. While a significant number of people were willing to risk arrest and possibly torture, this is far from a sufficient number to represent a threat to the regime.

Kifaya held its first public demonstration on 12 December 2004. Slogans and chants opposed Hosni Mubarak running for a fifth presidential term in the September 2005 elections and the grooming of Gamal to succeed him. While *Kifaya*'s national organizational capacity was limited, the slogan caught on in Egypt and abroad. For the next two years, the movement inspired offshoots such as Youth for Change, Workers for Change, Journalists for Change, etc. But after the 2006 Lebanon War, *Kifaya* lost steam. From then until Israel's invasion of Gaza in 2008, it turned out no more than 200 people for a demonstration.

Hosni Mubarak tried to outflank *Kifaya* by announcing in February 2005 that Article 76 of the Constitution would be amended to permit direct, competitive election of the President. The NDP majority in the People's Assembly duly approved the proposed amendment and submitted it to a popular referendum. Many objected to the limited constitutional change because it would make it nearly impossible for independents to stand for election after 2010 and did not limit the number of presidential terms or restrain the vast powers of the executive. Therefore, a measure promoted as an advance for democracy actually increased the likelihood that Gamal Mubarak would succeed his father in office. *Kifaya* and others called a demonstration on the day of the referendum. On 25 May 2005, subsequently dubbed "Black Wednesday", security forces chased demonstrators around the centre of Cairo. Some regrouped in front of the Journalists' Syndicate, where thugs of the NDP sexually assaulted women activists, a new low for the regime.[30]

The fate of Ayman Nur, the leader of *al-Ghad* Party and first runner-up in the 2005 presidential election, indicates the limits of the "democratization" the regime envisioned by amending the Constitution. Nur received 7 per cent of the vote. That was considered enough of a threat for him to be jailed after being convicted on manifestly ridiculous charges of forging signatures (including those of his wife and father) on the petition to establish his party. Signalling their impotence and near irrelevance, the political parties were unable to mount a united protest against this barefaced assault on explicitly legal forms of opposition.

The United States expressed periodic "concern" about Nur. Secretary of State Condoleezza Rice postponed a visit to Egypt scheduled for February 2005 in reaction to Nur's first arrest. By her February 2006 visit, the Bush administration was less assertive about the case; ensuring Egypt's support in the global war on terror and the non-existent Palestinian–Israeli "peace process" seemed more important to Washington than promoting democracy. Nur was released with no explanation in February 2008.

3. The New Business Class: Agent of Reform?[31]

The 1991 ERSAP agreement was reinforced by enacting Law 203/1991 permitting sale of public sector industrial, financial and service enterprises. By 2002, 190 of the 314 eligible companies were partially or totally privatized. Privatization slowed while the Egyptian economy experienced a recession and minimal or no growth during 2000–2003. In July 2004, a new cabinet headed by Dr Ahmad Nazif resumed selling off public sector enterprises with increased vigour and adopted other policies to encourage local and foreign investment. Within a year, it sold off 19 additional non-financial and financial companies.[32] Sales of public sector enterprises, high oil prices, remittances from migrant workers, a surge in tourism, and increased Suez Canal tolls, boosted Egypt's foreign reserves and current account balance. All these factors are rents or otherwise unsustainable. Nonetheless, the new policies produced impressive levels of annual GDP growth in the 7 per cent range. Egypt's macro-economic scorecard looked very respectable if one did not examine too closely levels of debt, trade deficits, inflation, unemployment, inequality and poverty.

The economic portfolios in Nazif's cabinet were entrusted to holders of Western PhDs or businessmen close to Gamal Mubarak, and this was widely understood as a statement about the likely succession of the first son to the presidency.[33] Gamal and his allies in the NDP leadership advanced the slogan of "new thinking". They are vague about what new thoughts they advocate, although it is clear they may not offend Gamal's father or Washington.

Many predicted that as Egypt privatized its economy, entrepreneurs with access to globalized capital and independent resources would seek access to political power. This has turned out to be wishful thinking. Anyone wanting to do business on a significant scale must have clientalist relationships or alliances with the ruling elite. The elder Mubarak son, Ala, is infamous for demanding a large cut in any enterprise an investor proposes to operate in Egypt.[34]

The emblematic example of an entrepreneur who benefited from the neo-liberal policies of the regime and became politically active is Ahmad Ezz, chairman and managing director of al-Ezz Steel Rebars. But rather than seek any independent political or social power, he became the NDP's secretary for organizational affairs and a close ally of Gamal Mubarak. Ezz's firm, established in 1994, is the largest steel producer in the Middle East; it controls some 60–70 per cent of Egypt's domestic steel market, which some believe constitutes a monopoly. But another of Gamal's cronies, Minister of Investment Mahmoud Mohieldin, assures us that "Ezz's dominance of the steel market does not constitute a monopoly because local buyers have unrestricted access to the international market".[35] When Ezz's business practices are debated in the People's Assembly, the NDP majority guarantees that he will come under no serious public scrutiny or censure.[36]

In the December 2005 parliamentary elections, Ezz stood for election in the Minufiyya constituency. He was opposed by another NDP businessman, Ibrahim Kamal, the former Member of Parliament (MP) in the district from 1990 to 1995. Kamal is the brother of Kamal al-Shazli, who remains a prominent member of the NDP "old guard" despite losing his cabinet post in the July 2004 reshuffle. Ezz was elected, largely on the strength of the votes of the approximately 11,000 workers he employs in his steel mills in Sadat City, a new city on the periphery of Cairo located in Minufiyya. To further secure his election, Ezz reportedly distributed large quantities of fertilizer to farmers in the rural areas of his constituency.[37]

In 2005, 12 of Cairo's 25 parliamentary constituencies were contested by businessmen. All but one were either NDP nominees or NDP members who ran as independents and rejoined the party after the elections. Samer Soliman concludes that businessmen were among the big winners in the elections. Their proportion in the People's Assembly increased from 12 per cent in 1995 to 17 per cent in 2000 to 22 per cent in 2005.[38] But political participation of businessmen may lead to less, not more, democracy. It is easier for them to buy votes and bus their workers to the polls to vote for them. Soliman argues that less outright vote falsification actually increases these phenomena.[39]

4. The Political Economy of Islamism

In the 1980s, some argued that Saudi petrodollars created the Sunni Islamist movement.[40] This instrumentalist view fails to historicize the aftermath of the 1967–73 conjuncture in which specific forms of Islamist mobilization emerged: secular Arab nationalism was defeated, statist import-substitution-industrialization development projects reached the limits of their capacity, and a combination of cajoling and pressure from the West was applied on the region. As the price of oil rose twenty-fold from 1973 to 1981, rentier coalitions based on petroleum revenues came to dominate Middle Eastern states. However, they did not establish a stable social structure of capital accumulation or a new political vision. The political, economic, social and moral crises of these states are the context for the rise of Islamism.

Economic stabilization and structural adjustment programmes imposed cutbacks in state budgets and social spending. Consequently, state efficacy became increasingly restricted to urban upper-middle-class and elite areas. Income distributions polarized. States became unable to provide previously established levels of services or to ensure adequate supplies of commodities to all sectors of their territory and population, undermining the terms of the social contract established in the era of authoritarian populism and state-led development. Limiting state capacity provided a windfall to Islamist movements, enabling them to speak in the name of resisting foreign domination and exploitation of "the people". A populist Islamist discourse linked the corruption and autocracy of state elites with their inability to provide social services and jobs.

In "informal" neighbourhoods ('ashwa'iyyat), where many migrants from Upper Egypt settled, and among the uneducated poor, the Islamic Group established itself by offering social services that the state could no longer afford to provide. The "Islamic Republic of Imbaba" (in western Cairo) was a base for armed militants, largely trades people and the unemployed in their teens and early twenties with less than a university education, until it was dismantled in 1992 by an invasion of thousands of security forces.[41] Blowback from the anti-Soviet *jihad* in Afghanistan fuelled armed insurrection based in Upper Egypt and urban peripheries until 1997.

Further up the class ladder, the number of university graduates nearly tripled from 1975 to 1985. But because of cuts in the state budget and commodity subsidies imposed by the IMF, public sector employment no longer provided wages adequate to marry and raise a family. Hence, fewer university graduates sought public sector employment, even though they were entitled to a position by law. At the same time, the declining price of oil on the world market after 1982 reduced opportunities for young men to migrate to oil-rich countries and amass savings to buy and furnish an apartment – the prerequisites of a middle-class marriage. The real unemployment rate in the mid-1980s was well over the official rate of 12 per cent and was concentrated among first-time job seekers with university degrees. This "lumpen intelligentsia", as Wickham dubs them, was deeply aggrieved that despite their hard work and academic achievements they had few prospects for material success.[42]

Many joined the Muslim Brothers and became cadres in its social service network. Janine Clark argues that middle-class Islamist networks are not sites of recruitment, and primarily provide services "by and for the middle classes".[43] Like many other things about the Muslim Brothers, there is no conclusive way to discover the extent of members or supporters of the society among the subaltern strata. Since Richard Mitchell's classic study of the Muslim Brothers, scholars have generally concurred with him that the society does not accept "uneducated" people as members.[44] But, Soliman argues that while 60 per cent of the 88 Muslim Brothers' MPs elected to the People's Assembly in 2005 are educated professionals, as Mitchell would have predicted, the urban poor are their principal constituents.[45] Only 9 of the Brothers' MPs are workers.

The society's activities are funded largely by its members in the Islamist business class. Muhammad Khayrat al-Shatir, the third-ranking member of the Muslim Brothers, exemplifies this element in the society. In 1992, he and two other principals of the Salsabil Co. (*Sharikat al-Umma*), a computer import firm and the largest economic enterprise associated with the Muslim Brothers, were jailed and the firm dissolved.[46] Although al-Shatir recovered financially, in December 2006 he was among 40 Brothers whose assets were frozen when they were arrested and charged with money laundering and financing a banned organization. In January, a civilian criminal court dismissed the charges against them, but before leaving the courtroom they were rearrested. They were retried in a military court, which imposed prison sentences of up to ten years on al-Shatir and 24 others in April 2008.

Al-Shatir's incarceration removed a powerful pragmatist from the active leadership and accentuated divisions among the Brothers along class and generational lines as well as between traditionalist conservatives and political pragmatists. Husam Tammam argues that the Brothers are losing touch with the popular classes and failing to maintain the strong organizational discipline for which they were once renowned.[47] Hence, the future direction of the society is unclear.

As the oil boom intensified and migrant labourers from Egypt, Sudan, Jordan, Palestine and Yemen found work in Saudi Arabia and the Persian Gulf, Islamic movements were often funded by recycling the earnings of these workers through informal exchange networks, some of which became major financial institutions known as "Islamic investment companies", another sector of the new Islamist business class.[48] In the mid-1980s, there were nearly 200 such firms of various sizes organized as individual proprietorships and joint-stock companies. Perhaps one million Egyptians had invested in them. Estimates of their total assets vary from 20 to 60 billion Egyptian pounds (EGP), based on little publicly available evidence. Minister of Social Affairs Amal Abd al-Rahim Othman claimed a figure of EGP 24 billion.[49]

In contrast to the Muslim Brothers, whose leadership is linked to old money and the educated middle classes, the Islamic investment firms were associated with the nouveau riche of the *infitah* era. They deployed a Muslim moral economy discourse of equity, mutual obligation, and mutual responsibility. But it is unclear how devout some of the principals of these firms actually were.[50] Moore suggests that, "The entrepreneurs wrapped themselves in Islam in the manner that US presidential candidates use the American flag".[51]

The Central Bank began trying to audit these firms and regulate the movement of their assets in November 1986. Most of the Islamic investment firms collapsed in May 1988, one month before enactment of a new investment law. However, it is unlikely that the government was motivated purely by the desire to uphold financial transparency. The regime suspected, though it never provided evidence, that its jihadist opponents were financed by the Islamic investment firms and came to regard them as subversive institutions that had to be crushed.

A third sector of the new Islamic business class is comprised of entrepreneurs who are Muslim-identified but not attached to any Islamist organization. The wealthiest of them is reputed to be Salih Kamil, the Saudi husband of Egyptian actress Safa Abul-Suud, whose assets are estimated at USD 2 billion.[52] To promote "Islamic economics", he endowed the Salih Kamil Center for Islamic Economics at al-Azhar University. Kamil's Dalla-al-Baraka firm began operating in Egypt in 1981 and engages in tourism, banking, insurance, industrial and agricultural production, transport, media, and health services. He owns the Middle East Broadcasting Center and is chairman of the board of the ART digital television platform in which his principal partner is the Saudi Prince Walid, whose fortune is estimated at USD 13 billion. ART targets the "conservative but silent majority of Muslims who [are] neither secularists nor so-called 'Islamic Fundamentalists'".[53]

There are also more local Muslim-identified entrepreneurs who have no known organizational affiliations. The largest construction company in Asyut, *Tali'at al-Iman* ("Vanguard of the Faith"), was established by the son of Abd al-Qadir Awda, one of the six Muslim Brothers executed for attempting to assassinate Gamal Abd al-Nasser in 1954. The firm requires that its clients be good Muslims with recommendations from persons with "Islamic connections". Male employees must have beards and women employees wear *hijab*.[54] The *Tawhid wa-Nur* ("Unity and Light") department store chain, which has outlets in both upscale and popular neighbourhoods, was established by Ragab al-Suweirki, who began by offering women free "Islamic dress" in exchange for handing over their Western fashions.

In the 1990s, what Haenni dubs "Islam of the market" emerged among the second generation of the post-*infitah* wealthy, who are more sophisticated and worldly than the first.[55] Umar Abd al-Kafi was the first in a line of preachers to appeal to this class. They typically have no formal Islamic education, wear Western clothes, speak in colloquial Egyptian Arabic, and valorize the moral and social stature of the wealthy, so long as they are socially responsible and give alms (*zakat*). A professional agronomist, whose business interests include land reclamation and pesticides, during the years 1990 to 1994 Abd al-Kafi turned the Shooting Club, located in the upper-middle-class Cairo neighbourhood of Muhandisin, into a religious centre.[56] Half his audience was reputed to be women, including repentant former actresses. Threatened by his popularity and unable to distinguish his message from that of the armed Islamists, the security forces forced Abd al-Kafi out of his position at the Shooting Club.

He was replaced by Amr Khaled, who began preaching at the Shooting Club around 1997 and soon became the most popular preacher in the Arab world. Khaled purveys a softer message than Abd al-Kafi, soothing the anxieties of his audience by speaking of love and moral personal behaviour. He proclaims unabashedly, "I want to be rich in order to use my money in the way of God [. . .] So that people will look at me and say, 'You see, rich and religious', and they'll love God through my wealth".[57] Khaled appeals to society ladies, former movie stars, and under-35 yuppies, including students at the American University in Cairo. In 2002, Khaled was "encouraged" to leave Egypt. Security forces were disconcerted by his capacity to draw crowds of tens of thousands, regardless of the apolitical content of his speech. He still reaches a huge audience through satellite TV.

Haenni and others dub this development "post-Islamist" because its proponents do not speak of installing *shari'a* rule or any other overt form of politics.[58] Islam of the market seeks a hip, consumerist, modern Islamic identity. It embraces personal improvement, business efficiency, and positive thinking, in a style reminiscent of Max Weber's "Protestant ethic", Dale Carnegie's *How to Win Friends and Influence People*,[59] and Stephen Covey's *The Seven Habits of Highly Effective People*[60] (Haenni argues that its translation into Arabic in the 1990s was a key development for this form of Islamism). One of its features is a new style of Islamic songs (*anshad*) similar to Christian rock. The star of this genre is Sami Yusuf, an English Muslim of Azerbaijani origins.[61] The ultra-posh Grand Hyatt hotel, whose owner flushed millions of dollars of alcohol into the Nile in the spring of 2008 to advertise his Islamic credentials, hosted Yusuf's debut Cairo concert. During Ramadan 2007, the Mobinil mobile telephone company, whose principal investors are Christian, advertised that customers could download Yusuf's recitation of the 100 names of Allah. Some Islamist yuppies are drawn to Magda Amr, who integrates chakras, yoga, reflexology and macrobiotic food into her New Age preaching. "Liberal" veiled women in this crowd shop for their *hijab* at boutiques like Petite Lune, Muhagaba Home, Flash, and L'Amour, which feature fabrics and brands imported from London and Paris.

The Muslim Brothers denigrate the message of Amr Khaled and its associated phenomena as "air-conditioned Islam".[62] Nonetheless, this trend is growing in popularity. However, it does not seek to mobilize its adherents politically. Its political expression might possibly be the New Center Party (*al-Wasat al-Jadid*), the third iteration of a group that left the Muslim Brothers to establish a socially conservative "Muslim Democratic" style party in 1996. However, the regime refuses to legalize *al-Wasat* in any form, fearing it would be a stalking horse for the Muslim Brothers, or even worse, that it might pose an alternative to both the regime and the Brothers.

5. A Social Movement of the Working Class

Fears about the loss of jobs and unwillingness of new private investors to pay fringe benefits, such as dividends in shares of firms owned by workers or contributions to retirement funds, which some public sector managers neglected for as long as a decade, were the main forces impelling a wave of strikes and collective action which began in the early 2000s and accelerated after the Nazif government's inauguration in July 2004. This is the largest social movement in Egypt in over half a century, involving over one million workers in some form of collective action by the end of 2007.

There were 265 strikes, sit-ins, protests and demonstrations in 2004, 193 of them following the installation of the Nazif government.[63] The Land Center for Human Rights reported 202 collective actions in 2005, 222 in 2006, and a staggering 614 in 2007.[64] In mid-2007, collective actions spread from their centre of gravity in the textile and clothing industry to encompass building material workers, urban transport workers, the Cairo underground Metro workers, railway workers, food processing workers, bakers, sanitation workers, oil workers in Suez, and others. White collar workers and civil servants, university professors, doctors, and other professionals joined the movement. Most notable in this sector was a strike of 55,000 real estate tax collectors throughout Egypt in December. The movement continued into 2008. The Egyptian Workers and Trade Union Watch reported that in February 2008 alone 42,000 workers took part in 68 protests, including 10 strikes, 22 sit-ins and 13 demonstrations.[65]

The most politically significant of the collective actions were two strikes at the Misr Spinning and Weaving Company in Mahalla al-Kubra in December 2006 and September 2007. The Misr complex is the largest industrial enterprise in Egypt and employs some 25,000 workers, about a quarter of all public sector textile and clothing workers.[66] The first strike mostly won its principal demand: that Prime Minister Nazif's announcement that public sector workers would receive an increased annual bonus from EGP 100 to a full two months' pay be honoured. The workers settled for 45 days' pay.

The victory of the Mahalla strikers reverberated throughout the textile sector. In the next three months, at least 30,000 workers in more than ten textile mills in the Delta and Alexandria participated in strikes and other forms of collective action demanding that they receive what the Mahalla strikers won. In virtually all cases, the government succumbed.

The most politically significant aspects of the Mahalla strike were the demand to impeach the local trade union committee because it opposed the strike, and the petition of some 14,000 workers to resign from the ETUF because it rejected their demand to impeach the local committee. The 4,200 workers at the recently privatized Shibin al-Kom Spinning and Weaving Co. and Kafr al-Dawwar Workers for Change, announced their solidarity with the call of the Mahalla workers for mass resignations from the ETUF following strikes in those enterprises.

A far larger proportion of the industrial workers' actions than ever before were in the private sector. This is one of the signs of the emergence of a broad social movement, not just a backward-looking effort by public sector workers to retain privileges from a bygone era. The largest private sector strike was at Arab Polvara Spinning and Weaving in Alexandria, a fairly successful enterprise privatized in the first tranche of the sell-off of the public sector in the mid-1990s. On 24 March and 2 April 2007, nearly half of the firm's 12,000 workers struck to protest against discrimination between workers and managers in the allocation of shares in the company when it was sold, failure to pay workers' dividends on their shares, and elimination of weekly paid days off and paid sick leaves. The last time workers had received a dividend on their shares was 1997, when they were paid EGP 60.[67] The Arab Polvara workers' demands indicate that public sector workers are justified in suspecting that, even if privatized firms initially offer decent wages and benefits, the requirements of competing in the international market, where China's low-wage structure dominates the textile industry, will eventually erode their wages and working conditions.

The government and the sensationalist press accused both the Muslim Brothers and the Communist Party of organizing the strike movement. But there is no evidence that either group initiated any of the actions since 2004. The Brothers have never had a strong base in the industrial working class; in the 1940s they assisted the government in breaking strikes and undermining the left in the labour movement.[68] However, there are policy differences within the society which apparently reflect its cross-class composition. The Alexandria Brothers are generally considered more militant, more confrontational towards the regime, and closer to the popular classes than the Cairo leadership.

In February 2007, the Muslim Brother MP from Kafr al-Dawwar, Abd al-Aziz al-Husayni, announced his backing for the walkout of the Misr Spinning and Weaving workers there. His parliamentary colleague, Sabr Abu al-Futuh from Alexandria, issued several statements supporting the Arab Polvara strike.[69] Abu al-Futuh coordinated the Brothers' campaign to run candidates in the trade union elections of autumn 2006 and announced that, if they were rigged, the Brothers would establish a trade union independent of the regime. They have not done so despite the undemocratic character of the elections.[70]

Nonetheless, the possibility that a trade union independent of the regime might be established in the coming period was enhanced by the outcome of the second strike at Misr Spinning and Weaving in Mahalla in September 2007. An exceptionally militant six-day walkout achieved impressive gains, including payment of a profit-sharing bonus equal to 130 days' pay.[71] Even more significantly for the political horizon, the workers compelled government representatives to negotiate directly with their elected strike committee, bypassing the discredited local trade union committee entirely. The demand to impeach the local union committee that had failed to support the September 2007 strike was renewed. In contrast to their previous reluctance to speak openly about political questions, several leaders of the strike announced their opposition to the entire regime. Muhammad al-Attar, a member of the elected strike committee, told a rally of workers: 'I want the whole government to resign [. . .] I want the Mubarak regime to come to an end. Politics and workers' rights are inseparable. Work is politics by itself. What we are witnessing here right now, this is as democratic as it gets.[72]

6. Conclusion

The neo-authoritarian phase of the Mubarak regime as it crystallized in the 1990s replaced the uncertainties brought about by the conjuncture of 1967–73. The contours of the new order were shaped by the 1991 ERSAP agreements, the defeat of the armed Islamist insurgency in 1997, the intensification of the neo-liberal economic orientation by the Nazif government installed in 2004, and the appearance of liberalizing the political order while retaining power firmly in the hands of the national security apparatus. The collapse of global financial markets in 2008, and with it the hegemony of neo-liberal ideology, will likely impose new strains on Egypt's political order with uncertain consequences.

Despite periodic expressions of opposition, the regime has shown a remarkable capacity to endure and renew itself despite a structural fiscal crisis, a widening gap between the rich and the poor, and an unstable regional environment. The conventional wisdom is that Gamal Mubarak's succession to the presidency is a foregone conclusion. A package of constitutional amendments adopted by a referendum in March 2007 with the usual low rate of participation made it much more difficult for independents and Muslim Brothers to run for office and is likely to enshrine abusive police practices that have been nominally illegal or legal only under the "temporary" state of emergency which has been in force since 1981 and was renewed for two years in 2008.

Since early 2007, the regime has demonstrated signs of desperation, internal division and weakness. Tolerance for expressions of political opposition diminished markedly as it lashed out at Muslim Brothers, NGOs, bloggers, journalists, workers, students and *Kifaya* members, and blocked oppositional websites. Street demonstrations and other public protests were increasingly met with repression reminiscent of the 1990s. In the spring of 2007, the Association for Human Rights and Legal Aid was closed. In the autumn, newspaper editors were hauled into court on spurious charges of "insulting leaders of the National Democratic Party" and "spreading false rumours about the President's health". The regime responded exceptionally violently to spontaneous demonstrations in Mahalla al-Kubra on 6–7 April 2008, protesting against the sharp increase in the price of food. Security forces arrested 331 people, beat up hundreds, critically wounded 9, and shot dead 15-year-old Ahmad Ali Mubarak, putting a bullet through his head as he was standing on the balcony of his flat. The protestors sent a clear political message by ripping down and trampling a poster of Hosni Mubarak and burning the banners of the NDP candidates in the fraudulent local council elections of 8 April.

The brunt of the repression was directed against the Muslim Brothers. Thousands of them have been detained, including many candidates for the 2007 Shura Council and the 2008 local council elections. As the largest opposition force with a wide network of institutions, the Brothers have a great deal to lose from a direct confrontation with the regime. They have apparently decided to back off and continue the mutually beneficial cat-and-mouse game that constrains their activity but ensures their survival.

We cannot know how the contradiction between the populist discourse and the business interests of the Muslim Brothers would be resolved in a democratic environment. Keeping this contradiction unresolved helps to project Egyptian political Islam as a social movement opposed to neo-liberal policies, although the Brothers may have already lost popular support because they are unwilling to confront the regime more forcefully. The trajectory of the Turkish Justice and Development Party suggests that business interests would ultimately prevail, while popular support might be retained by mobilizing around cultural issues and resentment against cosmopolitan elites, akin to what Thomas Frank describes in *What's the Matter with Kansas?*[73]

The strike movement, because it was generated locally and is not nationally coordinated by either the Muslim Brothers or the secular left, is more difficult to repress. The government accused the Center for Trade Union and Workers Services of provoking the strike movement, although there is no evidence that this is the case. On 25 April 2007, the Ministry of Social Solidarity shut down its headquarters in the industrial suburb of Helwan, south of Cairo; the offices in Naja Hammadi and Mahalla al-Kubra had already been closed on 29 March and 11 April.

These measures did not slow down the strike movement, nor did they thwart the second strike at Mahalla al-Kubra. They may even have contributed indirectly to its more militant oppositional political character. And after a year of legal struggle the CTUWS was reopened by a court order in July 2008.

Since 1967, the old forms of political mobilization animated by Arab nationalism and Arab socialism have been completely undone, except among diehard Nasserists whose inefficacy is symbolized by their division into two tiny parties (one legal and one illegal). Armed political Islam failed to overturn the order that emerged fitfully after 1973. Unarmed Islamism plays only the limited political role that the regime deems tolerable. Egypt shares these developments, modified by local particularities, with much of the rest of the Arab world. Among the specificities of Egypt are its less successful economic performance than Morocco, Tunisia, and Jordan – the other non-oil-exporting Arab favourites of the international financial institutions – or the oil-rich mini-states of Qatar, Bahrain and the United Arab Emirates; its utterly dysfunctional educational system; the exceptionally wide gap between the rich and the poor (in common with Morocco); as well as deep anxieties about its identity and political role in the Arab world, which are expressed by the often hysterical opposition to "normalization" of relations with Israel among the intelligentsia.

Despite the claims of the Egyptian regime, the administration of George W. Bush, and over-optimistic observers, neither the economic nor the political changes of the last three decades have fundamentally altered the contours of power. Rather, the neo-authoritarian Mubarak regime has adapted and become further entrenched. Cosmetic measures like amending the Constitution have actually enhanced the power of Gamal Mubarak and his business-class allies. However, unlike in Turkey, the Egyptian business class has little self-confidence and shows no sign of becoming a class for itself; it is largely an appendage of the state. For example, in 2010 a presidential candidate will need to be nominated by a party holding at least 3 per cent of the seats in the lower house of parliament and 5 per cent of the upper house; independent candidates will require endorsements from 10 local council members from 14 governorates. Postponing the local council elections for two years and rounding up hundreds of Muslim Brother candidates has virtually eliminated any but the NDP candidates.

Directly confronting this new business class and the government is a workers' movement handicapped by the global collapse of a credible alternative to capitalism and the lack of a significant left political pole in national politics. It cannot yet organize on a regional or national scale. Nonetheless, neo-liberalism does not eliminate the contradictions of capitalism. Egypt's future will likely be determined by how those contradictions play themselves out and the contest between an unrepentant neo-authoritarianism and political forces attempting to establish their legitimacy as representatives of "the people" – the business class, the Islamists, and a new left of some sort.

Notes

1. Thanks to Yoram Meital, Daniela Pioppi, and Faiza Rady for comments on a late draft of this chapter and to the research participants for providing a stimulating framework for thought and discussions at an earlier stage.
2. Pfeifer 1999.
3. US Government Accountability Office 2006; David R. Francis reported a figure of USD 117 billion adjusted to 2001 dollars in purchasing power ("Economist tallies swelling cost of Israel to US", *The Christian Science Monitor*, 9 December 2002).
4. This terminology is adapted from Schamis 1991. He argues that military regimes in the "southern cone" of Latin America in the 1970s were not "late" bureaucratic-authoritarian regimes, as O'Donnell suggests, but neo-conservative regimes.
5. Wickham 2002, p. 163.
6. For a full list of Human Rights Watch reports on human rights violations in Egypt since the early 1990s, cf. Human Rights Watch website, http://hrw.org/doc/?t=mideast&c=egypt (retrieved 15 October 2007).
7. Pripstein Posusney 1993, p. 221.
8. El Shafei 1995.
9. Beinin 1993.
10. Mustafa al-Bassyuni (labour correspondent for *al-Dustur*), lecture at Middle East Studies Center, American University in Cairo, 3 October 2007.
11. Pripstein Posusney 1993.
12. For details, cf. "Firebrand tamed", *al-Ahram Weekly Online*, 2–8 November 1995, http://weekly.ahram.org.eg/archives/parties/tagammu/firebrnd.htm (retrieved 2 June 2007).
13. El Shafei 1995.
14. Kienle 2000; Human Rights Watch reports on Egypt, op. cit.
15. Soliman 2006; Kienle 2000.
16. Gamal Essam El-Din, "Rulings confirm electoral fraud", *al-Ahram Weekly*, 19–25 October 2006.

17 Soliman 2006.
18 Ibid.
19 Ibid., p. 92.
20 Ben Néfissa *et al.* 2005; Abdelrahman 2004.
21 Other similar NGOs include the Egyptian Association against Torture, the Hisham Mubarak Law Center, El-Nadim Center, the Arab Network for Human Rights Information, the Egyptian Initiative For Personal Rights, the Foundation for Egyptian Woman's Issues, the Women and Memory Foundation, and the Egyptian Center for Women's Rights.
22 For details, cf. Human Rights Watch 2003; Women Living under Muslim Laws, "Egypt: The New Woman Research Centre (NWRC) has won its legal battle against the Ministry of Social Affairs", 31 October 2003, http://www.wluml.org/english/newsfulltxt.shtml?cmd%5B157%5D=x-157–27198 (retrieved 5 June 2007).
23 Prominent examples are Norton 1996; Kubba 2000.
24 Langohr 2005.
25 For details, cf. Howeidy, "A chronology of dissent", *al-Ahram Weekly Online*, 23–29 June 2005, http://weekly.ahram.org.eg/2005/748/eg10.htm (retrieved 3 June 2007). For a critical assessment of the Palestine solidarity movement, cf. Colla 2006.
26 Cf. Shaden Shehab's report on Haykal's September 2002 Dream TV appearance, "Dream's wake-up call?", *al-Ahram Weekly*, 7–13 November 2002.
27 Howeidy, op. cit; al-Ghobashy 2003.
28 Quoted in al-Ghobashy 2005.
29 Carnegie Endowment for International Peace 2005.
30 "Statement of Egyptian NGOs", *The Arabist*, 25 May 2005, http://arabist.net/archives/2005/05/26/egyptian-ngos-issue-statement-over-referendum-attacks-yesterday/ (retrieved 1 June 2007).
31 [Eds' note:] On the new business class, cf. Wurzel's chapter in this book.
32 International Monetary Fund 2005.
33 The ministers in Gamal Mubarak's entourage include Minister of Trade and Industry Rashid Muhammad Rashid (CEO of Unilever Egypt), Minister of Tourism Ahmad al-Maghrabi (CEO of the French tourism group Accor), Minister of Youth Anas al-Fiqqi, Minister of Finance Dr Yosuf Boutros Ghali, Minister of Investment Dr Mahmoud Mohieldin, and Minister of Communication and Information Technology Dr Tarek Kamel.
34 For a list of the business interests of the Mubarak family, the accuracy of which cannot be confirmed, cf. the "Free Egyptians" website, http://free.egyptians.4t.com/bayanmokata3aEn.htm (retrieved 19 October 2007); Kassem (2004) relates the story of Ramy Lakah, whose fate is an example of the "bad things" that can happen to businessmen who adopt an independent political position.
35 Waleed Khalil Rasromani, "Competition authority investigates claims against cement and steel producers", *The Daily Star* (Egypt), 20 July 2006.
36 Essam El-Din, "These shoes were made for talking", *al-Ahram Weekly Online*, 8–14 June 2006, http://weekly.ahram.org.eg/2006/798/eg5.htm (retrieved 1 June 2007).
37 Essam El-Din, "The business of taking over politics", *al-Ahram Weekly Online*, 2–9 November 2005, http://weekly.ahram.org.eg/2005/767/eg2.htm (retrieved 1 June 2007).

38 Soliman 2006, p. 167.
39 Ibid., p. 87.
40 Pipes 1983; Zakariyya 1986; Moensch 1988.
41 Haenni (2005a) is a fine-grained political sociology of Imbaba; cf. also Denis 1994; Ibrahim 1996; Ismail 2000.
42 Wickham 2002.
43 Clark 2004, p. 3.
44 Mitchell 1969.
45 Soliman 2006.
46 *al-Ahrar*, 16 March 1992; *al-Ahram*, 8 June 1992; *al-Musawwar*, 3 April 2002.
47 Tammam 2006.
48 For an overview, cf. Roussillon 1988.
49 Clement 1990, p. 238.
50 Ibid., p. 48.
51 Ibid., p. 250.
52 *Ruz al-Yusuf*, 12 July 1993. According to *Forbes*, 3 May 2008, Naguib Sawiris, a Copt, is the wealthiest Egyptian, http://www.forbes.com/lists/2008/10/billionaires08_Naguib-Sawiris_4MRK.html (retrieved 17 June 2008).
53 Salih Kamil quoted in Sakr 2001, p. 47.
54 Springborg 1989.
55 Haenni 2005b.
56 *al-Qahira*, 30 November, 7 December, 14 December 2004.
57 Excerpts from Khaled's sermon "Youth and Summer", cited in Haenni 2005b, p. 84.
58 Perhaps most prominently, Roy 2004.
59 [Eds' note:] Carnegie 1936.
60 [Eds' note:] Covey 1989.
61 See his cassette tape, *al-Mu'allim* ("The Teacher", referring to the prophet Muhammad).
62 Tammam and Haenni 2003.
63 *Markaz al-ard lil-huquq al-insan, Isdarat al-huquq al-iqtisadiyya wa'l-ijtima'iyya*, July 2004, No. 35; February 2005, No. 36.
64 Ibid., August 2005, No. 39; January 2006, No. 42; February 2007, No. 53; July 2007, No. 55 and February 2008, No. 58. The Egyptian Workers and Trade Union Watch (*al-Marsad al-'ummali wa'l-niqabi al-misri*) reported over 580 collective actions in 2007 (Egyptian Workers and Trade Union Watch 2008, http://arabist.net/arabawy/wp-content/uploads/2008/04/feb-2008–report1.pdf, retrieved 2 March 2008).
65 Ibid.
66 For details, cf. Beinin and el-Hamalawy 2007
67 *al-Misri al-Yawm*, 4 May 2007.
68 Beinin and Lockman 1987.
69 Cf. *Ikhwanweb*, 20 March 2007, http://www.ikhwanweb.com/Home.asp?zPage=Systems&System=PressR&Press=Show&Lang=E&ID=6687 (retrieved 3 April 2007); http://www.ikhwanweb.com/Home.asp?zPage=Systems&System=PressR&Press=Show&Lang=E&ID=6836 (retrieved 15 May 2007).
70 Center for Trade Union and Workers Services 2007.
71 For details, cf. Beinin 2007.

72 Stack Liam and Mazen Maram, "Striking Mahalla Workers demand Govt. fulfill broken promises", *Daily News Egypt*, 27 September 2007.
73 [Eds' note:] Frank 2004.

3

AN ANALYSIS OF POLITICAL CHANGE IN LEBANON IN THE LIGHT OF RECENT MOBILIZATION CYCLES[1]

Karam Karam

Introduction

The demonstrations of the "independence uprising" (*intifada al-istiqlal*)[2] which followed the assassination of the former Prime Minister Rafiq Hariri on 14 February 2005 and accompanied the withdrawal of the Syrian army at the end of April 2005 anchored the conviction that the political system was effectively changing in Lebanon.

The disappointments are already making themselves felt. The bloody civilian confrontations of May 2008 and the settlement of the conflict which followed attest to the system fragility. The Lebanese political scene in 2008 is perceptibly different from that of the post-civil war period when the Syrian Baathist regime took control of Lebanon with the assent of the international community in the context of the post-Cold war period, the liberation of Kuwait and the launch of the peace process. It is also different from the political set-up of 2004, when the Syrian President Bashar al-Assad imposed an extension of the term of the President of the Lebanese Republic, Emile Lahoud, in an unconstitutional manner.

The hypothetical indices of "democratic transition" in Lebanon – which could be represented by, for example, the end of the war in 1990; the dynamics of "reconciliation" and "reconstruction" of the country and the state institutions launched in 1992; the organization and holding of several presidential, parliamentary and local elections after a long period of interruption or boycotting of the process[3]; and the withdrawal of foreign troops – in reality do not prefigure in the least a reform of the Lebanese political system (and even less its potential for democratization). They do not prefigure a resolution of the endemic crises of the regime. In fact, since the adoption of Resolution 1559 by the United Nations Security Council on 3 September 2004, the Lebanese political scene has experienced a series of developments bringing somersaults of differing natures and reaches.

To the weaknesses of the political system, which shows little ability to regulate itself on the model of a "democracy of consensus",[4] are added the internal and often violent repercussions of conflicts and relationships of regional forces. These include: the war waged by Israel against Lebanon during the summer of 2006, the United Nations Resolution 1701 that followed, and the war between the Lebanese army and the Islamist group *Fatah al-Islam* in the Palestinian camp Nahr al-Barid in the north of Lebanon between May and August 2007, not to mention the indirect effects of the power struggle being played out on the subject of Iranian nuclear capability, the war in Iraq, the attempts at the international isolation of Syria or even the power clashes in Palestine.

This chapter discusses the transformations in political Lebanon from 1995 to 2008 in the light of three cycles of mobilization: a civil mobilization (1995–2000), a sovereign mobilization (2000–spring 2005) and a partisan mobilization (summer 2005 onwards). These three cycles of mobilization can be distinguished by the dominant problematic which animates them, namely the way in which they participate in the formation of political identities and in which they intervene in the definition of actors and dominant groups (group-related social forms of domination) and counter-actors.

This brings me to discuss the restructuring of the public space, the Lebanese political scene and the change of modes of government during these three periods. It is a question more precisely of examining the interactions during each cycle of mobilization between the logics of the governing elites and the forms of opposition, paying particular attention to the impact of the involvement of regional and international actors in these internal dynamics. The movement from one cycle to another can be seen to be determined to a certain extent by what is going on at the international level: in Lebanese political society, the complex influence of regional and international powers never ceases to play a role of prime importance, sometimes only dissociable with difficulty from the internal stakes; Lebanese political actors have recourse to external sponsors – Syrian, Iranian, Saudi, French or American as the case may be – to bring influence to bear in internal relations. The diplomatic representatives of these countries appear sometimes to play the role of actors among others on the Lebanese political stage.

Rather than the process of economic, social and political liberalization in which certain countries in the Middle East and North Africa (MENA) region are engaged, it would seem, in the light of the last 15 years, that Lebanon is engaged in different cycles of mobilization or dynamics of protest which are restructuring state power. Without prejudging the exemplarity or atypicality of the Lebanese political trajectory in the region – in particular in terms of "state resilience", monopoly of legitimate violence and/or personalization of the regime – the analysis of the interferences between the strategies of the regime (and the evolution of its contours), the transformations of the elites and their modes of participation and finally the mobilizations "from bottom up" in these three moments can suggest some routes to follow as regards the logics of "political change without democratisation".[5] One must examine these dynamics without being either Manichean or teleological: the hypothesis of an opposition between civil and political society finds itself particularly at fault in this regard. It does not allow one to grasp with nuance the complex articulations between electoral politics, issue politics and contentious politics. Such articulations, far from forming part of a linear history, are to be read on the contrary in their countersteps and advances and withdrawals, and the different strategies and return journeys which political actors make between these spaces. This brings me to pay attention particularly to the stakes of the successive positions of the actors, which make them moreover difficult to describe: who is "in power"? Who is the "opposition"? And so on.

1. Aspects of an Endemic Crisis

In order to understand how these three cycles of mobilization operate *vis-à-vis* the structures of the Lebanese political arena and how those structures in return impose constraints on them and provide them with resources and opportunities, it is appropriate first of all to examine the principal aspects generally used to describe the endemic crisis of the Lebanese political system. These cycles of mobilization and the transformations which they bring in their wake are closely connected to the context in which the "civil" war in Lebanon broke out in 1975 and to that in which it came to an end 15 years later in 1990 with the signature and application of the Taif Agreement. This immediately highlights the interrelations of national, regional and international issues and actors on Lebanese territory by mixing the internal stakes of reform and power with those of regional geopolitics.

Notwithstanding all explanations and analyses that have been made of the Lebanese war, its outbreak in 1975 showed the limits of "consensual democracy" as a mode of government and non-violent conflict management in a multi-confessional society capable of leading to its development and reform while maintaining the balance of the political system. Many had long wanted to believe in the virtues of the consociate formula employed by the founders of the Lebanese state. Political communitarianism had become an institutionalized, consolidated and stabilized political formula, in the shape of the system established by the National Pact of 1943 and confirmed by the Taif Agreement in 1989, "both constitutive at the same time of the political structure of the country, of the crises which beset it and of the resolutions of those crises".[6] Historically, the "National Pact [of 1943] expresse[d] the consensus by which the new elites of Great Lebanon solemnly consecrate[d] its existence and define[d] its basic orientations".[7] The then President of the Republic, the Maronite Bishara al-Khoury, and Prime Minister, the Sunni Riad al-Solh, defined in *al-Mithaq al-Watani* (the National Pact) rules for power-sharing on confessional bases and in accordance with the principles of a consensual democracy: the great state functions (the presidencies of the Republic, the Council of Ministers and parliament, parliamentary seats and positions in government, high-level functions, etc.) were to be divided between the different communities.[8] More generally, the political system was thus organized around a communitarian definition of political stakes, social interests and their modes of representation. Nevertheless, the confessional sharing established by the National Pact was presented as temporary by the independence government, led by al-Solh, insofar as the executive set itself the goal of the long-term deconfessionalization of the system.

The impasse in which the consensual system found itself at the time of the outbreak of the conflict encouraged, among several Lebanese groups, the choice of violence as the mode of management and regulation of political conflict and as the means of imposing or equally opposing change. However, the duration of the war and its permanence, the impossibility for each Lebanese group to impose its military supremacy over the others, the disintegration of the state and its institutions, and the division of the country into confessional territories controlled by militias, demonstrated the inappropriateness of political regulation by means of violence between groups of almost equal weight in a zero-sum game of alliances in constant change at national, regional and international level. The use of violence showed its limitations. From being an instrument of change, it became a mode of government of militia fiefdoms and reopened the way to talks with a view to a negotiated solution of the crisis by means of inter-Lebanese dialogue (at Geneva in 1983 and Lausanne in 1984) or by means of a bilateral agreement with one of the main external actors connected to the crisis, i.e. Israel[9] or Syria.[10] These various attempts underlined, on the one hand, the invalidity of solutions negotiated at national level without inter-communitarian agreement or external sponsorship, and on the other that even an agreement imposed by an external power was not viable without a regional and international compromise. Thus the former Foreign Minister, Elie Salem, who negotiated the agreement with Israel in 1983 under the presidency of Amin Gemayel (1982–8), states that:

> [f]ollowing the cancellation of the Israel-Lebanon Withdrawal Agreement, the US, the European states, and the Vatican began to acknowledge Syria's leading role in Lebanon, and began to coordinate with Damascus to preserve "an independent, sovereign, and democratic Lebanon". While Syria had been perceived by them in the early 1980s as a threat, by the late 1980s they began to see in the Syrian presence in Lebanon a source of stability. Soon there was much reference to "Syria's legitimate interests in Lebanon".[11]

The new circumstances of the end of the 1980s assembled the conditions necessary for the elaboration of a regional and international compromise to bring the Lebanese crisis to an end. For Paul Salem:

> [a]fter 1989, however, the regional and international situation changed rapidly. The Gulf War ended with an abject Iraqi defeat and a resounding American victory, while the Soviet Union collapsed as a unified superpower. Both events had a bearing on US–Syrian relations, and hence on Lebanon [. . .] After offering troops to fight alongside the Americans against a fellow Baathist regime, Asad agreed to face-to-face talks with the Israelis and agreed to join an American-dominated peace process without a central role for the

Soviet Union or the United Nations. In Lebanon, he was also key in resolving the long-standing hostage crisis.[12]

William Harris insists on the external conditions which helped to end the war, stating:

> Lebanon temporarily became more strategically salient in 1989 because of new local, regional, and international circumstances – the Lebanese presidential vacancy, the Iraqi assertion in Arab politics with the end of the Iran–Iraq war, and the recession of Soviet power. The Soviet retreat made American ambitions to tame the Arab hinterland of the oil reservoir seem more realizable than the condition of superpower competition. Lebanon's international significance stemmed not from its own utility – in this sense Lebanon was irrelevant outside the Arab–Israeli arena – but from the fact that it had to be neutralized to help settle more important matters.[13]

Such external compromise is illustrated by the inter-Lebanese agreement concluded in the town of Taif in Saudi Arabia in 1989. It was negotiated under the auspices of Saudi Arabia and the Arab League with the support of the US, and preserved Syrian interests within Lebanon. Salem reports:

> The US encouraged the Arab League to take hold of the Lebanese situation, and a committee made up of King Fahd of Saudi Arabia, King Hassan II of Morocco, and President Benjedid of Algeria, was formed in May 1989 to bring the Lebanese crisis to an end. Its efforts led to the meeting of the Lebanese parliamentarians in Taif, Saudi Arabia and to adoption of the National Conciliation Document by parliament on November 5, 1989.[14]

The task of applying the agreement was entrusted to the Syrian regime, which imposed it by means of the force of its army in 1990 by excluding and removing its detractors.[15]

Among all the constitutional reforms and fundamental principles introduced or approved by the Taif Agreement, some had a more structuring effect than others. The basic principles of the Lebanese political system, namely political confessionalism and consensual democracy, were reconfirmed at Taif. The communitarian and confessional sharing of power and political representation was retained, and prerogatives were redistributed between the three presidencies of the Republic, the Council of Ministers and parliament. A large part of the powers and functions of the President of the Republic, of Maronite confession, was transferred to the Council of Ministers, presided over by a Prime Minister of Sunni confession. The power and role of the leader of parliament, of Shiite confession, was also strengthened. Thus, in accordance with the constitutional reforms, parliamentary seats and positions in government were shared equally between Muslims and Christians, and proportionately between the different confessions within each community.[16]

Under the Syrian tutelage (1990–2005), the consensual regime was organized around this presidential troika. The three presidents established a system of personal negotiation under the arbitrage of the neighbouring regime, which ensured continuity and balance, outside the institutional framework, to regulate issues and affairs which were the source of conflict between them. It was the job of the members of parliament to ratify the results, be they conflictual or consensual, of their discussions. This legal practice denatured the representative institutions and the principle of balance and separation of powers. When the troika came up against a disagreement, and general crisis threatened, it was the turn of the Syrian regime to impose its solution. Some solutions were the object of constitutional modification often presented as "exceptional and temporary". For example, the conflict over the amendment of Article 49 of the Constitution to extend the term of the President of the Republic, Elias Hrawi, in 1995 by three years was only resolved after the direct intervention of the Syrian President Hafez al-Assad.[17] The same article had been amended in a similar way in 1998 in order that the Commander-in-Chief of the army, Emile Lahoud, could be eligible in the course of the exercise of his functions.[18] In September 2004, the Syrian President Bashar al-Assad imposed a new extension of the term of President Lahoud which was not in conformity with the Constitution against the will of a large part of the Lebanese political class and the "international community".[19]

Around such rules of the game, largely conditioned by the internal and above all international interests that had put an end to the war, arenas of power were thus organized under the tutelage of the Syrian regime and on the basis of arbitrary and partial application of the reforms introduced by the Taif Agreement.

> The new regime was the product of an agreement extracted by American, Saudi and Syrian officials from an assembly of Lebanese parliamentarians in the Saudi resort city of Taif over three weeks in

October 1989. The Taif Agreement, more a US–Syrian contract than a Lebanese one, provided for a Lebanese regime integrating remnants of the old elite with militia elements and operating under Syrian strategic hegemony. In exchange for American acquiescence regarding their extended influence, the Syrians were expected to stabilize Lebanon and to restrain parties that disturbed Israel or challenged the West and its Arab allies – Palestinian militants and Hezballah.[20]

This negative management of the consociate system generated new imbalances in the postwar political system, unveiling its limits and its inability to maintain a consensual mode of government and of conflict management without external imposition or arbitrage. A good example is the serious political crisis which degenerated into a civil conflict in the course of the first weeks of May 2008, when the armed forces of the "opposition" and of the "majority" clashed in the streets of Beirut and Tripoli and in the mountains. Only under Arab mediation did the protagonists finish by signing an agreement at Doha in Qatar to elect General Sleimane as President of the Republic after six months of power vacuum and to establish a national unity government.

This political history, traced very broadly, has not only influenced the formation of the recent institutions of the Lebanese political arena, but has also determined to a great extent the resources and constraints available to the different protagonists of policies and politics. In this context, what has recently begun to be called "civil society" at the international level in the wake of the East European revolutions in particular has very little scope for participation in the process of terminating war. The different cycles of mobilization which can be observed are on the one hand fashioned by these rules of the game, and on the other militate for their change and transformation.

2. Civil Mobilizations

The first cycle of mobilizations can be described as "civil". Between 1995 and 2000, several organizations, initiatives or social movements presenting common and particular characteristics emerged from the "margins" rather than from "bottom up". In a context where the governing elites tended to neutralize any sort of opposition coming from the interior of the system, such speaking out on the part of journalists, academics, lawyers etc. representing a superior middle class situated at the edges of that system had the effect of requalifying citizens' action and of mobilizing the Lebanese. It gave a politico-legal and constitutional meaning to participation in the public domain and reconciled citizens with political action, which had been disowned on account of the violence of the war and the practices of the political class at the end of the conflict.

Three categories of actor and protagonist in the internal political game can be fairly clearly distinguished during this period. This allows for some reflection regarding the transformation of Lebanese political elites and of their description: "governing elites", elites in "opposition" and "civil" actors, each having relationships of variable geometry with foreign actors.

The appearance of cohesion and of homogeneity to which the "governing elites" attest during this period derives above all from the homogeneity imposed on them by the actor dominating political society, in this case the Syrian regime. Thus, despite their divisions, officials of the public and political authorities were able to maintain the rules of the game and to impose them on the entirety of the political elites, while neutralizing the political space by means of several combined tactics: recourse to repression or exclusion (for example the imprisonment of Samir Geagea in 1994, the exile of Michel Aoun in 1990 or the bloody repression of *Hezbollah* demonstrations,[21] etc.), the locking of the political system by means of control of the electoral system and its process, which restarted during this period,[22] or the logic of cooptation and distribution within large programmes of work and reconstruction (reconstruction work began with the arrival of Prime Minister Rafiq Hariri in 1992, in particular through the intermediation of his company Solidere).[23]

The stakes of the exercise of political opposition during this period are complex and closely connected to the rules and conditions of participation in the political game. On the one hand, in a consociate system, the principle of power-sharing between the different representative segments renders the principle of opposition ambiguous. Either it is expressed through the exercise of the right of veto which each group enjoys: Syrian power gave or withheld this right to one or the other of the three Presidents in order to serve its own interests and maintain a sort of negative balance within the troika. Alternatively, it is expressed between those with competing claims to the representation of each group, or, within the government itself, between the representatives of each group. In return, opposition to the government becomes more costly. This was the case, for example, with the Lebanese Forces party when it tried directly to question the government and to oppose its policies: it was dissolved after the imprisonment of its leader Samir Geagea, who was accused of an attack against a church in 1994.[24] Despite the amnesty adopted by parliament in 1991 for crimes perpetrated during the conflict (with the exception of crimes against the state and politicians), several times during his imprisonment Geagea was charged with atrocities alleged to have been carried out during the war.

On the other hand, the period is characterized by the banning of political leaders, who thus found themselves *de facto* in the position of opponents of the regime. For these excluded or mal-integrated actors or groups, there were many arenas of opposition but none situated within the central institutions of representation or pluralism. When absent from government or barely or not present in parliament, they "opposed" the government and the regime at local level, by boycotting elections or in "virtual" arenas (from abroad, through intermediate communiqués, as General Michel Aoun was able to do from his exile in France for 15 years, etc.). This absence of representation in governmental institutions did not translate in the same way in terms of effective power. That was determined particularly by relations with the dominant actor, the Syrian regime: radical opposition for some (essentially the Lebanese Forces and the Aounist movement) and objective alliance for others (particularly Rafiq Hariri, who accepted Syrian tutelage in return for the position of Prime Minister and the launch of the project of reconstruction of the country through the intermediation of his private company Solidere).

In reaction to such a closure of the political field, civil actors organized themselves, "in the absence of anything better" for some, in the associative space particularly in order to oppose government policies, but not the government itself.[25] Far from being hegemonic, such initiatives remained marginal in a political space built around Syrian tutelage and mobilizing political leaderships. Openly non-violent, these initiatives set up in the collective cause problematics crucial to political society after 15 years of civil war; questions such as how to bring a collective crosscutting action based on the watchword "civil" in a society described before and during the war as segmented, conflictual and warlike: in other words, how to mobilize social groups in the face of this particularly dominant and determinative political and social form of organization. These initiatives faced three challenges: disputing religious and communitarian solidarities; marking out for themselves military, violent or, as the case may be, militia-based forms of action; and making political claims, bearing for example on human rights or political freedoms, in a "closed" political system.

This period bore the imprint of such initiatives insofar as they made claims for the deconfessionalization of the political system and for the development of a peaceful mode of political regulation audible, and as they opposed both the intervention of the security services in public life and restrictions imposed on the freedom of expression.

This "civil" mobilization took root among circles of intellectuals and the circuit of educated inhabitants of Beirut, who signed and circulated petitions and published articles denouncing the corruption of the regime, calling for respect for the law and opposing amendment of the Constitution for personal ends. This movement expanded in "civil" associations. Such associations developed at this time and were organized around various causes such as defence of human rights, defence of the environment, defence of civil and political rights and defence of public freedoms. They were involved in the placing on the agenda and treatment of dossiers concerning the electoral law, the law on associations, the question of civil status/the law on personal status, the question of those who disappeared during the war, environmental policies, etc.

In April 1996, following the bombing of the south of Lebanon by Israel, the Shiite majority population was massively displaced towards other regions. At that time, two civil associations mobilized a whole network of associations, creating a chain of solidarity under the name of the "National Assembly for support for the survival of Lebanon" to help and welcome displaced persons.[26] This movement can be considered not only as revealing the capacities of civil society, but also as a matrix, a "mother movement" for the social movements which would succeed it. Not only was it the first mobilization on a national scale since the end of the war which transcended the fragmentations and divisions of a Lebanese society weakened by deep crises, but it also formed part of the growing rift between the "civil" population and the formal political authorities in an unfavourable and hostile regional context.[27]

Many other movements of the same type would be initiated by civil associations: the Assembly for the Holding of Municipal Elections, launched in 1997; Mobilization for the Social Rights of Disabled Persons, launched in the same year; the Assembly for a civil law facilitating personal status, better known by the name of the "Assembly for Civil Marriage", launched in March 1998; the National Campaign for the Age of Political Majority at 18, launched in 1998; the Movement against the Death Penalty, launched in 1998; the "Right to Know" Campaign for those who disappeared during the war, launched in 1999, etc. Two more permanent movements developed in parallel, an environmental movement and a movement for the defence of public freedoms. Clearly, these were not the only forms of political contestation to exist during this period, which also saw demonstrations by students, unions and partisans. Indeed, civil mobilizations were deployed when the public authorities succeeded in defusing union movements by repressing or dividing them. The student movements of the immediate postwar period took over the action of political parties banned essentially for having questioned the Syrian tutelage (Lebanese Forces and the Aounist movement), but those movements were contained within the bounds of their universities. As far as union mobilizations – organized in particular by the General Confederation of Lebanese Workers – are concerned, they attacked the policies of reconstruction and were severely repressed.

These movements gave an apparent indication of the potential for mobilization of the Lebanese political scene by revealing an ability to react quickly to threats on a national scale, as if latent mobilization structures were putting themselves in place. They took different forms, raised different issues and were stretched out over long or short durations, but they presented common characteristics in their organization and modes of action, reinforced by the fact that they were all animated by civil associations. Beyond the fact that such associations found in them an effective means of bringing into the public domain certain of their claims, it seems that experience tended to be generalized and to become a model. Their actors gained and gradually built up knowledge in action in the same way that they established networks and brought in their wake a variety of actors.

Thus, the Lebanese Association for Democratic Elections, the Movement for Human Rights, Green Line, *Minbar al-Akhdar* (Green Forum), the Association for the Defence of Rights and Freedoms, the

Lebanese Association for Human Rights, the Union of Lebanese Disabled Persons, the Lebanese Women's Council, etc. were the vault-keys of the development of social movements enjoying extensive media coverage which reorganized the field of Lebanese protest.

Such civil movements raised real long-term political challenges: they pleaded on the one hand for reconstruction and reconciliation, and on the other for the rule of law and fundamental institutional reform. They thus took at their word the slogans of two Presidents in office, Rafiq Hariri and Emile Lahoud respectively. But they also proposed alternative modalities in relation to these issues which appealed for the taking into account of sensitive questions for the balance of the system: shedding light on those who disappeared during the civil war in order to find a lasting reconciliation; basing the construction of a civil peace on the communities' collective experiences of rapprochement; guaranteeing the conditions for balanced reconstruction and the preservation of the environment; encouraging the participation of young people, women and the disabled in public life; etc. They proposed substantial reforms of the system of political representation and of the functioning of the institutions that put under the spotlight the leadership not only of the representatives of the public authorities, but also of the opponents. Thus ideas for decentralization and amendment of the electoral law were put forward by these associations from the mid-1990s onwards. Such civil claims only rarely found the political support necessary to succeed. In certain cases, they were even confronted by a "social counter-movement". This was so for the movement defending the establishment of a civil personal status. With their core prerogatives threatened, religious and community leaders joined forces to rally the political elites to them and caused the movement to fail.[28]

In many respects, the development of these associations is comparable to the wave of associations observable elsewhere in the region and also in "Western democracies", or even in Eastern Europe, to take the closest examples. Moreover, such associations often feed on their respective experiences, South–South and North–South. They have the same financial backers and their agendas are often aligned around similar issues. Thus, as regards electoral reform and election observation, an "international" associative expertise has developed and asserted itself in the region. The same is true in the fields of human rights and even the associations of the families of the "disappeared". In all cases, recourse to the "associative" form to act on the collective has undeniable interests for these actors: in authoritarian contexts, it gives firstly an opportunity to avoid direct confrontation with the public authorities, and for certain actors the associative engagement is undertaken "in the absence of anything better". Furthermore, the associative framework is flexible and allows for ad hoc and quick action which allows for the targeting of different audiences according to the cause at stake. But it also presents major inconveniences in terms of public and political action, such as its fragility, its weak social anchorage and its lack of representativeness. Unlike other kinds of political organization, political parties or unions, these associations, as "political" as they might be, are not situated in the domain of the competition for power, or at least do not directly question the legitimacy of the governing class. They do not pretend either to expose major social splits around the formation of a collective political identity. Finally, some reproach them for obstructing the conditions for fundamental change of the system by mitigating certain of its weaknesses.[29] Nevertheless, the recent history of Eastern Europe shows that the activities of such civil associations can play a role in the laboratory of dissidence or at least that of reform of the political domain. In the case of Lebanon, the mobilizations of the 1990s impacted less on the structure of the political system than on its functioning. They led to the organization of municipal elections and the observation of elections, the placing on the public agenda of the question of associative freedoms, the adoption of rights for disabled persons and the creation of a Ministry of the Environment. In return, as far as their claims regarding decentralization, deconfessionalization and fundamental reform of the electoral law are concerned, they did not find an effective political sounding-board.

The 1990s ended with such a negative balance maintained in the interests of the Syrian regime and its Lebanese allies. Lebanon was rarely present on the international agenda before 11 September 2001 and the famous "great Middle East" project.[30] In such a context, civil movements were weakly supported by the international organizations that some years later would worship at the altar of democratization in Lebanon.[31] The political actors who had accepted the rules of game and were trying to benefit from it developed two strategies. Some played the Syrian card openly, particularly those who held the most important positions or who owed their power entirely to Syrian intervention. Others adopted a resigned or hopeless attitude: without clearly showing their allegiance to

Syrian power, they questioned neither its hegemony nor the organization of the management of power following the Taif Agreement.

3. Sovereign Mobilization

A second cycle of mobilization emerged at the beginning of the 2000s. It is "sovereign": various mobilizations were organized in effect around the principal objective of the "liberation" of the public and national spaces from the domination of Syrian power and the intervention of the various Lebanese and Syrian security and intelligence services. One can broadly speaking locate its catalysts or triggers in 2000–2001. It reached its peak with the great movements of spring 2005, following the assassination of Rafiq Hariri, and particularly the demonstrations of 8 and 14 March 2005, which saw millions of Lebanese take to the streets of Beirut. Attesting to the matrix-like character of these huge gatherings, Roger Naba'a notes that:

> Since the assassination of Hariri some two years ago, demonstration has become the sole mode of political expression of the Lebanese. It is to their rhythm – more than 40 in two years – that Lebanon lived between February 2005 and February 2007; it is beneath their sign that this period has gone down in the memory of these places, while two demonstrations, those of 8 and 14 March 2005, have given their "name" to two camps of antagonists. Thus the Group of the 8 March and the Group of the 14 March were born.[32]

This cycle is "sovereign" not only on account of the political forces of 14 March and those of the anti-Syrian coalition, but also on account of the forces of 8 March (in particular the two Shiite movements *Hezbollah* and the *Amal* movement), which while asserting their allegiance to Syria insisted on the independence and sovereignty of Lebanon *vis-à-vis* the interference of certain countries and more precisely the US and France.

The imposed cohesion and hegemony no longer held. Several factors contributed to the change in balance and the transformations in the power relationships within the regime and the Lebanese political space.

First of all, the parliamentary elections of 2000 indicated that there was a break as compared to previous ballots, particularly as concerned the recruitment and circulation of the elites in power. Competing lists putting up against each other great names of the system (in particular the three presidents of the troika) replaced the previous single and consensual lists imposed by the Syrian regime. As Picard indicates, the stakes in these elections were several. "New Members of Parliament, confident in their electoral legitimacy, opened up a public space which transcended the communitarian space and was abundantly broadcast by the media and by intellectual and student circles."[33] Moreover, in central Druze and Christian regions, the results of the vote "crystallised a rejection of the Syrian tutelage".[34]

The death of Hafez al-Assad and the withdrawal of the Israeli army from South Lebanon in 2000, and then the reorientations of the Near Eastern policy of the great international powers after September 2001, exacerbated by the war in Iraq from 2003 onwards, transformed the internal stakes and the power relationships between the Lebanese elites.

Thus a first questioning of the Syrian presence in Lebanon was brought about within the very heart of institutions such as parliament by individuals or groups who, by their participation and positions taken during the first cycle of mobilization, had indeed contributed to the rooting of the system of tutelage. The Druze leader Walid Joumblatt illustrates this: his critical positions taken after the elections of 2000 as regarded the Syrian presence in Lebanon earned him direct threats from a Member of Parliament from the Syrian National Party.

The tensions and divisions within the governing elites became more intense, as is shown by the electoral divisions, while the considerable changes taking place at national, regional and international level upset previous positions even more. France and the US found in Lebanon a ground for agreement to pass over their disagreement on the subject of the invasion of Iraq. This turned into Resolution 1559, adopted by the United Nations Security Council at the initiative of the two countries.[35]

In this context, certain leaders in either the "opposition" or the "government" changed strategy in order to derive benefit from the opportunities which appeared to be presenting themselves. Gradually a major opposition was organized around the pole of resistance to the dominant actor, Syria, which brought in its wake sometimes a jamming and in all cases a reformulation of political alliances.

In particular, the principal actors of the earlier "civil" movements allied themselves to the political elites who rallied to the watchword "sovereign" by assimilating those of their claims which related to public freedoms and non-violence, to those of the "political opposition". They left suspended, however, the part of their mobilizations which related to reform of the Lebanese political system. This strategy can be explained in several ways. On the one hand, during the first cycle of mobilization, they had tried to juggle between these two aspects of their mobilizations (the liberation of the political and national space from Syrian tutelage and the fundamental reform of the system). That tactic was no longer working. On the other hand, certain persons were looking for support among the "opposition" and even to carve out political careers for themselves. In both cases, it was a question of seizing the opportunity which was presenting itself for their causes with the emergence of an opposition. However, this strategy very quickly showed the misunderstandings on which it was based. The very name of their mobilization reflected different points of view: certain actors and the American administration called it the "Cedar revolution", while others called it an "independence uprising" (*intifada al-istiqlal*). The former group situated itself within the global language of "democratization", while the latter positioned themselves within a nationalist reference. The definition and fronts of the opposition therefore changed lines of demarcation. It was during this period that different political poles and groups were established. The *Qornet Shehwan* group was composed of about thirty Christian political personalities, all political functions confused. They adopted a common document which

> claimed in particular the restoration of Lebanese sovereignty and the redeployment of the Syrian army in accordance with one of the clauses of the Taif Agreement. In the course of 2000/1, the leaders of the group appeared to be pillars of the rapprochement between several segments (Druze, Christian and lay) which was coming about between the leaders of the Maronite and Druze communities, as well as within student circles and certain intellectual and political groups (such as the Democratic Forum or the Movement for Democratic Renewal).[36]

As regards the Bristol Group, named after a hotel in Beirut, it was made up of different political groups, all confessions mixed up, whose main aim was the application of the Taif Agreement in the context of a free and sovereign independent Lebanon and who were "reassured by the new posture of the international community with regard to the Lebanese file in a sense which converged with their sovereign claims".[37] This movement reached its peak with the independence uprising, which covered broad fringes of society. The detractors of these groups gathered in similar fora, such as the Ain al-Tineh meeting (named after the place of residence of the leader of parliament, Nabih Berri), which defended Lebanon's strategic alliance with Syria while rejecting the interference of the international community in Lebanese affairs.

Alongside these strategies of the political elites, this period is characterized by an evolution of the arenas of protest. The key point is evidently the cycle of demonstration and counter-demonstration of spring 2005. This logic was perceptible from 2001 onwards and contributed to the polarization of the political game around the split between those who are ironically called the "Group of the 8 March" and the "Group of the 14 March".

In this context, a misunderstanding arose between the political elites, who transformed their alliances and positions in strategies which were complex and sometimes difficult to read in the name of an agenda of national liberation on which they could not agree,[38] and a Lebanese society which had showed its politicization and capacity to react and mobilize around these problems by taking to the streets *en masse*. In other words, the reconstitution of the political space of the elites, and the rules and the norms on which those rules were based, did not necessarily coincide with the transformations of a society which was becoming poorer and whose expectations went beyond the sharing of power between governing and opposing elites.[39] A gap opened up between the expectations of reform expressed in the earlier mobilizations and the interests of the political leaders, who were anxious to preserve their privileges.

4. Partisan Mobilization

The balance imposed within the consensual system no longer held. The Syrian withdrawal translated into an absence of a referee. Between 1990 and May 2005, the dominant Syrian actor had been an off-field actor which imposed itself from the outside. Hegemonic, it had played the role of referee between the different communities, and in particular within the presidential troika. It had ensured the management and functioning of the system in such a way as to serve its own interests (political, economic, strategic, etc.) and the interests of its principal Lebanese allies. In other words, the Syrian regime had maintained the stability of the Lebanese system in a sort of negative equilibrium. The conflicts of interest and the political antagonisms which the Syrian cover had masked, albeit badly, began to express themselves openly, in particular within the political institutions. Thus the weaknesses of the consensual system resurfaced. The organization of armed resistance against Israel, the alignment of Lebanon behind the Syrian-Iranian axis or the pole gravitating around the US, and the opportunity to establish a special tribunal for Lebanon for the trial of the assassins of Rafiq Hariri, were among the principal strategic subjects of disagreement which gradually created a dividing-line between two partisan alliances. The Group of the 8 March, dominated by *Hezbollah* and General Aoun's Free Patriotic Movement (FPM), and the Group of the 14 March, bringing together Saad Hariri's Future Movement, Walid Joumblatt's Progressive Socialist Party (PSP), Samir Geagea's Lebanese Forces and Amin Gemayel's Phalangists, struggled to gain power over the institutions of state. Up until November 2006, each of these groups were represented not only in parliament, but also in the Council of Ministers (with the exception of the FPM), in accordance with the logic of consensus. After the entry of *Hezbollah* ministers into the government following the 2005 parliamentary elections, the FPM *de facto* occupied a position unique among the main political parties. In disagreement with the division of portfolios, it was the only party not to have any ministry, and therefore it concentrated its opposition within parliament and during electoral ballots. The participation of *Hezbollah* in government for the first time in 2005 (it had been present in parliament since 1992) can be explained as a consequence of the Syrian withdrawal: in the absence of its objective long-standing ally, the party entered the Council of Ministers in order to be able to defend its interests there.

In this context, a third cycle of mobilization began during summer 2005. It was a partisan mobilization opposing different political forces which sometimes played at violent confrontation and came close to civil conflict, before embarking on a mini-civil war for a few days in May 2008. This mobilization took up previous contours. It confirmed, or even reinforced, the political and segmentary splits of Lebanese society and its public authorities. This cycle of mobilization is in fact characterized by intra-community alliances (the *Hezbollah*/FPM pole as against the Group of the 14 March). However, what was at issue was competition between leaders or groups to represent the political community. The logics of patronage and the clan are determinative. In other words, each political leader is seeking to rally a community in the name of a partisan claim. Their objective is to strengthen their position and to maximize their gain on the political chessboard during the tumultuous period which the Lebanese scene and the region are going through, while waiting for the imposition of a new order, or even a new redistribution or restructuring of power, by external actors. In this sense, the Doha Agreement of May 2008 can only be seen a temporary pact reproducing this unstable equilibrium. It forbids recourse to weapons and violence, advocates the strengthening of the role of the state and calls for the election of the Commander-in-Chief of the army, General Sleimane, as President of the Republic. It allows for the formation of a new government of national union on a consensual model, giving a third of seats to the opposition. Finally, it adopts the principle of an electoral law based on a small constituency (necessarily communitarian), the *qada'*. If the terms of the Agreement constitute a contingent compromise allowing for an exit from crisis, they do not for that matter respond to the endemic problems of the political system, namely its political confessionalism and consensual mode of government, nor to the question of the insecurity and inability of the state authorities to control the entirety of the national territory.

In other words, in this new cycle of mobilization, partisan structures take different forms, reflecting the evolution of the Lebanese partisan scene. "Traditional" parties or parties born from the conversion of militias, such as the PSP or the Phalangists in the former case or *Amal, Hezbollah* or the Lebanese Forces in the latter, are organized around personalized leaderships, on a communitarian base and with a stated ideology. Political movements such as the Future Movement or the FPM were formally established in the postwar period. Such movements also have a personalized leadership and a largely communitarian base, but their ideological axis is less strong. Finally, parties such as the old Communist Party and the more recent Democratic Left Party, which aim at non-confessional mobilization, have difficulty in gathering support. Let us underline here that the fracture between the Group of the 8 March and the Group of the 14 March transcends such classifications.

This configuration saw the emergence of a more "classic" form of opposition, namely an opposition to the government devoid of Shiite representatives which was able to make its voice heard in institutional and non-institutional arenas since it had recourse to demonstrations, to the street, to sit-ins, etc. The five Shiite ministers in the Lebanese government, belonging to *Hezbollah* and the *Amal* Movement, resigned on 11 November 2006. In their struggle for power, the Group of the 8 March wanted to bring pressure to bear in order to increase its presence in the Council of Ministers and to reach a third of its members. This would have enabled them to block decisions, in particular on the subject of the strategic questions that divided them from the other clan. When this strategy showed itself to be ineffective, they made use of other political instruments, only returning to a government of national understanding in June 2008. This included for the first time representatives of the FPM. Once again, the notion of "opposition" was diluted.

Whatever the case may be, from December 2006 to May 2008 the Group of the 8 March made use of classic opposition tools, organizing a sit-in in the centre of Beirut beginning in December 2006 in front of the seat of government in support of the formation of a "national union government". Novel situations arose during this period: the government pursued its mandate while the ministers who had resigned threatened, together with their groups, to establish a parallel government. The system found no solution but remained on track while, in the absence of an agreement between the parties, the seat of the President of the Republic remained empty from November 2007 to May 2008. The political game returned to ways of violence, partisans belonging to the two camps dying during the demonstrations of 23 and 25 January 2006 and January 2008, and above all in the street-fighting of May 2008, which continued in Tripoli throughout the summer of that year.

In this tense context, some civil society actors tried to detach themselves from these petty local quarrels or communitarian splits and propose crosscutting actions to unite around either a common project or certain principles of coexistence. But their voices were barely audible, as the polarization of the political elites reverberated among the great majority of civil society associations and occupied the quasi-totality of the media.

In sum, following the withdrawal of the Syrian army in spring 2005, the Lebanese political representatives found themselves left to manage their conflicts on their own while ensuring their cohesion and the balance of the communitarian system. After several attempts, they failed to govern themselves for several reasons: personal ambition; intra-communitarian conflicts (in particular within the Maronite community and over political balance – what type of troika, which prerogatives and above all what type of legitimacy and representativeness should be pursued); and conflicts over policy and plans relating to the economy and to strategic conflicts (the Israeli–Arab conflict, alliances and allegiances). All these internal conflicts had regional and international ramifications which complicated their resolution in what was already a very tense regional situation.[40]

No dominant actor could impose itself on others without the risk of tearing apart the fabric of national life. The events of spring 2008 show that another civil war is quite possible, and that it would be as destructive for all groups and communities as the last one. The wounds and the memory of the past war of 1975 to 1990 act for now as a fragile and selective negative incitement holding the main actors back from launching themselves into a new fratricidal war. The interests of the various regional and international actors in concluding a compromise and imposing a solution remain for the time being divergent.

One could imagine for a moment that the Lebanese army might be capable of assuming the role of the hegemonic actor which imposes a solution or compromise on the totality of actors, while maintaining the balance of the system and the cohesion of society,[41] much as the Turkish or Algerian armies have done. But this hypothesis is barely credible in the case of the Lebanese army, which is the image of its society, divided and fragmented. If it has been able since 2006 to take on new tasks, particularly at the southern border where it has been deployed, or more recently in the context of the fight against *Fatah al-Islam* in the Palestinian camp of Nahr al-Barid, or even in interposing itself between demonstrators, it is far from being able to develop an '*asabiyya*, an *esprit de corps* which is stronger than the communitarian, confessional and other links. Its passive and embarrassed attitude at the time of the battles of May 2008, when it let the main fighting go on without intervening, illustrates this.

5. Conclusion

Lebanon has come close to a generalized violent crisis. While it may have temporarily saved the country from sinking, the Doha Agreement did not propose new rules of the game, but quite the reverse. Foreign interventions have been numerous but do not necessarily push for a search for new methods of political regulation. The clear intervention of the US and France, as well as of the Arab states and Iran, by means for example of the adoption of Resolution 1701 or the Arab mediation of May 2008, or by the indirect means of the financing of the reconstruction after the war of summer 2006, appears to illustrate this. One could equally refer to the Paris III conference of January 2007 on support for reform or debt finance. One should finally emphasize the controversial decision of the United Nations Security Council to place the creation of the special tribunal for the government under chapter 7 of the United Nations Charter. With the establishment of such a tribunal having stirred up profound differences in Lebanon and blocked the functioning of its institutions, it is the United Nations which decides, not without exceeding its prerogatives in the view of certain international lawyers.

This leads to the conclusion that Lebanon has been engaged for the past 18 years in a process of political change without democratization, or rather without reform. The interactions between these actors in these different spaces of the political domain are complex and far from being univocal. Their analysis allows us to understand the debates, dynamics and tension which have traversed, and still traverse, the Lebanese political scene. This perspective allows us to speak of "political spaces in the plural [where] political action takes place on a multiplicity of stages".[42]

We know that the relative atypicality of Lebanon in the region derives from its consensual political formula, which leads us to look at the restructurings of the public authorities and more broadly at the question of power in Lebanon. To what extent is "the exception" of the Lebanese trajectory really atypical?

The National Pact of 1943 and the Taif Agreement of 1989 established a system of political confessionalism. Within such a system, no hegemonic group can *a priori* acquire a position of exclusive power. On the other hand, the idea of "national" and "individual" citizenship is to some extent sacrificed in the name of the maintenance of peace between the groups.[43] However, in the famous "grey zone",[44] the syndromes of the "feckless pluralism"[45] of Lebanese political society are expressed in and transformed into the three cycles of mobilization.

On one hand, as a result of these rules of the game, the political elites of the main groups or parties are perceived by the majority of citizens as corrupt, selfish and inefficient. For some people, they have resigned from their public responsibilities. However, this does not prevent these same elites from showing a strong ability to mobilize *en masse* on bases of patronage and confession.

On the other hand, despite the consociate pluralist formula, Lebanese political society has not been protected from authoritarian logics and particularly "dominant-power politics":[46] from the end of the war in 1990 until 2005, Syrian power played, more or less directly, a predominant role in political decision-making. In the particular case, the dominant actor imposed itself from outside the national political space, partially determining the terms of the articulation between the elements of civil society and the structures of political society.

Finally, with regards to the three recent cycles of mobilization and current developments on the Lebanese political scene, a last question could be as follows: after the withdrawal of the Syrian army, is what is at stake today a competition about becoming the dominant actor in a political system so organized as to prevent the domination of a single group or person? If so, this could open the way to a new domination from outside.

Notes

1 This chapter was translated from French by David Ashton.
2 This name has been given to the demonstrations by the various Lebanese opposition groups gathered together in the Bristol Group (*Liqa' al-Bristol*).
3 No local election took place between 1963 and 1998. Parliamentary elections restarted in 1992 after 20 years of interruption (the last ones having been held in 1972), but the call by the majority of Christian political figures and the Maronite patriarchy for a boycott of the parliamentary elections of 1992 was obeyed by 70 per cent. The same call for a boycott was obeyed more moderately in 1996.
4 Lipjhart 1997; Picard 1997, 2001a.
5 Heydeman 2002; Albrecht *et al.* 2004.
6 Bahout 1999, p. 300.
7 Corm 2003, p. 96.

8   According to the "unwritten rule" which is the Pact and which has become legal custom, the Christians renounce Western foreign protection for Lebanon and the Muslims, in return, recognize the definitive existence of Great Lebanon and renounce any desire for the attachment of Lebanon to any Syrian or Arab entity. For analysis of the National Pact, cf. Corm 2003 and Rabbath 1986.
9   The agreement of 17 May 1983 was concluded between Israel, after its invasion of Lebanon in 1982, and the Lebanese state, and was rejected in particular by W. Joumblatt, N. Berri and S. Franjieh and annulled in March 1984.
10 The tripartite agreement of December 1985 was concluded between the three main Lebanese militia, the Socialist Progressive Party of W. Joumblatt (Druze), the Lebanese Forces of E. Hobeika (Christian) and the *Amal* movement of N. Berri (Shiite) under the auspices of Syria. It was rejected by the *Kata'ib* party and by the then second-in-command of the Lebanese Forces, S. Geagea.
11 Salem 1992, p. 26.
12 Salem 1993, p. 73.
13 Harris 1997, pp. 237–8.
14 Salem 1992, p. 30.
15 Essentially General M. Aoun, exiled to France, and the leader of the militia of Lebanese Forces, S. Geagea, condemned to imprisonment for an attack carried out after the end of the conflict.
16 For a presentation and critical analysis of the reforms introduced by the Taif Agreement, cf. Maïla 1990.
17 Al-Assad stated to the press that "there was unanimity in Lebanon in favour of an extension of the term of the President of the Republic" (*al-Safir*, 11 September 1995).
18 Under Article 49 of the Constitution, an outgoing President of the Republic can only be re-elected after an interval of six years. Under the same article high officials and the Commander-in-Chief of the army can only be elected if they resigned two years previously.
19 United Nations Security Council Resolution 1559 expressed in particular the disapproval of the American and French governments of this decision.
20 Harris 1997, p. 240.
21 In 1993, the government decided to ban public demonstrations following a deadly accident during clashes between the forces of law and order and *Hezbollah* militants who had come out into the street to protest against the Oslo agreements. This decision was regularly recalled whenever unions, associations, political parties or other organizations called for a demonstration. In 1995, a state of emergency was even decreed in order to prevent the huge public gathering for which the General Confederation of Lebanese Workers was calling in order to protest at the cost of living. This decree would be lifted by the government of S. Hoss in December 1998.
22 Parliamentary elections were organized in 1992, 1996 and 2000, presidential elections in 1995 and 1998, and finally local elections in 1998.
23 Beyhum 1991; Debié and Pieter 2003.
24 Moukheiber 2000.
25 Karam 2006.
26 For a chronology of events, cf. the report entitled "Crime de paix", *Orient Express*, 6 May 1996.

27 For an analysis of the behaviour of the militants of this mobilization, cf. al-Amin 1997 and Chamess ed-Dine 1997.
28 Karam 2006.
29 [Eds' note:] Cf. the analysis of the NGOs sector in Egypt by Beinin in this book.
30 Rougier 2005.
31 By way of comparison, cf. Carapico 2002.
32 Naba'a, "La crise libanaise dans le miroir de ses manifestations", 28 March 2007, http://www.peuplesmonde.com.
33 Picard 2001b, pp. 26–7.
34 Ibid., p. 23.
35 *L'Orient Le Jour*, 15 October 2005.
36 Favier 2006, p. 4.
37 Ibid., pp. 4–5.
38 This was the case in particular at the time of the parliamentary elections of summer 2005, after the withdrawal of the Syrian army, when the composition of the electoral lists gave rise to contradictory behaviour. The clear positions taken some months earlier seemed to be emptied of meaning by the political leaders.
39 For data and socio-economic analysis, cf. Nahas' chapter in this book.
40 On the game of the different international interventions, cf. Bahout 2005; Mermier and Picard 2007.
41 On this point see Picard's chapter in this book.
42 Geisser *et al.* 2006, p. 194.
43 Salamé 1994.
44 Carothers 2002.
45 Linz 1975.
46 El-Khazen 2003.

4
SAUDI ARABIA'S POLITICAL DEMOBILIZATION IN REGIONAL COMPARISON: MONARCHICAL TORTOISE AND REPUBLICAN HARES

Steffen Hertog

Introduction

No matter whether one is fascinated or repelled by Saudi Arabia's ruling elite, in any discussion of political mobilization and participation in Saudi Arabia, one will inevitably be drawn to pay homage to "the instinct of self-preservation of the great, flabby, but pervasive jellyfish of the Al-Saud".[1] I found this flowery turn of phrase in a British diplomatic dispatch from 1972, but it appears even more apt 35 years later.

Saudi Arabia has seen much less change in the conduct of politics and state–society relations than the republics under study in this volume. This does not mean that there has not been a certain convergence of systems in the Arab world, but is mostly because the republics have shed their populist mobilizational structures, which Saudi Arabia never had. Recent moves to create ostensibly representative, formal-corporatist institutions in Saudi Arabia have not resulted in substantial change in the paternal, clientelistic political strategies of the regime, which still are the essence of Saudi politics. The new corporatist institutions largely remain state-dependent and have little popular outreach, which makes them surprisingly similar to the formerly influential, but now largely disembowelled parties, unions and syndicates of other Arab states. One point in which Saudi Arabia paradoxically differs from both Morocco and the formerly populist republics is that it has been more successful in keeping up its distributional, inclusive socio-economic agenda – which has never been tied to political mobilization, however.

Continuity of both political actors and of the rules through which they operate is the underlying theme on all levels of analysis addressed in this book: Saudi Arabia's status as a large and fiscally autonomous rentier state shields it from most international and transnational forces of change.[2] On the regime level, the leading actors have come from the same group of princes for the last 45 years. There has been somewhat more change on the level of other elites, but this has been on the level of individuals rather than groups. Among the technocratic, religious and business clienteles of the regime, business alone has managed to somewhat improve its status, but without gaining a voice in politics at large. Finally, lower social strata in the kingdom remain politically inactivated, with the state continuing to support (and control) a large part of them.

To underline the deep-seated nature of recurring patterns, this chapter is somewhat more historically oriented than most of the others in this volume. A snapshot would not do justice to the Al-Saud's aptitude for reinventing themselves as paternal rulers, and for swiftly deflating any independent political mobilization, in very different historical contexts.

The chapter will therefore start with a substantial historical section that maps out how the paternal clientelism of the Saudi polity was constructed and expanded between the 1950s and the 1980s, and how non-state social actors were fragmented or coopted, leaving royalty and bureaucracy as main active constituents of the polity. I will then discuss a number of challenges to the regime, including non-state Islamist mobilization, and how these were dealt with through established structures of repression and, more importantly, cooptation. The empirical section of the chapter will conclude with a discussion of recent corporatist initiatives undertaken by the regime, explaining how thus far they represent a modernization of the regime's political paternalism at best, but no substantial political change. The final section will put the Saudi case in a comparative perspective, also briefly discussing other cases in the Gulf which are not addressed by this book in detail.[3]

1. Saudi History as History of the Saudi State

The history of modern Saudi politics is to a large extent the history of the modern Saudi state and its elites. A small elite created the early Saudi state through conquest and alliances with local notables in the 1920s and 30s. Before the new state could become an arena for truly national politics, oil income skewed relations of power between regime and society, allowing state elites quickly to build growing bureaucratic and distributive institutions without having to engage in negotiations with larger social groups.[4]

Non-state actors grew increasingly dependent on state and regime patronage and became (or remained) politically fragmented. Never in modern Saudi history have social forces formed or acted independently of the state at national level. Tribes were settled and coopted, with the tribal leadership remaining relevant only at local level.[5] Those urban notables who were willing to cooperate with the regime preserved their local status, but usually became clients of the royal family, their range of action typically geographically circumscribed to their region of origin. Business was allowed to thrive, but in the shadow of the state, dependent on various forms of handout and fragmented regionally. Between the 1950s and the 1980s, it was the regime and its distributional networks which largely defined Saudi politics.

1.1 Patterns of patronage: personalized
The system has held together through patronage of two kinds: personalized and institutionalized. Personalized patronage can be captured by concepts of patron–client relations as developed in the anthropological literature – princes as patrons, smaller princes, notables, bureaucrats or businessmen as clients; bureaucrats as patrons, aid recipients, small-scale shop owners or "paper pushers" in and around the bureaucracy as clients, etc. With the growth of the Saudi state, cascades of clientage have evolved at an increasing number of levels.[6]

It is important to remember that patronage in Saudi Arabia is multi-layered in various ways and should not be reduced to simple dyadic relationships. But even if understood as a complex phenomenon within a larger institutional context, it remains defined by inequality of resources and power, its small-scale nature and its capacity to undermine coalitions of equals.[7] Tokens of exchange from the patrons' side can take the form of jobs, bureaucratic protection and access, money, contracts and other state services. Clients reciprocate by spreading the word about their patrons, representing their interests in the lower reaches of the system, and gathering information for them (some princes go as far as keeping paid informants on their informal payroll). A larger clientele gives social and political prestige, which makes for competition in enlarging, and by implication bankrolling, one's clientele.

In the absence of other political institutions or groupings, structures of personal patronage have often been the defining feature of the politics of the Saudi elite. Similarly, it has been important in bringing ever larger numbers of Saudis into the fold of the state as clients of growing numbers of princes, bureaucrats and other figures with access to state resources. It has also been important in defusing political crises, as the regime has tended to prefer cooptation of opposition over outright repression – although this was less so under stern King Faisal than under his successors, who allowed former oppositionists back into the fold in the 1970s and 1980s, coopting many young Arab nationalists into the growing Saudi state apparatus.[8]

1.2 Patterns of patronage: institutional

Institutional patronage has become increasingly important with the expansion of the Saudi state and its "swallowing" of large swathes of Saudi society in the boom decade of the 1970s. "Institutional patronage" as used here denotes the formal structures of distribution, broadly defined, with which the increasingly complex Saudi state has been reaching out to various constituencies in society on a large scale and through formal means.[9] It is an unequal exchange involving specific groups of actors which, like personalized patronage, undermines the formation of autonomous horizontal groups. It usually involves jobs, subsidies and public services of various kinds. It can be intertwined with personalized patronage on a small scale, but cannot be reduced to it.

The most important means of institutional patronage has been bureaucratic employment, which has contributed to the "statizing" of social groups and to the creation of new, fragmented social formations dependent on the state,[10] most notably the so-called "new middle class",[11] which is not really a class at all, but an incoherent melange of various professional groups which are dependent on various state institutions. State employment has also helped to control and fragment tribes through employment in the National Guard.[12] Similarly, Saudi 'ulama' have been bureaucratized, not least by "granting" them control over a variety of state institutions such as the Ministry of Justice, the moral police and significant parts of the education system, which gives them local institutional power, but also makes them subservient to state leaders.[13] Different social groups were swallowed by different state institutions and networks, making for a set-up that was both fragmented and politically immobilized.

One might object that subjects in many other political systems play comparable roles as clients of state apparatuses and benefit from public services on a similar scale. What is more important, however, is the historical *proportion* of state to societal resources: Saudi societal resources have been much smaller than those of the state for a long time; for exactly the decades when the rules of Saudi politics were written and a national framework established. The state's oil income increased rapidly from the 1940s until the early 1980s, more or less uninterrupted.[14]

Considering the very low level of development of pre-oil Saudi society, relative dependence on the state has been much more pronounced than in any non-rentier state (as has the clientelistic entitlement thinking that goes along with sustained direct and indirect state support). The state has been the dominant channel of social mobility, whether through the bureaucracy or through state-sponsored business.[15] It gradually became the main or only vehicle to improve one's life for most Saudis.[16]

The corollary of omnipresent, state-centred patronage in Saudi Arabia is the absence of large-scale social movements with any serious claim to autonomy from the regime. With distribution as the prevalent mode of economic interaction, conventional class formation was stymied.[17] Distributional states allow structures of kinship and primordial identities to flourish, often to the detriment of programmatic politics.

Leftist and nationalist parties in the 1950s and 1960s were weak and fragmented in social and regional terms.[18] An incipient labour movement only existed in the Eastern Province, where US-owned oil company Arabian American Oil Company (ARAMCO) was the only entity to employ a sufficient number of workers in one place to enable attempts at unionization. As these attempts had little national resonance, they were successfully crushed.[19] While a labour class never developed, the business classes of the various Saudi regions quickly grew dependent on state and royal patronage, as the size of state and ARAMCO contracts outstripped any opportunities for private profit (as reflected in the table below).[20] Many of the big Saudi merchant families were "made" by the Al-Saud family or the senior gatekeepers and administrators around them.[21]

TABLE 4.1
Composition of the Saudi GDP in the 1960s

[Chart showing Private sector, Total GDP, oil sector, and government sector from 1962/63 to 1968/69. Total GDP rises from ~8500 to ~16000; oil sector from ~4700 to ~8500; private sector from ~2700 to ~4800; government sector from ~1200 to ~2400.]

Source: Calculated from Knauerhase 1977.

With old social actors losing their coherence and new groups growing up as creatures of the state, Saudi society in general remained fragmented and politically immobilized.[22] Independent organization of political interests was seldom demanded and never condoned.[23] As far as the Saudi regime experienced crises in the 1950s and 1960s, these resulted from conflicts within the royal family rather than bottom-up pressure from society.[24] Rather tellingly, princely attempts to mobilize wider constituencies outside the royal family during the royal infighting between 1958 and 1962 failed.[25]

Differently from all other socio-economic groups, business has developed some coherence as a class in recent decades, as sustained rent recycling has increased its autonomous resources and gradual maturation of its managerial capacities has made it capable of catering to private demand and competing regionally.[26] In terms of capital and expertise, it is probably ahead of its peers in the region. Its share of national investment is now considerably higher than that of the state. It remains, however, a class without politics, as its limited demands are channelled through corporatist institutions such as chambers of commerce or economic policy commissions.[27] These institutions generally have a more meaningful role in policy-making than the more recent non-economic "interest groups" the regime has created. Yet their political impact is that economic policy issues are taken care of separately from other political questions, reducing the risk of broader political mobilization among the bourgeoisie.

Business has not entered political coalitions with other social groups and has largely stayed aloof of the heightened political contestation of the 1990s. Despite its larger resources, the business class is still shot through with princely patronage and often dependent on it for smooth dealings with the administration. Industrialists are somewhat more entrepreneurial and independent of the regime than large contractors and commercialists, but this is a difference of degree, not least because different sectors overlap due to the conglomerate structure of many Saudi family businesses.

Most businessmen consider it too risky to make open political demands to the regime. Business is kept separate from politics at large[28] – a feat that is easy to achieve considering the underdeveloped state of other forms of political mobilization. The increased economic, but subdued political, role of business is in line with, but even more pronounced than, patterns in other Middle Eastern states.[29]

2. Mobilizing against the Paternal Order

All the above is not to deny that Saudi Arabia has experienced phases of salient oppositional mobilization. The fate of these movements, however, illustrates the resilience and flexibility of Saudi political paternalism more than the potential for broad oppositional coalitions.

The fully developed Saudi state saw its first political crises in late 1979 in the form of the uprising of Saudi Shiites in the Eastern Province and the occupation of the Holy Mosque in Mecca. Although they shook the ruling elites, both were delimited problems which did not prompt a politicization of the bulk of Saudi society.[30] Many Sunni Saudis have little sympathy for Shiite claims for recognition.[31] The absence in Saudi Arabia of political ideologies not related to identity, to which the Shiites could have attached their demands, has allowed the regime to play divide and rule. The problem could be neatly quarantined in the Eastern Province, and – in classical Al-Saud fashion – alleviated through increased expenditure on regional development, thus increasing institutional patronage.[32]

The occupation of the Holy Mosque in Mecca by Juhayman al-Otaibi and his followers delivered a deeper psychological blow to the rulers, not least as his movement had emerged at the margins of Saudi Arabia's official religious establishment, with some of the leading figures of the latter initially supporting the Juhayman's group.[33] Yet its very extremism also underlined the isolation of Juhayman's movement in Saudi society. Its retrograde and millenarian nature arguably reflects the unwitting success of Saudi state-builders in suppressing any broader-based, oppositional ideology with a concrete political agenda – at least for the time being.[34] Although the Mecca events made a significant dent in the Al-Saud's credibility as protectors of the holy sites, they had no problems in crushing the movement itself.

The Juhayman movement had no tangible socio-economic agenda and was dissimilar to the broader socio-revolutionary Islamist movements that developed in other Middle Eastern states.[35] As far as it made any non-religious domestic political demands, they were related to royal corruption, which has since then been the only political economy item that is regularly included on the agendas of Saudi opposition movements. Such half-articulated uneasiness about waste and embezzlement does not, however, constitute a programme, and it is difficult to mobilize specific groups around it, as it is a very diffuse phenomenon.[36] Saudi opposition has always suffered from a collective action problem in that it cannot cater to specific deprived or economically frustrated classes, as they are not clearly defined in the kingdom. Instead, one might argue, rentier states with their large redundancy of organizational resources, provision of non-meritocratic and vacuous jobs and lack of focal issues for socio-economic programmes create space for particularly unhinged, if localized, ideologies.[37]

True to form, King Fahd tried to deepen the cooptation of the religious establishment through allocating more funds to its institutions and giving in to its demands for tighter state control of social mores, lest another loose cannon emerge at its periphery. Fahd in particular, who had come into his own as a ruler in the oil boom of the 1970s, instinctively tried to buy off all potential troublemakers. When dissidents submitted anonymous critical essays about political modernization and the role of the Al-Saud to him through an intermediary, his only reported reaction was to ask how much land or money they wanted.[38]

The 1980s, although a decade of economic crisis, were calm in political terms. Political debate, as far as it occurred, tended to focus on cultural and moral issues, as a new generation of educated young Saudis questioned the relatively liberal attitudes of the socially mobile generation of the 1960s and 70s.[39] The locations for these debates were literary clubs and Islamic charities, not political organizations. These venues were all licensed and controlled by the state.

Despite this, the Islamic intelligentsia (known as the *Sahwa* movement) did have a rather large organizational leeway in various cultural, educational and charitable institutions. Although having no clearly defined socio-economic base, it still is the closest approximation to a "new middle class" movement Saudi Arabia has seen to date, consisting of students, educated professionals and lower-ranking Islamic scholars.

It was after the Gulf war of 1990/1 that a considerable section of the Islamic networks of the 1980s became politicized, openly demanding an Islamicization of the public sphere and an Islamic foreign policy, as well as an end to the corruption and favouritism of the Al-Saud state.[40] Economic crisis and reduced social mobility from the mid-1980s onwards had probably helped to create discontent and a sense of exclusion among the generation of "latecomers" entering universities at that time. However, it took a major foreign policy crisis to politicize them.

The emergence of the politicized *Sahwa* from within formally state-controlled institutions (universities, charities, etc.) once again revealed the ambiguity of the Saudi state's omnipresence: while its patronage reaches virtually all parts of Saudi society, it has in itself, in parts, become so amorphous and fragmented that the leadership cannot always control what happens in all of its sectors. This is particularly the case in relation to those sectors to which the leadership grants some internal autonomy on account of their specific role in reproducing the state's Islamic ideology, which requires some credibility and therefore freedom from overt interference on the part of the regime.

In Saudi Arabia more than perhaps anywhere else, politics often happens *within* the state. By holding positions within the fragmented state, actors can acquire resources and opportunities, which explains the *Sahwa*'s relative organizational successes. However, actors within the state also tend to have more to lose. This puts constraints on them to which groups outside the state would not be subject. One example is the political gag order on state employees that was apparently first issued in 1960,[41] but has been revived whenever opportune. With a large share of educated Saudis being public servants, this can heavily stifle political debate.

Politics within the state can force actors to engage in unusual tradeoffs – most saliently, they might decide to pursue their aims by having themselves coopted, a process that tends to appear at best peculiar and at worst duplicitous to outside observers, but which can be entirely rational and socially acceptable in the Saudi context. Oppositional bargaining with the regime in Saudi Arabia can be intricate and functions according to rules that are different from both democratic-pluralist systems and the harsher autocracies of the rest of the Arab world.

Such bargaining arguably helps to explain why the sahwist oppositional movement, which reached its apogee in 1994, subsequently fizzled out and has not been revived since. To be sure, the Saudi state deployed a measure of coercion to stop sahwist demonstrations, and a number of activists, including the two most prominent sahwist leaders (Salman al-Awda and Safar al-Hawali), were imprisoned for several years. At the same time, however, subtler means of pressure, such as threats to public sector careers, were applied to a larger number of dissidents, and incentives for cooperation were given.

Remarkably, both al-Awda and al-Hawali now have been more or less coopted by the regime, taking part in regime-sponsored intellectual events and abstaining from anti-government rhetoric. The strained fiscal resources of the 1990s made it harder for the Saudi regime to coopt whole social strata. Yet the princes kept sufficient discretionary resources available to capture specific actors and networks as clients, and the continuing role of state employment and resources in the lives of most political activists made them vulnerable to soft pressure.

The *Sahwa* once again was not a socio-revolutionary movement like Islamist movements in other states, but rather opted for a socio-cultural programme that could also be pursued from within the state, as now is arguably the case, with coopted sahwists being allowed to wield influence over educational and cultural matters. The cooptation of the *Sahwa* reflected the softness and flexibility of a fragmented Saudi state which can serve diverse interests at the same time while preventing the formation of broader independent coalitions against its core leadership. For good measure and in keeping with its tradition of divide and rule, the Saudi regime also supported the "Jami" trend of Islamic activism against the *Sahwa* in the 1990s, thus turning a previously rather marginal and rigid, but apolitical, religious ideology into a major intellectual trend.[42]

Many other sahwist preachers now are firmly in the government camp, some of them enjoying considerable prestige and resources as regime-sponsored intellectuals. The predilection of specific princes to act as patrons of intellectuals offered additional opportunities for cooptation. Once again, the Saudi leaders' paternal willingness to let unruly subjects back into the flock defused and divided opposition activism, as had happened several times before, be it with leftists or errant princes. The Saudi state easily had enough resources to cope with an opposition that only had a vague programme and a relatively thin socio-economic basis in the intelligentsia. Many stories of oppositionists being bought off circulate in the kingdom.[43] In a society in which state resources play such a prominent role, dissidence has both more to lose and more to gain through its relationship to the state.[44]

3. The Corporatist Reaction

King Fahd's regime also reacted with a number of institutional reforms in 1992/3, such as the promulgation of a "basic law", a new law on regional governance and the creation of an appointed quasi-parliament, the *Majlis al-shura*. The basic law more or less institutionalized authoritarian rules of governance which had long since been in force informally,[45] and the regional reform has had little impact on actual governance structures. The *Majlis* was a more innovative reform step, although one that had been considered on various occasions for more than 30 years. It also was a first significant step towards the institutionalization of public debate that has progressed further under Crown Prince and later King Abdullah.

As I have argued elsewhere, this institutionalization is best captured by the concept of state corporatism,[46] the state-led creation of various "interest groups" which are granted a representational monopoly by the state and organized along non-competing, functional lines in order to accommodate the various parts of society, while ultimate control of politics remains in the hands of the regime, which alone is able to reconcile the various interest groups.[47]

Saudi Arabia has not yet experienced a phase of oppositional mobilization like that of the early 1990s. It has, however, gone through a number of political crises since 2001, such as the soul-searching induced by the events of 11 September 2001 and the domestic jihadist political violence seen since 2003. The latter has no domestic political programme other than the liberation of Saudi Arabia from Western presence and has not enjoyed great support in society, but has nevertheless proved deeply unsettling for the Saudi regime, which has used many of the same religio-ideological sources for its own legitimation.[48] The events of 11 September 2001 and the 2003/4 bombings[49] openly put the ideological identity of Saudi state and society into question.

This identity crisis has emboldened Saudi intellectuals of various hues to relate the socio-cultural and political rigidities of the kingdom to recent events and once again to demand political reform. Again, Islamist elites – often with a sahwist background – have been the best organized and most persistent in their petitioning, although there have also been several petitions in which liberal and Islamist intellectuals have joined hands to ask for a political opening.[50]

Corporatism has been the regime's main response. With Abdullah at the helm, willingness to allow for controlled public debate has become much greater. At the same time, Abdullah's regime has worked towards channelling debate into state-controlled institutions, in line with his generally stronger reliance on formal mechanisms of governance (possibly a strategy to delimit the informal powers of other senior princes). Abdullah might also recognize that, as Saudi society has grown larger, more complex and better educated, it has become increasingly harder to accommodate all interest groups through princely or bureaucratic clientelism. Although the complex and fragmented Saudi state apparatus, with its various client groups, constituted a kind of proto-corporatism,[51] this offered no formal channels for negotiation or interest representation.

Abdullah's regime has created a number of new, formal fora for various interest groups, including a "National Dialogue", which meets roughly twice a year to debate specific social and cultural problems, and has successively invited representatives of groups such as intellectuals, women and youth. The state has also created a journalists' association, a human rights association and a pensioners' association, while student and teacher associations have been considered. Moreover, under Abdullah, the *Majlis al-shura* has been further extended. As it is explicitly recruited from various strata of functional elites (academics, businessmen, former bureaucrats, military and some *'ulama'*), this body is more corporatist in nature than a conventional parliament.

With the exception of the *Majlis*, which has become a real forum for technocrats to debate policy issues in specific areas determined by the regime, the above-mentioned exercises have aroused remarkably little interest in Saudi society. The state hand in orchestrating the new organizations might have been too visible, but, at the same time, it appears that large parts of Saudi society have little interest in formal, functional interest representation – the new bodies are not even seen as a chance to get a process of formal representation started. In the absence of a formal organizational tradition, the vast majority of Saudis seem to prefer pursuing their interests through established informal (and often multifunctional) channels. Active identification as a member of specific functional strata still seems alien to most Saudis.[52] Reflecting the low interest in formal political mechanisms, the 2005 municipal elections – the first since the early 1960s – produced a turnout of less than a fifth of eligible voters in most places.

Needless to say, desultory attempts by dissident intellectuals to set up independent organizations or to take public collective action have been suppressed by the regime. Attempts to set up an independent human rights group in late 2003 led to the arrest of several activists, as did a summer 2007 sit-in protest by a handful of women requesting that their husbands or brothers be released or formally indicted.[53] The small scale of mobilizations seems to reflect the fact that the organizational resources of opposition beyond Islamic opposition are more or less absent, while the independence and political outreach of Islamist networks is, at least currently, also rather limited.

The one area in which the new corporatism really reaches beyond a small number of regime-sponsored client actors is in economic policy-making, where the regime has created several new channels for the representation of business interests. Although this finds considerable resonance in business circles – Chambers of Commerce are by far the oldest corporatist institutions with the largest outreach – it takes place in a separate area disconnected from the political and cultural debates taking place in the rest of society. The one political consequence this seems to have is to prevent the politicization of business. More generally, a comparison of business with other corporatist initiatives shows that without an organizational tradition, top-down institutionalization of political debate is unlikely to have much resonance in a fragmented society used to operating in a clientelistic fashion.

4. Conclusions and Comparative Discussion

With the exception of business inclusion and the *Majlis*, recent corporatist initiatives have been rather inconsequential. At the same time, however, Saudi Arabia has not witnessed successful oppositional mobilization. Saudi dissidents are adrift, having no broad social base and independent national organizational structures to call upon. As the economy has been doing well for several years, not even the ritual, unspecific denouncements of regime corruption has much resonance. After the events of 11 September 2001, a liberalization of the national debate on cultural and social issues has set in, allowing more space for critical discussions of educational issues, social reform and intra-Islamic pluralism, the latter being debated for the first time in modern Saudi history. Through this qualified socio-cultural opening, the regime has however also managed to deflect public attention away from politics proper. Moreover, due to the polarization of Saudi Arabia between a broad conservative base and a smaller group of elite liberals (often with a technocratic background), "culture wars" type debates on schooling and women's issues can be continued endlessly without political consequences for the regime.

The most recent threat from domestic jihadists has had limited political impact: since 2005, such groups have been largely under control and have failed to recruit significant new numbers.[54] The return of veterans from the Iraqi *jihad* could create a new security problem, but this is unlikely to have much greater resonance. So far, the jihadist movement has been dealt with as per usual: hard-core activists have been killed or imprisoned, while those with a more peripheral role as sympathizers or logistical supporters have been involved in a programme of ideological re-education.[55] Newly reformed activists are not just released from prison, but are frequently provided with housing and jobs, while their families are supported materially during their time in prison.[56] This is very different to the re-education programme in Saudi Arabia's poor neighbour Yemen, where jihadists are usually simply allowed liberty in return for a pledge not to engage in political violence again. The Saudi deal is more in the classical patron–client mould that creates material dependence and an expectation of long-term gratitude.

4.1 Comparative remarks
Saudi Arabia has seen less substantial change in its political institutions than the impressive formal record of reform initiatives would suggest. With visible corporatist reform, but little change in actual participation and mobilization, it might represent the inverse of what has happened in other Arab states: there, older corporatist institutions have seen substantial change – they have been undermined – but in a stealthy fashion.

Differently from other Arab states, there has been no demise of mass-based political organizations in Saudi Arabia because it never had any. Conversely, its cautious political liberalization has not been accompanied by depoliticization and elitization of political confrontation. Politics has always been an elite affair, although political elites, by means of their clientelistic networks, have usually made great efforts to get a sense of social desire so that they can react to it with paternal largesse.

It is also difficult to discern a higher level of intra-elite competition in Saudi Arabia. The elite has of course grown in size, but the plural nature of princely fiefdoms is nothing new. It has been part of Saudi politics since the inception of the modern Saudi state in the 1950s, when Saudi rule acquired an oligarchic or "dynastic" character.[57] Princes do compete for enlarged clienteles, including also among the lower classes, but this kind of paternalism is as old as the Saudi state. Neither is it new that much of Saudi politics, even oppositional politics, happens within the state as opposed to between clearly delimited constituencies within state and society, or between different groups in society. Similarly, the growth of business resources and their influence on economic policy-making does not denote a new centre of political power, at least not one that is in open rivalry to other political institutions. If anything, it has become harder to carve out new niches in the Saudi elite since the early 1980s, as socio-economic mobility has decreased considerably due to slower state growth. It is too early to tell whether the current boom will change anything about this.

With some delay, Saudi Arabia has gone through a measure of political liberalization like other Arab states, culminating in municipal elections in 2005. In this, however, it has been able to sell very modest steps as progress, as its point of departure in formal-institutional terms was that of an absolutist monarchy. It has therefore had the advantage of being able to give tokens of liberalization which other regimes already gave a long time ago.

At the same time, the Saudi regime has not had to resort to repressive policies on the scale seen in Egypt or Syria in the 1980s and 90s. It has maintained a paternal and cooptative political tradition which is rooted in the historical conservatism and gradualism of the Al-Saud dynasty and which has been made possible by oil income. But under Abdullah as under his predecessors, smaller numbers of too vocal or – more importantly – too independently organized dissidents have spent short stints in jail.

The clientelism which many decry as politically regressive in other Arab states has always been the dominant mode of politics in Saudi Arabia, and has been widely accepted. In this sense, the kingdom has a comparative historical advantage in the way it conducts its politics, which it possibly has in common with other monarchies which never promised mass-based, mobilizational politics.

Paradoxically, the distributional commitment of the Saudi regime is more resilient and serious than that in the "progressive" Arab republics. Wide-reaching distribution is of course made possible by oil income, but it has remained a very serious consideration even at times of strong economic pressure. Subsidy cuts tended to hit business and higher income brackets rather than lower social strata, and as far as the latter are concerned, austerity measures were often repealed.[58]

The current oil boom has not led to an explosion of distributional entitlements as occurred in the 1970s, but the Al-Saud have nonetheless carefully stabilized and adjusted existing distribution policies to increased costs of living and a larger population, increasing for example welfare and wage rates that had been frozen in nominal terms since the 1980s and initiating a new national housing programme. This carefully tailored welfare overhaul has been accompanied by much paternal imagery and language in the Saudi media, which documents an Abdullah incessantly touring the country and looking after his "children".

Although public employment guarantees are not given anymore, public services remain strongly subsidized, and social expenditure has recently increased more rapidly than any other type of expenditure.

Lower and middle social strata were always meant to be included, but never to be mobilized, and the regime still holds true to that.

That no strand of opposition ever managed to mobilize the lower and lower middle-income strata is testament to the Al-Saud's continuing grip over a clientelistic society. Thanks to the large resources accumulated over the last seven years, distributional paternalism is set to continue for a considerable time, no matter how soon the king finds a successor. Differently from other Arab states, intermediation through non-state elites has not increased in importance. Intermediation of state resources through princes, bureaucrats or notables is significant, but not new.

As it has not re-engineered its socio-economic basis, the regime also has not had to de-ideologize its discourse to a significant extent: it can by and large stick to its Islamic-conservative guns, which continue to suit the paternal monarchy. The recent opening away from rigid Wahabi discourse, allowing for a restricted intra-Islamic pluralism, is limited. It is rooted in Saudi Arabia's specific security problems, namely the use by a circumscribed jihadist movement of some of the regime's own Wahabi rhetoric which has forced a public ideological self-examination, an opportunity which Abdullah seized on to obtain reformist credentials. Although the regime's language has changed considerably, it does not reflect a new paradigm of rule: the change is discursive rather than structural.

One development that other Arab states and Saudi Arabia have in common is that only Islamists have come to constitute a serious opposition. The socio-economic base of the broader networks of Saudi Islamists engaged in petitioning and peaceful protest is comparable to that of the Muslim Brotherhood in other states: students, academics and middle-class, educated professionals are strongly represented. What Saudi Islamists lack, however, is the backing of a strong Islamist bourgeoisie – which might help to explain their lack of perseverance as opposition. Moreover, they do not gain legitimacy from the provision of social services to the lower classes, certainly not on the scale witnessed in poorer countries such as Egypt, Palestine, Morocco, etc. The Saudi state has not failed to such an extent as to provide space for this.

With the exception of Lebanon, the state is "over-developed" everywhere in the Middle East, i.e. it dominates formal associational life in society and plays an overbearing role in the life of most people. This phenomenon is particularly pronounced in the more autocratic Gulf monarchies, i.e. United Arab Emirates, Qatar, Oman and Saudi

Arabia. Saudi Arabia's private sector and notable families have recently increased their charitable activities, increasingly complementing state provision with more specialized initiatives. But all such activity is state-licensed and controlled and, although touching some sensitive social issues, stays clear of politics.[59] In order to set up a charity on a more meaningful scale, moreover, the formal or informal patronage of a prince or – quite frequently – a princess is needed. To date, private charities have not replaced state provision of health and education, but rather complement them.

The relative lack of international pressure and globalization-induced socio-economic changes that other Middle East and North Africa (MENA) states have gone through has probably contributed to the relative continuity of the Saudi system. Rich rentier states like Saudi Arabia keep larger distributional resources, have greater ownership over their fiscal policies and economic adjustment processes, can privatize with local capital, and do not have to liberalize at the expense of lower social strata. US pressure and the negative external image Saudi Arabia earned internationally after 11 September 2001 have had a surface effect in terms of prodding the regime towards announcements of reform and symbolic gestures. But insofar as there was any substantial pressure, this dissipated after 2005 when the US became definitively mired down in Iraq. Today more than ever, Saudi Arabia appears as a relatively successful model of rule compared to other MENA states.

This chapter does not argue that state–society relations in Saudi Arabia are completely different from those in other Arab states. The point is slightly more complicated: the way politics is nowadays being conducted in Saudi Arabia and elsewhere in the Arab world – in an authoritarian-clientelistic fashion, with formal-corporatist institutions little more than embellishment – is similar. Low levels of political mobilization, neo-patrimonial regime structures, and a larger role for the private sector are all shared by the rest of the contemporary Middle East to various degrees. What differs are the routes by which the different states arrived at this set-up. The different histories in turn explain why the Saudi regime appears more comfortable with this style of politics: it did not have to go through a crisis of legitimacy and the painful dismantlement of formal-inclusive institutions to reach it, but adopted it as the natural form of politics of a rentier monarchy. Therefore its new corporatism is not suffering from a full-blown legitimacy crisis, but rather from a (clearly delimited) crisis of irrelevance.

NOTES

1 "Confidential letter from AD Parsons to Mr Le Quense", 12 October 1972, Public Record Office (PRO), London/Kew, FCO 8/1906, Political Situation in Saudi Arabia.
2 The converse is not true, however: powerful networks of transnational actors have emerged from Saudi Arabia, on levels as different as that of regional business and of international Islamic jihadism; Luciani 2005; Hegghammer 2007; Hertog 2007a.
3 The sources for this chapter consist of press and government material, interviews with "civil society" and regime representatives in Saudi Arabia as well as oppositional documents. I will also draw on the growing theoretically informed secondary literature on political change in Saudi Arabia, which is much more substantial now than only five years ago. In its historical part, the chapter draws on archival material from the Institute of Public Administration in Riyad, the Public Record Office in Kew/London, US State Department documents from the National Archives and Records Administration in Washington, as well as the Mulligan Papers collection at Georgetown University and a number of other private paper collections.
4 For a detailed account, cf. Hertog (forthcoming), chapters 2–4.
5 Cf. El-Farra 1973; al-Seflan 1980.
6 Cf. Hertog (forthcoming).
7 Eisenstadt *et al.* 1981; Eisenstadt *et al.* 1984; Schmidt *et al.* 1977.
8 Fahd himself boasted to diplomats of how gently the Saudi state treated its opposition in the 1970s. "Prince Fahd, the King, and the Inner Circle", 26 September 1973, US National Archives and Records Administration (henceforth NARA), College Park/Maryland, Record Group 59, box 2584, folder POL 2 SAUD (1/1/70). His claim is to a considerable degree borne out by the facts; many dissidents were allowed back into business and government after doing some jail time; cf. "The Rehabilitation of Salah Ambah", 18 April 1973, NARA, RG 59, box 2586, folder POL 23 SAUD (1/1/70); Lacey 1981.
9 Roniger 2002.
10 What Ross calls the "group formation effect" of rentier states (Ross 2001).
11 Rugh 1973; Seznec 2002; Abir 1988.
12 Hertog (forthcoming), chapter 3.
13 Lacroix 2007; al-Fahad 2005; Piscatori 1983; al-Yassini 1985.
14 For times series from the late 1960s onwards, cf. Saudi Arabian Monetary Agency (various issues).
15 For some early examples of this, cf. Hertog 2007b.
16 Armitage to Foreign and Commonwealth Office (FCO), "Saudi Arabia – The Al-Saud and Internal Affairs", December 1973, PRO/FCO 8/2105.
17 On this process in rentier states in general, cf. Vandewalle 1998.
18 Folders on oppositional activity in international diplomatic archives consistently document paltry activity (cf. NARA, folder POL 23-10 SAUD, 1/1/66); Hertog 2007b.
19 Vitalis 2006.

20 Despite accounts to the contrary (cf. Chaudhry 1997), business became dependent on the modern state pretty much from its creation ("Brief for talks with the USA", January 1956, PRO/FO 371/120754, ES 1015/3). Many merchants were coopted into administrative structures through bureaucratic posts ("The new reign in Sau'di Arabia", 21/1/1954, GB 165–0229, Philby archives at St Antony's College/Oxford, 1/4/9/3/28/39).
21 Hertog 2007b.
22 "Impact of Youth and the US National Interest – Phase II", 17 December 1970, NARA, RG 59, box 2584, folder POL 7 SAUD (1/1/70).
23 Even sports clubs were dissolved and reconstituted under state control in the 1960s; ("Monthly review for April 1968", NARA, RG 59, box 2470, folder POL 2 SAUD, 1/1/68). King Faisal also prohibited the wearing of tricots for soccer for fear of creating too strong a corporate identity among the youth (Interview with US official who served in Saudi Arabia in the 1970s and 80s, New York, May 2007).
24 Yizraeli 1997.
25 "Free prince" Talal failed to rouse support when touring the provinces to mobilize the young Saudi intelligentsia; "Complete Powers" (n.d.), Mulligan Papers, Georgetown University, box 6, folder 12; "Saudi National Legislative Council", 2 August 1961, Mulligan Papers, Georgetown University, box 3, folder 8.
26 Luciani 2005.
27 Like other corporate bodies, the various regional chambers of commerce were set up under state supervision from the 1940s on ("Chambers of Commerce in Saudi Arabia", 14 April 1956, Mulligan Papers, box 2, folder 51). They have, however, recently increased in importance as relatively autonomous locales of articulating the economic policy interests of Saudi business.
28 Hertog 2006a.
29 Bellin 2004a; Heydemann 1993.
30 Ibrahim 2006; Hegghammer *et al.* 2007.
31 Ibrahim 2006.
32 Abir 1988; Ibrahim 2006.
33 Hegghammer *et al.* 2007.
34 The movement did not have a defined political project and had its roots in networks of rejectionist activists who originally had preached total withdrawal from society. It was a millenarian sect rather than a political movement and its resonance in Saudi society was accordingly limited.
35 Cf. Kepel 2004.
36 According to some strands of rentier state theory, an anti-corruption agenda is the only economic item which oppositions in rentier states can easily agree upon, as this agenda does not require specific class interests (cf. Luciani 1990).
37 Rentier theorists have made the related but somewhat broader argument that identity rather than economic politics determines contention in rentier states (cf. Shambayati 1994; Delacroix 1980).
38 Interview with a US official stationed in Riyad in the 1970s and 80s, New York, May 2007.
39 Lacroix 2007; Hegghammer 2007.
40 Teitelbaum 2000; Fandy 1999.
41 "Extracts from the Saudi press", 24 July 1960, No. 37, Mulligan Papers, box 3, folder 6.

42 This trend of Islamic activism is named after Sheikh Muhammad Aman al-Jami, a former professor at the Islamic University of Medina. It is part of the broader "*ahl al-hadith*" Islamic trend inspired by Sheikh Nasir al-Din al-Albani that rejects doctrinal innovations of modern political Islam and puts particular emphasis on *hadith* handed down from the time of the prophet as guides to pious behaviour, to the exclusion of logical reasoning and analogy as sources of doctrine. Emerging after the Juhayman events, the "Jami" trend went out of its way to underline its loyalty to the al-Saud (Lacroix 2008).
43 Interviews, Riyad 2005–7.
44 A full political economy of the Saudi opposition has yet to be researched, as most works thus far focus on intellectual rather than structural factors.
45 al-Fahad 2005.
46 Hertog 2006b.
47 Schmitter 1974.
48 al-Rasheed 2006a.
49 Jihadi activists calling themselves "al-Qa'ida on the Arabian Peninsula" conducted more than 20 operations against mostly Western targets between 2003 and 2007, the largest ones happening in 2003 and 2004. Their prime objective seems to have been the ejection of Western "occupiers" from Saudi Arabia (cf. Hegghammer 2007).
50 Lacroix 2004.
51 Chaudhry 1997.
52 Interviews with journalists and civil society activists in Saudi Arabia, 2003–6.
53 *Kuwait Times*, 22 July 2006.
54 Hegghammer 2006.
55 Discussions in Riyad, February 2007.
56 Boucek 2007.
57 Herb 1999.
58 Hertog (forthcoming), chapter 4.
59 Montagu 2006.

Part II

Changing Patterns of Wealth Accumulation and Distribution

5
THE POLITICAL ECONOMY OF AUTHORITARIANISM IN EGYPT: INSUFFICIENT STRUCTURAL REFORMS, LIMITED OUTCOMES AND A LACK OF NEW ACTORS

Ulrich G. Wurzel

Introduction

President Hosni Muhammad Mubarak came to power in 1981. After some half-hearted reform efforts undertaken by his predecessor President Sadat in the 1970s, the economy was characterized by an unhealthy mix of state planning and market regulation in the early 1980s. Mubarak was unwilling to change fundamentally the economic system in order to avoid undermining what came to be known as "Egypt's stability" – a euphemism for the power of the ruling authoritarian regime. Egypt's basic economic structures continued to deteriorate and the gap with other parts of the developing world widened, but increasing economic and political rent income helped to overcome the worst symptoms of crisis. However, the major feature of the "Mubarak era" has been the dominance of just one policy concern among the top leadership, namely staying in power. The regime's obsession with power, control and security also explains the design and implementation of all major economic policy measures during the last 30 years. By the time of the so-called "bread riots" of January 1977, security concerns had begun to shape economic policy and often to overrule policy proposals made by domestic and external "technocrats", including agencies such as the World Bank and the International Monetary Fund (IMF).

Due to a massive budget deficit and external debts of USD 50 billion at the end of the 1980s, economic stagnation turned into an acute crisis. A first reform attempt in the late 1980s, supported by international financial institutions (IFIs), failed due to a lack of commitment on the Egyptian side. In 1990/1, after renewed negotiations, the IMF and the World Bank imposed a Stabilization and Structural Adjustment

Programme (SSAP) on Egypt – an external intervention designed to ensure that the Egyptian government remained a major ally of the West.[1] The economic policy reforms called for by international creditors were a precondition for debt relief of more than USD 25 billion (50 per cent of Egypt's external debt and equal to its annual budget), new loans and other financial and technical support. Since 1990/1, consecutive cabinets have implemented different approaches to reform. During the early 1990s, a hesitant approach prevailed. Increasing donor pressure, however, led to a more active attitude in the mid-1990s. While still trying to delay, water down or obstruct those reforms that could undermine the political stability of the regime, other, less controversial measures demanded by external agencies were implemented, if also in an unsystematic and sometimes contradictory way. Finally, in the second half of the 1990s, due to massive relief and restructuring of its external debts, Egypt's macro-economic stability seemed to have been restored, and the country possessed substantial foreign currency reserves.[2] With the final debt write-off under the Ganzouri cabinet in 1996, donors and creditors lost the leverage with which to pressurize the Egyptian side to continue with the reform programme. Since the late 1990s, Egypt has experienced a recurrence of earlier macro-economic problems and a substantial crisis of its domestic economy.

With the appointment of Prime Minister Nazif in mid-2004, a cabinet was put together that came to be known as "a team of young reformers", as some well-known businessmen together with neo-liberal intellectuals, such as Yusuf Boutros Ghali, Minister of Finance, came to office. But the "young reformers" were neither really young nor radically reformist. The new ministers promised to break dramatically with the past and presented themselves as energetic agents of change who would revive the stagnant reform process in order to transform Egypt into a functioning market economy. The international community applauded once again, but clearly did not recall that most of the newly announced measures, according to the initial plans, should already have been implemented years earlier[3] and, in the case of Ghali and Mahmoud Mohieldin, Minister of Investment, by the very same individuals who now claimed to be the first and only serious reformers in the country for decades.

This chapter will show that socio-economic reform in Egypt has been designed and implemented in order to stabilize the authoritarian regime in the face of increasing economic and political problems. The major objective of the regime concerning its economic reform programme has been to reorganize and consolidate its power system and not to lay the foundations necessary to make the national economy more competitive on the international scene.[4] In particular, section 1 shows that, despite a number of reform measures, there has been no fundamental reconstruction of Egypt's economy, while section 2 highlights that even a massive redistribution of decision-making power and assets does not necessarily imply the termination of the control and domination of the economy by the regime. Section 3 continues this analysis by showing that an independent entrepreneurial class – an emancipated and politically conscious modern bourgeoisie – has not yet emerged in Egypt, implying that Egyptian capitalists cannot be expected to push for substantial economic and/or political reform. Section 3 also briefly addresses the role of external actors regarding the current economic reforms. Section 4 provides a summary of the main findings and outlines the principal conclusions.

1. Have the Reforms Fundamentally Changed the Economic System?

The politico-economic system that produced the economic crisis of the late 1980s has been conceptualized as a rentier system – the combination of an authoritarian regime whose political power is based on the monopolization of economic and political rent income and a national economy in which economic activities are to a large extent either rent-based or rent-oriented. Massive direct and indirect control of the economy by the regime has been one of the foundations of its political survival.[5] The major criterion therefore in an assessment as to whether the economic changes introduced since the early 1990s have led to a fundamental alteration of this system is how far those changes managed to transform the regime-controlled rentier economy into a modern market economy. Whatever the assessment of the changes made since 1990/1 and/or since 2004, some important changes in Egypt's political economy have certainly been taking place. The question, however, is whether these changes have had a fundamental impact on the core economic structures of Egypt's system of authoritarianism and how far the heavy-handed control of the regime over the economy and its monopolization of economic power have decreased in practice. As shown below, by means of numerous instruments the regime still makes or breaks businesses and creates lucrative business opportunities for some whilst at the same time denying the most basic economic rights to others. As far as the issue of the regime's control over the economy is concerned, we will see that there has been little substantial progress in the transition from a state-controlled rentier economy to a functioning market economy. The measures implemented so far have not altered the system as such, even if the former direct control of the regime has been substituted to a certain degree by more indirect, less obvious means of control in parts of the economy.

1.1 Framework conditions for firms

Regulation and institution

Some progress in terms of streamlining the legal and institutional environment has taken place during the past 15 years. Among the more important changes of the earlier period are the privatization-related laws and the new banking law of the early 1990s, as well as some trade liberalization measures and the numerous (but rather unsystematic) changes to the system of administrated prices and subsidies.[6] More recent changes include, for example, tax and customs laws, the labour code and antitrust regulation. However, in an environment in which the law is not effectively enforced due to the weakness of the judiciary and where powerful players find ways to circumvent rules and regulations, the formal modernization and adjustment of the legal and institutional environment is necessary but not sufficient. The regime remains able to manipulate the business environment in ways which benefit its representatives and business cronies.

Competition

It is true that there has been some trade liberalization that, according to mainstream theory, should lead to greater competitive pressure in the local market. However, the Egyptian state has for decades granted import licences to certain businessmen in order to distribute privilege so that many import activities have been controlled by a small number of powerful and well-connected tycoons. Formal trade liberalization, in such an environment, does not necessarily mean that competition in local markets increases. On the contrary, there are many reports that a limited number of powerful players increasingly oligopolize or monopolize lucrative import businesses and systematically drive out smaller players. At the same time, small and medium-sized businesses complain about increased competition, mainly from Chinese and other Asian producers, suggesting that trade liberalization, at least in some markets, does lead to increased competition. There are substantial fears that the aggressive export strategies of Asian competitors may sooner or later lead to the collapse of whole branches of Egyptian industry, from traditional production such as textiles in the Delta to more advanced operations such as the production of automotive components in the new industrial towns. However, such competitive pressure is unequally distributed among different segments of the economy. The bigger and better-connected players have much greater leverage to keep up old barriers to external competition and erect new ones. And still there is no effective enforcement of antitrust regulation. Important provisions are formulated in very general, unspecific terms, including those on the amounts to be paid in fines by firms found to be engaging in illegal practices and the criteria to be used to determine fines.

Bureaucracy and corruption
The numerous corruption scandals uncovered in recent years have usually involved high-level administrators and relatives of office holders in the highest echelons of the state apparatus.[7] These cases highlight how rotten the state and administrative structures are and how little has changed since the beginning of the reforms. Neither have the series of so-called anti-corruption and clean-up operations of recent years fundamentally altered the situation. Such activities seem rather to have been elegant ways to replace members of old networks whose power and influence has decreased with members of competing power centres with more leeway and better connections. In addition, some legal and institutional changes in areas such as corporate taxation, customs and the General Authority for Investment (GAFI) were said to be aimed *inter alia* at reducing red tape and corruption. However, measures taken to

reduce bureaucracy and corruption have been rather limited compared to what seems to be necessary. Further, the benefits primarily accrue to the well-connected business cronies of the regime who have always been able to negotiate special arrangements with the authorities. Cumbersome bureaucracy and excessive corruption remain major reasons for the high share of informal economic activity in Egypt, estimated by some at 50 per cent of the total.[8]

Unequal access to financial services
Small and medium-sized enterprises which do not benefit from patronage, clientelism or corruption have had nearly no access to credit, while a small number of bigger and better-connected businessmen have received credits worth billons of dollars from Egyptian state banks, often without providing feasibility studies for their projects or sufficient guarantees or collateral. Major scandals erupted throughout the mid- to late 1990s. When minor players received loans, often the borrowing conditions differed from those the regime's business cronies would enjoy.[9]

One of the government's recent well-publicized reforms has been its attempt to restructure the financial sector. So far, banking regulations have been strengthened, supervisory bodies seem to have become somewhat more active and a number of smaller banks which were unable to cope with the new requirements have merged or ceased operations. The changes also seem to have led to greater transparency in the role of the state in the banking sector. However, it remains to be seen how far the measures taken have improved the conditions for the average Egyptian business. According to Egyptian businesspeople and analysts, there is still only very limited access to credit. It seems to be even more problematic for the ordinary Egyptian businessman to get a loan after the financial scandals.

Privatization of state banks: greater transparency or more corruption?
The privatization of one of the four big state banks (Bank of Alexandria) and the ongoing process of divestiture of former government shares in joint venture banks (JVBs) have been part of the recent banking sector reform.[10] However, also in this regard, some high-profile members of the "reform cabinet" as well as other individuals linked to the regime

have been accused of major corruption and self-enrichment through, for example, insider dealing.

The Stock Exchange: continued lack of transparency and the ripping-off of small investors
Ever since the Cairo Stock Exchange was revived in the 1990s, financial analysts and Egyptian small and foreign portfolio investors as well as policy advisers and donor organizations have been complaining about widespread irregularities at the exchange.[11] Up to today, the Stock Exchange – one of the major institutions of corporate capitalism – has an image of being corrupt and of being manipulated in the interests of a few well-connected players.[12]

1.2 Direct and indirect forms of the regime's continued control of the economy

Direct and indirect domination through ownership and networks
Since the early 1990s, the continuous change in the composition of the regime's domestic power base which began under Sadat in the 1970s went on, culminating in the appointment for the first time of a whole number of influential businessmen as cabinet ministers in 2004. The increasing role of business circles as active supporters of the regime has been paralleled by a process of accelerated merger of the former military-bureaucratic and technocratic elite (the rentier regime's "state class"[13]) with the newly emerging class of big private businessmen nurtured by the regime in the 1980s and 90s.

Until the mid- to late 1990s, the government's economic leverage was the public sector, including, above all, state-owned business enterprises (SOEs) and state banks. After some limited privatization during the mid-1990s, the government recently began a new round of SOE and bank privatizations. However, in many cases privatization "Egyptian style" led to a distribution of former state-owned assets to a limited number of well-connected business cronies of the regime and to friends and relatives of regime members, and allegedly also to the takeover of large parts of attractive state assets by high-ranking regime figures themselves. As regards asset sales to foreign direct investors, such deals have often been facilitated and arranged either by businessmen loyal to the regime or, again, by members of the "state class", who often managed to secure substantial influence over the businesses concerned for the period after the divestiture.

This pattern of privatization and of providing more room for what is misleadingly called "the private sector" has not fundamentally changed forms of regulation, control and domination. In many cases, the opposite is true. Previously, the regime's economic power was exerted directly through the public sector, whose laws and regulations, despite the fraud and corruption, secured at least a minimum of legality and transparency. Now, this channel of influence has been complemented and often substituted by a more indirect way of regulating affairs through networks of regime members and their business cronies.

Consequently, the increased share of "the private sector" in Gross National Product (GNP), employment (if any) and credit cannot be taken as a serious indicator of decreased economic power and influence of the ruling regime. In some areas, where high-ranking regime members or their relatives own substantial shares in privatized or newly established businesses, the direct control of the ruling elite over the economy may even have increased.

In general, concentration of economic power in the hands of a few with close links to the ruling regime has been sustained. This experience further undermines the naïve assumption that a greater role for "the private sector" will lead to the establishment of a real market system. While the regime's control and domination of the economy has been preserved (and sometimes even extended), new channels of influence such as ownership participation, networks of patronage and personal relations of actors to regime figures are less transparent than ever before.

Liberalization or partial adjustment of the patronage system?
Recently, some observers have seen a trend of economic liberalization in the sense of an increased role of markets in regulating economic activity. However, this is not necessarily in contradiction to what has been presented above. The competing claims of an increasing number of networks of privilege have in many instances led to an over-burdening of the regime as the final arbiter and power broker. Increasing signs of blockage and sclerosis of the overall system may have triggered the idea that "some more market" might be necessary, if only to prevent the state apparatus reaching total standstill as a result of the interference of

competing networks. At a certain point, rational calculations by the regime may have led to the conclusion that its capacity to accommodate all competing claims and to arbiter between the many networks it allowed to develop exceeded its already limited steering and management capacities. What appears to be a shift towards greater market regulation at the expense of state control may be just another measure designed to adjust an authoritarian regime to the circumstances at a given moment.

2. Redistribution: The Major Expression of the Dialectics of Stability and Change

Throughout the past decades, economic and political change in Egypt has been change from above. Regime-directed adjustment of the functional mechanisms of state and economy below the level of fully fledged system transition has been intended to keep the established power system functioning. This kind of change mainly materializes in ongoing processes of redistribution in the wider sense: a rearrangement of Egypt's authoritarian rule and the underlying resources in the face of multiple challenges. The contexts in which processes of redistribution are placed and the motivations for engineering redistribution activities are manifold. To a certain degree, in particular in the early stages of the so-called reform programme, instances of redistribution have often been nothing more than the limited and partially unintended side effect of the implementation of reform measures by the Egyptian government due to donor pressure, for example the partial privatization of SOEs in the mid-1990s. But, to a wider extent, redistribution has been part of a deliberate strategy of the regime of granting privileges to selected businessmen in order to buy domestic policy support. This has been accompanied by giving those businessmen more room in public debate and a bigger role in society in general. Further, the recently accelerated merger of the rentier regime's state class with big business – the merger of "guns and money" – naturally includes all kinds of redistribution process described above. The sections below will give an overview of the most important channels of such redistribution and show that the result is a strengthening of the current authoritarian regime and not a weakening of its ability to control either economy or society.

2.1 The redistribution of definition and decision-making power

The redistribution of definition power concerns the ability to formulate broader visions of the development of society and the economy, to identify relevant problems and to formulate priorities for action. It further includes interpreting events which happen to society and deriving conclusions for policy-makers (i.e. prescribing appropriate action in the form of policies, strategies, programmes and measures). A clear shift away from Egypt's earlier populist discourse can be observed in this respect. Thirty years of Mubarak's rule and nearly twenty years of talk of economic reform, together with more recent changes in the country's media landscape, have provided the framework for a sea change in economic debate as well as the representation of economic issues in public discourse. With the exception of some leftist and Nasserist newspapers, advocates of "the market" and entrepreneurship dominate the scene. In particular, new and privately run and financed newspapers, TV channels and radio stations seem to have changed the way public debate is presented and public opinion is influenced in Egypt, despite the fact that most of these outlets are backed and financed by well-known business cronies of the regime.

The redistribution of decision-making power concerns the ability to propose and push through decisions at all relevant levels of the policy process, from general decisions on the fundamental features of the system of state and society and basic principles for steering and managing public affairs (including the economy) to specific policy measures to be implemented in particular circumstances (for example the timing, speed and extent of privatization activities). A particular issue is the influence of different actors on legislation (e.g. tax laws and the labour code) and other forms of regulation, on foreign economic relations and on the concrete framework conditions for the behaviour of micro-economic actors (entrepreneurs and workers), their representative bodies and so on.

There is no clearer sign of the redistribution of decision-making power in favour of the regime's business elite than the fact that current cabinet members have been recruited from among well-connected business cronies. Businessmen also complement the members of the traditional, military-technocratic state class in high-profile positions in parliament, parliamentary committees and the ruling party's special committees whereas people officially referred to as "workers" or "peasants" previously served in these various functions. Despite the fact that the most important policy decisions are still made directly by the top leadership (Mubarak and his aides) this again shows the changing composition of the regime's domestic power base.

Further, with the advent of "young reformers" like Gamal Mubarak's men in the cabinet, those organizations that have been well connected to the President's son – such as the American Chamber of Commerce in Egypt (AmCham) – also seem to have gained a stronger and sometimes very direct influence on Egypt's economic affairs. Political and economic analysts in Cairo stress that drafts of some of the recent "reform laws", for example the new tax and competition laws, were provided by AmCham.

The redistribution of definition power, decision-making power and assets (see below) comes with the construction and reconstruction of ideologies, visions, discourse, meaning, concepts and terms by the most influential actors in ways compatible with their interests. Among other things, this includes the construction of overly positive – if not false – images. Examples are the images of a "clean" (corruption-free) and efficient government of experts, of the alleged success of the "economic reforms" (including fiddling the figures) and of the Egyptian regime as the leaders of a country that still matters internationally in economic, political, military and cultural terms. At the same time, the previous negative images of big businessmen – perceived as corrupt individuals by the majority of the population – or of "the market" – widely perceived as the sphere of exploitation of ordinary people by ruthless businessmen – is "corrected" (for example the "market" is now presented as the institution that is able to solve major social problems).

2.2 The redistribution of assets and means of accumulation
Change in asset distribution
The redistribution of assets can involve changes in the relative importance of the public versus the private sector in the economy or in the role of domestic versus foreign capital. Further, it can imply changes in the economic weight of the rulers' business cronies *vis-à-vis* new, independent entrepreneurs pushing for a more level playing field. The redistribution of means of accumulation can be limited to simple rearrangements among different networks of state officials and their business cronies, i.e. changes in the balance of power *within* the established politico-economic elite.[14]

*The relative importance of the public versus the
private sector in the economy*
Egypt is witnessing the emergence of a new private sector. Since the time of Sadat, the balance between the public and the private sector has been gradually changing, but rather slowly and only in relation to certain areas of economic activity. Only with the emergence of the so-called new communities in the 1990s – desert cities built to relocate substantial parts of the population and industry away from Cairo and the Nile Valley to the desert areas – did a new private sector come into being. A major reason for this was the support of the regime for new businessmen. Networks of patronage linking the regime and selected entrepreneurs date back to the time of Sadat. However, only with the availability of new forms of economic "incentives" and nearly unlimited credit ordered by the regime and provided by the state banks did substantial investment in production begin to take off. This has been accompanied by generous tax holidays of up to fifteen years, the provision of cheap land, usually equipped with basic infrastructure, to investors and bureaucratic procedures for start-ups in the new communities which were somewhat less cumbersome than usual.[15] In addition, in recent years public funds have been increasingly redirected away from improving the living conditions of Egypt's lower strata by means of public housing or infrastructure projects towards subsidizing the profits of private sector businessmen in real estate.[16] Often, the successes of new industrial enterprises have also been due to close interaction with the public sector, which has usually resulted in advantages for the private at the expense of the public firms.

At the same time, the opportunities for well-placed business cronies to make money have generally also increased as a result of changes in regulation. Areas which have been opened up for private sector participation include the telecommunication sector, including TV channels, "build, own, operate, transfer" (BOOT) infrastructure facilities such as airports, ports and power plants, the cement industry and land reclamation and development. Further, private companies have been allowed to deal in public sector imports, an indication of the rearrangement of the traditional relationships between public and private sector activities in Egypt, again to the benefit of the latter.

However, the public sector has continued to dominate in various fields, particularly industry. At the beginning of the 1990s, Egypt's

SOEs still produced roughly 75 per cent of the overall industrial value added.[17] When it became clear to the top leadership that privatization of the public sector could potentially undermine the regime's stability, they chose to postpone, if not abandon, important privatization steps. In dealing with external donors and creditors, this decision was disguised by a surprisingly effective "reforms-just-for-show" strategy. For about a decade, the Egyptian government successfully prevented comprehensive privatization and retained direct control over major parts of the economy.[18] In cases where the formal divestiture of some major SOEs could not be blocked on account of external donor pressure, various tactics enabled the regime to keep the greater part of the assets under the control of the public sector.[19] At the end of the 1990s, Egypt's privatization stagnated and in February 2002 the Egyptian government officially announced that no further privatization steps would be implemented. Egypt's privatization programme of the 1990s, therefore, did not result in a substantial change in the balance between the public and private manufacturing sectors. Sines calculated a public sector share of 68.5 per cent of the value added in industry for 1998 (compared to 75 per cent in 1992), and of 74.4 per cent of employment in larger enterprises.[20]

With a new round of privatizations in progress since about 2004 and the ongoing investment of the Egyptian private sector as well as of foreign investors, the public–private sector balance seems to have been affected again. However, public sector companies, too, sometimes heavily invest in new projects, not to mention the expanding activities of the huge military-industrial complex in military production, consumer goods and land reclamation and real estate.[21] While the major concern of the regime during the 1990s was the prevention of large-scale SOE divestiture, the cabinet of the "young reformers" seems to be interested in maximizing privatization revenue as a way of covering the increasing fiscal deficit, while any privatization process also offers numerous opportunities for semi-legal or illegal self-enrichment by bureaucrats and politicians. The question, however, is how "private" the private sector in Egypt really is. As shown above, the formal distinction between the "public" and the "private" sectors does not say very much about control and the degree of market relations and competition in the Egyptian economy. The economic reforms implemented so far may have changed the balance between what is called the "private sector" and the public sector, meaning the part of the economy that is directly controlled by the state, but a fundamental transition from a rentier system towards a functioning, liberal market economy has not taken place.

Does foreign direct investment (FDI) contribute to structural change?
The Egyptian government regularly publishes data on FDI. On the one hand, increasing FDI figures are presented as proof of the success of the government's economic policies. On the other hand, high and increased FDI is referred to whenever supporters of the regime claim that the economic reforms underway will lead to real structural change. The main argument is that FDI leads to stronger competition and that foreign investors do not behave according to the rules of "the old system". In other words, increasing FDI is presented both as a result of successful economic reforms and as an additional driver for the continued structural change the so-called reforms are allegedly aiming for.

However, patterns of FDI so far do not suggest that foreign investors will substantially contribute to the establishment of new "rules of the game" or markedly increased international competitiveness. First, the total inflow of FDI is still limited compared to the size of the overall economy and to FDI in other developing countries. As a result of the small volume of FDI, potential positive effects on the business climate and business culture in Egypt seem to be rather limited. Second, the sources of FDI as well as the industries benefiting from investment do not suggest positive change.

Investment in modern production for international markets makes up a very small fraction of overall FDI. The bulk of investment still goes to the rent-generating oil and gas sector that has few backward and forward linkages. By its very nature, such FDI will reinforce – and not undermine – the rentier pattern of revenue generation. Other major investment seems to be concentrated in real estate, construction and tourism. These industries do not appear in general to have the potential for bringing about substantial structural change in a rentier economy, as investment in them forms part of established ways of making easy money without the need for significant investment in productivity, technology or innovation. Further, licensing processes for new tourism development zones and the allocation of land for new projects are constantly linked to allegations of corruption, violations of the law, favouritism, nepotism and so on. The real estate and construction business in Egypt has been characterized by speculation ever since Sadat opened it to the private sector in the 1970s. Egyptian industry insiders already admit that the large local and foreign investment in real estate and the resulting construction boom have produced a bubble that can be expected to explode rather soon, with potentially devastating consequences for the local economy. In addition, as a result of the high oil prices of recent years, a large proportion of FDI in the industries referred to above, as well as in trade, land reclamation and infrastructure, has come from oil-rich Gulf countries, themselves not particularly well known as transparent, liberal market economies.

The rulers' business cronies vis-à-vis the role of independent entrepreneurs: changing economic and political importance?
Redistribution processes could reduce the economic importance of the regime's business cronies as compared to the role of other, more independent businessmen. Quite naturally, the well-established and privileged business circles with their strong links to the politically powerful will try to preserve the special arrangements benefiting them. At the same time, less well-connected, newly emerging entrepreneurs could be expected to push for substantial reform. This could have a positive impact in terms of the transition of the Egyptian rentier system towards a market economy. However, an essential precondition for such change is the existence of a significant number of economically powerful, independent entrepreneurs. In the Egyptian case, such a minimum critical mass of independent businesspeople is lacking. Under the circumstances, it seems simply impossible for a businessman to be both economically successful and independent from the ruling regime, at least once a certain level of business activity is reached. The regime is still powerful enough to destroy the business operations of any entrepreneur who does not conform to what is considered appropriate behaviour. Business people of a particular standing are thus forced to play by rules set by the regime.

Redistribution in the sense set out above may include certain rearrangements of influence, leverage and economic resources among different factions and networks of state officials and their business cronies, i.e. rearrangements of privilege and economic means within the established elite circles. Egyptian analysts, indeed, have identified several waves of the building-up and destruction and substitution of generations of business elites by the rulers.[22] However, there is no indication that this leads to the emergence of a relevant number of Egyptian businessmen emancipated from the all-embracing regime. The few attempts of more powerful entrepreneurs to establish a certain degree of independence have been immediately punished by the regime.[23]

Means and instruments of asset redistribution
Since the time of Sadat, a traditional vehicle for the redistribution of economic resources towards selected business cronies of the regime has been the interaction of private firms with public sector enterprises. Further, government contracts of all sorts regularly provide private firms with ample opportunity to have access to public money. Often, state procurement or public construction projects help well-connected individuals to build their private business empires from scratch.[24]

The same applies to the numerous monopolies for trading or producing certain products or providing particular services in the Egyptian market which are granted and guaranteed by the state. A recent example is an oligopoly of three providers (initially of two) in the Egyptian market for mobile telephone services which, according to some sources, has allowed the businessmen involved to triple or quadruple their wealth within a period of less than ten years.

In addition, during the 1980s, but in particular in the 1990s, loans and credits handed out by state banks to private businesses, often after direct intervention from high-ranking regime figures, became a major source of asset accumulation and personal enrichment for certain businessmen.[25]

The complex system of tariffs and non-tariff import restrictions linked to the monopolies just mentioned serves as another instrument for the transfer of economic wealth from bigger parts of the population to a small number of privileged businesspeople. High import taxes for consumer goods guarantee high profits for those entrepreneurs who import the components at a much lower tax rate and assemble the products locally, for example cars or consumer electronics products.

With the revival of the Egyptian stock market in the early 1990s, another channel for redistributing wealth to a few well-placed regime members and their business friends has been opened up. Due to weak institutions and the related lack of transparency and control, some players are in a position to manipulate the trading process in a way that leads to the massive enrichment of a small number of investors at the expense of the majority, in particular small investors.[26]

With the recent boom in real estate speculation, tourism and construction, a very traditional asset has gained new importance as a means of wealth transfer: land. In Egypt, the state still controls major parts of the country's land resources and the regime is in a position to allocate land as it wishes. Within the framework of the new communities programme, investors could purchase huge plots of land, usually equipped with basic infrastructure, at very low prices. More recently, during the last three to five years, land has been given to Egyptian and Gulf investors for a wide variety of projects, ranging from the New Valley land reclamation project at Toshka to the establishment of gated communities for the affluent around Cairo. State land has become an essential instrument of accumulation.

A less direct but nevertheless very important channel of redistribution is the state budget. Egypt's fiscal policy is increasingly characterized by distribution that benefits the higher income brackets at the expense of the lower. A recent example is the reduction of the rate of corporate income tax from 40 per cent to 20 per cent, while the rate of tax on labour income did not decrease. The excessive use of domestic debt as a source of budget financing has been identified as another mechanism the benefits and costs of which are distributed among the Egyptian population in an unbalanced way.[27]

Further, inflation is considered to be a form of income tax, as it will cause wealth to be redistributed from wage earners to capital income earners (inflation rates between 2004 and 2007 were 4.3 per cent, 9.5 per cent, 4.9 per cent and 6.5 per cent respectively).[28]

Lastly, corruption benefits the rich and well connected and puts a disproportionate burden on the poor. Corrupt practices, in addition, often siphon off money directly from public enterprises, resulting in losses which impose additional burdens on the budget and thus on the ordinary taxpayer, whereas privileged actors have greater opportunity to avoid taxation. The lack of control and accountability at all levels of the state machine, a feature of a state that is strong in oppressing the population but weak in delivering proper administration and economic development, allows well-connected people to appropriate wealth in various ways.

3. Internal and External Actors

This section will show that neither the redistribution of definition and decision-making power nor the massive redistribution of assets and means of accumulation of recent years has led to a loss of power on the part of the regime or to the emergence of new independent actors such as a self-conscious class of capitalists emancipated from the political rulers. Furthermore, other domestic actors independent of the regime and/or in opposition to it do not seem to be strong enough to take any action that could substantially contribute to overcoming the established system of control and domination. Further, in contrast to the early to mid-1990s, throughout the so-called new reform period since 2004, pressure of external actors on the Egyptian government to implement decisive structural economic reforms seems to have been almost absent.

3.1 The regime, the "state class" and the business elite: new independent actors?

Splits, factions and competition
Throughout Egypt's modern history, economically powerful businessmen have established close links to the state in order to enjoy the government's support and protection.[29] However, there seems to be a tendency on the side of the regime to periodically shift privileges from older networks to younger generations of businessmen. It also seems that currently some representatives of the regime, such as Gamal Mubarak, regard younger, often more outward- and export-oriented entrepreneurs as being more capable of contributing to growth and employment than previous generations of business cronies, or at least of being better able to create the positive image of new economic dynamics in Egypt that is important in order to regain at least some domestic legitimacy as well as for relations with external supporters of the regime. This also implies better access by members of the business elite to the economic resources to be distributed by the state. In recent years, influential entrepreneurs have emerged as a strong domestic support base for the rulers.

However, despite the fact that business people have more room and play a rapidly increasing role in the economy and in politics, and that the political leadership, in turn, wants to be connected to business circles, the agenda of the ruling elite is clear: to keep the regime in an unchallenged position of power *vis-à-vis* all other actors in society. Consequently, the "new" business cronies are weak compared to the core decision-makers of the regime. In any potential clash, the top leadership will prevail.

Nevertheless, private businessmen linked to the regime have benefited from political patronage, economic privileges and favourable links to the public sector. Their economic interests, despite all the free market economy rhetoric voiced by some leading entrepreneurs in public, may result in economic and political action which opposes or obstructs any fundamental shift of the system that has nurtured them. However, this is not to say that all entrepreneurs who made their fortunes thanks to support and privileges granted by the regime would be against any kind of change. The debates over economic reform, including issues such as privatization, trade liberalization and financial sector reform, illustrate that many businessmen very much welcome changes that entail immediate improvement of their own business activities.

Despite the fact that the regime has been quite successful in preventing substantial change of the established system and that Egypt's entrepreneurs have not emerged as a class in itself and for itself, both the political-military-bureaucratic and the business elites are by no means monolithic blocs. As for the political elite, a clear distinction can be made on the one hand between the upper echelons of leadership and the domestic security apparatus as the core of the regime and on the other all its other elements. Major political decisions are made by the President after consultation with a small circle of advisers, including the heads of the security services. Other parts of the "state class", such as the economic administration and so on, seem to play only minor roles. Even the relative importance of the military, compared to the internal security forces, seems to have declined dramatically since the times of Nasser and Sadat. Besides the military, other subgroups of the state apparatus also have their special interests, but are even less in a position to pressure the top leadership in terms of decision-making.

The business elite is much more diversified and differentiated than the military-bureaucratic elite. There exist numerous, often competing power centres, networks and factions within the Egyptian business world. With the increasing number of well-organized networks, the regime's task to accommodate the different factions' demands in terms of privilege and opportunities for doing business has become more and more difficult.

At the same time, the lack of class consciousness and of a political project among Egypt's capitalists helps the regime to continue its policy of divide and rule *vis-à-vis* the country's business circles as well.

An alliance for system change from within?
As the military-bureaucratic administration has been increasingly marginalized and the domestic security apparatus has gained in importance, a major precondition for any fundamental reform of the established politico-economic system is that the relevant parts of the security apparatus be involved in a potential alliance for such change. Only if powerful actors from the intelligence and police organizations join an attempt to overcome Egypt's socio-political and socio-economic stagnation could such an attempt be successful, given the support and cooperation of other parts of the government machinery as well as of the business elite.

After a certain level of military strength and economic development was achieved in some of the most successful Asian "tiger states", such as South Korea and Taiwan, their military-autocratic leaders handed over political power to civilian democratic governments more or less voluntarily and also gave more room to market forces after decades of strong government intervention in the economy. The authoritarian leaders of South Korea and Taiwan well understood that such moves were necessary in order to facilitate the economic development of their nations and to enable them to withstand international economic and political competition, first of all from China. Implicitly or explicitly, the transition to democracy and a modern market economy was understood as a functional precondition for the further mobilization of human capital and other resources in the context of national development aiming at increased technological capability and economic competitiveness.

However, it seems that neither such far-reaching insights nor the corresponding policy scenarios can be expected in the near future in Egypt. As it is primarily the higher-ranking members of the security services who benefit from the established order, there seem to be only very limited incentives for the relevant actors to get involved in any potential attempt to overcome the system, even if only by evolutionary change. The same holds true for leading members of the private sector business elite, despite the fact that some of its representatives may have understood that substantial change is necessary to secure the country's future economic existence in an environment of global competition.

External actors and "economic reform" after 11 September 2001
It seems that global structural trends and international actors are not currently significantly affecting the process of the state's economic reorganization in Egypt. By contrast, in the early to mid-1990s, foreign creditors and donors who demanded that Egypt undertake major reforms as a precondition for debt relief, new loans and other external financial and technical support had relatively strong leverage. The Egyptian regime had to consider the pressure of the IFIs and of the United States (US) in negotiations on debt restructuring, new loans and so on, even if it turned out that the external pressure had only limited impact in terms of structural change.[30] With the overcoming of the external debt problem and some other positive macro-economic developments, including substantial foreign currency reserves, external influence on Egypt's economic policy diminished in the late 1990s.

It was only in the aftermath of the events of 11 September 2001, when President Bush announced his vision of democratization in the Middle East, that pressure on the regime increased. This time, Washington did not call for greater market or foreign trade liberalization, but for minimum levels of democracy and human rights. The regime felt uneasy, in particular when the Americans indulged in public speculation as to alternatives to Mubarak and directly intervened to free opposition politician Ayman Nur from an Egyptian prison in March 2004. However, with the increasingly visible disaster of the US policy of "democratization" in Iraq, the pressure on the region's authoritarian regimes once again declined. For the Egyptian rulers, this meant both the abatement of any criticism of how the regime deals with the opposition, Islamist or otherwise, and a nearly complete absence of any further pressure to continue or revive economic reforms. Further, the economic upturn experienced by the country due to very high oil prices at about the same time as the US failure in Iraq became visible and the so-called "young reformers" came to office in Cairo, seemed to relieve the regime from any immediate need to act. In this context, the reform measures of the Nazif government seem to have been initiated primarily by domestic actors such as Yusuf Boutros Ghali or Gamal Mubarak, who could, of course, count on the support of their friends in Washington as well as in the US embassy and the AmCham office in Cairo. Had the so-called reforms touched the core mechanism of the Egyptian rentier system – which, as shown above, was not the case – the top leadership would have intervened to stop them.

The regime seems to be very confident that it is safe from undesired external pressure to reform the economic or political system and from substantial organized domestic opposition. Egyptian observers, some of whom have close links to the country's highest decision-makers, share the view that leading regime figures simply do not care what outside observers, including major allies in the West or representatives of international organizations, think about their policies.[31] This is a rather unexpected finding for a rentier state like Egypt, and can only be explained in the context of the West's current obsession with security and political "stability" in the Middle East in the wider context of the Iraq disaster and the perception of an increased worldwide Islamist threat.

In brief, global structural trends and international actors have, of course, affected the process of the state's economic reorganization in Egypt. However, it seems that during recent years external influences have not been important in terms of the design and implementation of the restructuring of the authoritarian state. After the events of 11 September 2001, considerations of domestic politics, control and the preservation of power seem to have shaped decisions and the restructuring process more than external economic events and interventions.

4. Conclusions

4.1 Restructuring and adjustment of the mechanisms of authoritarian control

The rulers' preservation of the established power system has required some change *within* the authoritarian system. As a result, one can identify signs of both stability and change. "Stability" exists insofar as the Egyptian leaders have managed to secure the continuation of their own rule. However, change from above has also contributed to the regime's survival and preservation of its power. This change in order to prevent change also seems to contribute to the astonishing harmony between the representatives of the regime, who deny "their" citizens the most basic human rights and representatives of the West, i.e. US and European states' officials, who also seem to be more interested in "security" and "stability" than uncontrolled change. Limited adjustments within the economic system have aimed at and resulted in a shift of patronage towards particular segments of the private sector, including networks of high-ranking representatives of the state and the business community, without undermining the role of the state as the ultimate source of power and distributor of rent. This shift of patronage has been accompanied by and achieved through a massive redistribution of economic resources and influence over economic policy decisions in favour of the regime's business cronies at the expense of the lower strata of society. However, the increasing importance of well-connected businessmen in the economy as well as in the political sphere does not mean that the economic elite has been emancipated from the regime.

The externally imposed reforms of the 1990s and their local manifestations in this period as well as from 2004 onwards have contributed to a general restructuring of the state's economic functions. The most important new pattern is the establishment of additional *indirect* forms of control of the economy by the regime, mainly through the merger of the old (military-technocrat-bureaucratic) state class with the class of regime-connected big businessmen. At the same time, direct control of major parts of the Egyptian economy by the regime through the public sector has been preserved, despite recent privatization activities. Further, as a result of the privatization of former state assets, as well as of the establishment of new businesses by regime members or their families and their participation in other people's businesses, an additional element of control has emerged, namely the regime's *direct control* of parts of the "private sector".

The major objective of the regime in relation to economic reform was simply to reorganize and consolidate its power system. The Egyptian regime has in this respect pursued a number of clear objectives or intended outcomes. These include, on a more general level, restructuring external economic relations, for example by negotiating external rents and conditions, and restructuring the internal system of distribution of economic resources and privilege, for example by coopting new social groups and marginalizing others. However, it would be wrong to assume that the leaders would have been following a clear strategy.

Egypt's authoritarian regime has always resorted to ad hoc measures in the face of internal and external economic pressure.

After the termination of the previous social contract and in the absence of a new one, the legitimacy of the regime has dramatically eroded. On the one hand, the regime relies on the brutal suppression of any opposition by its security apparatus. On the other hand, it desperately tries to maintain, or re-establish, the image of a development-oriented national leadership that is able to deliver, if not prosperity and wealth for the majority, at least some relief from economic misery and social decline for the population.[32] The projection of such an image is itself an attempt to regain some legitimacy, not only domestically but also in the international arena which, under normal circumstances, is at least as important as the domestic audience for a rentier regime that receives geopolitically motivated rent transfers. For this purpose, the regime incorporates not only the elites of the security apparatus and higher-level technocrats, but also big businessmen who are seemingly loyal to it.

The shifts in the balance of power among different elite factions, including the rise of new power centres and influential networks at the expense of other actors, have only been possible due to the fact that the top leadership either did not intervene to prevent it, or even actively encouraged the redistribution of power and privilege to its new protégés. So far, it seems that the regime is still in control of the process of redistribution. If there is any change at all, it still seems to be controlled change. And, for the time being, there are only very few signs that such processes of intended change may get out of hand.

4.2 Socio-political and economic implications

Impact on the social situation and regime legitimacy
The social basis of the Egyptian regime has been changing in a way that increases the importance of the newly emerging elite composed of a mixture of higher government officials (civilian and military) and outstanding representatives of the property-owning classes. These new networks of business cronies and state officials with close business links have gained increasing importance *vis-à-vis* the former support base consisting of the rural population, the urban working class and lower to medium ranks of the public sector and civil service. The social actors who are increasingly marginalized are the landless labourers in the countryside,

small farmers and the lower and medium ranks of the public sector workforce, as well as civil servants and intellectuals of various professional backgrounds. Further, it can be assumed that a significant number of business owners and employees in the informal sector may also be negatively affected. The private sector workforce enjoys much less protection than the public sector workforce, unionization levels are low and labour code violations are widespread. Finally, the privileges enjoyed by certain big businessmen imply restrictions for the majority of small and medium-sized Egyptian entrepreneurs.

The massive redistribution of wealth in Egyptian society and the changing role of the state in the provision of public goods and social welfare services negatively affect social cohesion and further erode the legitimacy of the ruling elites. State–labour relations, among others, have been changing in ways which negatively impact on equality. The same holds true for the reorganization of asset ownership and tenants' rights in the Egyptian countryside.[33] Consequently, the authoritarian restructuring employed by the Egyptian regime leads to social conflict as well as to the reinforcement of clientelistic social relations and informal networks of solidarity (family, religious, etc.), which in turn might result in a further fragmentation of society.

As the massive strikes of 2006/2007 illustrate, the negative outcomes of authoritarian restructuring for large segments of the population can create their own dynamics of growing discontent and opposition. Under certain circumstances, the new dynamics of such opposition, together with the increased room for activists resulting from globalization (increased information, external support, protection through worldwide media coverage, etc.), can lead to a partial challenge to traditional power, albeit without implying a serious threat to the established system as such. The strikes made it clear that the former public sector work force could become a political factor again.

The prevention of change undermines Egypt's economic viability
The main objective of the regime has always been to prevent change, in particular change that might affect the basic pattern of social organization and regulation. In this sense, the regime seems to have been very successful: until now it has been able to stay in control of both society and the economy. However, the very framework that has been established in

order to implement that control is also the greatest obstacle to the mobilization of the country's economic potential. The established patterns of organization and regulation which the regime has been able to maintain despite all the talk of reform have produced the long-lasting economic crisis that the country has been suffering from. The remarkable capacity of the regime for management and steering is above all the capacity to prevent any transformation, be it disruptive or evolutionary change. It is the capacity to suppress any social and economic dynamic that could contribute to overcoming the sclerotic structures prevailing in the country at large. In this sense, the regime is still able to keep the country locked into a situation where the most basic foundations of international competitiveness cannot be established.[34]

Consequently, the regime seems so far to have been unable to produce any meaningful results in terms of development, either alone or in cooperation with its new business cronies. Some observers advance the argument that strong direct and indirect government control of the economy can help to make use of resources so as to produce positive development outcomes, citing examples from South-East Asia. However, the adjustment in Egypt of forms of control from the earlier overt and direct mechanisms to more disguised and indirect forms does not necessarily imply that the regime could now start a sustainable process of economic development, even if only to increase its legitimacy. On the contrary, important economic indicators have recently shown negative trends. The regime is still failing to deliver sustainable, positive economic results. In relative terms, i.e. in comparison with other developing economies, Egypt is clearly continuing to lose ground. In relation to regime legitimacy, the question primarily is to what extent the larger segments of the population experience an improvement in their material and immaterial standard of living, but also in this respect the regime cannot deliver.

Notes

1 Suleiman *et al.* 1990; Weiss *et al.* 1998.
2 Ibid.
3 Cf., among others, International Monetary Fund 1996.
4 Cf. also Wurzel 2000 and 2004.
5 Ibid.
6 Weiss *et al.* 1998.
7 Cf. among others "Kifaya's corruption report and more", *The Arabist*, 7 July 2006, http://arabist.net/archives/2006/07/07/kifayas-corruption-report-and-more/ (retrieved 20 October 2008).
8 According to the World Bank's and IFC's report *Doing Business 2007*, Egypt's overall ranking in terms of ease of doing business is rank 165 in a sample of 175 countries (cf. World Bank *et al.* 2006).
9 Interviews, Egypt 1992–2007.
10 According to the reform agreement of the Egyptian regime and the Washington institutions, these reform steps should have been finalized already in the mid-1990s.
11 Wurzel 2000.
12 Interviews, Cairo 2007.
13 Cf. Elsenhans 1981.
14 Heydemann 2004.
15 Cf. e.g. Knaupe *et al.* 1995.
16 Cf. e.g. Salheen 2007.
17 World Bank 1992.
18 Weiss *et al.* 1998.
19 For details, cf. Wurzel 2000 and 2004.
20 Sines 1998, p. 93.
21 [Eds' note:] Cf. Droz-Vincent's chapter in this book.
22 Interviews, Cairo May 2007.
23 Cf. Wurzel 2000.
24 Cf., among others, Mitchell 2002.
25 It is estimated that not more than about 1,000 Egyptian businessmen received roughly one third of all public sector bank credits.
26 Interview, Egypt 1992–2007.
27 Abdel-Khalek 2000.
28 Cf. Index Mundi n.d.
29 Cf. Springborg 1989; Wahba 1994; Amin 1995; Zaki 1999.
30 Weiss *et al.* 1998; Wurzel 2000 and 2004.
31 Interviews, Cairo 2007.
32 In this respect, the Egyptian state shows some striking similarities with O'Donnel's descriptions of the exclusionary and repressive Latin American bureaucratic authoritarian state during the phase of its final decline (O'Donnel, cit. in Fahmy 2002, p. 26).
33 Cf. Mitchell 2002; Bush 2007.
34 Cf. Wurzel 2000.

6

THE LEBANESE SOCIO-ECONOMIC SYSTEM: 1985–2005

Charbel Nahas

1. Characteristics and Functioning of the "Lebanese System"

The recent history of Lebanon, at least since the early 1970s, presents a striking contrast: on the one hand, remarkable "technical" successes in various fields: attraction of capital and financial management, social and communitarian resilience, military and civil resistance, worldwide political polarization, etc. and, on the other hand, a persistent and dramatic institutional and human failure.

Such a strong, widespread and persistent contrast cannot be considered as accidental and be attributed to exceptional individuals or events. It requires a drastic reallocation of factors, energies and resources towards specific ends. This reallocation is at the core of the economy and in its deeper meaning. It constitutes a "system".

The purpose of this chapter is firstly to explore the inner "mechanics" of this system from an economic perspective, from the side of the engine, and secondly to look at it from the outside, from the driver's point of view.

What is intended by "system" is an intellectual construction, a model which allows for an acceptable level of integrated understanding of a given social-historical situation through the interpretation and anticipation of the set of discourses and behaviours that are observable and expectable within it or towards it.

The Lebanese economic and political situation surprises the observer with a set of striking features:

- An exceptional resilience towards the accumulation of debt (the highest debt to Gross Domestic Product GDP ratio in the world for several years, above 200 per cent in 2006) that recalls the resilience to the war that lasted 15 years.

- A low level of growth[1]: in spite of very favourable endowment with capital and labour, levels of consumption are nevertheless sustained by the attraction of capital flows that cover an exceptional current account deficit (20 per cent to 30 per cent of GDP).
- Particularly high levels of consumption among a privileged class and an exceptional level of inequality in wealth[2] and income that threatens social stability and leads various political forces to provide their services in return for communitarian or partisan allegiance.
- Persistent losses in factors: emigration flows are higher than during the war and inflows of capital are added to banks' liabilities and used to finance private and public consumption with no economic counterpart.
- A lack of legitimacy of the state, its administration and its services, commonly dominated by communitarian or partisan groups, leading to the interpenetration of public and private concerns and to persistent calls for the liquidation of the state's social functions.
- An endemic inability to produce efficient government structures that has shown to be deeper than the effects of direct external domination (notably in the Syrian era). Internal political precariousness is proportionate to external support intervention.

These features, although striking, do not mean that Lebanon is exempt from the common rules of political economy. They are controlled by two powerful and dominant factors, as follows:

- Lebanon attracts a specific submarket of capital (that of its diaspora and of wealthy individuals from the Gulf countries).
- Labour is exceptionally mobile in the region as a whole and in Lebanon in particular (foreign workers with low qualifications and wages at entry into Lebanon and all categories of Lebanese at exit).

Internal policies have not tried to mitigate or channel the effects of those two factors. On the contrary, they have constantly striven to amplify them through:

- a monetary policy based on extensive dollarization (since the mid-1980s) and pegging the local currency to the US dollar (since the end of 1992) to attract capital; and

- a generous public spending policy, based on powerful and massive redistributive mechanisms and aiming at buying political allegiances and preventing resistance.

1.1 Main characteristics of the model and its primary rules of operation

Lebanon shows, with some particular modalities, a severe case of what economists call the "Dutch disease". This generic name applies to a situation where massive inflows of funds, generally but not necessarily related to very large exports of raw materials, lead, paradoxically, to a severe and lasting deterioration of the sectors that produce internationally tradable goods.

Official estimates for the accounts for 1997, the most recent base year for national accounts, show a current account deficit of USD 4.8 billions, representing 30 per cent of GDP. This is an aberrant situation by any standard. One half of the deficit comes from the public sector and the other half from the private sector (savings and investment). The accounts show a corresponding inflow of capital and transfers for an amount that is close to the deficit in goods and services. Year after year, the two phenomena, both being unusual, repeat themselves, and the balance of payments, more or less, is balanced.

This mechanism works as follows: capital inflows swell the liabilities of the banks that reuse them domestically as loans to the state and the private sector. Through various channels, this flow of lending ultimately feeds consumption and, to a much lesser extent, investment (as far as real estate can be amalgamated with productive investment). The mechanism supposes that three conditions are met: firstly, that the inflow be perpetuated; secondly, that the banks find advantage in placing almost the entirety of the capital inflows domestically; and thirdly, that borrowers and final beneficiaries are not prevented from using funds to finance final consumption. Respect for these conditions is at the heart of the management of the model.

It follows that domestic demand is boosted by the inflow of capital and clearly exceeds domestic production. This "excess" in demand concerns tradable goods and services, i.e. goods and services that can be imported and exported, as well as non-tradable goods and services. Lebanon being a "small country", the excess in its demand for tradables has no influence on international prices (even though it could have some influence on prices for some import niches for specific goods or factors) and translates fully into an increase in the volume of imports. The situation is different for non-tradables. In their case, prices increase the more supply is inelastic, in spite of the tendency of available resources, labour and capital to concentrate on their production.

This gives several easily recognizable consequences:

- Domestic resources (labour and capital) are massively reallocated to the production of non-tradable goods and services (commerce, education and health, construction, restaurants and personal services, financial intermediation, etc.). On the other hand, job opportunities in the sectors that produce tradable goods and services are reduced (unless funded by subsidies that add costs to the taxpayer).
- The increase in prices of non-tradable goods and services exerts pressure for a rise in prices of domestic goods and services without an equivalent increase in their production. The purchasing power of residents who do not profit from the inflow of capital is reduced. This favours the entry of non-resident workers and lowers the competitiveness of tradable Lebanese products both on the domestic and the export market, unless assisted by protectionist measures that are costly for the consumer and aggravate distortions of costs and prices.

This type of evolution generally occurs in countries that undergo a rapid rise in their exports of raw materials in proportions that are large compared to the size of their economy. The classic case is that of small oil exporters. The risk for such countries is that the distortions in their economy induced by those exports tend to rigidify and become permanent and therefore expose them to serious difficulties once the exportable resources are exhausted.

In this respect, the "Lebanese case" shows two particularities that should be noted:

- The inflow of capital is not linked to the export of non-renewable resources, but to a persistent outflow of Lebanese emigrants sufficient in size to allow enough of them to succeed in accumulating capital that can feed transfers to Lebanon.

- If and when, in the case of oil-exporting countries, resources are exhausted, nobody will raise any claim on them. In Lebanon, the capital attracted accumulates in the form of bank deposits and financial claims whose owners retain the right to claim them, at any moment, with interest.

1.2 Effects on the economy: prices, activity and income
This model has produced sizeable and durable effects on the economy:

- Domestic financial aggregates swell up regularly, with no absolute nor relative limit, generating, even with constant interest rates, a burden of interest (predominantly renewed)[3] that is disproportionate to the economy and considerable losses (that remain latent) in assets.
- Prices of non-tradable goods and services are pushed upwards, as are those of domestic goods and services (land and, in proportion to negotiating power and stress of impoverishment, labour). In spite of the stabilization of the Lebanese pound against the US dollar since the end of 1992, and even its revaluation, domestic consumption prices increased by 80 per cent between 1993 and 1998 and more than doubled over the period 1993–2004.
- Patterns of allocation generate over-investment (capital and labour) in the production of non-tradable goods and services and under-investment elsewhere. In the case of previous investments or of new investments based on stubborn decisions or on erroneous anticipations, heavy losses are incurred unless specific subsidies or protections are provided, as happened in the case of industrial projects launched in various sectors (furniture, construction material, mechanics, clothing, etc.) since the early 1990s.
- Such over-investment in non-tradables, along with massive recourse to cheap non-resident labour, lowers costs, keeping productivity low. Tariff protection also encourages production with low added value.
- Activity tends to concentrate on the final stages of transformation of products so as to incorporate the maximum amount of non-tradable input. Inter-business trade remains minimal, reducing demand-driven effects and hindering sectoral and spatial diffusion of activity. Employment outside the public sector tends to concentrate in areas where the wealthiest live, close to demand, which exacerbates

regional disparities. This creates an increased pressure to hire in the public sector and fierce competition for the implementation of public goods and services contracts which have little economic justification beyond the jobs they create.
- Income sources are precarious and the proportion of wage-earning remains small outside the public sector. Permanent wage earners account for 46 per cent of active residents and close to 40 per cent of the total workforce, including transient Syrian workers. Wages, including social contributions, do not exceed 23 per cent of GDP and, if one retains this aggregate, 19 per cent of gross national disposable income. One third of those revenues come from the public sector. The narrow base of waged labour and the low level of its remuneration restrict women's labour to a small number of professions and, in spite of equivalent levels of education and a favourable social environment, the global participation of women in economic activity remains very low and does not exceed its level of thirty years ago.[4]
- Businesses are heavily indebted. According to available data, the average interest burden in most sectors exceeds 70 per cent of "earnings before interest, tax, depreciation and amortization" (EBITDA) after allowing for a "reasonable" remuneration for the individual entrepreneur; the ratio of debt to EBITDA is often above 8, which exceeds usual standards by far. These indicators stress the under-capitalization and over-indebtedness of Lebanese businesses.
- Businesses remain of the small family type. In 2004, businesses with more than 50 workers (excluding the public administration) accounted for 520 out of a total of 175,000; among these, 244 (about 50 per cent) were in the social services sectors (health, education, associations, etc.). In peripheral regions, the share of such activities among businesses with more than 50 workers becomes insignificant. Private businesses with 50 workers or more account for only 5 per cent of the private sector workforce, while those with 5 workers or more account for 19 per cent.
- The Lebanese are pushed to emigrate massively. More Lebanese have emigrated in the 15 years that followed the end of the war than during the 15 years of war. Kasparian estimates the annual gross outflow of Lebanese migrants at 32,000 between 1996 and 2001.[5] The comparison of age pyramids between 1996 and 2004,

once mortality rates per cohort are accounted for, would put the yearly net outflow at around 40,000. According to the same data, the population aged between 15 and 64 naturally increases by 40,000 every year. Hence most of the natural increase in the Lebanese working age population is cancelled out by emigration. The fact that emigrants are more skilled and have higher labour participation rates than residents further aggravates this worrying picture of a stagnating and ageing labour force. Emigration is due to sluggish growth and the existence of high reservation wages stemming from alternative employment opportunities abroad, as suggested by continued private investment in education in spite of poor domestic returns, and the high domestic cost of living. The fact that, as shown in Table 1, unemployment declines strongly with age might suggest that unemployment is temporary for new entrants due to opportunities for emigration. Under current migration patterns, approximately half of a given generation will have left the country by the age of 59 (see Table 2).

FIGURE 6.1
Age and unemployment rate

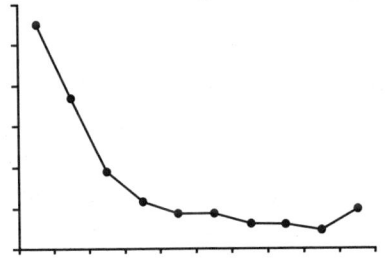

Source: Berthélemy *et al.* 2007.

FIGURE 6.2
Cumulative migration rate

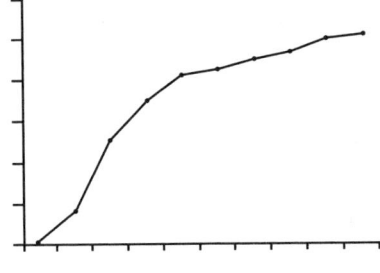

Source: Berthélemy *et al.* 2007.

1.3 Effects on society: redistribution, waste, exclusion and corruption

The "Lebanese model" cannot function and cannot even have emerged without powerful and effective redistributive mechanisms. If not, most attracted capital would remain concentrated in the hands of a few and the only part that would be transformed into income to finance consumption and imports would be a proportion of what the owners of that capital and the beneficiaries of those transfers spent directly; considering the very high concentration of capital inflow as inferred from the concentration of deposits, this would only represent a small part of the inflow. The domestic assets of the banking system would have no reason to swell systematically.

Since private economy is structurally unable to provide a sufficient number of Lebanese, from all categories, communities and regions, with revenues, it rests with the state to provide a double form of redistribution: it must first pay significant amounts of interest on public debt to keep the financial mechanism working, interest being the first form of redistribution, and it must secondly inject considerable amounts of subsidies to cater for the needs of the large categories of the population who suffer from the negative effects of the model on their jobs, revenues and cost of living.

These redistributive mechanisms are the necessary complement of the financial mechanism since they divert a significant part of attracted capital to meet the needs and cover the private financial debt of a large number of residents; they also constitute the basic condition for the security of the financial mechanism since they are key for ensuring social and political stability in a country living with a model that generates serious inequalities in revenues and living conditions without facilitating the social and economic links and ties that stem from work relations. In fact, the two sides of the redistributive mechanism, economic and political, are permanently intertwined. This interrelationship leaves its mark on social and political life as a whole.

It is neither surprising nor an accident that the Lebanese model provides considerable amounts in subsidies and redistribution. Although equivalent in economic terms, such subsidies and redistribution follow different channels that can be categorized, in socio-political terms, using two main criteria: the visibility and contestability of the transfer (legality, legitimacy, tolerance) and the political precision and efficiency of its targeting.

Along these lines, one can distinguish between various types of redistribution, as follows:

- Some redistribution is declared, visible and legal. It is usually aimed at general targets, as in the case of "social" public services such as public education or the coverage of the costs of hospitalization by the Ministry of Health, but in some cases it is also aimed at specific targets, such as social contributions for taxi drivers supported by the budget, subsidies for hundreds of "charitable associations" that have clear political motivations, discretionary "public works" allocations given to elected Members of Parliament (MPs), subsidies for tobacco growers who were fortunate enough to be granted a licence for cultivation, schooling indemnities for the children of civil servants or specific exemptions or privileges given to this or that project or company.
- Some redistribution is formally legal but remains invisible because the subsidies do not appear as such in any budget or balance sheet but translate into an increase in the operational costs of the administration or of some public enterprise or into insufficient social and economic returns; this is mainly the case for over-staffing and for public investment that is not justified by recognized needs.
- Other redistribution is illegal but visible and widely tolerated, such as the robbery of electrical current or water or the occupation and exploitation of public property, including the greater part of the seashore. Interesting variants are some channels that are formally legal but widely considered to be illegitimate, such as compensation for squatters within the operation of the "return of the displaced".

Beyond all those cases there are of course the cases of theft, extortion, misappropriation of public funds and so on.

2. Modes of Management of the "System"

The management of the system, and more obviously of society, requires many local adjustments that do not appear integrated and also some subtle mechanisms of global regulation. The global level is a direct determinant of the political scene. Being the most sensitive and the most vital element of the system, the regulation process is naturally at the source of the distribution of power.

2.1 Need of and pressure for adjustment

It is natural to distinguish between two types of cause that make adjustment of the system a naturally permanent necessity. One type of cause relates to changes that occur in the system's external environment and the other to the peculiarities and weaknesses or accidents of its internal operations.

While it is easy intellectually to understand the first type of cause, the second type requires more explanation. To say that one can explain to a reasonable extent the functioning of and behaviours within a given society does not mean that such functioning and behaviours must be smooth, non-contradictory and non-violent. The explanation would be very poor if it could not take into account the expression of conflicting interests within the society in question. In this sense one has to bear in mind that social conflicts have a dual meaning: they are usually functional *vis-à-vis* the system, in the sense that the system incorporates the framing of oppositions and gains credibility from their resolution, but they can also be antagonistic or slip out of control and become dysfunctional, bringing major changes in the social and political system. The difference is not one of degree. Conflicts that become dysfunctional generally express the exhaustion of the conditions of survival of the system as such. There are also cases where poor management can accelerate such an outcome.

Types and forms of conflict, resistance, claim and worry

The joint management of exceptional flows of capital and labour characterizes the "Lebanese system", but this is not perceived by the various actors, including most policy-makers. The Lebanese do not recognize that a part of the revenue they derive from their daily labour, a part of their income and expenditure, comes from the redistribution of capital inflows. They do not see a link between the permanent emigration they see around them and the "excess" of their consumption over production; they are happy with the remittances they might individually receive from a relative as a means to finance additional purchases for their household, and they miss their children who live abroad, but perception of any more general causal link is missing. The direct index for everyone is liquidity: delays in payment from both private payers, even the wealthiest, and public entities are a general phenomenon. Its intensity closely reflects the size of capital inflows and fluctuations in oil prices, but only initiates make the link.

Four stages in the system should be distinguished: that of the building-up of the system (1985 to 1992); that of its unconstrained expansion before the recognition of fiscal and financial difficulties under Syrian arbitrage (1992 to 1997); that of its financially constrained management under Syrian arbitrage (1997 to 2005); and that of its constrained management without Syrian arbitrage (2005 to the present). Under conditions of the normal running of the system, putting aside the phase of its building-up and some accidental crisis situations, the core difficulties relate to the allocation process.

The most obvious characteristic of the allocative redistributive process is its politicization. This serves the interests of politicians both because they gain support from their ability to bestow advantages on their clientele and because warlords who lack legitimacy and who agreed to disband their militia organizations and join the state on the condition that they would hold privileges in the redistribution process have a greater need to rely on patronage. This has been called "the price of peace". There is also another reason, the importance of which should not be ignored or minimized: the channels of redistribution of attracted capital are complex and can in no way be reduced to public expenditure, and most of their final effects are felt by a limited segment of society on account of the weak links in the production process, a phenomenon that is accentuated by the increasing weight of interest payments on the public debt, which is itself due to the extremely high concentration of deposits in the financial system. This situation generates a feeling of deprivation that expresses itself through the available socio-political structures and requires direct public and politicized intervention in the process of redistribution.

Direct distribution of revenue by the state or by state-owned agencies is the most elementary form of redistribution. Although widely used, especially in the phase of expansion of the system, it remains precarious and its obviousness imposes an uneasy mixture of concealment and justification. The beneficiaries are not unaware of this precariousness and their ambitions go beyond an occasional gain or an unstable complement to their income: a job is much more valuable, a job in the private sector is better, and property even better still. They try to obtain permanent and indisputable gains.

The clearest examples are the Displaced Fund, the Council for the South and the *Régie des Tabacs*. Other cases could be cited, but these three examples persistently come under the fire of critics.

- The Displaced Fund was created in 1991 to compensate for houses destroyed during the civil war and to allow their occupants to return to their original regions. Many cases of unjustified compensation have occurred, and compensation was extended to those who illegally occupied the houses of the displaced after removing them by force at the end of the fighting. In the regions of Shouf and Aaley specifically, compensation was disbursed by village, but only after "reconciliations" between the "displaced" and the "residents" took place under the direct patronage of Walid Joumblatt. Thus the allegiance of both groups was channelled to the man who commanded the militia which won the war and provoked the displacement and the occupation. The post of Minister of the Displaced has persistently been held by Joumblatt himself or by members of his party, while the Fund has been headed by people close to Rafiq Hariri. Twenty-five years after the displacement, the process is not yet finished, and very few people have returned effectively.
- The Council for the South was created in 1970 when Israel began its incursions into South Lebanon. Its responsibilities were increased as a result of the Israeli invasion and occupation of 1978. It was supposed to compensate for the destruction and to rehabilitate infrastructure and public services and, due to the emergency, was given large financial and administrative autonomy. It was headed directly by the Minister of Social Affairs during its first years of existence. Then, in the wake of the increasing influence of Musa al-Sadr as religious leader of the community, the post of president was created and entrusted to a Shiite personality close to Sadr and acceptable to Kamel al-Asaad, the traditional political leader in the South. In 1984, Nabih Berri, leader of the *Amal* movement,

a Shiite political party and militia, became Minister of State for Affairs of the South. Since then, all presidents of the Council have been prominent members of the *Amal* movement. The Council has been active in performing its duties, but in its actions, from staffing to the selection of beneficiaries and contractors and the assessment of compensation, it has clearly and consistently been oriented towards the reinforcement of the political base of the *Amal* movement.

- The *Régie des Tabacs* used to be a company enjoying the monopoly right, imposed during the French Mandate, for the growing of tobacco and the fabrication and import of cigarettes. After independence, it was acquired by the Lebanese state and new factories and warehouses were built, but local cultivation declined steadily. During the war, local production of cigarettes almost disappeared and the *Régie* became the formal channel for the import of foreign cigarettes alongside extensive smuggling under the control of militias. The company was wound up in the 1980s and has since had no defined legal status. It nevertheless shows significant profits due to the fact that excises on imported tobacco appear as a commercial margin in its books. This apparent income has allowed it to offer a wide range of subsidies to farmers, who, due to the monopoly, are required to have a licence to grow tobacco that the *Régie*, using tax proceeds, then commits to buy well above international prices. Tobacco growing has progressively disappeared from most parts of the country and has been concentrated in the south, the subsidies being justified by the need to maintain farmers in land under Israeli occupation. The *Régie* is consistently managed by members of the *Amal* movement, and has proven to be an efficient vector for the reinforcement of the political base of the movement as its peculiar legal and financial situation gives it exceptional room for manoeuvre.

Direct distribution faces obvious limits which have become much tighter since 1997, with the "worsening" situation of the public finances.

Redistribution and the conflicts surrounding it take place at two levels: a lower level where the issue is how much can be given and to whom, and a higher level where the issue is who can manage the allocative process and within what limits. There are conflicts about the redistribution of income and about the distribution of power to redistribute income and status. This dual level of conflict is a decisive factor in maintaining the cohesion of communities around their political leaders. A united community is a good answer in this type of situation. However, its smooth running requires several conditions to be met.

- Strong reciprocal fidelity between the members of the community so that the leader behaves faithfully towards it and derives from its mobilization behind him the strength to impose advantageous terms on other players. This condition has consistently been fulfilled.
- A reasonable assessment of the balance of power by politicians so as to use intimidation without slipping into open conflict (the availability of ample resources and of a strong arbitrator clearly make things easier in this respect). This condition has no longer been met since the fiscal situation tightened (thereby imposing the need for external and subtly politicized assistance), and since the Syrians were pushed out. It was therefore completely fulfilled until 1997 and partially until 2005.
- A good prediction by politicians of the evolution of economic and also social and political conditions: deals than can be cut, at a given moment in time, as to the allocation of specific instruments and institutions to a political leader or a coalition of political leaders, and that are based on an assessment by the other players, who are not party to the operation, of the advantages given. Since such allocations can to some extent be irreversible, if those advantages turn out later to be significantly larger or smaller than anticipated, and if the party who holds them refuses or is not allowed to review the sharing, major crises can occur, the most common outcome of which is a deadlock situation. This is precisely what happened with the cell phone "build-operate-transfers" (BOTs).

The need for clear predictions makes the management of allocation go hand in hand with the management of expectations. In this game, some players have shown more talent than others, but it has often led to crises and violence. The more the instruments and institutions of allocation – including special councils, autonomous public entities, publicly owned commercial enterprises, including the interesting cases of fictitious entities derived from expired concessions, contractors and private enterprises enjoying licences or monopolies – are distant from the core of the state, the more efficiently they can be used for political purposes and the more accurately they can target specific social groups including segments of the "elite", but also the more irreversible they become as long as the Prince cannot easily seize assets and reverse what was originally a political allocation of power.

The climax of this process of graduation, away from the uncertainties related to the direct redistribution of public money, is reached when tangible and stable positions are secured and legalized in the private sector.

This graduation makes the concept of corruption, when it goes beyond cases of characterized theft, look very ambiguous insofar as it opposes public and private sector behaviour: many prosperous private entrepreneurs obtained the original and decisive push towards their wealth as a result of a dated political arrangement, and both politicians and the public, at least in the first generation, do not make a significant distinction between the corporate advantages of those entrepreneurs and direct "rent-seeking" from public and para-public channels.

This insidious relation of overlapping and differentiation between the public and the private spheres gives a specific content to the debate about "reforms", "privatization", "downsizing the state" and so on. The incestuous relation of power and wealth blurs the debate about public–private relations and distorts the effective meaning of several widely publicized and fashionable concepts.

All the above-mentioned strategies apply to the powerful. The rest go on living with their ambitions and anxiety, and the more they feel ambition and fear, the more they are pushed to stick to their "community" as the most convenient and readily affordable framework for gain and protection.

Apparently paradoxical and contradictory behaviour designed to face the overwhelming feeling of precariousness can be noticed: clinging to real estate, fleeing towards dollar-denominated deposits, striving to obtain a foreign citizenship; all are individual strategies aimed at securing the future to the best knowledge of the actor concerned. Patterns of behaviour and opinion polls show that the banking sector, including the Central Bank, which is dissociated from the state, is seen as a haven of security and regarded as sacred; bankers have understood the advantages of this perception and are keen to feed it.

Emigration is the most decisive factor. Reasons for emigration are economic and political and are interrelated. Job opportunities and differences in income and the cost of living are obvious causes. Anxiety about the future is also a major driver: escaping the debt burden through repayment by an increase in taxes or through a crisis and gaining a citizenship that provides protection against the political hazards that stem from the unstable communitarian system are inseparable factors.

Beside the claims for greater shares or more power in the distribution process, there are *worries* that can relate to much more serious matters but that must remain silent. The virtue of the system is precisely in encircling those worries and keeping them "private" or too costly to express. As long as questioning the system is considered to lead possibly to chaos, the failure of the system to provide tranquillity becomes the major source of its stability.

This resilience shows clearly in moments of great tension. Fears focus on exchange rate risk, as happened in 1998 when Lahoud was elected President and Hariri left office as Prime Minister, and again in 2005 after the assassination of Hariri. It shows also in the face of external shocks such as wars (that of summer 2006 is a good example) and natural disasters. This vulnerability is accentuated by the extreme dependence of the system on inflows of capital and labour. It should be noted that capital inflows are of three different types: family remittances, being the most stable and even showing countercyclical features; financial capital inflows, being the most volatile and showing pro-cyclical features; and political inflows, whether civilian or militarized, being an instrument of control. It is interesting to note that, during the recent political crisis, all parties agreed to a "political ceasefire" during the Christmas and New Year holidays in order not to disrupt the usual inflow of expatriates and tourists. This recalls the *modus operandi* that prevailed during most of the civil war period, when fighting used to begin in the mid-afternoon and stop at dawn to allow people to go to work or to school.

Apart from cases of irreversibility and the occurrence of shocks, the system has a particularity that causes one more type of worry: its financial cumulative nature. The fatality of cyclical crises reduces the ever-increasing gap between financial claims and economic counterparts, and the system thereby regenerates itself. Such corrective crises can be postponed for a long time if the system is managed well and if external conditions are favourable, i.e. principally if there is an abundance of funds on regional capital markets that are likely to be channelled to Lebanon. However, regeneration of the model is subject to limits: it has to have lasted for long enough, it has to be able to produce credible scapegoats, it has to leave little room for breaches, and so on.

Stakeholders, advocacy and political relays
Instability and communitarianism are commonly put forward as obvious and permanent characteristics of the Lebanese political scene. This "fact" is usually linked either to external interference or to internal cultural specificities, or to both. There have been few attempts to address the subject from a simpler, more "functional" point of view.

Visible and significant wealth appears to be available to the Lebanese, but it does not seem to come from work and saving or from building and managing institutions, but by chance, some say as "an honour vested by God". This way of looking at things has increased during the last two or three decades. Any idea of "exploitation" is therefore out of the picture, or at least fading away, but so is any idea of rewarding investment or accumulation over time. Those who were not yet chosen remain, of course, the overwhelming majority. They can simply not acknowledge the fact, but this does not help them avoid the effects of the recurrence of capital inflows on their economic activity and on their absolute and relative social status. This is the effect of the small size of the economy and of society as compared to the volume of the inflows and to the number of rich. They can accept the fact and try to adapt by changing their activities, their allegiances and, progressively, their convictions; this is what many did or tried to do once they understood that the changes were lasting and not just accidental; some succeeded but many could not find the opportunities they looked for. This is due to the size of the economy and of society as compared to the number and quality of the jobs and positions that a "Monte Carlo" or "Dubai" model can offer.

The simultaneous rise of passive discontent and of active disappointment opens the way to a third rational attitude: being strong enough to force those who won the jackpot and want to use it in Lebanon to share it. This means the constitution of political pressure groups that are coherent and organized for that specific purpose, implying the presence of mutually loyal leaders and followers. The suitability of a community to fulfil this function is probably not sufficient to create communities from scratch in a society that does not have any historical or sociological experience of politicized communities, but it is sufficient to make communities adapt to this role and prosper in the course of its performance. Such communitarian mobilization satisfies both the discontent of the "deprived" and the ambitions of the "unsatisfied" and creates a permanent link between them.

This does not turn the game into some kind of caricature ransoming; it rather leads to a joint management of complex political and economic equilibria. These equilibria, to be stable, reliable and mutually binding for both parties, have to translate on both the "supply" and the "demand" sides, and have to take institutional forms.

This is a good reason why, on the "demand" side, political representation and advocacy is communitarian-territorial. Electoral constituencies are based on the 1932 census and polling stations are segregated along sex and sects. Each station groups the whole of a family; people therefore vote mostly in the villages where their grandparents used to live, the principal remaining and active link between them and those villages being clannish ties that are revived by the political process and that allow politicians to exert a high level of control over the support they get from a given family group. This means that, in a country more than 75 per cent of which is urbanized, the majority of the population resident in the large agglomerations do not participate in the election of those who influence their daily life, while in rural zones permanent residents are subject to a choice of representatives imposed by non-residents who outnumber the residents. Bearing in mind that rural areas used to be populated by a single community and that most mixed areas were the theatre of communitarian strife that ended with the clear domination of the victorious community, it is no surprise that the greater part of redistributive claims appear to be territorial and that "balanced development between regions" has been adopted as a constitutional principle, giving a respectable face to communitarianism.

The demand side alone cannot achieve a stable equilibrium on account of the dissymmetric nature of the redistribution. Hence an equivalent set-up needed to be achieved on the "supply" side. This set-up is achieved by the permanent allocation of key institutions to communitarian parties, forcing the partners to engage in permanent negotiation. This political-communitarian allocation of general public functions goes far beyond the quota principle in the public administration: quotas regulate the overall distribution of public offices in each category among communities, while allocation permanently links a given function to a given community, from the top positions down through most of the hierarchy, with a particular reliance on contractual "experts" and "advisers" who overshadow normal civil servants. In this sense, finance and reconstruction were allocated to the Sunni Hariri group, social affairs and social security to the Shiite *Amal* group, and so on. This allocation extends to private companies under the influence of the state (Middle East Airlines for the Sunnis, Intra Holding Company for the Shia, the *Casino du Liban* for the Maronites, and so on), and is in addition to the allocation of the specific redistributive agencies already mentioned (the Council for the South, the Displaced Fund, etc.) and to that of the major institutions of the state (the presidency of the parliament for the Shiite *Amal* leader, the presidency of the government for the Sunni Rafiq Hariri, the presidency of the Republic, with reduced powers and political influence, and the post of Commander-in-Chief of the army remaining in the hands of the Maronites). This set-up is at the root of the present political deadlock in the country. It forces a permanent "Coasian" bargaining that leaves little room for the public formulation of policies and alternatives, the electoral process no longer being concerned with testing the popularity of policy options, but with asserting and weighting the cohesion and strength of communitarian political parties.

Viewed from the perspective of the "elites", this set-up leads to a clear distinction between several categories of players. The first category, in order of importance, is that of the "communitarian emblems", which have three main names: Hariri, Berri and Joumblatt. With Aoun being exiled and Geagea imprisoned, the Maronites have two substitutes, the Patriarch and the President of the Republic. The second category is that of the "professionals" who are in charge of the regulation of the whole system and who therefore hold decisive powers, but who have to stay away from the political scene: the governor of the Central Bank, the commanders of the key Security Corps and, of course, until recently, the Syrian security officer in charge of the "Lebanese file". The third and largest category is that of the "lieutenants" of the communitarian emblems, who constitute the bulk of the political and high administrative personnel; they are not allowed to have any autonomous political status (cases of treachery have been very rare and immediately sanctioned).

The fourth category is that of the "small barons", who come mainly from the remaining old political families which still hold some local influence and representative legitimacy, and who managed to find some arrangement either with the "communitarian emblems" or with the "professionals" to hold seats and to keep some limited margin of manoeuvre on the political scene but without any influence over decision-making; this category includes some businessmen who "bought" seats from the leaders, and some representatives of old political parties that have been instrumentalized by the system. The configuration not being symmetric, the Maronites and the Greek Orthodox are over-represented in the last category to "compensate" for their exclusion from the first.

This configuration should not be seen as locked. It is a fact that some political forces have been consistently excluded and repressed: Aoun, Geagea, Islamists, pro-Arafat nationalists, Iraqi Baathists, etc., while some other parties and organizations have been fought, besieged and dismantled; this applies mainly to leftist and anti-sectarian groups and to trade unions. But the configuration has given many opportunities to "elite" candidates and newcomers to enter the game, mainly as "lieutenants", most of whom would have had little chance of gaining equivalent prestige and wealth in the market. There is also room for survivors of excluded political forces to repent and reach agreeable arrangements with the system, sweetened by the appropriate mix of political justification through arguments of wisdom, pragmatism and efficiency and of personal advantage; the most prominent examples in this category are the late Elie Hobeiqa and the leaders of the Islamic *Tawhid* movement (Shaaban, Minqara, and so on).

In spite of its dominance, this dynamic does not embrace all public life nor cover the whole socio-political scene. Old-style unionist or categorical conflicts continue, but for smaller and smaller stakes and with poorer and poorer advocates. Social riots occur and can be repressed and turn tragic, as in the case of the riot of taxi drivers over the price of gasoline in March 2004.

New types of claim and conflict, linked to the environment or to specific social categories such as the handicapped, come to the surface and gain audience mainly among the young. But the old and new types of conflict become marginalized or are instrumentalized by the protagonists of the dominating dynamic, the most striking example being that of the unions.

Workers' unions used to be powerful in Lebanon and played a significant role before and during the war.[6] They have been deeply weakened by the operation of two factors: a socio-economic factor, namely that industry has been on the decline since the end of the war and has employed an increasing number of immigrants while, more generally, the size of businesses has decreased; and a political factor, namely that the system has deliberately fragmented the unions and imposed substitute or parallel sectarian unions structures fully devoted to their patrons, while in addition the Ministry of Labour was firmly held during the whole period by some of the closest politicians to the Syrians. Union strongholds have become isolated and are concentrated among teachers in the public and private sectors, the large public utilities, and the banks. On the other hand, professional unions (journalists, engineers, lawyers, doctors, etc.) remain active and enjoy an enviable status mainly on account of their financial autonomy, the privileges they have obtained from the state and their external exposure. They respect precise rules concerning sectarian quotas within their institutions and defend with efficiency their corporation's interests, and they also provide cover for certain democratic activities and an interesting laboratory for political alliances, and in fact the prevailing political alliances of today – such as those between *Hezbollah*, the Free Patriotic Movement and the Left on the one hand, and Hariri, the Lebanese Forces, Joumblatt and *Amal* on the other – were prefigured at the level of the professional unions several years ago. Chambers of commerce and employers' associations are active but generally weak, with the exception of the Bankers' Association, which exerts considerable influence and enjoys exceptional prestige that is easily understandable in the context of the prevailing economic system: the Association is formally (and informally) consulted by the Central Bank, the Ministry of Finance and parliamentary committees on all sensitive economic or fiscal issues, and has an influential say in the nomination of key officials, including the Governor of the Central Bank and his deputies.

2.2 Fields and means of adjustment: desired and undesired effects
Public services: between norm and subsidiarity
According to the latest survey by the Central Administration of Statistics carried out in 2004/2005, 57 per cent of resident households have their

own private supply of electricity and 24 per cent have their own private supply of water.[7] Private institutions are predominant in education, accounting for 62 per cent of total enrolment. The role of public hospitals is incidental and in practice restricted to certain rural areas.

Total "social" expenditure (including health, education, social security and unfunded public sector pensions) is high in Lebanon both in nominal terms and as a percentage of GDP, standing on average at 24 per cent over the period 2000–2004.[8] Two-thirds is covered directly by the private sector, while the one-third covered by the public sector is much lower in value than in comparable countries but still constitutes about half of primary expenditure at the equivalent of USD 2.2 billion.

In practical terms, public services in Lebanon cannot be seen as representing a decision to provide the whole community of nationals and/or residents with a defined set of services according to defined standards through taxes. They act as a complement to the private provision of the services concerned and are only targeted at those households which cannot afford the private services. To be stable, such a dual system supposes either a severe and persistent shortage or rationing in the provision of public services (which is not the case), or a considerable and persistent difference in quality, whether real or perceived, between the private service, that is costly and desirable, and the free public service. It is worth noting that this difference in quality fits quite well with the over-staffing, under constant budgetary constraints, of public services with under-qualified personnel for clientelistic purposes. The redistributive role of hiring and the subsidiary status of public services reinforce and justify each other.

The state's subsidiary role has deep effects on its institutional status. The "production" of public services is different from their mere "redistribution", whether it takes the form of free access to those services or that of partial or total reimbursement of their costs. Redistribution occurs through the delivery of services and should not come about through an alteration of their conditions of production implying an increase in their costs or a decrease in their quality. Mixing redistribution with production is harmful to both, as well as to the legitimacy and authority of the state, which appears at best incidental and often useless or even detrimental to the well-being of its citizens.

Public administration: a channel for providing services or a field for redistribution?

The deterioration in the quality of public services leads to their being restricted to those who cannot afford to dispense with them. Public administration and public services tend to be perceived as a useless and heavy burden by everybody else. Even those who have no alternative resign themselves but share the negative assessment of the wealthier.

For this reason, calls for the reduction of the competences and responsibilities of the state abound in every domain. Despairing of having a "better" state, citizens ask for "less" state. Such calls can be justified in many specific fields but their generalization is excessive because it affects the basic sovereign functions of the state and paves the way for uncontrollable formulae for social and political segmentation that can be extremely dangerous.

An intermediate solution that is gaining more and more ground consists in keeping public services as they are, with their weaknesses, but building parallel systems that are more costly and are supposed to provide a better quality of service. This dual action can take place through the creation of specific institutions that enjoy specific privileges (for example the Council for Development and Reconstruction, the Central Bank or the regulatory authorities), or through extensive recourse to "experts" who are paid from the budget through indirect "technical assistance" formulae, as is frequently the case with United Nations Development Programme (UNDP) projects. A more effective method is simply the transfer of competence to private entities under cover of "privatization" or "management contracts".

Wages in the public administration have been blocked since 1997. The wage increase voted for by parliament in 1998 to compensate previous price increases had to be paid "as soon as the financing is available",[9] which is rather meaningless given the peculiar nature of the budget and has not yet been applied, with the exception of the teaching sector, which forced a decision from the government in 2000. All previous wage corrections, mainly during the hyperinflationary period of the 1980s and the beginning of the 1990s, were capped and have led to a marked narrowing of the wage scale.[10] At low levels of qualification, public wages clearly stand above equivalent remuneration in the market, but the contrary is true for high levels of qualification, where the recruitment of qualified staff is more difficult.

Public investment: the lever for reconstruction and the trap of erroneous choices[11]

Unlike total social expenditure, that is very high, public investment in Lebanon is remarkably low as a percentage of GDP, especially for a country that has experienced a destructive war and several subsequent large-scale attacks.

Since 1997, investment expenditure has been on a downward trend. Since 2001 it has stood at a level of about 2.7 per cent of GDP, or 7.8 per cent of total public expenditure, or 14 per cent of primary expenditure. Net investment expenditure (accounting for depreciation) does not exceed 1.7 per cent of GDP. All these levels have fallen further since the Israeli attacks of 2006. The low quantitative levels of investment are aggravated by low global efficiency.

This set of dysfunctional data is not fortuitous, but results from the conjunction of several factors that appear independent but are usually connected to different, not to say mutually antagonistic, political factions, as follows:

- There is, on one hand, "political" pressure from communitarian and local leaders to use public investment as a means of clientelistic distribution. This pressure uses the argument of "balanced development", added to the preamble of the Constitution after Taif, to demand for the "region" (the "region" being a clear cover for the "community") the same equipment that can be found in any other region, and specifically in Beirut. Given that political representation is based on the 1932 census, rural areas therefore get a much higher share than their real population would warrant, while peri-urban areas are under-weighted and under-equipped. This leads to glaring cases of redundant and unjustified projects with consequences in terms of excessive costs and harmful environmental impacts.
- There are also, on the other hand, "financial" tricks used by technocrats and "pro-economic reform" parties, who are in search of real or fictitious fiscal performance. For this reason, public investment projects financed by external loans are kept outside the budget and external financing is presented as a windfall that should not be refused or called into question by parliamentarians, while local expenditure is cut wherever is easiest, without regard for

the technical or economic consequences of such cuts. This leads to investments that are not operational or that lack basic maintenance, and to delays of several years in the payment of indemnities for some expropriations and in the disbursement of the local counterparts of external loans, thus hindering the effective use of contracted loans and leading to the cancellation of some.

In practice, the two factors complement each other, and their conjunction is in keeping with the logic of the socio-economic system and the difficulties of its management. It leads to a situation where firstly, the process of planning is completely paralysed: not a single investment plan has been approved by the Lebanese government since 1991 (when a national Emergency Recovery Programme was discussed and adopted); secondly, the efficiency of public expenditure and the quality of public services is low; and thirdly, the selection of projects depends on the bargaining power of political lobbies both domestically, in relation to budgetary expenditure, and externally, in relation to external extra-budgetary funding, and specifically on the ability of local politicians to market to external lenders or correspondingly on the political interests of certain lenders or donors in local politics.

The fiscal system (taxes and expenditure)[12]
In broad terms, and taking 2004 as a reference (given that later years have witnessed exceptional turbulence), "revenues" (taxes, both central and local, non-tax public revenues and mandatory social security contributions) represent about 30 per cent of GDP, as compared to about 18 per cent in 1997.[13] Total expenditure (including social security provision and the Central Bank share of interest payments) is about 42 per cent of GDP. The Lebanese public debt is the highest in the world, standing at 200 per cent of GDP.

On the revenue side, the tax system is socially regressive in that it is essentially based on consumption, raising revenue through value added tax (VAT), customs duties and telecom taxation. It is also detrimental to economic activity on account of its effects on rising domestic prices, while any correction on the exchange rate market is blocked due to dollarization and the peg to the US dollar. This aggravates price distortions and the loss of competitiveness.

The limited share of income tax is imposed almost entirely on wages and the profits of formal companies; all other forms of domestic income are only marginally subject to tax (interest, real estate appreciation, capital gains, profits of family businesses, etc.). Income arising abroad is fully exempt. This happens at a time when disposable income significantly exceeds GDP, the share of wages of GDP and the proportion of wage earners in the population of working age are remarkably low, and formal companies, outside the banking sector, are becoming rarer while most businesses are family businesses, over-indebted and under-capitalized.

On the expenditure side, Lebanon devotes very sizeable resources to redistribution. About 29 per cent of GDP or 70 per cent of total public expenditure is redistributed (45 per cent of redistribution takes the form of interest payments on public debt or Central Bank deposits, the latter of which are paid to the local holders of claims; 20 per cent goes on the various social transfers and services and categorical economic subsidies; and 5 per cent on clientelistic hiring, over-expenditure and so on). This high level of redistribution reflects the basic rule of the economic model based on the attraction of capital inflows and their domestic redistribution, and addresses the very high level of inequality that such a model spontaneously generates between different social categories and regions.

The redistributive effects are either inter-categorical, when financed by taxes, or inter-temporal, when financed by debt and according to the realization and maintenance or otherwise of investments. The redistributive impact of the fiscal system has not been formally studied along the two lines of income (levels and types) and age. It is likely, however, that the net result follows a U-shaped curve along both the revenue and the age axes. Intermediate income groups and young resident households with few children in the current and future generations are financing the lowest income groups and old or large households in the present generation, and are also financing, due to the extreme concentration of bank deposits, the wealthiest households in the present generation.

Official "safety nets"
The institutional system of social security is inadequate and suffers from major problems, as follows:

- Its coverage is limited both in terms of services (pensions are only available for public servants, while no protection at all exists in case of unemployment or work accidents) and in terms of categories (only civil servants, representing 6.2 per cent of the workforce, and permanent wage earners in the private sector, representing 20.4 per cent thereof, are entitled to benefits); on top of this, operational costs are high and the quality of the services is below the minimum standard.
- It is exposed to major financial risks. The state has not made contributions for several years, funds regularly show deficits and technical reserves are either inexistent or fall far below the level required. Existing funds are invested in public debt paper.

This situation of deficiency and high exposure to risk explains to a significant extent why relatively large monetary savings are common in Lebanon.

Here again, one sees an example of systematic arrangements between apparently opposed political groups. For the past 15 years, everybody has been complaining about the social security system and vehemently calling for its "urgent reform". The basis of the arrangement is simple: management of the system, exercised by the directors and the representatives of the unions and the government on the board, is allocated to the Shiite *Amal* group, whilst management of the public finances is allocated to the Sunni Hariri group. The first group has an interest in extending clientelistic services to its political base by means of recruitments, contracts with hospitals and doctors, extensions of coverage and so on, whilst the second group has an interest in lowering nominal public expenditure by not paying contributions and by financing debt using existing reserves. The arrangement is made easier by the fact that the National Social Security Fund comprises, side by side, a fund for "end of service indemnities", which is an accumulation fund, and a "health as family indemnities fund", which is purely redistributive. Deficits in the latter fund are covered by amounts present in the former, thus depleting the technical reserves of the former fund.

Privatization and monopolies[14]

In Lebanon as elsewhere, relations between public and private are focussed on by the media through the theme of privatization. Some present it as the miracle solution to every problem, while others see it as the conclusion of a long conspiracy. Neither attitude helps a great deal in making a rational assessment either of the general phenomenon or of specific cases.

The public sector is extremely limited in Lebanon and does not cover either basic utilities or social services. The few commercial enterprises that belong to the public sector do so by accident. Lebanon has followed a strictly orthodox liberal policy since its independence, dismantling protectionist measures put in place by the French. It did not participate in the wave of socialist nationalizations of the 1960s, and did not even have any recourse to Keynesian policies. No nationalization ever took place in Lebanon.

On the contrary, the private sector is widely involved in the provision of public services. Service contracts and concessions are widespread, health and education are mainly private and private capital has been extensively involved in reconstruction, the main two examples of this being Solidere and cell phones.

With the worsening of the public fiscal situation, BOT projects are becoming increasingly popular and are presented as a miracle solution for the realization of costly investments "for free". In the same vein, the privatization of existing investments was put at the top of the agenda of the so-called "economic reforms" presented to the conferences of Paris 2 in 2002 and Paris 3 in 2007.

What privatization in Lebanon really amounts to is two cell phone BOT projects terminated in 2001, two years in advance of the end of the contracts, giving the operators huge compensation for assets that they would have had to give up for nothing two years later. No privatization has taken place since then.

In practical terms, privatization has very little to do with improving economic efficiency or with broadening the capital base of corporations. There are many cases of natural or quasi-natural monopolies, partly because of the small size of the economy and partly because of several legal or practical dispositions; but this is only a small part of the story. The management of the system is fundamentally based on an interweaving of the public and private spheres. For example, most non-governmental organizations (NGOs) are financed from the public budget and are openly linked to political communitarian forces, and television licences have been granted by the Council of Ministers to all its prominent members. Such management is not easy and can produce both desired and undesired effects, so correction is necessary.

Two cases deserve to be studied because they have dominated the political scene and they illustrate the difficulties and the strength of the management of the "Lebanese system".[15]

Cell phones: under-estimation of profits leading to deadlock
In 1994, an international tender was launched to build and operate two GSM networks under a BOT scheme for a duration of ten years, extendable to twelve, with a revenue share for the state of 20 per cent climbing to 40 per cent in the last two years and 50 per cent in the case of extension beyond the tenth year. After submission of offers, negotiations led to the formation of two syndicates of tenderers, with whom the final deal was cut. Both groups included, openly or covertly, influential Lebanese and Syrian politicians.

The fixed network was still in very poor shape and demand took off. The tariff scale provided for an entry payment by each subscriber of USD 500; the amounts collected easily covered investment costs and the shareholders did not need to inject capital, even though the injection of private capital instead of scarce public capital is the basic justification for a BOT. During their entire lifetimes the two companies proposed absolutely identical products and applied the same tariffs. There was no possibility of, or reason for, moving from one operator to the other. There was no trace of competition whatsoever.

It was no surprise that the businesses proved prosperous. A tax on tariffs was introduced in 1997–9 when the fiscal situation began to deteriorate, but this did not curb demand. Such prosperity proved harmful by exciting appetites, notably those of the power groups who had not been associated in the initial deal. Pressure was exerted through the issue of two penalty warrants in 2000 that remained outstanding for several years until their invalidation in an international arbitration in 2004. Financial results were exaggerated by ignorance or on purpose through the amalgamation of taxes and earnings, and many politicians, being unable to enter the deal, tried to block the situation by setting the stakes too high: cell phones became "the oil of Lebanon" whose privatization would wipe off the public debt.

The government share should have passed from 20 per cent to 40 per cent in 2002 and the contracts should have terminated in 2004 with physical and immaterial assets being transferred to the state without any compensation. Nevertheless, the contracts were repudiated in August 2002, leading to the payment of about USD 500 million in compensation both immediately and as a result of the arbitration.

The Lebanese government presented the "privatization" of the mobile phone companies as its leading economic reform at the Paris 2 conference and again at Paris 3, four years later. A confused formal privatization process was launched with no results, as expected, because no operator was interested in paying, on top of the licence for the phone business, the price of the right to collect taxes.

The vital spurt of the system: September 11, Iraq and Paris 2
The second example illustrates adjustment not of erroneous financial expectations but of erroneous economic choices.

The successive Hariri cabinets from 1992 onwards decided to lower taxes and to adopt an expansionary fiscal policy that allowed wide redistribution at the cost of rapidly increasing public debt, although such policies are highly unusual in phases of reconstruction. In 1997, debt was accumulating dangerously, Central Bank reserves were depleting and economic activity was becoming sluggish. The deviation from expectations was becoming too large to ignore, and the critics (mainly from international institutions, local criticism having been suppressed as anti-reconstruction) could no longer be dismissed. Some timid corrective measures were adopted in 1998 in the form principally of a slight tightening of expenditure (at a significant political cost) and an accumulation of arrears. Massive manipulation in the budget figures for 1997 and 1998 showed an apparent improvement.

In 1998, with support from Syria but also with wide local support largely due to the failure of current socio-economic policies, Emile Lahoud was elected president, and Salim Hoss appointed prime minister. The government announced its will to carry out deep fiscal and economic reforms, and a comprehensive programme was drafted. Income tax was readjusted and VAT introduced, but the main dogmas of the Hariri period (pegging the currency, borrowing in foreign currency from the banking sector to reconstitute reserves at the Central Bank, etc.) were retained, and the Governor of the Central Bank was reappointed.

The opposition presented these timid and reasonable actions as an unjustified and deliberate austerity policy, their only result being to seize up the economy; they claimed that public debt was not a problem, and adopted a programme based on new tax cuts. The elections in 2000 brought them a sweeping victory and Hariri returned to office. In the first months he swiftly took some expansionary measures (repealing the VAT law, lowering social security contributions, reducing tariffs, etc.), but as early as January 2001, James Wolfenson, then president of the World Bank, told Hariri during a private visit that the "boat was sinking". A creeping financial crisis developed over more than a year. The government completely reversed its policy and went along with the ideas of the previous government that it had fiercely opposed, reintroducing the VAT law, which it presented as a major achievement. But this was far from enough to curb the crisis.[16]

The attacks of 11 September 2001 created a fear of future developments in the region. The whole political class felt an increased need for cohesion. In a historic meeting in October, attended by the main political leaders, the governor of the Central Bank and the Chief of General Security, a package of decisions was agreed upon: an anti-laundering law would be passed to meet American pressure, a mandatory reserve of 15 per cent of banks' foreign currency deposits would be constituted with the Central Bank, and a 5 per cent tax on interest income would be included in 2002 budget.

This major turnaround in fiscal policy was exceptional and paved the way internally for an additional important step towards rescuing the system, namely the Paris 2 conference, which was held in November 2002 under the auspices of French president Jacques Chirac at the time of the preparation of the American attack on Iraq which itself pushed regional fears a step further. USD 2.6 billion was lent to Lebanon, with no conditionality and at concessional rates. The internal political conflicts had been silenced and Lahoud and Hariri had been reconciled and had "washed their hearts". A few months later, there was a change of government.

It appears from this episode that, taken as a whole, the system feels internal problems and external threats and reacts to them. Internal threats and opportunities are spotted at an early stage and managed within the political scene, with varying degrees of success, on a very "Coasian" basis of allocation and bargaining and with extensive reliance on public financing. A failure to anticipate can have adverse consequence. It appears also, on the other hand, that systemic threats are more difficult for politicians and public opinion to spot. Reactions do occur, but they are beyond the range of the political factions, which have little choice but to keep a low profile while the "professional operators" take over. No surprise therefore that, in general terms, the programmatic content of political discourse is of little significance: a government which failed completely and which had to reverse its position remained in office, while a government that successfully carried out an "exceptional rescue" was removed from office. Politicians and political discourse fit "within" the system and do not pretend to control or even change it.

NOTES

1. Real growth over the period 1993–2006 stands below 2.5 per cent in spite of the natural postwar recovery effect (cf. Berthélemy *et al.* 2007).
2. In mid-2007, about 800 banks accounts, belonging to no more than 200 families, cover about 20 per cent of the total deposits, i.e. USD 14 billion.
3. By mid-2007, the domestic assets of the banking sector amount to USD 65 billion and bear an average interest close to 10 per cent, leading to an annual interest bill that represents 30 per cent of the GDP.
4. Women's participation in the resident active population stands at 22 per cent (2004 and 1996). Considering the presence of large numbers of foreign female domestic workers, the participation of Lebanese female workers does not exceed 20 per cent compared to 18 per cent in 1970 (Administration Centrale de la Statistique 1998).
5. Kasparian 2003.
6. [Eds' note:] For an analysis of the workers' movement in Egypt see Beinin's chapter in this book.
7. Central Administration of Statistics 2006.
8. World Bank 2005.
9. Law 717/98, dated 5/11/1998.
10. The nominal minimum wage has been fixed at USD 200 since 1996. In real terms, it decreased by 24 per cent between 1996 and 2006. Compared to 1983, in the middle of the civil war, the minimum wage in 2006 stood at 30 per cent of its real historical value and less if compared to the prewar period.
11. For data on public investment, cf. Council for Development and Reconstruction 2006.

12 For a detailed presentation of the fiscal situation in Lebanon, cf. Nahas 2003.
13 Ministry of Finance n.d.
14 [Eds' note:] Cf. privatization policies in Egypt and Morocco in Wurzel and Catusse's chapters in this book.
15 The case of Solidere provides another example of the management of the Lebanese system by politicians.
16 For a detailed account of this period and to access the text of the *Financial Correction Program*, cf. Nahas 2003.

7
GLOBALIZATION AND THE SAUDI ECONOMY: GAINS AND LOSSES

Tim Niblock

Introduction

The focus of this chapter is on how economic globalization will affect the course of development in Saudi Arabia, both socially and economically. A central concern is whether an economic framework which will enable Saudi Arabia to exploit its comparative advantage in some specific fields of industry will lead on to a wider process of industrialization and modernization. It is usually assumed that such a process of development is likely. International trading patterns which enable countries to exploit their comparative advantage, therefore, are seen as positive for the development of the countries concerned. This, indeed, has been the experience of the newly industrialized developmental states of the Far East and South-East Asia.

Inherent to the success of an industrial development strategy that gives emphasis to exploiting a specific comparative advantage are the knock-on effects which follow from the initial developmental effort. The effective development of some core areas of industrial and/or service activity leads on to a broader industrialization. Industries and services emerge that feed off the success of those in the core areas. The skills and training needed in the core areas encourage the development of programmes of industrial and service training, and these benefit the development of the economy more generally. New areas of comparative advantage emerge as the industrial base expands. Agriculture becomes more efficient and mechanized, with significant numbers of people moving to the cities. Important social benefits ensue for substantial parts of the population: more employment, better educational and training opportunities, and a higher standard of living. There may at the same time, of course, be some social and political tensions that accompany this process of change and development, but in most cases the spread of social well-being has ultimately enhanced social stability and strengthened the foundations for a settled and representative polity.

This chapter will contend that, with regard to the process outlined above, Saudi Arabia presents a more complex picture (as it does in so many other ways). The international trading frameworks that underpin economic globalization, together with the country's resource base, provide Saudi Arabia with a major industrial opportunity. To an extent that has not yet been fully recognized in the outside world, Saudi Arabia has the potential to emerge as a significant industrial power. It is poised to gain a substantial share in a critical sector of global industry. The Saudi government is currently implementing a coherent economic strategy well geared to achieving this objective. Yet the knock-on effects that normally follow in the wake of such a development strategy will not necessarily arise in the Saudi case. The social outcome that the country most needs – a population gainfully employed in economic activity that benefits the country's development – may not be attained. Failure to achieve the desired social outcome is likely to have far-reaching social and political effects, with an outcome that may be politically destabilizing.

The problems that are likely to inhibit the wider industrial development of Saudi Arabia, it will be suggested, stem more from structural difficulties than from policy failure. They have their origin in the oil-induced structure of social and economic development that the country has undergone over the past four decades, and especially in the impact this has had on the cost, quality and expectations of Saudi labour. One outcome of this oil-induced structure is that Saudi labour is unlikely in the short term to be globally competitive. Industries that do not have an established and clear resource-based comparative advantage, therefore, will have difficulty in gaining a place in global markets on the basis of Saudi labour. They can solve this problem by employing foreign labour, to the extent they are permitted to do this, but this will not satisfy the social needs of the Saudi population.

The field of economic activity in which Saudi Arabia can gain a substantial share of global industrial markets is that of petrochemicals and downstream production based on petrochemicals.

"Petrochemicals" are defined here as chemical products made from raw materials of hydrocarbon origin. The downstream processing of petrochemicals leads on to the production of plastics, resins, fibres, solvents, pharmaceuticals and detergents. Global trade in petrochemicals is currently valued at some USD 300 billion annually. Given the importance of this industrial sector, supplying so many of the basic consumer needs of society, Saudi Arabia's capture of a major share in the global petrochemicals market would clearly give the country some significance in world industry – certainly greater than that which any other Arab country currently possesses.

The major part of this chapter will be taken up with a consideration of the effects that follow from Saudi Arabia's accession to the World Trade Organization (WTO). Although there are many other ways in which the process of economic globalization impinges on Saudi Arabia, the accession agreement is of overriding importance. It provides a prism through which the factors surrounding Saudi Arabia's links with, and absorption into, the global economy can be viewed and analysed in depth. The factors that shaped the ultimate agreement, the way in which it affects different sectors, and the dynamics which will determine how it is implemented, all need to be given detailed attention.

1. Saudi Arabia's WTO Accession: The Dynamics and the Significance

Before looking at the terms and conditions under which Saudi Arabia acceded to the WTO, it is worth giving some attention to the national and international dynamics surrounding the accession.

Saudi Arabia's admission to the WTO involved a longer process of negotiation than that for any other country. In fact, its application for membership predated the formal establishment of the WTO itself, being submitted to the General Agreement on Tariffs and Trade (GATT) in June 1993, one year before the WTO came into institutional existence. Negotiations between Saudi and WTO negotiators in the Working Party on Saudi Arabia's Accession began in May 1996 and continued in a desultory fashion through the late 1990s and into the decade that followed. Agreement of the terms on which Saudi Arabia could be admitted was not reached until November 2005, with the country becoming the 149th member of the WTO on 11 December 2005. At the time of accession the Saudi economy was the second largest in the world outside of the WTO, exceeded only by the Russian economy. Many of the key elements in the eventual agreement on accession did not fall into place until the middle of 2005.

The reasons for the lengthy period of negotiations are important. They reveal some important factors affecting the modalities of Saudi Arabia's integration into the global economy. First, the initial Saudi approach to the WTO was not pursued with much determination or urgency on the Saudi side. There seemed to be good reason for this. Saudi Arabia's economy relied primarily on the export of hydrocarbons, and it was clear from the outset that this sector would not be affected greatly by WTO membership, whether positively or negatively. Although trade in oil and gas were not formally excluded from the trade rules of GATT and the WTO, a combination of factors has, *de facto*, brought the virtual exclusion of petroleum products from the rules of the trading system. The most important ones in this respect include the absence of petroleum export interests from GATT's origins, the consequent lack of specific trade/import liberalization commitments by GATT/WTO members, and the system's inherent market access bias.[1]

In practice such tariffs as exist on imports of oil are low, such that their abolition would make relatively little difference. The main duties affecting the oil trade are the domestic duties and taxes that oil-consuming countries levy on refined petroleum products. Many governments in the developed world, especially those of the European Union (EU), depend heavily on this source of revenue to maintain their fiscal balance. WTO rules, however, do not cover domestic taxation systems, provided they apply equally to nationals and non-nationals. The Saudi government knew from the outset, therefore, that its main exporting activity would draw no significant benefit from WTO accession. For the government, therefore, the immediate disadvantages of accession were perhaps more apparent than the advantages. The social and economic disruption that might follow from the opening up of Saudi markets could easily be envisaged, whereas the economic gain seemed remote.

The Saudi government's understanding of the treatment that Saudi oil exports would receive after accession remained unchanged throughout the negotiations, and the terms of accession duly reflected this understanding. This raises the question of what other factors and motivations were at work, affecting both the Saudi government's determination to press ahead, and the enthusiasm of existing WTO members to accept

Saudi Arabia into membership. In practice there were both domestic and international factors shaping Saudi policy.

Domestically, many of the economic reform measures that the Saudi government needed to take in order to comply with WTO regulations were ones that reform-minded members of the government believed were desirable and necessary in their own right. The measures were in effect taken forward by a coalition of interests that straddled government and business. The King, whose "door [. . .] was seen as being open to the private sector", was himself explicitly favourable to reform.[2] Supporting this line there was a grouping of ministers led by the Minister of Commerce and Industry (Dr Hashim Abdullah Yamani), who was responsible for the WTO negotiations. The ministerial grouping included some of the most prominent commoners in government, such as the Minister of Economy and Planning (Dr Khaled al-Qusaibi), the Minister of Information and Culture (Dr Iyad Medani), the Minister of Labour (Dr Ghazi al-Qusaibi), the Minister of Finance (Dr Ibrahim al-Assaf) and Minister of State Abdullah Zainal. Also important were the leading figures of major state corporations, such as the Saudi Arabian General Investment Agency, the Saudi Arabian Mining Company (MAADEN), the Saudi Arabian American Oil Company (ARAMCO), and the Saudi Arabian Basic Industries Corporation (SABIC). In business, it was the larger corporate groupings, especially those with interests in the petrochemicals sector, which were actively supportive. Among those known to have pressed the reform case were the al-Faisalia Group, the Binzagr Group, Kingdom Holdings, the Xenel Group, and the Zamil Group.[3] The need to cohere with WTO regulations and practices became in practice an instrument used by business and government elements to promote their own agenda for change. The necessity for reform could be argued not in terms of its intrinsic merit but of what would satisfy the WTO.

Without this combination of support for the reform case, the desired reforms may not have been enacted, given that they were challenged by some important social and religious groupings in the country, allied to specific factions in the government. The more conservative parts of both the society and the polity disparaged the idea that opening the Saudi economy to global forces was either desirable or in the interest of the population. Within the government, this attitude appears to have been strongest in the ministries dealing with internal security and religious affairs: the Ministry of the Interior, the Ministry of Justice and the Ministry of Islamic Affairs, Endowment, *Da'wa* and Guidance. Opposition also came from some of the smaller business organizations.[4] The case against the WTO reform package was in fact a rational one, from the point of view of the interests and groupings concerned. The package would indeed constitute a bridge across which wider forces of social and cultural globalization could enter the country. The Kingdom's ability to maintain its established cultural mores would be affected, as perhaps also would the political balance which underpinned the ruling establishment. It will be shown later in this chapter, moreover, that much of the small business sector was not capable of meeting global competition and would not survive the opening up of markets.

After 11 September 2001, there came to be an important international factor causing the Saudi government to treat the issue of WTO accession more urgently than before. The country needed to escape from the ostracism in, and isolation from, the Western world (in particular the US) that had followed from 11 September. Given that many of the political reforms which the Western world was pressing on Saudi Arabia were unacceptable to the Saudi government, economic reform provided an easier option in regaining international acceptance. WTO membership would be a symbol both of the country's integration into the accepted framework of international contacts, and a means of showing material policy change.

The international factor became most apparent in the role played by the United States in the negotiations. Accession required Saudi Arabia to reach bilateral agreements with its main trading partners, and it was the bilateral agreement with the US that proved most problematic. Through most of 2003 and 2004 the US was demanding far-reaching changes in the Saudi economy as a prerequisite for the necessary bilateral agreement. This formed part of the US's wider campaign to press political, educational, social and economic change on a country whose lack of democracy and openness were deemed to have fed into the extremism of the 11 September hijackers. It was only after US–Saudi relations had recovered from the shock of 11 September that the remaining issues in the bilateral agreement were resolved. The key event in moving the relationship, and the agreement, forward was the visit of (then) Crown Prince Abdullah to President Bush's Crawford ranch in April 2005. The joint communiqué which followed the visit gave an assurance that "we welcome the renewed determination of Saudi Arabia to pursue economic reform and its quest to join the WTO". There was a specific commitment to work towards "welcoming Saudi Arabia into the WTO before the end of 2005".[5]

A second reason for the length of the negotiations was the substantial impact which Saudi accession could have on established interests, both within Saudi Arabia and in existing WTO member-states. The character and strength of the impact would depend, of course, on the terms of accession. A significant number of developed countries had large petrochemicals industries of their own, and there was widespread recognition that these would be at risk if Saudi petrochemicals were allowed into their markets with no quantitative restrictions and at a low tariff rate. The case put by these countries was that admitting Saudi petrochemicals on this basis would constitute unfair competition. The Saudi petrochemicals industry benefited both from cheap (subsidized) energy and also from cheap (subsidized) feedstock. There was also a suggestion in some quarters that the employment of cheap migrant labour in the Saudi industry added to the unfair element of the equation. There were predictions that Saudi access to Western markets for the sale of petrochemicals would have catastrophic effects for employment and industrial well-being in the Western world.

The concern on the Saudi side was that the opening up of the Saudi market would lead to the destruction of large parts of the country's industrial, agricultural and services sectors. These were currently protected from competition by high tariffs on some goods and by a range of measures that supported and subsidized their activities. They were, it was said, not strong enough to face competition from outside companies. Many enterprises would cease to exist, leading to higher unemployment and a spread of social instability. Incoming companies, moreover, would bring with them values and practices that were out of keeping with those of Saudi society.

In the negotiations on Saudi accession, not surprisingly, the leading members of the WTO and Saudi Arabia pursued mirror-image strategies. The leading members of the WTO sought to restrict the entry of Saudi petrochemicals into their markets, while ensuring that the Saudi economy was opened up to competition in all major respects. Saudi Arabia sought to ensure that its petrochemicals were given access to all markets, at relatively low tariffs, while limiting the opening up of its domestic market to competition. Most important of all was that the liberalization of its economic organization should not lead to social disruption.

As each side jockeyed to promote its own side of the equation, an extensive amount of documentation was generated. The Saudi government was required to answer 3,400 questions on its trade regime, leading it to produce some 7,000 pages of documentation.[6] Given that the Saudi economy was heavily bound up in restrictive legislation, subsidies and uneconomic practices, a large range of issues on which practices were at variance with WTO regulations needed to be raised. For the Saudi negotiators, cognizant of the importance of the subsidies for large parts of the population, this presented formidable problems. All 148 existing members of the WTO had to agree to Saudi Arabia's trade regime before it could be admitted, and this led to a total of 38 bilateral agreements being signed. The most significant of these were those with the two trading partners which accounted for the majority of the Kingdom's imports (the US for 25.6 per cent and the EU for 32.5 per cent in 2004).[7]

2. Saudi Arabia's Accession to the WTO: Terms and Conditions

The deal which was eventually struck was one in which both sides (those negotiating on behalf of the WTO and the Saudi government) made considerable concessions. The Saudi government agreed to a very substantial opening up of its own domestic markets, together with changes to its investment laws and regulatory framework. Foreign companies would now find it easier to operate in the country, under conditions which in most respects were the same as those affecting local firms. Later in this article it will be shown that the legal and regulatory changes were perhaps not quite as bold as they initially appeared. Some of the detail in the accession texts, and in the laws passed, suggest that the government has left itself with considerable room to shape and control the country's domestic market. For the moment, however, the emphasis will be placed on the main sweep of policy and the radical change which it seemed to (and to some extent did) represent.

It should, first, be noted that many of the changes which WTO accession helped bring to Saudi Arabia predated the actual accession agreement. In practice they should, nonetheless, be seen as part of the accession process. Agreement would not have been reached without them being in place first. As has been noted earlier, much of the new legislation which was passed was in keeping with the reform agenda of parts of the governmental and business elite. In 2001 the Saudi government introduced an important new Foreign Investment Law. This made it possible for companies registered in Saudi Arabia to be 100 per cent foreign-owned, except in certain specified sectors. It guaranteed that such companies would be treated on an equal basis with Saudi companies, and that for the first time they would be entitled to own land. Between 2001 and 2005 a series of other laws were passed, most of which were geared to facilitating and encouraging foreign investment: a Real Estate Law (a corollary to the Foreign Investment Law, enabling foreign nationals to own real estate for their private residence); a Corporate Tax Law (specifying in detail the procedures by which foreign companies' taxation was charged, and reducing the tax to 20 per cent in non-hydrocarbon fields of investment – as against the 45 which had been the level prior to 2000); a Capital Markets Law (regulating the capital markets and creating a formal stock exchange); a Copyright Law (protecting intellectual property rights in a wide range of fields where property rights were previously unprotected); a Patent Law (spreading the coverage of patents to a substantially wider range of products than before); and a Cooperative Insurance Law (regulating the sector and opening it up to competition).[8]

Much of this legislation did indeed provide foreign companies with a reasonable basis on which to enter the Saudi market. One area where it seemed that there might be some inequality as against local companies was in taxation, where Saudi companies did not have to pay corporation tax. They did, however, have to pay *zakat* at 2.5 per cent. The latter was a tax on the value of the company and not on its profits. The Saudi government argued in the course of the WTO negotiations that the burden of this tax was no lighter than that of the corporate tax which foreign companies were paying on their profits. Besides this, the main difference in the conditions facing foreign firms lay in the areas in which they were not allowed to invest. The "Negative List" which defined these areas initially defined 23 areas, but by 2005 these had been reduced to 18. Many of the barred sectors were in fields of activity which are barred by many other WTO members (such as defence and security). Nonetheless, some were more significant, such as those covering oil exploration and production, trade, and land and air transportation.[9]

Besides these major pieces of legislation, which attracted the major attention of external observers, there were also a large number of smaller changes in regulations and procedures. The Saudi American Bank (SAMBA) reported that Saudi Arabia had, in preparing for membership, enacted 42 new trade-related laws and created nine new regulatory bodies. Over the period of the negotiations, furthermore, there had been a steady reduction in the country's external tariffs. Whereas in the mid-1990s Saudi tariffs stood at 12 per cent for some three-quarters of imports, by 2003 they stood at 5 per cent for the same proportion of imports.[10]

The actual agreement took matters further. Customs duties were to be reduced over a five-year period on 870 industrial and agricultural commodities. These made up 12 per cent of the commodities listed on the Saudi tariff schedule. This may seem a small part of the total but they in fact mostly comprised the commodities that had retained a high tariff barrier – around the 20 per cent level rather than the 5 per cent that applied to most imports. The industries affected by this were those producing confectionery, plastics, paper, metal, steel pipes and lubricating oils. In some other cases tariffs were to be reduced to zero, as in telecommunications equipment, computers and computer accessories. The only significant items that could continue for the moment to maintain higher tariffs were those covering some key agricultural products, as the Saudi government argued that it had invested heavily in the development of that sector. With regard to the latter, there was nonetheless a commitment by the Saudi government to reduce its domestic support for agriculture (which had been declining in any case) by 13.3 per cent over a ten-year period.[11]

In the services sector Saudi Arabia agreed to open up[12] main fields of service activity, together with 155 subfields and four administrative or delivery structures. In practice this covered most of the major fields of service activity. These fields now became free for cross-border delivery and for receiving foreign investment. While not all restrictions were to be removed, there was nonetheless an extensive opening up of activity, especially in the banking, insurance, wholesale and retail trades, and franchising. One of the most crucial elements was the removal of the requirement that foreign companies should act through Saudi-owned agencies. They could now act as agents themselves as well as establish joint-venture partnerships with Saudi companies. As the private sector in Saudi Arabia had been built up around agencies for foreign companies, this measure constituted a major change to established practice, the social and economic effects of which were likely to be substantial.

Perhaps recognizing that it had already made many of the critical rule-changes prior to accession, the Saudi government agreed to implement all WTO rules from the date of accession, rather than for them to be put into effect in the course of a transitional phase. All of the regulations on intellectual property rights, foreign investment, transparency in trade issues, legal recourse for trade partners, and the elimination of technical barriers to trade, therefore, were applied from 11 December 2005. Changes in tariff levels, subsidies etc., however, were to come into effect over a four-year transitional period.

The changes that the Saudi government agreed to were far-reaching. The dynamics and character of the domestic Saudi economy would be significantly changed by the new regulatory frameworks and by the lower tariffs. Quite apart from intended changes to economic practice, however, there was the simple fact that regulations had now been made explicit, published in English as well as Arabic. The bodies responsible for implementing them could therefore be challenged if they were not operating according what was required in the written texts. This had not always been the case before. All future regulations would similarly have to be published both in English and Arabic.

The gains which Saudi Arabia drew from WTO accession were also significant, and indeed were greater than might have been expected at the outset of the negotiations. These gains related primarily to the country's petrochemicals exports. Full access to global markets was assured once the transitions to the conditions of membership had been completed in 2009. The government was not required to give a commitment to change the pricing of feedstock or energy for Saudi-based industry, given that Saudi and non-Saudi companies were to be treated on an equal basis. ARAMCO would, therefore, continue to supply natural gas and natural gas liquids to the petrochemicals industry at prices that were substantially less than global prices. This represented a substantial achievement for Saudi Arabia. The value of the arrangement was enhanced by other developments that had been occurring in the global petrochemical market. Under the Chemical Tariff Harmonization

Agreement, initially signed by a number of chemical-importing countries in 1995, tariffs on imports of chemicals coming from WTO member-states were to be reduced steadily. This was to take place over a period extending to 2010. Tariffs on chemicals, which had previously been high in many countries, were to be reduced to a maximum of 6.5 per cent. The objective of the International Council of Chemical Associations was to seek further reductions leading to the elimination of all chemical tariffs for WTO members. All of the 64 chemicals produced by the Saudi petrochemicals industry are covered by the Chemical Tariff Harmonization Agreement, such that the gains to Saudi Arabia from this process of global tariff reduction will be extensive.[12]

3. The Financial Resource Base

Before looking at the impact that WTO accession will have on Saudi Arabia's economy and society, it is important to take note of the substantial increase in the country's financial resources in recent years. How the Saudi government chooses, or is able, to use these is of course crucial to how the country's further integration into the global economy proceeds. Oil revenues for 2001 stood at Saudi Riyal (SR) 183.9 billion (USD1= SR3.75). In 2003 they reached SR 231.0 billion, rising further to SR 330.0 billion in 2004, SR 505 billion in 2005, and SR 604 billion in 2006, falling back slightly to approximately SR 560 billion in 2007 (the latter figure is a calculated estimate at this stage as the exact breakdown between oil and non-oil revenues has not been disclosed at the time of writing).[13] The 2008 Saudi budget estimates likely oil revenues for that year at approximately SR 390 billion.[14] This figure, however, is very unrealistic. It is based on an oil price of USD 45 per barrel, whereas at the time of writing the oil price is more than twice that. The likelihood is that oil revenues will exceed SR 600 billion for 2008. Over the next three years, moreover, there will be a substantial increase in Saudi Arabia's oil production capacity, from 10.8 million barrels a day in 2007 to 12.2 million in 2012.[15] Given that the rise in oil prices since 2003 stems as much from rising demand as it does from supply problems, the likelihood is that revenues will remain in excess of USD 500 billion annually for the remainder of the decade and probably into the one that follows.

Saudi government expenditure has risen significantly since 2003, but the increase has not been commensurate in any way with the rise in revenues. Two factors explain this. The first is that Saudi Arabia has been using the revenues to improve its international fiscal and financial position. Whereas the level of government debt stood at 115 per cent of GDP in 1999 (a total of SR 620 billion), this had declined to 28 per cent of GDP in 2006 (SR 366 billion). The projections for 2007 were that it would decline further to 18.9 per cent of GDP by the end of that year.[16] The debts had been accumulated during the late 1980s and through the 1990s, when the price of oil was relatively low. At the same time, the government has been substantially increasing its foreign assets. Between 2002 and 2007 the foreign assets held by the Saudi Arabian Monetary Agency more than quintupled, reaching some USD 233 billion in the first quarter of 2007.[17] In January 2008 it was announced that Saudi Arabia would be creating a sovereign wealth fund, which would initially be capitalized with some USD 6 billion.[18]

A second factor is that the Saudi government has deliberately avoided investing directly in the economy. Saudi government policy today reflects the economic philosophy of the international financial institutions and of global capitalism generally, namely that governments should leave economic production to the private sector. This is a very different approach to that which the Saudi government pursued in the 1970s. At the time of the first oil boom, government investment in industry and oil extraction was deemed critical to the country's development. Most of the major development projects announced since 2005 have been dependent on private investment. The bulk of the investment going into the six new economic cities, where most of the major new industrial developments will be located, is expected to come from private investment. In the case of the King Abdullah Economic City in Rabigh, the largest of the projects, the private sector is expected to provide the entire infrastructure of the city. The Saudi Arabian General Investment Authority is to play the role of regulator, facilitator and promoter, while the private sector acts as the capital provider, landowner and developer.[19] This Public Private Partnership, where the private sector would contribute some USD 27 billion, is on a scale that has not been attempted elsewhere in the world. Total investment in all the six cities is expected to come to about USD 86.6 billion.[20] The reliance on private capital, at a time when the government itself is awash with money, is given justification on the grounds that it is more likely to ensure success.

The government has not, however, devolved all responsibility for development to the private sector. As will be shown later in this chapter, the government retains an important (and perhaps enhanced) role in regulating the domestic market. Through the award of contracts it can determine how the gains from government spending affect society and economy, and a wide range of regulations can still be used to channel, restrict or shape decisions made in the private sector. The level of government expenditure on human resource development and social and physical infrastructure has been increasing steadily since 2003. Actual expenditure in 2007 came to SR 443 billion, as against SR 257 billion in 2003. The budget for the 2008 fiscal year, announced in December 2007, indicates that substantial new capital programmes will be initiated in education and manpower development (SR 39 billion), transport and communications (SR 14.6 billion), water, sewage and desalination (SR 13.3 billion), municipality services (SR 14 billion), and health and social affairs (SR 6.3 billion). The sums allocated to industrial and agricultural projects amounted to only SR 7.6 billion.[21]

While the Saudi government has ample resources with which to promote development, therefore, it will not do this by investing directly in economic production. The private sector is expected to take the lead in all industrial, agricultural and commercial undertakings, as well as in services. The percentage of the development budget devoted to economic resource development has steadily declined over the years and will continue to do so. The ability of the government to influence the domestic market, however, will remain substantial.

4. The Problem of Labour

In practice, the most critical factor that will affect the impact of WTO accession on Saudi Arabia's economy and society is that of labour. If the economy is to benefit from lower global tariff rates internationally and from the removal of other restrictions on trade, much will depend on the quality and cost of the labour available to employers. Labour that is more expensive, less proficient and less flexible than that which can be found in countries which produce similar goods, or supply similar services, will frustrate economic growth. Manufacturers and service-providers who supply the local market will find it difficult to compete with goods and services coming from abroad, and those who export will find their products priced out of global markets.

Saudi Arabia's labour market is, at least in the short term, ill-suited to a competitive environment. The task of identifying and describing the labour problem is not easy, given that the country's employment figures are in some disarray. This disarray may in fact be an outcome of the problem itself. There is a wide gap between what the government is seeking to achieve and what actually exists. Employment figures produced by the Ministry of Planning reflect the most optimistic assessment. They show an overall total of 8,281,000 in the labour force in 2004, where Saudis made up 42.7 per cent of the total.[22] The Ministry of Labour figures for the same year give an overall total of 6,754,904, of which only 20.5 per cent are Saudis.[23] No doubt part of the discrepancy can be explained by the two ministries defining "civilian employment" (the concern of both) in different ways, but as neither provide a clear definition of the term it is difficult to be certain of that. There may also be different practices in counting labourers who are employed in the absence of legal authorization. One indication of the greater accuracy of the Ministry of Labour figures is that these are the ones used by the Saudi Arabian Monetary Agency. There is a possibility, therefore, that Saudi labour makes up little more than 20 per cent of the country's civilian workforce.[24]

The significance of the imbalance between foreign and Saudi labour lies in the difference between the rates and conditions of pay for each. In all but high professional occupations, the rates of pay for Saudi labour stand at some two to three times that of foreign labour, based on the same levels of skills, qualifications and experience. Foreign labour, moreover, tends to be more flexible (in terms of where and how it is used), and more easy to dismiss if it is no longer needed. In short, foreign labour in Saudi Arabia tends to be competitive with that which is found elsewhere within the region, whereas Saudi labour is not.

What makes this problem more intractable in the case of Saudi Arabia, as against other Gulf States, is that Saudi Arabia has a fast-growing population with large numbers of young people who are (or will be) seeking employment. The rate of unemployment already appears to be relatively high. The unemployment estimates are as questionable as those on employment, but the statistics which are produced (together with the anecdotal evidence) suggests an upward trend. In 2002, when the government for the first time released data on unemployment, overall unemployment was put at 8.1 per cent. The figure was based on data that had been gathered in 1999.[25] Despite concerted attempts to boost Saudi employment, the statistics released by the Central Department of Statistics and the Ministry of Labour show a steady year-by-year increase in unemployment since then. In 2002 the figure stood at 9.7 per cent, in 2004 it had reached 10.9 per cent, and in 2006 12.02 per cent.[26] A 2007 figure prepared by the chief economist of the Riyad Bank (Zahid Khan), using data from official sources, put the rate of male unemployment at 9 per cent, and female unemployment at 22 per cent.[27] Khan was of the view, however, that these figures under-estimate the real numbers. Given the unclarity as to who is "available for work" (especially in the female part of the population), it is difficult to be sure. There is little doubt, however, that unemployment does constitute a problem in the Kingdom.

The impact of unemployment is intensified by the character of the age-groups most affected by unemployment. It is highest among those in their twenties. Almost 75 per cent of the Saudi population are under thirty, and some estimates have suggested that the rate of unemployment for the 18–30 age group is about 30 per cent.[28] The social effects that follow from high youth unemployment cannot be ignored. It has been the under-30s, and predominantly those who have failed to find satisfactory employment, who have fed the stream of Saudis travelling abroad to fight for radical Islamist causes. The impact of unemployment, moreover, is beginning to be felt more acutely as a result of rising prices. After years in which inflation posed no threat to living standards in the country, Saudi Arabia had an inflation rate of 4.4 per cent in 2007.[29] In reality, however, the impact of inflation on the poorer parts of the population is much more significant than this, especially in the cities. The largest increases in prices and costs are in those products and services which affect the poor most: food and rent. Rental prices increased by almost 7 per cent in 2007 and are expected to register an even higher increase in 2008.[30] Over the 2005–6 period many Saudis sought release from their economic problems by borrowing money and investing it on the *Tadawul* (the Saudi stock exchange), confident that the sharply rising market would leave them with a substantial profit. In the course of

2006–7, however, the stock market declined in value to about one-third of the level attained at the end of 2005. Poorer Saudis were unable to repay their debts without selling their possessions. Given that some dealers had made substantial profits by selling their stocks at the height of the market (perhaps with foreknowledge of what was to come), a strong feeling of injustice arose from this. Unless the economic order can provide reasonable employment opportunities for those graduating from the country's schools and universities, the survival of that order and the legitimacy of the regime itself will be in doubt. A dynamic creating alienation among a significant part of the population forms an unstable basis on which to construct or maintain a polity.

Another aspect of the employment problem is the low labour force participation rate. That is to say, the percentage of those Saudis who are classified as available for work is low. In fact, according to statistics produced by the Saudi Central Department of Statistics in 2002 only 19 per cent of the Saudi population is classified as such, which constitutes one of the lowest participation rates in the world. For Middle Eastern countries overall the rate stands at an average of 33 per cent, while the figure for Europe is 45 per cent. The Saudi figure is of course in part accounted for by the relatively small percentage of Saudi females who are employed. In 2002, only 6.6 per cent of Saudi females above the age of 15 were employed. Even if the male population is taken by itself, however, the participation rate remains low in comparison to other countries. Among those Saudis who are employed, furthermore, productivity tends to be low. Significant numbers of those employed in the public sector, which probably accounts for more than half of the Saudi labour force, could be more gainfully employed elsewhere.[31]

The government does not have the option of standing back and allowing employment to be governed simply by cost-effectiveness. Such an approach would be neither just to its population nor politically feasible. The Saudi government has sought to resolve the employment problem by promoting Saudization, which is given emphasis in all recent development plans. The Ministry of Labour has taken a wide range of measures to impel business to employ Saudi labour and to reduce the employment of foreign workers. Over half of the allocations for development expenditure in the last two development plans, moreover, have been for human resource development, which is clearly intended to give Saudis the skills, training and specializations that they need if they are to provide the economy with cost-effective labour. These policies are laudable but they will not solve the problem in the short or medium term. As far as education is concerned, radical change is needed to the quality and content of education and training, not just in its quantity. The gap in cost-effectiveness is still very wide and will take considerable time to be bridged, and pressure on businessmen to employ the less cost-effective labour will make it more difficult for them to compete in global markets. Nor could the government realistically resolve its dilemma by lowering Saudi wages and salaries. It is difficult for any government to reduce the wages of its citizens, and the Saudi government is in this respect no different from others.

The implications of WTO accession, and the globalization process as a whole, for the labour problem will be discussed further after the details of the accession agreement have been covered.

5. The Impact of WTO Accession on the Petrochemical Industry

The effect of WTO accession on the petrochemical industry, within the parameters of the financial resource and labour factors which have just been covered, will now be addressed.

Overall, WTO accession is highly favourable for the Saudi petrochemical industry. It provides access to the markets that the industry needs, and enables it to compete on a very favourable basis. For reasons that will be explained below, the factors that restrain and restrict growth in other parts of the economy do not, and will not, significantly affect the development of the petrochemical industry. The extent of the comparative advantage that Saudi Arabia enjoys in petrochemicals outweighs the additional costs stemming from Saudi labour practices (i.e. requirements to employ Saudis rather than the cheapest labour available). The impact of labour market restrictions, in any case, impinges less on the petrochemical industry than on other parts of the economy. The opening up of international markets will enable Saudi Arabia to emerge with a major share in the global petrochemical market.

A comparison between the price of natural gas supplied as a feedstock to the US and Saudi petrochemical industries makes clear the extent of Saudi Arabia's comparative advantage. ARAMCO supplies ethane and methane to the Saudi petrochemical industry at a rate of USD 0.75 per therm. The US petrochemical industry buys natural gas at USD 14 per therm. In the course of the WTO negotiations, the Saudi government maintained that its pricing of natural gas did not run counter to the principles of fair competition. Saudi natural gas, the government pointed out, is not sold for export due to the high cost of the infrastructure that would be needed to do this. The gas had previously been flared as a waste product, so there was no reason why it should be sold at global prices. It would, moreover, be supplied at the same price to Saudi and non-Saudi companies within the Kingdom, so there was no discriminatory practice present in that respect. Despite considerable initial opposition from developed countries, this position was ultimately accepted by the WTO. The position over natural gas liquids was more complex, insofar as Saudi Arabia does export these. The issue of fair pricing therefore was relevant here. The price which ARAMCO charges for the supply of natural gas liquids to industries within the Kingdom is about 30 per cent lower than the international market price for naptha (the normal benchmark for natural gas liquids). The Saudi government successfully contended that it was permitted to do this, as the price within Saudi Arabia reflected the lesser cost of marketing it in the country, with savings that stemmed from the less substantial infrastructure that was required, large-volume purchases, and arrangements whereby secure long-term contracts could be made. Again, this pricing practice was accepted.[32]

This basis of comparative advantage is not significantly undercut by domestic Saudi factors. The petrochemical industry constitutes one of the "islands of efficiency" within the Saudi system, which has been able to operate effectively with a minimum of interference from the wider governmental machinery. It is significant that the industrial areas of Jubail and Yanbu, where most of the petrochemical industry has so far been located, operate according to regulations and procedures which are outside of Saudi Arabia's normal local administrative system. The parts of the public sector which the petrochemical industry relates to most, moreover, are ones that can also be seen as islands of efficiency: the Saudi Arabian Monetary Agency, the Saudi Arabian General Investment Authority, the mining company MAADEN, the Royal Commission for Jubail and Yanbu and others.

Nor does the labour problem impinge seriously on the effective running of the petrochemical industry. This is one of the few areas where the Saudi educational system is producing expertise of the highest calibre. The King Fahd University for Petroleum and Mining, where the instruction is in English, and the specializations studied are predominantly in the scientific and technological fields, produces graduate engineers who are as good as those graduating in the developed world. The petrochemical industry, moreover, does not require a large workforce. It needs a small number of highly skilled and qualified personnel, and these are mostly available within the country. Their rates of pay are comparable to that which would be available on global labour markets. Where outside personnel are needed, the links which the petrochemical industry has within government and the resources at their disposal ensure that it can recruit from among the best.

The regulatory changes affecting foreign investment are also beneficial to the petrochemical industry. It needs to expand through alliances with foreign companies and the involvement of investors who bring with them technological knowledge. This will, in particular, be a necessity with the pursuit of a strategy aimed at obtaining major shares in global petrochemicals markets. The presence of foreign partners may also shield the Saudi companies further from unwarranted interference by the government in their activities. Their ability to cut through bureaucratic obstruction, and to seek legal redress if they are wrongly treated, will be enhanced. Saudi Arabia will also, increasingly, become a major investor externally in petrochemicals projects. SABIC's involvement in a major petrochemicals project in China, announced in the course of 2007, is a harbinger of that.

Substantial parts of Saudi Arabia's physical infrastructure are inadequate by global standards. The heavy expenditure in this sector during the 1970s was not followed through properly in the next two decades. There was, as a result, some deterioration of parts of the existing infrastructure and a failure to develop the new infrastructure and facilities needed by the population. A report by the National Commercial Bank in 2004 suggested that a total of USD 267 billion of investment would be needed to cover basic infrastructural improvements over a 20-year period.[33] Subsequent reports have suggested that the need would be significantly more than this. The financial resources which the government now has at its disposal, however, are sufficient to meet this need, and the government appears intent on doing so. For the petrochemical industry, moreover, the key elements of infrastructure have generally been maintained. Some of the new developments which are planned, such as the industrial cities, will further enhance the provision.

The industry has, therefore, a very strong potential to benefit from WTO accession and to use its comparative advantage to obtain a substantial share of global petrochemicals production. It already has 10 per cent of this market, and that percentage seems likely to grow significantly. Some other industries will also enjoy a comparative advantage on the basis of the cheap supplies of petrochemicals that they can obtain within the country. Among those that are currently being promoted for the new economic cities are factories for fertilizers, packaging (310 plants), tyres, and toys. Cheap energy, together with the plentiful supplies of bauxite within the country, will also give the aluminium industry a substantial comparative advantage. There are at present plans for 10 alumina refineries (refining bauxite into alumina) in the new economic cities and 10 smelters (refining alumina into aluminium).[34] The objective is for Saudi Arabia to produce some 6.25 million tons of aluminium per annum – a substantial amount given that it would make Saudi Arabia the second largest aluminium producer in the world, after China. These developments will clearly be important, but as with petrochemicals it is unlikely that they will employ large numbers of Saudis, and the multiplier effects on the economy may be limited.

6. Prospects for the Wider Economy

As for the wider economy, there may be a gain from WTO accession in terms of economic growth, but it seems unlikely that this will greatly facilitate the resolution of the Kingdom's social problems – especially that of unemployment. Some assessments of the impact of WTO accession on the Saudi economy have suggested that there is no major sector of the economy which will not benefit in some way.[35] This may be true. It does not follow, however, that a coherent strategy towards enhancing the employment opportunities for the Saudi population is now in place.

For an understanding of the above point, further consideration is needed of the terms and conditions of accession. The broad sweep of the measures which were agreed, as outlined above, no doubt create a strong impression. The headlines focus on the new openness to foreign investment, the reduction of tariffs, the facilitation of procedures, and the creation of conditions for foreign companies. The climate created by these measures helps to explain why Saudi Arabia has risen so quickly in the league tables which rank countries according to the ease with which business is conducted. The rise has been particularly marked in the years since 2003. The World Bank's *Doing Business Report* for 2007 ranks Saudi Arabia as 23rd in the world for ease of doing business, out of a total of 178 countries covered.[36] The report was prepared under the joint auspices of the World Bank and the International Finance Corporation. In 2004 the Kingdom had ranked 64th, and in 2006 38th. The 2006 report placed Saudi Arabia as the best country for doing business in the Arab world, and ahead of some developed countries. The 2007 report positioned Saudi Arabia as the best country for doing business in the Middle East generally, and internationally it stood ahead of many developed countries – including France, Austria, Portugal and Spain. Strangely, even the Saudi labour market is rated highly in these rankings.

If the opening up of the Saudi economy to foreign competition was indeed as extensive as the Doing Business ranking seems to suggest, the fate of existing Saudi companies would not look bright. Given that the latter would be competing against some highly efficient international companies and corporations, they would have limited prospects of survival. It would still be true that the economic sector concerned would experience growth, but the beneficiaries of that growth would be the incoming foreign companies rather than Saudi companies.

In practice, however, the headlines are misleading. The fine print of the accession agreement indicates that the Saudi government was able to retain significant control over the domestic market – especially with regard to the role that foreign companies could play. The Saudi government's handling of the negotiation, indeed, was managed skilfully: the market was opened up, but the government retained instruments to protect Saudi business.[37] Some examples will now be given of what the instruments are and how they can be used. Given the importance of the labour issue in Saudi Arabia, it is not surprising that this was the one area where the Kingdom sought, and was granted, a "national treatment" exemption. The framework within which all companies in Saudi Arabia are supposed to operate with regard to labour is laid out in the country's

Labour and Workers' Regulations. These require that for any enterprise, Saudi or foreign-owned, the percentage of Saudi workers is not less than 75 per cent of the total workforce and that they receive at least 50 per cent of the total payroll. In practice very few companies meet this requirement. The Minister of Labour has the authority under these regulations to reduce the required percentage in circumstances where qualified Saudi workers are not available, and in practice such exemptions are common. It seems, however, that foreign firms entering the services sector will be held to the 75 per cent requirement from the beginning when starting up a business, and that the makeup of the remaining 25 per cent will also have limitations (relating, for example, to the proportion of executive positions held by Saudis). Expatriate workers, moreover, will still need a work visa, and the sponsorship system remains unchanged (with the requirement that employees who change employment have to obtain release letters from their employer).

It may be significant that the latest employment figures from the Ministry of Labour show a substantial rise in the number of Saudis employed in the private sector. Between 2004 and 2005, the numbers rose by 27 per cent.[38] As the total number of Saudis employed in the private sector is small (591,280 in 2005, according to the Ministry of Labour), the significance of the increase for the employment of Saudi citizens in general should not be overstated. It does suggest, however, that the measures the government has taken to boost Saudi employment in the private sector are having some effect, and that the continuing controls which the WTO accession permits will be important. Saudi labour, then, may be employed even if it is more expensive than labour available on the international market.

The government has retained the ability, moreover, to favour local firms when awarding contracts for government procurement. Given the substantial role that government procurement plays in the Saudi economy, and will do increasingly over the coming years when the new financial resources at the disposal of the government will be spent, this leaves an important instrument in its hands. It should also be noted that the Foreign Investment Law imposes significant minimum capital requirements for foreign companies entering the county. In wholesale and retail distribution investors have to provide a minimum of SR 20 million in paid-up capital, and the government can specify the minimum size for outlets. There is also the requirement to hire and train Saudis.

With regard to agencies, foreign companies no longer need to have a Saudi agent to bid for government tenders but all non-Saudi contractors must assign 30 per cent of their work to wholly owned Saudi companies. Contractors are obliged to purchase the tools and equipment that they use for performance of their contracts with the Saudi government from Saudi agents in Saudi Arabia.

7. Conclusion

Saudi Arabia's integration into the global economy, therefore, presents a paradox. On the one hand, it will enable the economy to make the critical gains that governments hope will accrue from globalization. The key sectors of the industry where Saudi Arabia enjoys a comparative advantage will benefit greatly. Saudi Arabia, indeed, looks set to become one of the world's major industrial powers, taking a major share in the global petrochemicals market. It will be able to use its resources, expertise and market position to invest abroad in this field. Some downstream industries, making use of cheap and available local petrochemicals, will also benefit from developments in this sector. Cheap energy supplies and available local mineral sources will also give the aluminium industry an important stake in the global aluminium market.

On the other hand, the wider social and economic developments that usually accompany economic success in leading areas of comparative advantage are unlikely to occur in Saudi Arabia. To the extent that globalization impinges on the rest of the economy, indeed, the effects may well be problematic. The key factor here is the labour market. The more the economy is opened up to the forces of global competition, the more difficult will Saudi business find it to employ Saudis. Using costly Saudi labour, rather than cheap migrant labour, will price Saudi products out of most global markets. Even domestically, many local businesses will be unable to compete with companies which are based outside of the country. GDP statistics may show that all sectors are growing, but the reality will be that local businesses employing local labour will be in difficulty. Increasing unemployment will intensify social and political problems in the country. In practice, the outcome is unlikely to be as negative as this, but this is because the terms of Saudi Arabia's accession to the WTO will enable the government to retain substantial control over the domestic market. The impact of globalization, then, is reduced by limiting its scope. The possible gains which tend to ensue from globalization elsewhere, however, also become more limited.

The dilemma in which the Saudi government finds itself is not the effect of policy failure. It is structural. The labour market and the problems that arise from it have arisen from the rentier dimension of the economy. The government itself is a victim of these dynamics.

NOTES

1. Desta 2003.
2. Niblock *et al.* 2007, p. 148.
3. Information from interviews conducted with businessmen in Saudi Arabia, February 2006 and February 2007.
4. Niblock *et al.* 2007.
5. "Joint Statement by President Bush and Crown Prince Abdullah", 25 April 2005, from White House website http://www.whitehouse.gov/ (retrieved 20 October 2008).
6. Saudi American Bank 2006, p. 6.
7. Ibid., pp. 3–9.
8. For further detail on these laws, cf. Niblock 2006, pp. 126–30.
9. Ibid., pp. 131–2.
10. Saudi American Bank 2006, p. 3.
11. The information given on the accession agreement here is taken from the Accession Protocol, which is made up of the Schedule of Concessions and Commitments on Goods; the Schedule of Specific Commitments in Services; and the Report of the Working Party. However, it should be noted that a convenient summary of the changes introduced can be found in Saudi American Bank 2006.
12. Information on the Chemical Tariff Harmonization Agreement is taken from the website of the International Council of Chemical Associations, http://www.icca-at-wssd.org/about_us.html. That on the impact on Saudi Arabia is taken from Saudi American Bank 2006, p. 17.
13. Saudi Arabian Monetary Agency 2007, Tables 2.1 and 8.4.
14. Kingdom of Saudi Arabia, Ministry of Finance, 2007.
15. *Economist Intelligence Unit Briefing*, 18 January 2008, www.economist.com/displayStory.cfm?story_id=10552721 (retrieved 26 January 2008).
16. EFG Hermes Bank 2007, p. 11.
17. Saudi Arabian Monetary Agency 2007, Table 8a.
18. "Saudi Arabia plans its first Sovereign Wealth Fund", *Bloomberg*, 18 January 2008, www.bloomberg.com/apps/news?pid=20601104&sid=aSt3V9yQJo6o&refer=m (retrieved 20 January 2008).
19. Saudi Arabian General Investment Authority n.d.

20 Saudi British Bank 2007, p. 41.
21 Kingdom of Saudi Arabia, Ministry of Finance 2007.
22 Kingdom of Saudi Arabia, Ministry of Economy and Planning 2006.
23 Saudi Arabian Monetary Agency 2006.
24 The background behind these figures is covered in greater detail in Niblock *et al.* 2007, pp. 191–4.
25 Saudi American Bank 2002, p. 1.
26 Saudi Arabian Monetary Agency 2007, Table 28.
27 Khan Zahid, *Riyad Bank Weekly Briefing*, 7 April 2007.
28 "A Tipping Point in Saudi Arabia", *Christian Science Monitor*, 15 August 2007.
29 *Arab News*, 25 December 2007.
30 Jadwa Investment 2007.
31 Kingdom of Saudi Arabia, Central Department of Statistics n.d. The figures are based on information gathered in 2002.
32 Saudi American Bank 2006.
33 National Commercial Bank 2004.
34 Saudi British Bank 2007, p. 34.
35 Saudi American Bank 2006.
36 World Bank *et al.* n.d.
37 In view of this, it is perhaps surprising that the Saudi government has not seen fit to publicize more widely the role that it played, and the gains it achieved. Up to the time when Saudi Arabia joined the WTO, no detailed information was available to the Saudi public as to the content of the agreement. Even in the period since then, the material made available through public channels has been very limited.
38 Saudi British Bank 2007, p. 34.

8

MOROCCO'S POLITICAL ECONOMY: AMBIGUOUS PRIVATIZATION AND THE EMERGING SOCIAL QUESTION[1]

Myriam Catusse

Introduction

Morocco is in tune with the international neo-liberal agenda. The politico-economic trajectories of the Kingdom, while they do not arouse analyses as trenchant as in Tunisia,[2] which is presented alternately as a model pupil of the development therapists and as a counter-example of the democratic virtues of the "Washington Consensus",[3] are in many respects remarkable. The different reform measures in the arena of economic policy which have been put in place for more than 20 years lay claim to the dogmas of neo-liberal development. Resonance chamber, sometime laboratory, of this "modern religion",[4] Moroccan society lives its hopes and its disappointments.

In these terms, the Morocco of structural adjustment, of privatizations and of economic liberalization presents an interesting post from which to observe the reconstitutions of the powers of the state over economic regulation in the context of globalization. The nature and resources of public power are put to the test of the opening of economic borders and the normalization of markets at international level. In terms of political economy, alongside its historical and institutional specificities, Morocco can be considered in many respects to be a "paradigmatic" case within the Middle East and North Africa (MENA) region: the Kingdom is exemplary with regard to the modalities, the breadth and the effects of the economic reforms in which it has been engaged since the beginning of the 1980s. It sometimes fulfils the role of a laboratory, testing the effects of the exercise of new instruments of economic policy.

This chapter examines the logics of regulation which have developed since the abandoning of the "state-developmental" model and of Fordism,[5] and also in the face of the weaknesses of the "neo-liberal" compromise itself based on the classic figures of the "state as corrector of the market" or the "state as inciter or manipulator of incitement". By studying the interactions of the economic and political arenas, I will discuss in particular the falsities of the hypothesis of "regulation through less state". Rather than a macro-level analysis of the effects of the economic reforms, of their winners and their losers, of their perverse effects and even of their dysfunctioning,[6] the recent trajectory of Morocco calls for an examination of how public action in the economic and social sectors is being transformed in terms of distribution of resources, decision-making and finally the exercise of power.

A priori, within the region, the history of Moroccan political economy presents specific characteristics with regard to such questions. Firstly, the analysis in terms of a rentier or post-rentier economy such as has developed in the region is inopportune. Certainly, the modern Moroccan economy is largely based on a public sector rich in abundant mineral resources. By means of the *Office Chérifien des Phosphates* (OCP), a public company, the public sector has provided a manna to successive Moroccan governments from the 1970s onwards.[7] The OCP remains today the primary company in Morocco, with more than 300,000 employees, producing 3 per cent of its Gross Domestic Product (GDP) and exporting almost 30 per cent of its total exports. In terms of exogenous revenues, the capital transfers of emigrant workers also represent an important inflow of currency, which the public authorities try with varying degrees of success to capture and channel by means of favourable policies.[8] Tourism, principally European tourism, represents today the primary source of currency for the country, but is not monopolized by the public sector and cannot simply be a source of profit in the hands of the political authorities. In parallel, through the development of the food-processing and textile industry in particular, the Moroccan state has also been a "productive state" and still is, based on a widespread indirect fiscal system.[9] It has moreover only been slightly redistributive, ensuring neither high salaries nor generous social policies.

Secondly, the contemporary trajectories of Morocco document in an original fashion the relationship between economic and political reforms. Rather than an analysis of the "democratizing" effects or, on the contrary, of the "authoritarian" logic of economic liberalization, which is in any case partial or selective, and rather than an analysis of the effects of liberalization or deliberalization[10] of economic policies, the contemporary transformations of the political space in Morocco suggest an examination of the metamorphoses of public institutions and of the modalities of public action. Several correlated hypotheses can be put forward to analyse the reconstitutions of the economic power of the Moroccan state in the name of "less state", an argument which everyone puts forward in order to enter the "black box" of the state[11] and its institutions. By examining the means of privatization of public action, I will show that the powers of the state are decentralized and delegated and even disguise themselves beneath technical rags, but remain of prime importance.

The logics of "privatization" of public action are striking. They consist in forms of "discharge", to borrow the Weberian expression revisited by Hibou.[12] In such processes of reform, the metamorphoses of social regulation through the political rests perhaps less on a disengagement of public power than on forms of subsidiarity or delegation. The prior resources and regulatory capacities of state institutions are eroded, but their points of intervention multiply and shift. One should therefore speak of a redeployment of public action. In the case of Morocco, the discussion is much more interesting in that the programme of privatization of the public sector launched in 1990 has shown itself to be ambitious and has concerned the principal economic and strategic sectors of the Kingdom.

Standard neo-liberal theory and coordination "by the market" are indeed unable to explain these transformations. This explains the renewal of references to the work of Polanyi, who emphasizes instead the fundamentally dual character of the liberalization of the market, which has to be accompanied by the economic intervention of the state. Neo-liberal institutions themselves have revised their analyses.[13] The Moroccan public authorities remain central actors in economic policies. Reference to the state continues to inform the expectations and practices of actors confronted with the deinstitutionalization and destabilization of previous systems. This is, furthermore, not unique to Morocco. Over the course of the decades of structural adjustment, "the equation 'more market' equals 'less state' has been very widely assumed by default, and not only in Latin America".[14]

Decentralization and devolution are the cornerstones of the techniques of discharge in terms of policies of investment and of social policy. The spheres of public action change with its delocalizations and relocalizations of economic policies: new spheres of economic modes of regulation are mapped out, as are possible new splits and causes of deregulation.

Finally, beneath the surface, ambivalent attempts at the "depoliticization" of economic policies play out – the desire to set out and treat questions of economic choice beyond the sphere of politics and political competition. This clearly belongs to a relatively classic process proper to development and to the progressive sophistication of public policies leading to a call to experts or "technocrats". But this process is situated also in the logic of antipolitics,[15] which tends to marginalize the elected and the partisan in the construction of the public space.

Examination of Moroccan economic policies, and in particular of its privatizations, therefore allows us to examine the construction of new spheres of public action and the use of new tools of government. Behind the slogans of adjustment, privatization and *mise à niveau*, the powers of the state are restructured. The strictly political notions of public good and general interest are revisited. On the one hand, whether it be to deplore its faults or to praise its qualities, entrepreneurship has become over the course of these years in Morocco an "affair of society".[16] On the other hand, by means of decentralization, of fragmentation of spheres of action and of recourse to/seizing of "private" actors at national or international level, the public authorities have discharged themselves of aspects of the political economy while at the same time retaining control upstream and downstream. In the domain of social policies and welfare, they even sometimes redeploy themselves behind the administration or the royal figure. In this game, representative political institutions are by contrast marginalized.

In order to analyse how the catchphrase "less state" has reorganized the economic capabilities of public power in Morocco, and how the logics of privatization, decentralization and even depoliticization fit together, we will look in turn at the transformation of the modalities of the accumulation of wealth and of redistribution, at the evolution of the role of the state in social security, and finally at the reconstitution of wage and union relations in the context of rapid economic liberalization.

1. From One Form of Capitalism to Another: Accumulation of Wealth and Redistribution in the Economic Reforms

The neo-liberal turning-point of Moroccan economic policy can be described as the passage from one form of capitalism to another: a metamorphosis, with some adaptations, but certainly not a radical transition from one economic state to another different in all respects; not really a transplant or even less the importation of a mode of production, but an adjustment to new internal or external constraints. Contrary to what can be seen in the regimes of Central or Eastern Europe, for example, Morocco has not recently converted, properly speaking, to the market economy: property rights have not been restored or fundamentally transformed; before the train of neo-liberal reforms was undertaken, enterprises, businesses and private services prospered or survived alongside state enterprises. Moreover, the reforms undertaken from the 1980s onwards signalled the abandonment of the idea and of the promises of the "developer state" in terms of collective reference-points, representations and economic strategies. The norms of the "economically legitimate" changed rapidly and in a significant fashion between different borrowings and, in particular, between local reinventions of capitalism.[17] They were also accompanied by substantial transformations in forms of accumulation and redistribution and in modalities of economic government: public employment contracted,[18] and with it not only the quasi-assurance of a post for young graduates, but also privileged access to the modest system of social security. Customs protection for local production was to a large extent dismantled, which altered the balance of power in terms of the extraversion or introversion of the local productive tissue.

Figuring among the 15 most heavily indebted countries at the end of the 1970s,[19] like several other countries the Kingdom was forced to submit to shock therapy under the auspices of the unholy trinity: The International Monetary Fund (IMF), World Bank and World Trade Organization (WTO).[20] In 1983, a programme of structural adjustment was negotiated with the IMF and the World Bank, one of the first plans of its kind in the region. The principles are familiar: restructuring of the instruments of state intervention and reform of public finances, monetary policy and external trade arrangements. These decisions translated into a reduction in tariff protection for national production and the adjustment of exchange rate regulation. Foreign investment was again encouraged.

If only 38 per cent of imports were free in 1983, they reached 90 per cent in 1995. Exchange rate policy was liberalized and, in 1983, the dirham depreciated. In parallel, price control and subsidies for products of prime necessity were substantially reduced. New laws were adopted in 1993 to organize the banking sector and the Stock Exchange, and in 1996 to normalize and to *mettre à niveau* public companies, investment and trade. In 1989 parliament adopted a law designating 112 enterprises, among them the jewels of the public sector, for privatization.

In terms of its integration into the world economy, Morocco fulfilled the necessary conditions and acceded to the General Agreement on Tariffs and Trade (GATT) in 1987. It was furthermore at a conference in Marrakech in 1994 that the GATT became the WTO. The Kingdom signed a Partnership Agreement with the European Union (EU) in 1996. In the framework of the Euro-Mediterranean process started at Barcelona in October 1995, the Agreement provided for the establishment of a free-trade area between Morocco and the EU by 2010. The economic fabric of the country started on a process of *mise à niveau*, an imprecise leitmotiv with promising overtones used with regard to almost all sectors, including the economic fabric but also justice, education, the associative fabric, etc.[21] In 2004, the Kingdom signed a free-trade agreement with the United States which confirmed the option "of the integration of the Moroccan economy with the world economy".[22] In other words, the protection of Moroccan production appeared to be dismantled while, in accordance with the new canons of development, expectations turned towards the development of a "national class of entrepreneurs [. . .] fundamentally wealth creating".[23] Would this result in the formation of an "enlightened bourgeoisie"[24], bringing in its wake a liberal revolution? Would the ferment of a "market democracy" be put in place, as those who preached the "new orthodoxy of development"[25] then hoped, or at least appeared to believe?

1.1 At the origin of the "great transformation": structural adjustment
Appraisals of the structural adjustment programme launched in 1983 are mixed. For the Ministry of the Economy and Finance, it achieved its macro-economic stabilization objectives: external debt (the current account balance) was reduced from 12.3 per cent of Gross Domestic Product (GDP) in 1983 to 0.9 per cent in 1987 and to 0.7 per cent in

2003.[26] Thanks to the devaluation of the dirham between 1983 and 1985, exports increased. The growth in tourist revenues and in transfers from Moroccans resident abroad also helped, together with debt reduction, to re-establish external balances. But despite the exceptional revenues brought in by the privatizations, the state budget is still today in deficit.[27]

The *Association pour la Taxation des Transactions pour l'Aide aux Citoyens* (ATTAC) in Morocco highlights instead the worsening indicators of teaching, health and unemployment during the years of "liberal policies".[28] In 2007, the rate of unemployment officially bordered on 10 per cent[29] of the population, but this indicator is contested. In reality it evens out very marked disparities between town and country, young people and adults and also men and women. It does not take account either of situations of under-employment, informal employment[30] or unwaged forms of employment.[31]

As for World Bank experts, they are of the opinion that "the 1980s were a period of macro-economic stabilization, gradual liberalization and deregulation of the economy which brought about dynamic growth".[32] But if the "stock of Morocco has without doubt gone up among foreign investors", they too can only deplore the slow rate of growth and high rates of unemployment.[33]

In any case, structural adjustment, strengthened by the measures of *mise à niveau* introduced in the wake of the free-trade agreements with the EU, was an affair of state in all senses of the term: on the one hand, it was a question of transforming the economic structures of the state, and on the other, the Moroccan state controlled the process upstream and downstream. As Dillman indicates in relation to the Maghreb regimes put to the test by the globalization of economies:

> Regimes have been quite adept at maintaining patronage coalitions and determining the mechanisms by which public and external resources are divided up. The more they "deregulate" the more they "reregulate" by determining precisely who can most easily benefit from change and join distributional coalition to tap profits in the market.[34]

More perhaps than the relative decrease in the level of public expenditure,[35] the programme of privatization and the reduction of the state sector from the 1980s onwards were the pivots of the reforms. In fact, apart from its social consequences, to which we shall return, the structural adjustment programme smoothed the way for transformation of state interventionism in the economic arena, which illustrates particularly well the routes that the privatization of the Moroccan public sector took.

1.2 The crucible of privatizations[36]

The policy of privatization on which Morocco embarked at the end of the 1980s took several forms which, taken together, transformed less the sociological fabric of the elites than the modalities of public action. If such modalities were the instrument of a reproduction of the elitist system, the privatizations were also the backyard of a transformation of the resources of the state, of a redefinition of levels of intervention or even of the formation of new systems of reference for public action, copied from the metaphors of the market. The emergence of the category of "entrepreneur" as the archetype of success and power is an example of its effects.[37] In the image of what Boltanski described in relation to the middle classes in France during the 1930s, one can say that the 1990s figure among the "numerous cases where the appearance of a 'new' group is the product of a structural rearrangement of long duration exercised at the same time over objective properties and representations".[38]

A law made-to-measure

The programme of privatization of state-owned companies was initially set out in the framework of Law 39-89, which listed an initial 112 and a further 114 companies to be ceded. Taking into consideration the financial holdings of these companies in other companies, they represented 40 per cent of the portfolio of the state in 1989 when the law was adopted. Far from being lame ducks of Moroccan industry, this list put up for sale some jewels of the Moroccan public sector.[39] It included the country's big industrial businesses (particularly in the cement, steel, petrol, phosphate and mining sectors), and also four of the main banks, insurance companies, finance companies and service companies. The range of privatizations was moreover extended in particular in the area of public services (post and telecommunications, transport, abattoirs, state-owned water and electricity companies, and so on).

The sale of public companies was swiftly carried out by means of assignment by private contract, calls for bids, public offering on the

Casablanca Stock Exchange and – to a limited extent – the allocation of shares to employees. It took its course through the assignment or concession, in the form of the delegation of management but principally of concession, of public services such as the distribution of water and electricity and sanitation, energy sectors, the treatment of household waste, public transport, telecommunications, and so on.

Social reproduction and crony capitalism
In the majority of cases, in the short term at least, the sale of the public patrimony became the occasion for often opaque recycling operations. It showed itself to be "a decisive means of redistributing resources, of reformulating social contracts and even of resettling the legitimacy of governments in office".[40] The public authorities mastered the rhythm and extent of the process.[41] They could choose the companies and sectors to cede, and controlled upstream and downstream procedures to a great extent.

However, the privatizations, and the neo-liberal turning-point more generally, concealed a double facet: on the one hand, the public authorities could nurture the existence of complex politico-economic networks by engaging in "crony capitalism",[42] while on the other they could also obtain additional funds in a period of budgetary reduction so as to establish new economic means of regulation.

Bearing in mind the speed with which the privatizations were carried out in Morocco, they profited first of all the elites and those who already held concentrations of considerable personal capital and significant material or social resources. Stark comes to the same conclusion as regards the countries of Central or Eastern Europe, where the elites in place before the transition towards a market economy captured the benefits of the privatizations where they took place most quickly.[43] In the case of Morocco, the "incestuous" nature of the procedures is all the less astonishing in view of the fact that the economic transition did not bring about, nor was it accompanied by, a major transformation of the political system, a rupture of the political system or even a removal of the regime's personnel.

In general terms, the privatizations at the halfway stage have been fruitful for a limited number of Moroccan investors and major foreign groups.[44] Far from achieving the avowed aim of extending the country's entrepreneurial class, they have had the opposite effect of yet further concentrating the country's capital. An examination of the principal transactions reveals how just a few groups were consistently involved, both in offers for sale and purchases. *Omnium Nord Africain* (ONA), the "jewel in the crown",[45] and SIGER (anagram of *regis*, "of the king"), the private holdings of the royal family, were certainly the principal national winners from the privatizations by dint of their purchase of the National Investment Company, privatized in 1994. For ONA, it was the occasion to deploy a "multi-sectoral strategy [in] food processing, mining, automobiles, deep-sea fishing, the textile industry, tourism, real estate, communications and high technologies".[46] Together with a few other large conglomerates (Benjelloun, Kettani, Akhennouch, etc.), they were able to "reinforce their acquired positions and diversify in all directions".[47] Keeping to this level of analysis, it is clear that neither the practices of overlapping power and economic accumulation, nor the logic of rent-seeking, have been eliminated in Morocco by means of the privatizations. Quite the reverse.

The mechanisms of concentration of capital and accumulation of wealth and power have, primarily, political explanations: assignments were made in the majority of cases by private contract, often at the Palace and rarely transparently. The institutions created as occasion demanded were made up of personalities chosen at the discretion of the King: this was the case with both the Committee of Transfers – charged with giving its opinion on the programme – and the evaluation body whose role was to fix the minimum offer price for a shareholding or for the establishment to be ceded. The management (i.e. directing) of state-owned companies and services subject to concession is under the direct control of the Minister of the Interior, who supervises the management (i.e. running) of outsourced public services.

The logic of reproduction also has more structural stimuli, relating in particular to the conditions of access to credit, which have been controlled by the big banks of the Kingdom, themselves either public establishments (in particular the *Banque Populaire* Group) or privatized for the benefit of the principal groups of the Kingdom (the *Banque Marocaine du Commerce Extérieur* for the Benjelloun Group, Attijariwafa Bank for the Kettani group and ONA).

Other practices surround privatization, accentuating these tendencies. Examples of public companies repurchased by their former managers or shareholders are numerous, particularly in the hotel and petrol industries.[48] Sometimes, today's purchasers are the European companies that had been forced to cede to the Moroccan state a significant share of their capital during the 1970s, in accordance with the provisions of the Moroccanization laws of 1973 – so much so that the privatizations have been described as the "demoroccanization" of the public sector.[49] Far from being a source of clear and decisive rupture, from this point of view the privatizations ensured above all the passing of the baton of continuity.

Finally, the modalities of the restructuring of the powers of the state through privatization express themselves most particularly in the political uses of the resources produced by the assignment of public companies. This question, raised by opposition Members of Parliament at the time of the adoption of the law, was reawakened in 1999/2000 by the allocation of a substantial part of the sale of the second GSM (mobile telephony) licence to the Hassan II Fund for Economic and Social Development, an institution created ad hoc by the Palace in 2000. This decision, taken at the Palace, had the result of removing from the budget the profits of the privatization without any governmental or ministerial control. Criticized by financial backers as well as within ministerial cabinets, according to some press information, it clearly showed a "strategy of confusion of existing budgetary procedures as a form of privatization of public action".[50] The Palace relieved the government and parliament of any say in the management of this manna by taking privatization of the licence out of their hands. In the face of complaints, the Hassan II Fund was eventually reintegrated into the budget, but in the form of a special account managed by royal advisers.[51] It should be noted that apart from *Maroc Telecom*, the Hassan II Fund also received part of the receipts of the privatizations of the *Régie des Tabacs* (the state-owned tobacco company), the four sugar refineries and the *Société marocaine du thé et du sucre* (SOMATHES).

The privatizations therefore allowed for the reinforcement of certain economic structures of the Moroccan state, but also contributed to undermining other tools of public action in the longer term, or even to inaugurating new ones. They were also a means for the public authorities to direct social and political claims towards intermediary targets, designated as those chiefly responsible for the economic state of the country.[52]

The varied territories of economic regulation
The economic context has evolved, and not only in incidental detail or appearance. Earlier techniques of enrichment are adapting. One has to adjust to the liberalization of trade and the disappearance of sectoral monopolies. Privatizations have been the tool of choice for reinforcing mutual dependencies, sanctioning and correcting the economic fabric "top down". Like the earlier processes of Marocconization they have proven providential for the fortunes of certain families and groups, but they have also permanently and structurally changed the rules of the game.

If large transfers of resources from the "public" to the "private" sector have concentrated power and wealth, they have also shifted the site of the political control of the economy and changed the instruments of that control: for example, the slow development of the Stock Exchange is solidly supported by Stock Exchange companies themselves, in the lap as they are of banks and large private groups within the Kingdom. Nevertheless, the Exchange welcomes a generation of economic operators attempting new routes to success. In all cases, whether in the large-scale assignment of public companies or more modest sales, transactions were negotiated or disputed even when they were made by private contract or outside the frameworks fixed by the law. The shadow of ONA and the royal interests in these reconstitutions of capital is determinant, although this does not prevent them from being subject to competition from other groups, for example the Benjelloun family in the banking sector.

Other observations deserve attention. Cammett shows that:

> The combination of a new export-oriented trade regime and rising international manufacturing opportunities initiated important changes in the composition of the private sector [. . .] Thus a substantial group of small-scale producers from modest backgrounds emerged alongside traditional protectionist elites, who dominate the textile sector.[53]

In the field of professional relations, such transformations of the economic fabric translated into new types of conflict, which could be observed for example at the time of the negotiations for the adoption of a new labour code in 2003, when the *Fédération des Industries Textiles et de l'Habillement* (AMITH) led a revolt against the positions taken by the management of the *Confédération Générale des Entreprises du Maroc* (CGEM). While the then prime minister, Driss Jettou, who was heavily involved in the social discussions, was nothing less than the former president of AMITH, its president, S.E. Mezouar, future Minister of Trade and Industry and currently Minister of Finance and the Economy, virulently disputed certain measures, in particular as regards union representation and above all the decision to increase the guaranteed minimum wage. Together with other internal splits in the business world, this dispute seriously endangered the re-election of the president of CGEM, H. Chami, some months later.

Moreover, after almost twenty years of privatization, the public authorities are no longer the principal employers in the country, all the more in that they are no longer in charge of the provision of basic public services. Added to reform of public administration, this has led to a remarkable reduction in political power deriving from the ability to employ a large number of people in the public sector, and has impacted, as we shall see, on the field of wage and union relations.

Economic liberalization has also been accompanied by a shifting of the territories of investment policies. In the context of off-shoring at the Euro-Mediterranean and global levels, the reorientations of Moroccan economic policy have given shape to new levels of governance, as follows.

On the one hand, the devolution to multinationals of the provision of collective services, previously in the hands of state-owned companies, has, although not new, taken on remarkable proportions. It has been accompanied by a transfer of competence over issue areas of collective interest to national or international private groups (e.g. water management), often to the detriment of the local collectivities.[54] Those collectivities impose themselves like private actors in the reconstitution of public policies. Their measures, strategies and territories of intervention do not necessarily contradict the public policies of national development and urbanism, but they can generate conflicts over the occupation and/or use of space: for example, the territories of intervention of the private electrification company are not the same as those of the electoral ward, nor, to an even lesser extent, as those of the "legal" or "illegal" town.

On the other hand, in January 2002, the Royal Letter concerning the "decentralized management of investment" and its implementing decrees redefined the relevant territories of economic policy by entrusting to the *walis* (prefects) of any given region the decentralized management of investment ("local economic and social development"). Dispossessing the economic ministers of certain of their prerogatives, the King ordained the creation, under the tutelage of these local authorities – which were placed under his authority – of Regional Investment Centres (RIC) to act as single points of contact for Moroccan and foreign economic operators wishing to invest locally. Sixteen RICs were created in 2002/2003. In this new cartography of economic policies, the *walis*, charged normally with security policy in the Kingdom, gained significant competences in the field of economic policy as power was decentralized.

Finally, privatization interfered in the more individualized relations of the citizen with the administration, not without notorious instances of resistance. It transformed users and right-holders into "clients", which incited numerous mobilizations. Zaki for example shows how the programmes of electrification of the shantytowns of Casablanca, following the signing of a contract of delegated management with Lydec, subsidiary of the Suez group, provoked local mobilizations, pillaging, and negotiations between the local authorities and representatives of the private companies.[55] Similarly, Allain Mansouri emphasizes the role that the mobilization of unhappy users played in the renegotiation of the contract of REDAL (the state-owned water company) at Rabat-Salé.[56] This renegotiation has contributed, without any doubt, to transforming the terms of the social contract and the exercise of economic citizenship.

Structural adjustment and the policy of privatization have therefore ploughed new furrows for the Moroccan political economy. Fixed on the recommendations of development institutions that worship at their altar, their reorientations are ambivalent. The social performances of the Kingdom are in the spotlight. Growth rates are weak. But the rhythm and extent of its privatization programme are unique and acknowledged by the reformers as essential tools for the relaunching of the economy and of investment in the face of the incompetence of public actors. Neither the structures nor the actors of the Moroccan economy have been subject to radical shocks during the reforms, but Moroccan capitalism has nevertheless undergone significant transformations.

2. From the Abandonment of Regulation by the State to the Stakes of Regulation by the Market: The Role of the State in the Reconstitution of Social Security

Among other changes, structural adjustment and privatization to stimulate the private class of entrepreneurs signal the abandonment of a model of welfare by means of public employment.[57] This model, less decisive in Morocco than in other countries in the region, had greatly influenced representations and practices surrounding social expectations with regard to the state.[58] The reorientation of economic policy had at least two consequences in this regard: on the one hand, rates of unemployment increased, and on the other, social risks accrued. From the end of the 1980s, protest against the repercussions on employment of economic liberalization became a permanent feature of the landscape of Moroccan social movements due to "unemployed graduates".[59]

At the same time, as in several countries in the region, the policy of debt reduction entailed, at its very beginning, a suppression of, or drastic reductions in, consumption subsidies. Combined with political claims, these measures rapidly incited popular movements that certain observers called, a little hastily, and with little regard to the political claims that accompanied them, "bread riots" or "IMF riots".[60] Followed by severe repressions which extended the powers of the Minister of the Interior, D. Basri, this "revision of policies of compensation connected to the contraction of rentier resources broke the tacit pact of state clientelism and rendered the perception of inequalities intolerable", as was observed in the case of Tunisia by Camau and Geisser.[61]

The social malaise is far from having disappeared. It is not a residual problem of adaptation quickly to be resolved by policies which are compensatory in the short term while waiting for the virtuous benefits of liberalization to profit everyone. As in several countries subject to such drastic and speedy reforms, 25 years after the adoption of the programme of structural adjustment social risks seem to have been exacerbated. This is shown by mobilizations from autumn 2006 onwards against the high cost of living by human rights associations, unions, radical left movements and alter-globalization associations. Behind slogans such as "a privatized Morocco is a deprived Morocco", the demonstrators demanded the improvement of public services, an increase in salaries and an end to "the process of erosion of purchasing power". Alongside social movements for or against the plan to integrate women in development, or mobilizations for the recognition of the years of terrorism, or even behind Islamic or Berber identity reference points – themselves crucial poles of political protest at the turn of the 2000s[62] – social problematics impose themselves as collective causes of the first order: the pauperization of society, unemployment of young graduates, reduction in purchasing power, access to basic public services – water, electricity, health, education, transport, etc. – are now on the agenda of protest. The harsh repression to which protesters are subject increases the importance of the question and its political weight.[63]

The placing on the agenda of the social question in Morocco is therefore very closely connected to the transformations that its capitalism is undergoing. But the search for solutions and innovative means of social regulation, on the labour market or elsewhere, is conditioned by the constraints that weigh on the political economy of the country. When trade is liberalized, the importance of foreign direct investment (FDI) increases.[64] This constitutes a serious obstacle to the developments of social safety nets. Competing with East European or Asian labour markets for comparative advantages, the countries of the Maghreb seek to make use of structures and forms of employment. According to this way of thinking, low-salaried workers and flexible labour law are advantageous. Cleaning up the public sector obstructs access to employment for an increasing number of active workers. The effects of the transformation of labour markets in a society with not only very low wage levels but also a short-term comparative advantage in international trade that rests largely on the logic of social dumping complicate the "social question".

It is in such a context that, since the beginning of the decade and the ascendancy both of a new sovereign to the throne and of the Secretary-General of the *Union Socialiste des Forces Populaires* (USFP) to the head of government from 1998 to 2002, a triple train of reform was undertaken: firstly, in the field of professional relations, negotiations became triangular, with employers included as a "social partner". Secondly, in the legislative field, new important social laws, in particular a new labour code,[65] a new law on accidents in the workplace[66] and a law on compulsory sickness insurance,[67] were adopted after years or even decades of blockage. Finally, welfare for the "unprotected" was reorganized with, as a beacon measure, the announcement in 2005 of a National Initiative for Human Development (NIHD): orientated towards private actors and institutions, it is strongly and very ambitiously organized by the public authorities, for whom it is a priority.

Alongside the implementation of generic models of treatment of social risk proposed by international financial institutions which privilege methods of welfare through insurance (which are therefore individual and private), the metamorphoses of social regulation through the political in Morocco rest above all on forms of subsidiarity or delegation, in other words, through forms of discharge. The ambivalences of regulation "through less state" are flagrantly exposed. In place of a schema of binary regulation, whereby the social developmental state protects wage earners through the extension of public employment and the offer of social and health services, while local or national charitable institutions take care of the "rest", new arrangements emerge, employing several methods of co-management of social risk.

2.1 Failure of the social state

We should note that during the preceding decades, differently from other countries in the region, the Moroccan state showed itself particularly modest in terms of providing social security for its citizens. If one could have thought of the state, during the golden years of development, as "the alpha and omega of the moment, under the double aspect of the state as demiurge and the state as provider",[68] the model of regulation of social risks by the state in Morocco was very modest and collapsed.

If the seeds of a social question emerged with the globalization of the Moroccan economy, it is less the result of a brutal disengagement on the part of the state than because economic liberalization accentuated the weaknesses of an already modest state social security system. The Kingdom is badly placed on the Index of Human Development of the UNDP, including among Arab countries. It is classified, together with its neighbours Tunisia and Algeria, among countries with "average human development". From 117th place globally in 1995, Morocco slipped to 123rd in 2005 out of 177 countries ranked.[69] In particular, its scores for education were adverse. Morocco is placed among the worst in the world as regards the level of education rurally.[70] In 1998/9, 48.3 per cent of the population aged 15 and above was classified as unable to read or write, 83 per cent of the women living in a rural environment. If the 1980s were marked by a lowering of the indicators of relative poverty, the following decade saw a significant increase in the percentage of the population living beneath the poverty line. According to a survey of the domestic standard of living carried out in 1998/9,[71] 19 per cent of the Moroccan population was living under the poverty line, as opposed to 13 per cent in 1990/1, while the "economically vulnerable" population living just above this line had also increased. By 2005 the figure would be 25 per cent.[72] The worsening of these indicators, which went on beyond 1992 and the end of the main programme of structural adjustment, indicates that they could not simply be imputable to the short-term consequences of neo-liberal reform.

In this context, the idea of a "social question", "itself sowing the seeds of a questioning of the existing system",[73] emerged around the discourse of the "endangering" of society and even of its regime.[74] With the new forms taken by Moroccan capitalism, the previous social compromises appeared suspended in a "time of doubt"[75] which accompanied the search for innovative tools of regulation. The "social", up to now essentially envisaged as a question secondary to growth and economic performance, became a source of major political concern at the top of the state's agenda.

2.2 The seeds of a social question

Beyond the movement of unemployed graduates, what worried the public authorities, and incontestably destabilized the regime, in the 1990s and 2000s was, on the one hand, the intensification of the effects of media coverage of clandestine migration to Europe – in particular, that of young people who took to the skiffs of fortune to cross the straits of Gibraltar, risking their lives – and on the other the increasingly noticeable levels of participation in religiously motivated political mobilization.

If it is necessary to examine these two phenomena and their sociological motivations very carefully, let us simply underline that the one as much as the other is the object in the Kingdom of the same kind of – strongly debatable – dominant explanation that puts the "social state" and its (under-)performance in the spotlight. The fight against emigration (clearly subject to international and particularly European pressure) takes the form not only of security measures in the form of border controls but also of establishing social protection networks that identify likely candidates for departure on a local basis. Islamic political mobilization has been ostensibly expressed, for example, by the results recorded by the Justice and Development Party in the last local and parliamentary elections, and by the speeches of unofficial organizations, such as the Justice and Charity Association (*al-'Adl wa'l-ihsan*).[76] Without any direct link, other, more violent, political forms of action have mobilized Islamic references in recent years, like the attacks carried out at Casablanca in May 2003. Certain hasty analyses connect extreme poverty, social malintegration and Islamic engagement. The public authorities, like the majority of the Moroccan media, explain this sort of action in terms of the instrumentalization of social exclusion associated with acts of charity and mutual help in disadvantaged areas.

Of course, radical engagement or engagement behind populist ideologies does not necessarily directly correlate to socio-economic data.[77] The equation "Islamist mobilisation equals the expression of social misery" requires some nuancing.[78] In the shantytowns of Casablanca, political mobilization is far from being reduced to the Islamic option and even less to the passage to violence.[79] But one must conclude that it is a dominant explanation for the reorientation of public measures of social risk management.

In this context, new political methods of taking charge of social issues emerge. As often in developing countries, the under-performance of public measures to ensure real and tangible social security for all citizens encourages the return of private, public or mixed charity. Alongside the strengthening of social rights, public welfare, unfortunately presented as harmful and secondary by neo-classic theory, is strengthened in new ways, opening new spaces of intervention for the state.

2.3 Co-managing social risks

The creation of quasi-public institutions which are not subject to parliamentary control and involvement with the world of associations or, to a lesser extent, with that of "local communities", like the failure of partisan governments and ministers to follow through the reforms they instigate, has led to the formation of public arenas for the treatment of social policies characterized by their apparent depoliticization, their sectorization and a heightened recourse to discharge.

In the area of the fight against exclusion and poverty, recourse has been had to welfare and solidarity, ad hoc and private, supported by the development of local or international associations, and to sponsorship or private financing. As regards the remarkable development of associations with economic or social vocation, some are of the opinion that "the decline of the provider state and the progress of liberal economic ideology have been accompanied by a rehabilitation of the notion of profit, a new eulogy of private initiative and a re-evaluation of the company", which has been particularly important in the creation of associations giving help to micro-enterprises.[80] In this arena, the initiative has not always come from the public authorities. In several cases, reconstitutions of public action have been fed by effervescent associative activity, which such action encouraged to develop and sought to capture, as is indicated by the adoption of a new law on associations in 2002. If certain of its provisions were judged positive by the world of associations, others provoked reservations or even mobilizations within this dense fabric of organizations: the text was "liberal" as far as the exercise of the freedom of association was concerned. Nevertheless, the Minister of the Interior remained the organ of government responsible for the regulation and supervision of associations. Above all, "foreign financing" and "political" activities could be heavily sanctioned, which "placed the associative movement in a situation of provisional freedom and under constant threat of sanction and dissolution".[81]

The metamorphoses of public action have sometimes found fertile ground of a particular sort in the vagaries of the "enlightened entrepreneurs", a collection of individuals or groups who, modernizing the classic practices of notables, have taken the floor and moved to action in the public arena with more or less elitist and political motives.[82]

Foundations giving help in the form of microcredit[83] have developed at the interface of classic forms of sponsorship, social development and the promotion of the entrepreneurial spirit. If some such foundations have clearly been "private", others have been much more closely tied to political and public institutions. The Zakoura Foundation, the *Banque Populaire* Foundation and the *al-Amana* ("insurance") Association have been supported by Moroccan banks, the Hassan II Fund and numerous international development agencies. In 1999, a new law gave a boost to microcredit associations, framed their development and gave them an institutional dimension. These are active and effective bodies, counting thousands of lenders among their number. Their development, at the intersection of institutions and public and private initiatives, shows how new niches of public action develop where hybrid forms of management of social development are used.

The metamorphoses of government in this domain are articulated around two main fault-lines: on the one hand, a seizing of private, individual and associative activities to discharge itself not only of social mechanisms but also of social responsibilities; on the other, new methods of control, in this case less through constraint than through centralization of resources. If social policies are increasingly co-managed on the basis of partnership, it is by means of a capture and redistribution by the central administration of private or international resources. The state, whose budget is contracting, disposes of external capital to redeploy its social action: the public authorities try to position themselves on the chessboard of social policies as coordinators of the action of the associative fabric which has developed as a new privileged and credible recipient of international development aid.

Together with the development of microcredit, this phenomenon has been particularly visible in the most recent reorientations of social welfare policies. The announcement by King Muhammad VI in May 2005, two years after the attacks at Casablanca, of the NIHD constituted a key point in these adjustments. No fundamental reform of employment policy, no change in the chosen macro-economic model – it was a question instead of treating, by means essentially of housing policies and policies of encouragement for microcredit, the problems of "poverty", "social exclusion" and "insecurity".

The World Bank began to offer technical and financial assistance to the NIHD from September 2005 onwards. Its proposed objectives were extremely ambitious and grouped around three priorities financed from the budget and also from redistribution of international development aid: "strengthening the fight against poverty in rural areas", "reducing social exclusion in urban areas" and "stepping up the fight against precarious living conditions".

The first institutions established in the framework of the NIDH were created "top down" and supported by decentralized administrations of the Ministry of the Interior. Celebrated in the media, glorified by the royal seal and reported very ambitiously, the NIDH signals a reorientation of public action with respect to Moroccan social security. The initiative is still in its infancy, but one can already discern certain elements. Its function is to centralize and coordinate action. In this respect, it is an extension of the creation of several institutions in recent years, namely the Agency for Social Development of 1999 and the Ministry of Social Development, Family and Solidarity of 2004. Above all, the NIDH follows on from the creation of two beacon institutions of the reign of Muhammad V: the Muhammad V Solidarity Foundation and the Hassan II Fund for Economic and Social Development.

The Muhammad V Foundation and the Hassan II Fund were inaugurated amid great celebrations at the end of the 1990s. They are hybrid structures directed by advisers close to the King and by bank managers, private and public positions. They are financed through exceptional channels, making use, more precisely, of an exclusive method of management of funds of often public origin. This is particularly so in the case of the Hassan II Fund, which benefited from a significant part of the concession of the second GSM licence in 2001. These two bodies, the spearhead of the "social monarchy", have not so far been subject to any governmental or parliamentary control or any other similar control, and function essentially in a discretionary manner under the royal eye. Nevertheless, they have been gradually integrated within the public institutions, for example by the transformation of the Hassan II Fund into a public body in December 2001. Their status, between public and private, is ambiguous. Their field of action is not regulated by law, nor by a relationship with citizens, as if one was trying to define and supply services to the "needy" without giving them rights over the state in return.

As is the case with the 26/26 Fund in Tunisia, the institutionalization of the Muhammad V Foundation, the Hassan II Fund and the NIDH has had a populist function, namely to show that social questions are on the public agenda and that the Palace, as the principal promoter of such questions, is involved as leader in the affair, although at the same time the direct financial resources of the state are being reduced. Their titles themselves confirm the implicit recognition of collective problems sufficiently wide for each person to see himself in them: "human development", "economic and social development", "solidarity". The multi-sectoral character of the NIDH has reinforced this feeling. The machinery of these Moroccan social institutions is clearly less well oiled than that of the Tunisian 26/26 Fund, at least in its repressive and coercive aspect.[84] Indeed, the solidarity campaigns of the Muhammad V Foundation have been based on collective popular participation and on an appeal to national solidarity in which each citizen can play their part and show their support for the programme. Unlike what could be observed in relation, for example, to the obligatory subscriptions for the construction of the Hassan II mosque in Casablanca,[85] in this case the collection of funds have not taken place by means of a systematic and "obligatory gift" by all companies. The resources of these institutions do not rest on a disguised and subjugated system of taxation, but rather on the capture of public goods and international aid.

Whatever the case might be, since their creation, the Muhammad V Foundation and the Hassan II Fund, presented as "crisis authorities" created in the name of national solidarity to confront growing social insecurity, have acted by regularizing and placing on contractual terms their partnerships with associations and big private groups. The Muhammad V Foundation, like the Agency for Social Development, is managed by mixed administrative councils bringing together representatives of the public administration and an adviser to the King, as well as representatives of the private and associative sectors.[86] As far as the operation of the NIDH itself is concerned, it is based on the principle of decentralized partnership with the economic and associative sectors.

Not only do these recent institutions render private activities public, but they institutionalize those activities and regularize them in a mechanism of action which is alternative to that of the representative political institutions. It would evidently be necessary to bottom out the analysis of each of these new mechanisms, their methods of financing and logics of redistribution. They give birth to new forms of state interventionism in domains where one generally speaks, conversely, of its disengagement. It is not a question of overstating the competences and resources of public power, but of showing that, behind the reforms, the Moroccan public authorities are redeploying economic and social institutions by having recourse to the private and by capturing national and international resources directed towards development.

Without being anachronistic, certain parallels could be drawn with the "social intervention" in the Europe of the Industrial Revolution. This constituted to a great extent a paradoxical solution found by "bourgeois" legislators to contain the political pressure of the masses, confront the risk of revolution and silence workers' claims in France, for example.[87] The quest for social peace becomes a priority for the public authorities.

In the developing "partnerships" between public authorities and private actors, the discussion of the modalities of help for the least protected seems to become situated in a depoliticized context. This does not mean either that it is not political, or that the state is detaching itself from it: quite the contrary. In this sense, the privatization of public action consists in redistributing responsibilities, in redrawing the boundaries of what belongs to the public and what to the private, and finally in transforming the modes of regulation of social risk. The public authorities find other instruments to exercise their authority and control the basic mechanisms of the reconstitution of Moroccan capitalism. A range of actors, having flexible relations with the political and with the administration, find niches for their aspirations – their appetite for power, their desire for action or, in certain cases, their search for social recognition.

3. From Class Conflict to Social Dialogue: Reconstitution of Professional Relations

The metamorphoses of Moroccan capitalism have also been the theatre of important changes in unionism and workers' institutions. The expressing "of a concern about the ability to maintain the cohesion of a society", to borrow the phrase of Castel,[88] and the conviction that the forms which the working class takes cannot ensure the social integration of the great majority of the population, had already been formulated during the colonial period, when they were closely associated with the nationalist movement. In the developmental period, they were rather overwhelmed by the construction of the independent state. With neo-liberalism, they have been exacerbated in several areas.

Wage relations have become more flexible, been individualized and protect workers less and less. The "social worlds of business"[89] have been put to the test of liberalization, privatizations and increasingly savage forms of capitalism. As if by a balancing effect, this has been translated, on the stage of professional relations and business policy, into the precarious but lasting establishment of new institutions of regulation of the labour market. At the end of the 1990s, novel structures of tripartite negotiation – workers' unions, public authorities and employers – were organized which inaugurated a mode of political management of wage policies that openly broke with the tradition of direct face-to-face confrontation between workers' unions and the employer state.[90] The emergence of such structures of social dialogue is evidence less of an effective pacification of the business world than of a political will to pacify it by means of instruments that have shown their worth elsewhere.

Morocco presents an interesting observation-post in this respect as well. As a result simultaneously of its own historical trajectory – particularly the history of its unionism, which is pluralist and political – and of the particularities of the emerging social configuration, the routes which wage-related and professional negotiations have taken against this background are, if not atypical, at least remarkable.

The triangulation of social negotiations consisted in the entry of the employers' class, specifically the CGEM, then in 2003 of the Chambers of Commerce and Industry, as an institutionalized and normal "partner". Indeed, the GCEM had already been associated with social discussions in the past, but in the context of discussions between the public authorities and the workers' unions. From 1996 onwards, separate consultation authorities established the spheres of influence of the social "partners" and the public authorities, who have sought the role of arbiter of interests at stake (particularly the Minister of the Interior and then the Prime Minister). Other than the assumption of the participation of employers in business policy, this appears to me to have two important consequences in terms of public policy and the restructuring of the powers of the state: firstly, in a context of aggravation of social contradictions and rapid transformation of the labour market, the wage discussion is removed from the political arena and relegated to the business world. Secondly, the recognition of this third social "partner"/"opponent", which is based on the voluntary promotion of a pacified model of social relations, has presided over an important legislative output in terms of labour law. The adoption after several decades of blockage of a new labour code in 2003 and a law on compulsory sickness insurance are the most striking examples of this.[91]

The mode of social representation sketched out in these reforms attests to at least two dynamics: on the one hand, it has strengthened the formation of the interest group of "entrepreneurs", who are put to their collective responsibilities and summoned, finally, to play a role in a co-management of economic and social policies; on the other, it has formed part of the search for mechanisms of neutralization, depoliticization or even "disciplining" of wage conflicts. In other words, if it politicizes the employers' class by accelerating the assertion of a legitimate political and social identity thereof in wage-related transactions, it distances the treatment of social conflicts from strictly political arenas towards "spheres of public non-decision", spheres "through which one directs the protagonists towards private initiative or negotiation".[92] In the case in hand, this does not indicate that there has not been any public policy in the matter, but rather that the public authorities have diverted workers' claims, directly addressed to them, towards badly placed market institutions. Whatever the twists and turns of the "social dialogue" might be (a social dialogue that reeks more sometimes of a collective fiction to which few adhere, or even of propaganda, than of the real transformation of ad hoc practices of the treatment of conflicts), workers' unions and employers have acquired in the space of a few years a normative power and a certain autonomy solidly flanked by the executive instigator and arbiter.

The speedy passage from the dominant paradigm of "class conflict" to that of "social dialogue" in the name of the "economic growth", "securitization" and "pacification" of society should not mislead. It represents less the transformation of social cleavages or the attenuation of conflicts inherent in capitalism than a change in the political vision of the possible and the thinkable. The mechanisms favoured for the regulation of wage conflicts borrow more readily from neo-corporatist representations of the social world. This change in regime, sensitive to the business environment, is organized around the promotion of "privatized" procedures and transactions. "Rather than isolating public action from private initiative",[93] on the contrary it unites and mixes them. The political mechanisms which emerge are based on a political engineering of social regulation according to which the administration wishes to arbitrate and transfers social demands and tensions to third parties, particularly industry leaders, who are identified as legitimate social forces.

4. Conclusion

This chapter has tried to explore the transformations of the economic capabilities of the Moroccan state in the face of the rapid liberalization of its economy. The changes which its capitalism has undergone denote less a return of the market and a "retreat of the state"[94] than a diversification and redeployment of public power by means of new techniques and modalities of the government of economic activity.

The analysis of the different aspects of reform and privatization shows in particular that if the sun of the state bourgeoisie is indeed "setting", it is in the effects of contexts and generation rather than in the morphology of the social strictly speaking. What has changed? The social structures of the *ancien régime* have not been weakened by the structural adjustment but have showed themselves capable of adjustment and, in certain areas, have consolidated themselves. The heirs of the great families of the Souss region and of the city of Fez have been able to modernize their activities. Returning from studies abroad in Europe and increasingly in the United States, they are the "golden boys" of a rapidly evolving capitalism who do not hide their success. Their sources of accumulation diversify: alongside inheritance and rentier proximity *vis-à-vis* the administration, new opportunities open up for them, as well as new risks, as customs protection crumbles, international competition becomes stiffer and the state keeps hold of a certain arbitrage to rein in or encourage the affairs of this or that person. Alongside their triumphant success, the vast fabric of small and medium-sized enterprises (SMEs) has also had to adapt, not without difficulty, in the spaces which have been restructured to a greater or lesser extent in the face of increasingly international competition.

Rather than fall apart, the engineering of power has adjusted to the new constraints and opportunities. This does not mean that nothing has changed. We have seen on the contrary that a variety of shifts have taken place and that the normative system has evolved. At the end of the reign of Hassan II, the ministries opened their doors to the parties of historical opposition in a sort of consensual reconciliation. The tools of public action have been transformed, although in the end the Palace continues to exercise little-shared authority, while the business world in particular has increasing control over the instruments of fabrication of public goods. The "establishment of original mechanisms whose aim is to regulate the behaviour of individuals and to make new modes of constitution of private property and inequality possible" has pushed the political economy of the Kingdom towards a mode of "indirect private government".[95] Alliances for profit are made and undone. As far as the political scene is concerned, it has pluralized, which does not necessarily indicate that the regime has become more pluralist. If according to the liberal ideal the state has less legitimacy in economic policy, the control exercised by the administration and the country's political leaders has changed without their losing their power of influence or coercion over the market.

In this sense, social and economic policies in Morocco in the 2000s have a clear political significance, and their implementation cannot be reduced to questions of technical choice. The new institutions which have seen the light of day, explicitly straddling the "public" and the "private", are in part "apolitical means of intermediation between the interests at stake, with the principal effect of reinforcing the strictly political prerogatives of final arbitrage, which is the principal means of control of the Moroccan monarchy".[96] Under the cover of managerial realism or economic efficiency, recourse to business — virtual or real as the case may be — has served to marginalize political institutions and to de-ideologize the question.

To finish with, one could also reflect with caution on how the hypothesis of a "third way" could be heuristically interesting for an understanding of the modes of regulation in play in the reform of economic policies by means of "less state". Clearly, there is no question in this case of glimpsing the beginnings of a social democracy, dirigiste or liberal, between the contemporary transformations of capitalism, as Giddens was able to do in other contexts.[97] Far from it. However, one can see in the case of Morocco that the reconstitutions of public action have been based on a model which goes down tracks close to those cleared by the British sociologist. This does not, of course, prejudge the local result of the reforms, but one must conclude that the privileged mode of political regulation values the individual who organizes himself and builds up his own capital but entrusts to institutions the task of guaranteeing the quality of services by evaluating and measuring them and even by regulating them and arbitrating over them. Examination of recent social security policies in Morocco shows in particular a recourse to new tools and paradigms of action, whether it be in a localized manner or at national or even international level: contractualization versus institutionalization; universalization/generalization versus individualization/commercialization; insurance versus assistance; sectorization versus desectorization of public action. Original spheres of public action have been established for example in terms of wage negotiations, as the "social partners" became producers of norms in the context of the elaboration and adoption of a new labour code in 2003, or even in terms of social policies, as the beginnings of a right to welfare have emerged.

NOTES

1. This chapter was translated from French by David Ashton.
2. Hibou (2006) sets out a subtle and well-documented analysis of the political economy of repression in Tunisia, the economic "good student".
3. Williamson 1990.
4. Rist 2001.
5. This model is based on the principles of the internal market as driver of growth and the "Taylorist" organization of work in a business in return for salaries and growth in productivity (El-Aoufi 1998 and 2000).
6. For a discussion of the recent literature on this subject, cf. Catusse 2006.
7. Morocco has 75 per cent of the world's phosphate reserves and the OCP holds a position as leader in the international market in phosphate fertilizers. In 1973, following the unilateral decision by Morocco to increase the price of phosphate by 200 per cent, prices rocketed, ensuring for the Kingdom a substantial profit throughout the 1970s. But the price of phosphate was lower during the 1980s, at the same time as the second petrol shock of 1979 weighed heavily on the commercial balance of the country.
8. Brand 2006.
9. On fiscal policies in the Arab world, cf. Heydemann 2004 and in particular the excellent study by Cammett (2004) of the Moroccan textile sector.
10. Kienle 2000.
11. Signoles 2006.
12. Hibou 1999.
13. Hibou 1998.
14. Bafoil 2006, p. 135.
15. For a case study of the "antipolitics machine", see Ferguson 1990.
16. In the sense in which Sainsaulieu (1990) develops this metaphor in the case of France: it is a question, for this business sociologist, of showing how far the society in which a company operates influences its organization, life and even culture.
17. Bayart 1994.
18. Between 1984 and 1985, public sector recruitment fell by 80 per cent (Akesbi 2003). The slowing was maintained, at a less extreme pace, in the following years.
19. Outstanding external debt rose from 12.9 per cent in 1974 to 43.8 per cent in 1982. Cf. Kingdom of Morocco 2006.

20 Peet 2003.
21 This has been more closely studied in the case of Tunisia, where the expression has had a very similar fate: see Camau 1997; Cassarino 1999.
22 Ministère des Finances et des Privatisations (n.d.).
23 El-Malki 1989, p. 213.
24 El-Malki *et al.* 1990, p. 291.
25 Laïdi 1993.
26 Ministère de l'Economie et des Finances 1995.
27 Debt service as a percentage of GDP and exports rose between 1990 and 1999 (ATTAC Maroc 2005). In 2006, debt service remained high insofar as the Annual Report of the Moroccan Central Bank underlined that outstanding external debt represented 21 per cent of the entire debt of the country and 15.1 per cent of GDP. The total outstanding direct public debt of Morocco reached 327,400 million dirham and increased by 11.3 per cent, bringing the rate of debt to 71.6 per cent of GDP.
28 ATTAC Maroc 2005.
29 Haut Commissariat au Plan 2007.
30 According to the Direction de la statistique (2003), the contribution of the informal non-agricultural sector to GDP is 17 per cent.
31 El-Aoufi *et al.* 2005/2006.
32 World Bank 1999, p. 2.
33 Ibid.
34 Dillman 2001, p. 202.
35 Mouline 2005, p. 54, shows that "the structural adjustment plan 1982–92 and the reforms carried out afterwards did not allow for a considerable decrease in public expenditure in terms of percentage of GDP. This ratio, which was 29.9 per cent during the 1970s, was brought to 26.2 per cent during the 1990s and only to 28.7 per cent during the period 2000–2".
36 [Eds' note:] Cf. privatization policies in Egypt and Lebanon in Wurzel and Nahas' chapters in this book.
37 Catusse 2007.
38 Boltanski 1979, p. 75.
39 Bouachik 1993.
40 Bafoil 2006, p. 135.
41 Kernen (2004) demonstrates the same thing as regards the policies of privatizations in the industrial town of Shenyang in China.
42 Sadowski 1991.
43 Stark 1996.
44 For further details of later operations, see Catusse 2007.
45 Diouri 1992, p. 178.
46 Saïd Saadi 2006.
47 Ibid.
48 There are the cases, for example, in the petrol sector of assignments by direct allocation from *Shell Maroc* to Shell Petroleum International, from the *Compagnie Marocaine des hydrocarbures* (CMH) to Hogespar, from Dragon-Gaz to Dragonifa, from *Mobil Maroc* to Mobil Petroleum Corporation, and from *Total Maroc* to *Total outre mer*. One can also cite the purchase of companies, such as that of Sochepress, a press distribution company, by its own general manager from the time when it was public. The same type of case can be found in the hotel industry.

49 Salah, "La privatisation fait tomber la marocanisation", *L'Économiste*, February 1993.
50 Hibou *et al.* 2002, pp. 112–13.
51 Ibid.
52 Leca 1990.
53 Cammett 2004, p. 246.
54 Catusse *et al.* 2005.
55 Zaki 2005.
56 Allain Mansouri 2005.
57 On this point see Catusse 2005.
58 Destremau 2004.
59 This movement was studied first by Bennani-Chraïbi (1995) and then by Emperador Badimon (2005). Organized since 1991 and always active despite the intermittent but punctual waves of recruitment of its militants by the public administration (in particular in the framework of the national programme of integrations of unemployed graduates), the movement is remarkable for its longevity and its relative political independence.
60 Le Saout *et al.* 1999.
61 Camau *et al.* 2003, p. 188.
62 Vairel 2005.
63 Cheynis 2005.
64 According to the United Nations Development Programme (UNDP) in 2004, net receipts of FDI as a percentage of GDP went from 0.6 per cent in 1990 to 1.2 per cent in 2002 in Morocco and from 0.6 per cent to 3.8 per cent in Tunisia. They were 1.9 per cent of GDP in Algeria (UNDP 2006).
65 Law 65/99, adopted in 2003.
66 Law 18/01, adopted in 2001 and revised in 2003.
67 Law 65/00, which entered into force in 2005.
68 Roussillon 1996, p. 18.
69 UNDP 2006.
70 Mouline 2005.
71 Direction de la Statistique 2000.
72 UNDP 2003.
73 Didry 2001, p. 236.
74 Hirschman 1991.
75 Castel 1995.
76 Tozy 1999.
77 Traïni 2003.
78 Burgat 2005.
79 Zaki 2005.
80 Denoeux 2002, p. 37.
81 Akesbi, "La loi sur les associations: la copie est à refaire", *Le Journal*, 18–24 January 2003.
82 Catusse 2007.
83 Among others the *al-Amana* Association, the *Banque Populaire* Foundation, the Zakoura Foundation, the *Association marocaine d'appui à la petite et moyenne entreprise* (AMAPPE), etc.
84 Hibou 2006.
85 Cattedra 2001.

86 The King is the president of the Administrative Council of the Muhammad V Foundation and the Prime Minister is the president of the Administrative Council of the Agency for Social Development.
87 Donzelot 1994.
88 Castel 1995, p. 39.
89 Franckfort *et al.* 1995.
90 Menouni 1979; Catusse 2001.
91 Catusse 2005.
92 Offerlé 1994, p. 135.
93 Sgard 1997, p. 64.
94 In the sense for example of Strange, 1996.
95 Mbembe 1999, p. 103.
96 Ferrié *et al.* 2004, p. 63.
97 Giddens 2000.

Part III

Changing Patterns of Globalized Security

9

THE SECURITY SECTOR IN EGYPT: MANAGEMENT, COERCION AND EXTERNAL ALLIANCE UNDER THE DYNAMICS OF CHANGE[1]

Philippe Droz-Vincent

Introduction

The Arab regimes are in a process of adjustment to the dynamics of change. Two dimensions of this are examined in this book, namely the role of external actors and the changing structure of the state. Authoritarianism carries an image of rigidity and continuity by means of coercion. Yet the political, economic and security sectors (in the real world of politics, "border crossings" are numerous), are subject to heavy change. The security sector, acting as the ultimate recourse for a regime, is at the heart of the political equilibrium in many Arab polities. For historical reasons, it is primarily related in Egypt to the army, but the regime has evolved from a military-dominated regime to a "strong" civilianized state with a ramified security sector. The army has retained an essential role and security has gained a very broad meaning. The Egyptian security sector also relies on an external alliance with the United States in a model of "dependent security" that may pose risks for the regime. As change in Egypt is not predetermined and can be turbulent in other sectors, the importance of the security sector is increased. There are transitions within authoritarianism or translations of authoritarian rule that represent new ways of keeping control over a given polity. As cumulating processes of change are now reaching "a critical mass" in the Egyptian system, the security sector as an essential tool for holding together a polity subject to change remains the preferred shortcut solution for the regime.

1. The "Strong" State: Military Origins, Restructured Security Sector and Heightened National Security Concerns

The security sector is closely related to the structure of the state.[2] Any "modern" state contains in its functional ambit a supposedly "strong" security sector (the army and the police), buttressed by a discourse on national security priorities and acting as the ultimate tool for the enforcement of the "legitimate right" to the use of violence. Yet the security sector is not just an institutional (static) sector. It relates in more or less expansive ways to the course of "political development" in any given polity. Therefore we have "to bring the regime back in": the security sector in Egypt is related to the way the polity is subsumed within the state with the regime at its helm.[3]

1.1 The regime's military genealogy and the diminishing role of the army

To analyse the security sector in Egypt means assessing the place of the army in the Egyptian polity. The 1978 Camp David peace accords remain the backbone and fundamental context for Egyptian security policy. But Egypt has proclaimed the need to maintain a large and competitive military establishment and to pursue a "militarization" policy, i.e. the accumulation of a capacity for organized violence at times of peace. Egypt's armed forces have numbered between 420,000 and 450,000 since the end of the 1970s and are a real burden on the country's dwindling financial resources, with the defence budget on a slightly downward trend but still amounting to USD 2.7 billion annually, i.e. 4.5 to 4.7 per cent of Gross National Product (GNP).[4] The Middle East plays a key role in arms markets and Egypt, though handicapped by short resources, is trying to ensure continued access.[5] Egypt's indigenous arms industry, essential to bridging the technology gap (with Egyptian eyes turned to Israel), is the largest in the Arab world.

The military's position and self-image are closely related to its role in Egypt's political development.[6] The Egyptian military made an important contribution to Egyptian national unity and to the consolidation of the modern Egyptian state. The crucial place of the military sector was established in the war-prone 1950s. There is a kind of "path dependence" from this "praetorian era" that explains many subsequent developments.

Things have changed since, but the military has remained a key actor in the Egyptian polity and the Egyptian regime still views a strong military as its greatest asset. The Egyptian officer corps, where most officers were for a long time influenced in military academies by a generation of old-fashioned Arab nationalists, is sensitive to this genealogy. Officers portray themselves as professional actors at the service of the polity (they boast about their involvement in "national development", a vague term which does not have only economic connotations) and are deeply concerned about their role and position in society. The new generation, that came to the fore in the 1980s in a re-islamized Egyptian social context, has remained sensitive to nationalism (or a mix of Arab nationalism and Islamic feelings)[7] and to the army's "positive" role in state and society.

Yet the military in Egypt is no longer an actor undistinguishable from the state, as compared to the 1950s and 60s, when the officer was a modernizer, a nationalist and a ruler. There has been a "civilianization" of the state under President Mubarak. Military men no longer dominate the top positions in the Egyptian state (ministers, directors of public sector companies, high-level bureaucrats or governors, etc.), and the days have gone when a small clique of officers could seize power by mobilizing a few military units. The regime has increased its distance from the military establishment. The military has lost much of its direct clout over the Egyptian political system and has been "tamed" since Sadat strongly regained control of the armed forces (Mubarak, who comes directly from the armed forces, understands their psychology). Middle Eastern states are now huge Leviathans with large bureaucracies and differentiated security forces where the military is too weak and ineffective to control the whole state apparatus. It is rather the presidency that assumes full control in Egypt, with its own network of trusted individuals, security networks, "crony capitalists", the National Democratic Party's (NDP) high nomenklatura and the new technocrats promoted in the NDP by Gamal Mubarak. Although the Egyptian authoritarian regime suffers from "a crisis of legitimacy",[8] it has been able to secure more "legitimacy" than its potential competitors or opponents in the eyes of key social groups. The Egyptian regime has been able to (imperfectly) "institutionalize" itself, in contrast with states where the army remains the only effectively functioning institution (Pakistan). In this sense, we can say that the ascendancy to power (and limits thereon) of Gamal Mubarak represents a symbol of regime civilianization *à la égyptienne*. In 2005, Mubarak's surprise announcement that he would ask for amendment of Article 76 of the constitution to allow for multiple presidential candidates and to open up the presidency to competition, though without himself losing control over it, was an astute move to reinforce the cohesion of the "relevant elite" and to neutralize the military's reluctance to his son's candidacy.[9]

The regime's new-found stability can be explained to a significant degree by the restructured security sector. Paramilitary forces play an increasingly important role in Egypt. The Mubarak regime has maintained a division of labour between the military and the security/paramilitary forces (the Central Security Forces, established in 1977 and numbering between 300,000 and 400,000 personnel, which are part of the Ministry of the Interior). The paramilitary forces have been the regime's primary internal-security instrument for dealing with political demonstrations or social unrest and for leading the battle against Islamist militancy. The Ministry of the Interior and the increasingly powerful secret services (General Intelligence or *Mukhabarat*, attached to the president, State Security Investigations or *Mabahith Amn al-Dawla*, attached to the Ministry of the Interior) have gained a growing influence, as have a small special branch of the army, the Presidential Guard (the current Minister of Defence and army chief of staff both come from this special unit) and the Military Intelligence (attached to the Ministry of Defence). Within the so-called "paramilitary sector", the regime and its high-level "security bureaucrats" seem to make distinctions among units and services, in terms of reliability (effective repressive capacity) and hence equipment and missions assigned to them.

Contrary to all theories of the "weakening" of the state, the dangers of internal implosion have been resisted by the Mubarak regime with the help of the restructured security sector, whose resilience was tested in the 1980s and 90s. The Egyptian state waged an all-out war against Islamist militants (*al-Jama'a al-Islamiyya*). The fighting left 1,300 civilians or policemen dead and 15,000 to 20,000 Islamists in jail. The regime chose to rely primarily upon the security forces, gave free hand to them to combat Islamist groups (with massive arrests, generalized torture, etc.) and implemented amendments to the penal code and to the law on state security courts to combat terrorism by allowing the President to bypass the ordinary courts and refer terrorism suspects to any authority of his choosing, including military and specially constituted "emergency courts".[10] The Ministry of the Interior had direct command, under the supervision of the President, over counter-terrorism operations. The army often stepped in to assist the badly trained Central Security Forces. Hundreds of civilians were transferred to military courts with less legal protection. And whenever terrorist threats peaked, military top brass commissioned articles in Egyptian (Arabic) newspapers explaining their concern about stability in the country. Since the Islamist challenge has subsided, the restructured security sector has been instrumental in preserving the established pattern of containment and control that has sustained the political status quo in Egypt. Its resilience has allowed the regime to maintain its political domination and monopoly over power at small cost.

1.2 The military's residual role and the army's economic "spill over"
Nevertheless, the military remains an important component of the Egyptian authoritarian apparatus. The continued reliance of the regime on the armed forces mirrors the Mubarak regime's lack of accountability, which in turn increases the army's weight within the political system. The main strength of the military is not its own action within the political system, but the weaknesses and apathy of the civilian political system. The armed forces remain the last resort for the regime in times of need. The regime has called on the army in numerous situations when it was about to lose control, such as during the Islamist uprisings following the assassination of President Sadat in 1981 or the riots started by the badly paid Central Security Forces in 1986, or when the police proved unable to quell Islamist attacks in the 1990s, especially in Upper Egypt or at crucial moments when Islamist groups seemed able to strike at the top of the state apparatus. The military establishment has always answered positively to the President's requests. The difference between the military and civilian channels of influence is blurred at the top of the Egyptian state. The endeavours of the Egyptian regime are thus not so much geared towards "demilitarization" or pushing the military "back into the barracks", but rather towards the progressive (and cautious) "institutionalization" of the military apparatus within the authoritarian Egyptian state.[11] The trend of the disappearance of uniformed men from high posts is not in contradiction with the thorough integration of the military, or at least some high-ranking officers, in the formal and informal authoritarian

decision-making networks. We can call this process a "civilianization without retreat".

Armies behave differently in different institutional and hence political contexts or regimes. Years of interaction with the Mubarak regime have left their mark on the Egyptian armed forces, which are now characterized by over-centralized authority, hidden lines of command (i.e. the monitoring of military activities behind the scenes) and rivalries between different organizations of military and security/paramilitary services that keep each other in check. The presidential or royal palace is the centre of power. Promotions of military personnel are based on loyalty to the regime or at least passivity, rather than on field ability or skills. The top brass of the military is often enticed by material and immaterial benefits and has become an integral part of the regime's networks. Officers of lower rank keep a lower profile and are primarily concerned about their personal economic interests, while otherwise acting as docile yes-men who lack the will and/or capacity to take the initiative, preferring not to be identified as innovators and restricting themselves to the role of quiet modern technocrat and apolitical specialist in keeping with the military's self-image as a body of professional officers.

The army's institutional role in the Egyptian state is more restricted. It presents itself as an institution with an increasingly professional outlook. Officers have developed an emphasis on equipment, training and education (a high percentage of them hold university degrees). The reliance on conscription has dwindled (only one in two men on duty in the armed forces are conscripts; 80,000 conscripts are enlisted per year) and the Egyptian army is now characterized by professional officers. Corporatism and military privilege are the military's new features in relation to the state, varying in kind and size from the top brass to more junior officers, which is quite different from its interventionist outlook of the past, characterized by coups and military rule. Army officers are now a privileged group living in a kind of "military society", i.e. a closed social group living in seclusion from civilians in exclusive suburbs or residential areas, further distinguished by corporate privileges such as access to military-only facilities (schools, hospitals, clubs, leisure facilities, military shops, etc.), cheap housing, transportation facilities, easy access to low-interest credit, access to scarce consumer goods at cheap prices, better medical care and relatively higher salaries than employees in the civilian public sector (half of the average Egyptian household's budget goes to cover the cost of food, while the other half covers that of housing; public sector employees lost more than half of their purchasing power in the 1990s, which saw very high rates of inflation). The army's corporatism and privileges have protected the living standards of military personnel from the adverse effects of economic liberalization (*infitah*).

The corporate interests of the military mean that it is among the main beneficiaries of the authoritarian status quo and is wed to that status quo. The political quiescence of the military is not the product of its "(re-)professionalization" or of its return to an external mission (the defence of the country), but the result of its close relationship to the regime and the benefits it gains there from. The military as a whole continues to have access to a large share of scarce available resources, even at times of fluctuating national incomes. It has loosened its grip to some extent on the wealth of the Egyptian state and can no longer, as the Pakistani military still can, ensure a constant flow of resources for "high" strategic reasons. The Egyptian regime was forced to curb military expenditure in the 1990s when its capacity to engage in military spending came into conflict with financial constraints.[12] Nevertheless, relatively high levels of military expenditures have persisted, and the military remains a well-serviced, budget-hungry sector. The military has escaped austerity measures to a greater extent than other sectors of the Egyptian polity and has continued to escape accountability (there is no legislative oversight of the military budget and no monitoring of military industrial capacity).

The Egyptian army does not play its more proactive role at the centre of the political system but at the periphery, in areas of society where its political clout is important. The Egyptian army was increasingly involved in the 1980s and 90s in economic activities that extended beyond traditional perceptions of the military's role or the military's strictly corporate privileges, and were justified in the name of the necessary "self-sufficiency" of the Egyptian military or in the name of "national" help for the needy. The army has expanded its activities in the economic sphere (production of cement, fertilizers, spare parts, etc.) or has shifted the production of military firms to supply lucrative niches in the civilian market, to the chagrin of civil ministries who have no say in the matter. The assets of the military run into millions of Egyptian pounds with hardly any trace of accountability.[13] Some of the army's operations have created monopoly situations, are harmful for private sector operations and force private firms out of business due to its capacity to hide overheads, fudge other costs and bridge financial gaps. Statistics are not available, but the army may account for 15 to 20 per cent of Egyptian agricultural production. Land reclamation in the Sinai or the Western Desert province is another lucrative business for the army. The military knows how to make use of its comparative advantages such as the cheap manpower of its conscripts, its access to technology and highly qualified civilian engineers, its heavy equipment infrastructure, its privileges such as disguised subsidies, tax exemptions and absolute financial autonomy, its monopolistic right to produce goods of "strategic interest", and its sheer size, which enables it to alter market conditions and circumvent regulations. The army has become an economic entrepreneur of a different kind, knowing better than others how to play by and benefit from the intricate rules of the game of the reforming Egyptian economy. This is an accepted burden for the Egyptian state (the growth of a military economy is inconsistent with a privatized economy linked to globalization) and a way for the Egyptian regime to protect the army and reward the officer corps (generals and a limited number of middle- and lower-ranking officers) for their exceptional obedience toward the regime. Any successor to President Mubarak will have to service the military one way or another.

1.3 The regime's pervasive discourse on national security

The place of the restructured security sector in Egypt is backed or legitimized by a pervasive discourse on national security, sustained by an image of Egypt as an insecure "strong" nation-state. In sociological literature, the provision of security is said to be at the centre of the process of state-formation.[14] Egypt is a strong "nation-state" as compared to other Arab states of more recent origin, which are often considered to be artificial creations prone to internal fragmentation (Syria, Iraq, Saudi Arabia or Jordan). Security has nevertheless retained a specific and pervasive place in the vision of Egyptian decision-makers, as shown by the various issues of the "Arab Strategic Reports" published by the al-Ahram Strategic Center in Cairo. Threats are not so much actual as a range of potential challenges that are alleged to have a negative effect on the Egyptian internal, regional and international position in the unstable Middle Eastern region. Arab regimes have a great propensity for the "securitization" of many issues,[15] i.e. for presenting them not just as topics requiring public policies, but for constructing them as existential threats. And a deeply nationalist society, or at least a society endowed with a strong sense of "Egyptianism", can buy some of the arguments.

On the one hand, Egypt sees itself as a natural leader of the contemporary Arab world. In the past, Arab states showed a great propensity for regional projection in self-defined regional "missions", such as Arab nationalism, Arab unity, help to the Palestinian cause, etc. The current Egyptian "projection" is different from the flamboyant Arab nationalism of the Nasser years. Yet the ability to pursue an active foreign policy, or at least to get some diplomatic room for manoeuvre in the Middle East, which is equated with a desire to enhance the Egyptian position, is considered an essential strategic/security asset in Cairo. In this sense, the Egyptian military build-up should not be taken at face value as preparation for war in a region plagued by threats. The most symbolic aim is to keep Egyptian armed forces commensurate with those of Israel. This is not deterrence, or even conventional deterrence, something which Israel and the US would not allow. The maintenance of a potent Egyptian military is related in Cairo to Egypt's self-perception as a regional broker, and military capacities are seen as a way of enhancing the Egyptian diplomatic position.

The security discourse serves an important function for Arab regimes with obsessive concerns about making themselves secure within the state at the helm of the political system. The wide array of threats, alleged or real, in a volatile Middle East that are regularly evoked by Egyptian decision-makers ranges from foreign interference in the region, suspect Israeli behaviour, Iran's bid for power in the Middle East and threats by Sudan to the country's water supplies to Islamist plots in Egypt or elsewhere in the Middle East (plots which are alleged to originate in Sudan or Iran or in fears of Islamist waves in Algeria in the 1990s or Gaza in the 2000s)[16] and to a mounting "Shiite crescent/arc" emerging in the Arab world and contesting the status quo, as evidenced for example by the civil war in Iraq of 2005–6 or the war between *Hezbollah* and Israel of July 2006. The pervasive and vague discourse on Egyptian security commands full allegiance to the state and blurs the distinction between actual threats and security. Yet it is never just a one-sided game: for instance the abundance of violent regional conflicts reinforces the legitimacy of the regime's securitization policies and, hence, authoritarianism, but its inability to meet external threats may also become a liability in its relations with society.

On the other hand, Egyptian internal "weaknesses" are constructed as security challenges. Political violence has decreased steeply and no acts of armed violence by the followers of *al-Jama'a al-islamiyya* or *al-Jihad* took place in Egypt between the Luxor massacre of 1997 and 2004. Nevertheless, the Egyptian state has made great use of the myth of an Egyptian secular state besieged by violent Islamists and threatened by regional Islamist plots. The Egyptian regime has also used the new international security agenda to regain the upper hand by stressing its track record in fighting terrorism. The American "war on terror" has created parallels with the Egyptian regime's war against radical Islamists, as Egyptian officials have ironically alluded to, even if the loose American interpretation of terror has created rifts. A wave of bomb attacks on tourist destinations took place in October 2004 in Taba, in April 2005 in Cairo, in July 2005 in Sharm al-Sheikh and again in April 2006 in Dhahab (Sinai). The Egyptian government claimed that the Sinai terrorists were linked to *al-Qa'ida*, although this claim has not been substantiated by any "neutral" evidence. The discourse on national security, with its vague meaning, helps to shift the issue from the contestation of corrupt and inept authoritarian rule to one of radical challengers whose aim is to overthrow the regime. The blurring of the distinction between repressive missions and national security missions, and the equation of internal enemies and *al-Qa'ida*'s networks, justifies repressive moves.

The discourse on security has much wider significances. The Egyptian social fabric is in a process of gradual disintegration into ugliness, hypocrisy and cynicism amid growing sectarian tensions, for example between Copts and Muslims in the context of a reawakened Coptic question. There is growing social violence in Egyptian society (tribal vendettas in Upper Egypt, police brutality, political repression, etc.), and corruption has reached a massive scale. There is a growing sense of neglect in Egyptian society: the state has succeeded in its war against "terrorism" but has failed to protect the lives of its citizens. The hundreds of passengers burnt to death in a third-class train in Upper Egypt in February 2002 were a metaphor of the government of the Egyptian people by an incompetent and corrupt regime. The "retreat of the state" is not just physical – as evidenced, for example, by the privatization of parts of the state-run economy, the relinquishing of basic welfare state functions and the cessation of social services – but is also conceptual (a policy of neglect). The regime's answer has been a "security"-oriented one. The Egyptian regime has never addressed the ongoing internal challenges with adequate reforms, but has contained them within a "security order". Even the state's strong interference in the economy is justified in Egyptian public debate by reference to security concerns.

The Egyptian state's discourse on national security is related to the regime's authoritarian nature. It cultivates a "security atmosphere" in the country in perfect accordance with the regime's heavy and parallel reliance on emergency laws, censorship, control of the public space, preventive arrests against "terrorist cells" and massive police deployments. The regime's "authoritarian contract" is increasingly security-based, rather than distributive or ideological, as other sources of legitimacy erode. The Egyptian regime's main claim to power or legitimacy lies in its ability to maintain "stability" in the country. The flows of images coming from Iraq, Lebanon or the neighbouring Palestinian territories, engulfed in violence since 2000, has allowed the Egyptian regime to justify its model of rule. There is a strong tradition of managerial rule by the state bureaucracy in Egypt and a long history of corporatist political engineering on the part of the state. Political regimes in Egypt have made use of this "statist culture" or what al-Bishri describes as "the consent the Egyptians have expressed to be governed".[17] It is nowadays based on a "saviour model" justification, that of a Mubarak regime that "protects" the Egyptian polity from foreign and internal threats. This model took the place of the "realization model" used in the 1960s and 70s by numerous regimes with military roots, namely the enduring claim that they have achieved something for their people, for example by building roads, bridges, hospitals, schools, factories, etc. That model was gradually eroded by economic reforms and privatizations, the growth of the private sector, and globalization, which "hollowed out" the state apparatus and its hegemonic reach in Egyptian society. In Egypt, the so-called and enduring "Third World security predicament",[18] i.e. the concern of Third World state elites to accelerate the process of state-making and sustain their place in the system of states in the face of the heightened economic and political globalization that began in the 1990s, is therefore answered by a pervasive discourse on Egyptian national security and a strong process of "securitization" of state–society and regional relations, and not by political reforms or processes of adjustment to external and internal dynamics.

2. The "Dependent" State: The American–Egyptian Alliance and Security

Egypt is located in a Middle Eastern region plagued by threats of all kinds. The region has no security system comparable to that of Europe for instance, no stable balance of power (Israel has opposed any system of deterrence and has claimed a right to preserve all-out superiority on the ground) and even has no boundaries, because ideological influences and transnational mobilizations cross borders from Morocco to Pakistan. Identities such as Arab solidarity and Islamic attachments and actors have a strong potential for mobilization in Egypt in relation to specific issues such as Palestine and Iraq under embargo and then American occupation. The Middle East remains a very volatile security system (even the Maghreb is a more stable regional system, not just because of its own dynamics – the Union du Maghreb Arabe does not work – but because of its connection with Europe and especially Spain). The specific characteristics of "the Arab state" (if there is any such thing as a generic "Arab state", although there is a definite "view from inside the Arab world" on this)[19] are letting their weight be felt in Middle Eastern configurations. Arab states have a different genealogy and are vulnerable to specific types of conflict which are different from the geopolitical conflicts at the basis of classical national security definitions and which are connected to internal, religious, identity-related, political, cultural and socio-economic fragmentations. No wonder then that these features are at the core of Egyptian decision-makers' security concerns and explain their propensity to look for external alliances and resources.

2.1 Strategic American alliance

The Egyptian security sector has an essential external component, a close strategic American alliance. This alliance has been instrumental in the Egyptian regime's attempt to enhance its security. A qualification should be made: the Egyptian case is different from that of the Gulf states, chief among them Saudi Arabia. The latter have "outsourced" a large part of their security to the American hegemon.[20] Egypt shares with the US numerous strategic/security objectives: the settlement of the Israeli–Palestinian conflict, security in the Gulf, broader stability in the Middle East, the fight against extremism, and the country's economic and political development.[21] Egypt's role as America's partner in the Middle East has reinforced Egypt's standing as a regional leader. The Egyptian–American alliance has also brought concrete gains for Egypt's national interests. The alignment ("bandwagoning") with the United States has earned Egypt some of the largest US economic assistance aid in the world.[22] Egypt's economy is its biggest source of weakness.[23]

The Egyptian army is at the forefront of the Egyptian–American alliance. The United States is an essential part of Egypt's "militarization" policy. Egypt's close defence ties with the US have allowed it, despite its scarce internal resources, to bolster and have confidence in its huge conventional armed forces. US military aid doubles official Egyptian spending on defence, with US Foreign Military Financing (FMF) currently at USD 1.3 billion per year. US–Egyptian military cooperation has helped Egypt to modernize its armed forces and to retain its status as a significant military power, and has provided the Egyptian military with arms procurement and additional know-how (training, weapons maintenance, etc.). The United States has also provided training, military advice and expertise during the biannual "Bright Star" military exercises.[24]

The Egyptian officer corps and their American counterparts enjoy close relations. The Egyptian security services in the army watch the military-to-military exchanges closely and the top management of the Egyptian armed forces chooses carefully who benefits from them. Such relations have been essential to the transformation of the Egyptian army from an old-fashioned Soviet model to a modernized and technological force.[25] In modernizing its forces in accordance with the requirements of the "revolution in military affairs" and in transforming them into a Western-style military, the Egyptian military has tried to build up a "capital-intensive" force. In 1991, the Egyptian officer corps witnessed the quick defeat of the Iraqi army, which was viewed as the fourth most powerful army in the world, and once again witnessed the technological superiority of the American-British forces in 2003. There is indeed strong resentment within the Egyptian military of American unilateral interventionism in the Middle East and its close ties with Israel, and the

Egyptian–American alliance openly contradicts the Egyptian military's discourse on national pride and self-sufficiency. Yet in the eyes of Egyptian officers the US remains a reliable source of modern weaponry and substantial assistance for the modernization of the Egyptian armed forces.

2.2 Dependent security
"Dependent security" is the other facet of the US–Egyptian alliance. Egypt has gradually given up any claim to an autonomous security policy without openly acknowledging it. With Camp David I it lost the ability to define its security mission autonomously. The peace with Israel may be "a cold peace" just ahead of normalization, but Egyptian decision-makers have complied with many Israeli demands (the Egyptian–Israeli peace treaty lies at the core of the US–Egyptian alliance).[26] On numerous occasions in the 1980s and 90s, Egypt found itself in complete opposition to some Israeli (and American) positions that may have been construed as security threats in Cairo. Yet Egypt faithfully kept to the letter of the peace treaty. "Dependent" or "restrained" Egyptian security is best exemplified in the 1990s by the debate on the nuclear issue in the multilateral bodies established by the 1991 Madrid conference, in the 1995 Non-Proliferation Treaty "review and extension conference" and in the 2003 Chemical Weapons Convention. Egypt had every reason, in its national interest, to match Israel's nuclear weapon capability. Egypt fitted the profile of a country likely to pursue a nuclear weapons programme according to the so-called "security dilemmas" that were instrumental in initiating the Israeli, Pakistani and Iranian programmes, as well as the Iraqi programme of the 1980s. Yet Cairo reached the conclusion that such a programme would undermine its economic development, peace and stability, and above all its close ties with the US. Therefore Egyptian decision-makers accepted the "nuclear gap" with Israel.

The main rationale behind Egypt's position of "dependent security" lies in the symbolic and material value attached by Egyptian decision-makers to the American alliance. American support for Egypt is largely a function of Egypt's willingness to live in peace with Israel (something strongly resented on the Egyptian side). The alignment with Washington has helped to promote Egypt's vital interests (although Egypt has struggled to stay on an equal footing with Israel in terms of aid allocations, a very sensitive issue), but Egypt has failed to resist the involvement of Israel as a powerful third party in Egyptian–American strategic relations. Egypt has never managed to match Israel as a strategic ally for the United States. And Egypt has never hoped to counterbalance Israel's strategic relationship with the United States.

The security dynamics associated with an autonomous "regional level"[27] also receded in the 1990s as a consequence of the increasing American tutelage. Egypt's regional role was one of its main international assets in American eyes. This was a key calculus in Sadat's shift toward an American alliance in the 1970s. Egypt managed to benefit from its regional importance in American eyes to play a role in the Middle Eastern region as a security "agent". Egyptian diplomacy made use of the special characteristics of the region as an incomplete security system "to put Egypt in its right place" and to square them with the regime's security interests. After the removal of Iraq from the Arab concert in August 1990, the main Arab powers, Egypt, Syria and Saudi Arabia, engaged in "triangular" relationships to smooth security relations in the Arab world. Egypt might have dreamed of a greater role after it was able to play a key diplomatic role in forging a coalition between the United States and the Arab states. It was able to draw ahead somewhat of Israel in its relationship with the US in 1990/1, when Israel was behaving more as a burden for the US, and in return received economic benefits, debt relief, compensation for war-related losses and new loans from the International Monetary Fund. Yet, with the end of the Cold War, US diplomatic and military activities in the Middle East have increasingly focused on stability in the Gulf and "free access to oil", as well as on the peace process, leaving only a secondary role to Arab partners such as Egypt.

With the direct American sponsorship of the Oslo process and contrary to previous developments (the peace efforts by President George Bush and James Baker, the Madrid conference), Egypt's role has gone from that of a full partner to one of a useful facilitator (a meeting place, a mediator on specific matters) or a fireman unable to engage in the basic questions. As the peace process with its parallel paths (the peace treaty between Jordan and Israel, direct negotiations between Israel and the PLO, Syrian–Israeli talks) gained momentum in the 1990s, Egypt was sidelined. With its political weaknesses and ailing economy, Egypt was not the preferred choice in the "New [economic] Middle East". The derailment of the Oslo peace process illustrated by the failure of the Camp David II summit in 2000, and the subsequent eruption of the second *intifada*, did not restore any leverage to Egypt. It left Egyptian diplomacy in disarray. The ability of Egypt to swim in the troubled waters of the Arab world, an asset in building close relations with the US hegemon, decreased, as did its ability to find solutions to the Palestinian problem and to intercede between Syria and the US. American foreign policy also took a more assertive direction as the policy of "dual containment" of Iran and Iraq was carried out with military means in 1993. Latent tensions and disagreements and mutual scepticism were prevalent as the Egyptian government tried to rehabilitate Libya, Sudan and Iraq, considered by Washington as "rogue" or "backlash states" throughout the 1990s. The daylight between the positions of Cairo and Washington was never recognized. Furthermore, American ambition to reform the Middle East in accordance with a broad vision of international order became apparent, even if the Clinton administration remained cautious in practice. The rhetoric of democratization and pressure for economic reforms (the US–Egypt Partnership for Economic Growth or "Gore–Mubarak dialogue" of 1994) played an increasing part in American foreign policy in the Middle East.

The risks of dependent security
Egyptian "dependent security" has become a dangerous trap for the Mubarak regime. Authoritarian regimes have no problem with "public opinion", but are subject to a mix of national mobilization and transnational influences in the so-called "Arab street". The ruling elite is under strong scrutiny from Egyptian society, even if the channels of influence are not the accountability mechanisms seen in democratic polities, especially from intellectuals who profess to speak on behalf of the "Egyptian street" and who deeply resent "the selling of Egyptian basic interests" for other considerations. The Egyptian regime has been trying to square the circle by using flamboyant rhetoric and to appeal to Egypt's strong sense of self-esteem, and has invoked external conspiracies. It has been forced to a cautious alignment with US positions and has always resisted overt "subcontracting" for the US (i.e. carrying out US missions in return for political, symbolic or economic support). Security may be the preserve of an authoritarian regime, but too close an association with the US is leading to a weakening of the regime by fuelling a heightened debate in the Egyptian public space. And the volatility of the Middle

Eastern system increasingly weighs on regimes that no longer claim a broad political project which can "saturate" their public space. The adverse conceptions of Middle East security that pervade Arab and Muslim societies (Arab security, Muslim security, Mediterranean security, etc., along with Western definitions of security) are colliding and adding internal stress.

Egyptians resent the fact that American support for Egypt is largely a function of Egypt's willingness to live in peace with Israel. The idea of not having peace "at the expense of Egypt" in the 1980s is widespread in the Egyptian public sphere. In the debate on nuclear weapons in the 1990s, criticism was levelled against Egyptian decision-makers for having given up the nuclear option and forfeited an important source of "security leverage" for Egypt. The failure of the Camp David II negotiations and the start of the second *intifada* opened the way to a dangerous distancing between the official position of the Egyptian government and the mobilization of the "Egyptian street" (exemplified by the consumer boycott against US and Israeli products) at a time when violent Israeli retaliation was broadcast live by new Arab satellite media such as *al-Jazeera*, which broke the state's information monopoly in Egypt. A new generation of Islamist militants, together with intellectuals and social activists, has been instrumental in working out in the public sphere new themes such as "Egyptian sovereignty", by which they mean independence from the US. Fear of a loss of control over its destiny (Egypt possesses a strong sense of destiny) and resentment of the strong constraints faced by Egypt are aired in the Egyptian public debate, either implicitly (Egypt needs the economic and military assistance that the US alone can provide, yet it resents being treated like a small client by an American side that seems insensitive to local perceptions) or directly (especially in political opposition circles by Islamists who denounce "the colonization of Egypt").

Strains have deepened in the post-September 11 era with the new "offensive" American interventionism in the Middle East (the "Bush revolution" in foreign policy). Egypt declared its opposition to war against Iraq and to regime change by foreign diktat, a radically new approach for a country that in the recent past stood firmly behind the American projects in the Middle East. Yet Egypt remained committed to its strategic relationship with the United States and provided the American armed forces with discrete essential assistance and logistics in 2003. Egypt did not buy the new American agenda (the fight against a new "global enemy", i.e. terrorism): the Egyptian regime might have followed the US on "soft security issues" (fighting Islamist uprisings, securing transnational flows, etc.),[28] but the substitution of a new global agenda that appeared to be a political means of justifying US primacy created strains between the US/Western and Egyptian/Middle Eastern security agendas. Anti-American and anti-Israeli sentiment (America and Israel being seen as one) have skyrocketed in Egyptian society and found new fuel with the Bush administration's unqualified acceptance of Israel's interpretation of its own "war against (Palestinian) terror". The gap between regime and society has widened. In 2000/2001 the government subdued demonstrations in support of the second *intifada* with an overwhelming security presence. But the regime showed growing tolerance for public demonstrations in January, February and March 2003, a clear sign of its need to let public anger express itself. The National Democratic Party staged its own demonstration to stay in line with public opinion, and the regime coordinated with the Muslim Brothers to channel the anti-war movement into peaceful demonstration. The Iraq war sparked off a lively debate regarding the regime's ability to promote national interests, and Egyptian intellectuals of various political hues (such as Muhammad Hassanein Haykal or Tariq al-Bishri) denounced "Egypt's withdrawal from history", i.e. Egypt's marginal positioning in the region, its subservience to US interests and its inability to chart an independent course or even a coherent foreign policy, with the controversies reverberating in parliament. The Egyptian–American relationship has never relied on broad-based public support and has always been an elite bargain. Yet after September 11, negative feelings have openly surfaced. Egypt's strategic relationship with the United States has remained the primary determinant of Egyptian regional policy, but Egypt's "security dependence" has also become a hotly debated topic and a liability for the regime.

3. The Difficulty of Adjusting to Change: The "Security State" or the Role of the Security Sector in Egypt's Neo-authoritarianism

Longevity promoted by a "strong state" buttressed by an external (though "dependent") alliance is not synonymous with stability. The Arab states are experiencing changes under the effects of economic and political globalization. Authoritarianism remains deeply entrenched in the Arab world. Yet the huge increase in cross-border flows of capital, people, technologies – including new information technologies and ideas – is impacting on the ability of regimes to manage their polities and maintain their monopolies. Creating fear and political apathy and demobilization in society is essential for authoritarian regimes. Yet their "management" or "statist" tradition (notwithstanding the debate on the genealogy of the "Arab" state in the twentieth century as between an "Arab realm" and an "Islamic *umma*") faces increasing challenges. Hence regimes are forced to adapt and to shift to new forms of control. The Arab authoritarian state is not "retreating" but is repositioning itself, replacing one form of control with others in a kind of translation of authoritarianism.[29]

3.1 The "security state" or the "brutalization" of politics as a shortcut solution

Regimes have been forced into economic reform (marketization and privatization) and political opening. They are struggling to avoid losing control over the pace of change. Political opening made under pressure has left the dominant party struggling to maintain its dominance in a pluralized public sphere, and privatization has left the state with a majority shareholding in a nationally private sector. The Egyptian regime is able to counter-react so as to rein some groups back and to jolt others by setting the rules of the game to benefit those in power and protect its own position. The Egyptian economy is more pluralistic than in the 1970s or 80s in that there is a greater number of economic interests. Yet the rate of change has been mitigated by the political logic that underlies the management of economic change. The same holds true for the political sphere. The press sector has gained a degree of freedom but the opposition press circulation is not broad. Social sectors that were not regarded by the regime as the subject of a national agenda have gained increasing autonomy (many grassroots activities fitted into the regime's agenda because they alleviated the suffering of the parts of society that were abandoned by a "hollowed" state). Many societal actors (Islamist groups or non-governmental organizations, NGOs) are circumventing the state and its regulations in social or cultural activities and are challenging the authoritarian cadre. The Egyptian regime has counter-reacted with a creeping "authoritarian functionalism" that hinders the emergence of autonomous organizations (opposition parties, workers' unions, professional associations, NGOs, human rights groups, etc.) with restrictive laws. Yet the regime has been less and less successful in its containment policy designed to ensure that the system of power remains unchanged, and relies increasingly on the security sector as a shortcut solution in the newly "turbulent polity".

Despite the end of the war against Islamist groups of the 1990s, rampant repression, differentiated and no longer an all-out war against an "identified enemy", has persisted. The legacy of the 1990s has been a state apparatus whose brutality has become routine practice, or what is called in Egypt a "security state". The security sector has taken a new "regulative" role in the containment of political and societal activities and as the ultimate defender of the regime. The prolonged state of emergency has criminalized public life. The 1992 anti-terror law (law no. 97) has been used to arrest and prosecute not only those accused of committing violence but also those affiliated to the Muslim Brotherhood. The state security courts were abolished in 2004, but an emergency law has been in force since 1981. Generalized torture has been a hallmark of President Mubarak's regime. Military courts have tried numerous civilians. The police force has been expanded for reasons ranging from safeguarding "public security" to protecting "public order". The much-despised emergency law that grants security forces wide-ranging powers to detain terrorism suspects was reinstated in April 2006, despite Mubarak's promise during the 2005 presidential campaign to replace the emergency law with "anti-terrorist legislation". The amendments to the constitution approved by the National Democratic Party-dominated parliament in a referendum held in March 2007 and boycotted by the opposition gave the security services unprecedented powers to carry out arrests and to refer any suspect to the military courts under Article 179, "the big disaster Article" as it is referred to in Egypt. The security presence has always been (since the 1970s) an Egyptian feature, exemplifying the so-called "*mukhabarat* state". But there is nowadays a more dense and changed "security atmosphere" on the ground: with the prevalence in public spaces of numerous un-uniformed men from the security services (often an indicator of a more pervasive and generalized trend) and with the new technologies involved (see the Internet control campaign). The security sector's interventions are prominent in two very symbolic social sectors: electoral periods and social mobilizations.

On the one hand, police forces have taken a prominent role in supervising voting in nationwide legislative elections and in local elections. They have ensured that the candidates of the National Democratic Party have secured large majorities. During the 2000 parliamentary elections, the Egyptian regime, facing difficulties with the judicial monitoring of polling stations,[30] chose to revert to heavy-handed techniques: the police barred voters from entering polling stations and carried out massive arrests of potentially popular opposition candidates (truckloads of Central Security Forces were deployed at each polling station). In November/December 2005, violence and irregularities increased in each of the legislative elections' three successive phases. After the government failed to stop the Muslim Brothers winning a historic 88 seats, crackdowns by Egyptian security forces resumed, and in 2006–7 the Muslim Brothers were subject to massive arrests that severely crippled their capacity to mobilize. This is a reversal of the trend of gradual "controlled liberalization" of the 1980s.[31]

On the other hand, the latent mobilization that has developed in Egypt since 2000 has been increasingly contained by the security services. Political and social changes have given birth to rising expectations. In the *Kifaya* movement, activists of past generations, the leftists of the 1970s and the Islamists of the 1980s, have joined hands with a younger generation of students and social activists. They have shown a new boldness in breaking the ban on demonstrations and in trying to recapture some freedom in a public space that was monopolized by the state (see the foundation document of the *Kifaya* movement written by Tariq al-Bishri). Protesters are moved by calls for civil disobedience against a repressive, manipulative and personalized state (with the slogan "*hadha mesch balad-na*", "this is not our country"), publicly indict the government in a way that was unimaginable a few years ago and demand domestic political reforms (the lifting of the state of emergency, more safeguards for free and fair elections, the transformation of Egypt from a presidential republic to a true parliamentary republic, a fundamental overhaul of the constitution to allow for multiple presidential candidates). Demonstrations are also held by popular committees in support of the Palestinians or the Iraqi people under occupation, but usually spill over into direct criticism of the Egyptian government and of the President (a political taboo in Egypt for a long time, broken with new slogans like "*Mubarak zayy Sharon*", "Mubarak is like Sharon"). The year 2005 marked the end of the political lethargy of the Egyptian masses, held in a deadlocked situation whose main beneficiary was the regime.[32] The regime's response has been the massive use of security services to curb demonstrations, matched by preventive arrests and transfers to the emergency state security courts. And before every demonstration, central Cairo has been inundated with security forces.[33]

This new form of control or re-regulation by the security services remains unstable. The Egyptian model is different from the Moroccan one, where the regime has been able to internalize the global discourse on reform and democracy, to renounce massive and open repression against political opponents (and to open some past files with the *Instance Équité et Réconciliation*) and to give concrete results so as to sustain its promises (without renouncing its exclusive hold on power).[34] The Moroccan ruling elite has accepted turbulence as a way to keep control and to slow the pace of change. This does not hold true for Egypt, though Egyptian rulers know that they can no longer rule their country as they did in the 1970s. Egyptian decision-makers do not benefit from the strengths and capacities of monarchical rule[35]: the Saudi rulers for instance oscillate between the model of the "modern statesman" (in an authoritarian setting where control of the state gives a steering capacity to those at its helm) and the "traditional" ruler (related to a kind of anthropology of monarchical rule with its capacity to generate face-to-face interactions in different *majlis* or grassroot interactions between the ruler and the ruled). Hence in Egypt the resort by default to the security sector to "meet the ends of the regime" (or to square the circle of the regime, which means staying in power), and the "brutalization" of politics to "subsume" the mobilized Egyptian polity with the help of the security sector.

Two factors are instrumental in explaining the enduring performance of the Egyptian regime. Firstly, the security sector has kept a vested interest in the status quo and has become a strong interest group (of a special kind) in the Egyptian polity. The security sector has remained coherent, has not fragmented and has retained the capacity to strike when matters get out of hand (and increasingly when some interest groups make gains which are unacceptable in the eyes of the presidency). In particular, the army and the security forces, though sensitive to re-islamization, have remained largely immune to subversion by Islamists (close scrutiny in military and police academies is also instrumental in explaining this result). Secondly, the Egyptian regime, though subject to very turbulent change, has been able to benefit from the reconfiguration of the international security structure.

3.2 External challenges and short-term opportunities for the "security state"

The American–Egyptian security alliance has proved dangerously unstable. As a consequence of the events of 11 September 2001, numerous criticisms (and expressions of contempt) were levelled in Washington at the authoritarian, stagnant and corrupt Egyptian regime.[36] The US accorded a new prominence to political reform, a subject that almost never ventured onto the agenda of high-level discussions with the Egyptian government during the 1990s as it would have disrupted efforts at Arab–Israeli peacemaking, a point Egyptian decision-makers were making, along with waging all-out war against Islamists. President Bush broke the deadlock when he made public statements expressing expectations of reform and, in a very symbolic move in the summer of 2002, threatened to block USD 130 million in economic aid to Egypt if a well-known liberal opponent, the American-Egyptian sociologist Saad Eddin Ibrahim, who had been jailed after his involvement in the independent monitoring of the 2000 elections, was not released. American pressure indirectly bolstered the new boldness of Egyptian social mobilization against authoritarianism by weakening a regime under close American scrutiny and making it cautious when repressing opposition movements. While "democracy" seemed to be advancing in Saudi Arabia, Lebanon, Iraq and Palestine, Secretary of State Condoleezza Rice cancelled her scheduled visit to Cairo in February 2005 to welcome the first grant made directly to an Egyptian NGO by the United States Agency for International Development (USAID) without the approval of the Egyptian government after the arrest of another liberal opponent (Ayman Nur). The Egyptian regime began to think that the Bush administration was sincere in its admonitions. The new consensus in policy-making circles and in Congress blamed the spread of terrorism and violent Islamism on political repression and economic stagnation in Arab countries. Neo-conservative intellectuals were at the forefront of the "democratization" offensive. Egypt under "security dependence" had no alternative option to the American alliance and was subject to the possible threats of Congressional backlash or of increased disagreement as to the pace of Egyptian political reform.

Yet, incidentally, the regional context created by "the American/Bush moment in the Middle East" has shifted and has worked to the benefit of the Egyptian regime. Regional developments have pushed the Bush administration to set aside aggressive "democracy-promotion".[37] Since 2005 gradual change and dialogue on reform with the Egyptian regime have become the first choice for an American administration engulfed in the Iraqi "civil war" and in a regional quagmire. Whereas in June 2005 Condoleezza Rice had outlined democratization goals for Egypt, at the end of that year the Bush administration seemed to make too much of minor achievements (a multi-candidate presidential election) and too little of major failures (the crackdown on the opposition) following Mubarak's clear victory for a fifth term in the presidential elections. A few months later in 2006, the Bush administration became even more cautious after the Muslim Brothers won a historic 88 seats in the 2005 parliamentary elections and after "democracy-promotion" gave power to Islamists in the Iraqi parliament and in municipal elections in Saudi Arabia, and turned *Hezbollah* into a pivotal group in Lebanon. Since *Hamas*' victory in the January 2006 Palestinian elections and the war between Israel and *Hezbollah* of summer 2006, the Bush administration has given the impression, something well noted in Cairo decision-making circles, that its tepid support for democratization and even its enthusiastic embrace of elections has diminished. Conversely, the Egyptian government has intensified its crackdown on the opposition, while Washington has remained silent.[38]

All in all, a strong strategic alliance between the United States and Egypt remains of prime importance, although some in Washington continue to level "soft criticism" against Egypt.[39] The Egyptian regime has striven to demonstrate its "utility" to the diminished American hegemon in the Middle East since 2004/5. The Palestinian–Israeli file has been a prime example of the attempt of Egyptian diplomacy, by means of a pragmatic foreign policy, to fill the vacuum left by the "hands-off policy" of the Bush administration. Numerous regional mediations have been held by the Egyptian Foreign Minister and by the intelligence chief Omar Soleiman. Egypt took the "road map" in 2003/4 as a workable plan (even if it was strongly biased toward Israel), and worked with Israel on a plan for its withdrawal from some Palestinian territories. Egypt was involved in 2004/5 in preventing the smuggling of weapons through the Philadelphia corridor (the border between Gaza and Egypt) and in the training of Palestinian security forces in accordance with the basic tenets of the "security reforms" advocated by the Quartet. It was pivotal in the efforts to organize a ceasefire between various Palestinian factions when the Palestinian authority began to collapse. The international management of the situation in Gaza after Israel's unilateral withdrawal in summer 2005 was conducted with Egyptian help. Egyptian diplomats held numerous talks with the Israeli government of Ariel Sharon, and in February 2005 Egypt held its first summit with Sharon since he came to power. Egypt was instrumental in brokering ceasefires between Palestinian factions after *Hamas* took over Gaza, then the (six-months) ceasefire between *Hamas* and Israel in 2008. Since its legitimacy has decreased and its capacity has been crippled by the war in Iraq, the United States can no longer reject Egyptian help or ignore internal Egyptian developments.

4. Conclusion

The Egyptian regime has managed to consolidate its hold over the Egyptian polity by strongly integrating the security sector within its ruling apparatus. Authoritarian reflexes persist with an ageing President Mubarak, and the rigidity of the whole system hampers the injection of "new blood", notwithstanding the preparation of a kind of "dynastic" (father to son) succession that is likely to bring continuity rather than rejuvenation and reform.

The regime has not strengthened institutions. Instead it has sought to "depoliticize" the country and to impose order top down. As the regime has not been successful in containing change and related political expectation, the security sector has gained crucial importance. The robustness of the system is called into question because it is politically debilitated.[40] Politics is not just about who benefits from what (the basic question in political science), but also requires giving direction to a political community. Herein lies the blame for an Egyptian regime that has lost its capacity to impose a project on the Egyptian polity and only manages competing forces and groups in such a way as to protect its own grip on power.[41] The slow rate of change encouraged by the

Egyptian regime weakens the Egyptian social fabric. The middle classes, a pivotal group in Egyptian history, suffer from the economic reforms. Hence the regime's increased dependence on the security sector, while the latter's proper "institutionalization" into the regime would call for careful management (see the "successful" Chinese or Russian examples). In the meantime, everybody seems to be waiting for the successor to the President.

NOTES

1. This chapter benefited from discussions held at the workshop *The Dynamics of Change in the Arab World: Globalisation and the Re-Structuring of State Power*, organized by the IAI of Rome and the UI, Rome, 23–24 February 2007. Thanks to all participants for their comments and special thanks to Laura Guazzone for her help in improving the arguments of my chapter and to Elizabeth Picard and Joel Beinin for their close reading of an earlier draft.
2. Tilly 1985.
3. On the distinction between the state defined as institutional positions and the regime defined as the "roads" to fulfil these positions, cf. O'Donnell 1973.
4. The International Institute for Strategic Studies (IISS) 2004.
5. In the 2000s, Egypt has supplanted Saudi Arabia as the primary recipient of US armaments in the Middle East (cf. Grimmett 2005).
6. Droz-Vincent 2007a.
7. Ayubi 1995 and Salamé 1996.
8. Hudson 1977.
9. The military resisted Gamal Mubarak's attempts to take a political role in 1999–2000 when speculations mounted that he might lead a new party *al-Mustaqbal*.
10. See numerous reports by Human Rights Watch 2001, 2005a, 2007.
11. Bellin 2004b.
12. Sadowski 1993.
13. Droz-Vincent 2007a.
14. Tilly 1990.
15. The expression is borrowed from Buzan 1991.
16. Egypt was especially worried by information about the Iranian clandestine nuclear programme in 2002 (Iran is seen in Cairo as a political and ideological rival and a potential security threat in the Middle East) and by the Libyan disclosure (and elimination) of its weapons of mass destruction and long-range missiles programmes in 2003.
17. al-Bishri 2002.
18. Ayoob 1995.
19. Bilgin 2004; Korany *et al.* 1993.
20. [Eds' note:] See Aarts and van Duijne's chapter in this book.
21. Quandt 1988 and 1990.

22 The three sources of national income (tourism, remittances from Egyptians working abroad and taxes from the Suez Canal) plus shrinking oil exports do not allow for a freehand financing of the Egyptian system.
23 Waterbury 1983.
24 Egypt doesn't host permanent US bases even if it has a highly supportive role as US partner. Egypt has continued to show sensitivity about any permanent US presence on the Egyptian soil.
25 Under the International Military Education and Training Initiative (IMET), 6,600 Egyptian cadres have participated since 1995 in US education courses (House of Representatives, Audition in the Armed forces Committee, 17/05/2006).
26 The problem was levelled during the peace negotiations in early 1979 when Egyptians opened the possibility of conflicts between the Egyptian–Israeli treaty (especially article 6) and other Egyptian commitments (more specifically if Egypt could send troops to defend another Arab country that had been attacked by Israel). The American position has remained that the peace treaty prevails over other previous Egyptian commitments.
27 Buzan *et al.* 2003.
28 Scores of Egyptian Islamists suspected of links to terrorist groups have been sent back to Egypt (what the US calls "renditions") without due legal process and have been held by in jail.
29 For further developments see Droz-Vincent 2004.
30 In July 2000 the Egyptian Supreme Constitutional Court passed a decision that required judicial supervision of elections (it took ten years to hand down this ruling). A kind of liberalization movement from within the state (the so-called "*intifada* of the judges") has tried to put back some form of rule of law, denouncing the instrumentalization of justice.
31 Springborg 1989; Kienle 2000.
32 Heralded as "the year of elections in Egypt", with a referendum on May 25 on an amendment to the Constitution, presidential elections on September 7 and parliamentary elections in November and December, 2005 gave more salience to the protest movements.
33 [Eds' note:] Cf. Beinin's chapter in this book.
34 [Eds' note:] Cf. el Amrani's chapter in this book.
35 Anderson 1991 and 2000.
36 The United States came increasingly to see the authoritarian reform-proof Egyptian regime as a breeding ground for extremism (cf. the high number of Egyptians that took part in the September 11 attacks or the fact that *al-Qa'ida* had some connection with Egyptian nationals such as Ayman al-Zawahiri).
37 Droz-Vincent 2007b.
38 Municipal elections were postponed in February 2006 without any American rebuttal.
39 Cf. US GAO 2006.
40 Springborg 1989.
41 Even very narrowly based military regimes in the 1950s and 60s found ways to create around them a "moment of enthusiasm" (Binder 1978) and to mobilize their people with an internal (reformist) project or with projections of "regional missions" (Arab unity, the liberation of Palestine).

10

THE VIRTUAL SOVEREIGNTY OF THE LEBANESE STATE: FROM DEVIANT CASE TO IDEAL-TYPE

Elizabeth Picard

Introduction

Almost two decades after the end of the Cold War, the Arab world may be characterized by a renewed Western political and military penetration, of a kind reminiscent of the post-World War I period and sometimes described as neo-imperialist. The result is more than often the loosening of the functional interaction between the authoritarian state and its security sector, the withdrawal of national armies into the domestic arena and their mingling in civilian and economic affairs, while security missions are being partly fulfilled by foreign, international, private or para-statal agencies. These trends require a political accommodation of the armed forces either in a move towards democratization or through an authoritarian pact.[1] In both cases, change in the structure and functions of the security sector closely mirrors the transformation of the authoritarian state and its adaptation to values and practices imposed by globalization. In return, the restructuring of state power results in the securitization of state–society relations, the extension of police power and the judiciarization of politics; the level of physical violence decreases while the regimes' symbolic violence increases.

In this respect, although Lebanon is sometime characterized as a "deviant" case with respect to other Arab cases, its political and security priorities became aligned with those of neighbouring states after the end of the civil war (1990), to the point that Lebanon may be seen as a laboratory for future developments in the security sector in the region.

First of all, institutional realignment occurred as prewar institutions were restored and inter-communal consensus re-enforced. The Lebanese political elite found their way out of the long civil conflict by reasserting the principles of the constitution of 1926 organizing "consensus democracy", and by institutionalizing the tradition of communal power-sharing, thus giving rise to further communal bickering and state paralysis.[2] Beyond the institutional changes – the Taif Agreement of 1989 and the Brotherhood treaty binding Beirut to Damascus in 1991 – Lebanon's power balance underwent a fundamental practical change when Syria took control of the Lebanese polity and society, subjecting the Lebanese to arbitrary rule and state violence through its armed military presence and control of the Lebanese judiciary and military.[3]

Although Syrian rule officially ended with the final withdrawal of the Syrian military in April 2005, Syrian influence remains in the form of agents and state clients interested in preserving Damascus's domination. This significant factor influences Lebanese political culture as well as the practices of both pro- and anti-Syrian factions in society. As a result, Lebanon is not exempted from the twin problems that plague so many Arab states today: the persistence of authoritarian rule through securitized state–society relations; and the risk of political destabilization inherent in a liberalized public space.

Secondly, Lebanon is a case study in foreign, especially Western military intervention in the Middle East. Its state institutions were largely shaped by the *Règlement organique* imposed by European powers on Istanbul in 1864 and the French mandate from 1920 to 1943. Independent Lebanon has a rich record of Western intervention, from the United States landing during the civil war in 1958, to the creation of the United Nations interim force in Lebanon (UNIFIL)[4] to ensure Israel's withdrawal in 1978, and the failed Multilateral Force mission in 1982–3. Western intervention seems to have accelerated and intensified recently. After the Israeli war in the summer of 2006, the United Nations mobilized UNIFIL II, a force of 29 nations to which European nations contributed the most.[5] Lebanon, then, is an exemplary case of the growing involvement of the West, and more specifically Europe, in Arab states' political and security issues.

As a reaction to Western intervention, Lebanon has experienced growing regional interference in its security affairs. In addition to traditional players like Syria and Iran – *Hezbollah*'s main supporters – there has been increased interest from Arab states like Saudi Arabia and Qatar – which have contributed to rebuilding the Lebanese Armed Forces (LAF) since 2006 – and from transnational anti-Western networks, mainly Islamist, organized from inside the Palestinian refugee camps and in remote training camps.[6]

As a result, threat assessments and the involvement of international and transnational actors in the reorganization of national security are taking on new meaning. First, these actors inevitably impact upon the restructuring of state power in Lebanon with consequences for the balance of power between sectarian and political segments. Secondly, Lebanese security issues have become closely linked to regional security issues through the financial and military networking of militant groups, as well as through the common symbolic resources that frame domestic conflicts all over the Arab Middle East.[7]

With regard to the restructuring of state power and the effects of external intervention, we could hypothesize that Lebanon "differs" from other Arab states, not so much because of the segmentation of its social fabric and political institutions but because of the peculiar temporality of its modernization process. In Lebanon, unlike other Arab countries where institutional and political change has been at work for several decades since World War II, these processes occurred over a limited time. As a result of this acceleration, two diverging and eventually antagonist processes can be observed simultaneously in the restructuring of the security sector.[8]

In the 15 years following the end of the civil war (1990), the reform of Lebanon's defence and security sector took two opposite directions. On the one hand, the military and security forces were reconstructed according to the already obsolete model of the national Arab army,[9] with security strategies closely linked to Syrian priorities. On the other hand, the changes occurring in the post-bipolar era and fluid political environment, marked by looming regional insecurity and growing Western and regional intervention, contributed to a "post-modern" renewal of security priorities and military options, and played against the state's official military doctrine inspired by its Syrian patrons.

These diverging trends resulted largely from ideological and power struggles going on within the state between pro-Western actors on the one hand and pro-Syrian and/or pro-Iranian actors on the other. At the time of writing, the outcome of this confrontation remains open. It has however proved rich in lessons for those interested in the implications of globalization and the restructuring of the state in the Arab East.

This chapter looks at the security sector in Lebanon, and more specifically at security sector reform (SSR) in order to assess the current restructuring of the Lebanese state in reaction to the Middle East's growing integration into the globalized order. For analytical purposes, the institutional and strategic dimensions of the security sector are considered successively. Together, they illustrate the wearing away of Lebanese sovereignty through interconnected domestic fragmentation and external intervention.

First, the reform process following the civil war is examined by comparing institutionalization, particularly the adoption of general conscription and the rehabilitation of the Internal Security Forces (ISF), with the growing fragmentation of the state's security missions under pressure of renewed sectarianism. The crisis in the state's legitimacy is analysed by looking at the failure of military institutions to revive the civic bond and at the looming conflict between security agencies before and after Rafiq Hariri's assassination in February 2005.

Then, change in security objectives, functions and procedures is examined. The precedence of domestic police over external defence is analysed in light of Syrian domination until 2005. Afterwards, the fight against Islamist groups and the siege of Nahr al-Barid in 2007 confirm the subordination of Lebanon's security policy – henceforth subordinated to Western strategic interests. The dwindling of Lebanon's sovereignty is revealed by contrasting the structure and activities of the LAF to those of *Hezbollah* in the confrontation with Israel. It is confirmed by the new rules and procedures of cooperation between LAF and UNIFIL II in South Lebanon after the 2006 summer war.

1. The Lebanese Security Sector since 1990

With the end of the civil war, Lebanon was confronted with a challenge antithetical to that of the majority of Arab states: it needed to "bring the state back in". In Lebanon as in Palestine, the main stake was less the opening of public space and introducing accountability to public policies than the reconstitution of a sound public administration with authority over finance, foreign affairs and security matters – an authority the state had lost at the hands of competing warlords and transnational networks. Lebanon's efforts to reclaim its sovereignty and reunify its security services shed light on the authoritarian practices of other Arab regimes. They also showed how the fragmentation of security has allowed these regimes to perpetuate their domination, even as it weakens them.

1.1 Armed forces and citizenship: the Arab Achilles' heel

The Lebanese army was not spared the division of the country. National security functions were progressively taken over by non-state actors while hundreds of troops and dozens of officers enrolled in sectarian militia groups. Most armed forces simply remained in their barracks or at home, untrained and under-equipped, and the government eventually had to appeal to private funds to pay them.[10] When the war ended, the Lebanese army had been devastated and polarized: The "Eastern" (Christian) branch remained under the command of General Michel Aoun while the other branch, under General Emile Lahoud, garrisoned the rest of the country.[11]

In the framework of the Taif Agreement (1989), the reunification and consolidation of national armed and security forces were intended as the main vehicle for the restoration of the state. The centrality of the security sector in the reconstruction process was a novelty for Lebanon – a country which had traditionally advocated that "its strength lies in its [military] weakness". The vindication of security issues likened Lebanon to other Arab states and signalled the enforcement of Syrian rule over the Lebanese polity, in much the same way as the military had characterized the Baathist state and the Syrian nation since 1963.

The project was not unprecedented, however, and was in fact, inspired by Fouad Shihab's presidential experience between 1958 and 1964. President Shihab, who had previously been Commander-in-Chief of the Lebanese army, had in mind the "neutral army" (*jaysh muhayid*) model as a way to challenge the traditional rule of notables. In Shihab's view, the army should be an independent centre of power and should project a public image as an institution with political and social stances that are distinct from those of civilian actors.[12] The model was tentatively reactivated under Amin Gemayel's presidency in 1983, with intense US support. Emile Lahoud, who became the first post-civil war Commander-in-Chief in October 1990, following the expulsion of Michel Aoun by the Syrian army, was in many respects inspired by the Shihabist doctrine of a strong army for a unified state.[13] The army and police forces were considered by the new Lebanese leadership and their Syrian patrons as privileged tools to control the state and enforce national development, much along the lines of the classical Arab military model.[14]

In the meantime, the project was impeded by a major obstacle: Western powers which traditionally supported Lebanon (France and the United States, in particular) were reluctant to help rebuild the Lebanese security sector so long as the state remained under Syrian control, with the Lebanese security sector tightly interconnected with and dependent upon the powerful Syrian forces stationed within the country's borders (30,000 men in 1990, still 20,000 in 2001). Neither the West nor Syria itself was willing to rearm the Lebanese military or render them operational. Each feared a reprise of the civil war, and each had concerns about the effect a reinvigorated Lebanese military empowerment might have on the Eastern Arab–Israeli front. As a result, security reform remained incomplete.

The new armed forces were also meant to be a melting-pot for Lebanese citizenship. The Shihabist tone of the Taif Agreement was especially illustrated by two initiatives related to the reconstruction of the armed and security forces. The first was the Disarmament, Demobilization, and Reintegration (DDR) of the confessional militias, swiftly but incompletely implemented in 1991.[15] The second was the adoption and implementation in 1993 of universal conscription in support of national integration.[16] Both initiatives appear to have missed their mark.

Only around 4,000 ex-militiamen (of whom 85 per cent were Muslim) and a few dozen officers joined the regular armed forces. The main Christian militia group, the Lebanese Forces (LF), remained excluded in retaliation for their opposition to Syrian rule, thus causing a deficit in Christian representation within the officers' corps.[17] More importantly, *Hezbollah*'s Islamic Resistance was exempted from demobilization in view of the persistent Israeli occupation.[18] Lebanon now had two armies – the regular army and the Islamic Resistance – and this duality reflected the contradiction within its national security doctrine.

As for conscription, it aimed at fulfilling an ambitious objective. In view of the sectarian division in society and the violence of inter-communal confrontation during the civil war, the troops were to become an example and symbol of social integration and national unity. It was assumed that their codes, values and norms, free of social bias, would provide an example to the nation.[19] However, the Arab record should have cast doubt on the Lebanese army's ability to contribute to national reconciliation and the rise of a civic culture.

Compulsory military service brought 10,000 into the army annually, peaking in the year 2000 at 20,000 recruits – three-quarters of whom were Muslims.[20] The institution was costly to the state[21] and raised growing protest among all sectors of society, especially among Christians, as young conscripts received only three months' training and remained idle the rest of the year. After ten years, compulsory service was abrogated by a non-controversial parliamentary vote undertaken with Syrian agreement in January 2005. Since then, the deflation of the armed forces has been partially compensated by the annual recruitment of 5,000 men (of whom 80 per cent are Muslim) under short-term contracts.[22]

Beside DDR and conscription, a stream of reforms shook the Lebanese armed forces, in anticipation of state reform. The new army underwent several important changes, including sending dozens of officers into early retirement, providing intensive training for new recruits and old cadres at the Fayadiyeh military academy as well as at "friendly" military schools (IMET programs in the United States, the École de Guerre in Paris, and staff schools in Damascus and Aleppo),[23] reinforced discipline and (re-)training of men who had previously been confined to barracks, selective recruitment and new assignments. All in all, rapid promotion allowed for the professionalization of an officers' corps of some 3,000 men – half Christians, half Muslims. "Expertise, responsibility, corporateness",[24] appeared to be the watchwords for this postwar army.

While these reforms were supposed to herald the reconstruction of the nation-state in Lebanon, institutional changes put the Lebanese armed forces under the tight control of the pro-Syrian government leadership. The Defence High Council, re-established in 1991,[25] was composed of the President, the Ministers of the Interior and Defence, the Prime Minister (PM) and Vice Prime Minister, the Commander-in-Chief, the Chief of Police (ISF), the Director of Internal Security (*Sûreté Générale*) and the Director of State Security. Its composition indicated a highly hierarchical chain of command under close Syrian supervision, designed to centralize previously competing networks as well as to coordinate military and civilian security services inside Lebanon. A Directorate General for State Security was created in 1994 and attached to the office of the Prime Minister to advise the High Council. Army intelligence and the *Sûreté Générale* were reformed respectively in 1990 and 1998, and successively entrusted to the same pro-Syrian officer, Jamil al-Sayyid.[26] To complete the reorganization, the judiciary, one of the state sectors most damaged by the civil war, was placed under supervision of the Ministry of Justice, within the purview of the state executive. None of these reforms were discussed or voted in parliament. Clearly, national security and the definition of strategic priorities had become the monopoly of the ruling power.

Failed reforms and the assumption of security issues by a pro-Syrian leadership are worth analysing in comparative perspective both inside and outside of the Arab region. In contradiction to a growing demand for accountability, Lebanon was drifting toward authoritarianism and state/army symbiosis as illustrated by the accession of Commander-in-Chief Emile Lahoud to the presidency in October 1998. Although rebuilt after the bipolar era, the new Lebanese armed forces bore several characteristics common to those of the Arab states in the 1960s and 70s. Not only had their numbers increased fourfold from 1991 to 2003,[27] employing almost one tenth of the country's wage-earners and supporting nearly half a million people, but their resources had also augmented considerably. Their share of the government budget peaked at 25.9 per cent in 1992, and has remained over 15 per cent in recent years – an exorbitant figure given the government's budget deficit.[28]

The privileged status of senior officers was another indication of the regime's postwar transformation. Since 1992, Lebanon was living under dual leadership, with Prime Minister Rafiq Hariri ruling the economy while President Emile Lahoud attended to security interests. The duo – formed by the billionaire and the general – epitomized a kind of "Taiwanese scenario".[29] While the odds favoured the former, Syrian intervention managed to maintain a balance in favour of the President, and the military were also granted economic privileges.

These changes echoed a common development in the Arab world, where the military were losing their former centrality in the authoritarian configuration.[30] Economic leverage became a major instrument of power, with private actors as major partners and the officer corps one interest group among many. Military and security officers were granted various social and economic privileges. A foundation named *Iskan 'askari* (1994) after its Syrian model provided housing credits and financial support to members of the defence forces. Beside the special wage regime, officers benefited from a range of special allowances, from medical and social services to various domestic supplies and upgraded retirement pensions.[31] They were even provided with financial advantages linked to cooperation with Syria – namely the payment of a special allocation to officers attending Syrian military academies,[32] and invitations to join seaside military clubs. While improved material conditions enhanced recruitment of quality candidates, it also gave rise to a new corporatism, separating the armed forces from the political elite and the communal society at large. Rather than sharing a nation-at-arms ethic, officers now formed a kind of "military party" eager to protect their privileges.[33] In a context of aggravated budget deficit, they tended to stand up collectively for their corporate interests, openly defying civilian state authorities.[34]

The new Lebanese armed forces were rebuilt under tight Syrian political control. Syrian special forces and various intelligence services used a mix of corruption and threat to keep the Lebanese army and police in line. High-ranking officers did not escape the general atmosphere of corruption pervading postwar Lebanon and some were mentioned in bribe scandals alleged to have cost the Lebanese state over USD 1.5 billion per year.[35] Even the rank-and-file took advantage of police operations to blackmail ordinary citizens, imitating war-militia and trivializing their *khuwa* practices.[36]

On the whole, the security and political sectors in postwar Lebanon adopted several characteristics inherited from the authoritarian Arab nationalist traditions of the 1960s and 70s, while adapting to the new context of economic liberalization and forcing military participation in the clientelist distribution managed by the pro-Syrian "loyalist" power. Rather than strengthen state institutionalization, reform of the armed forces became a venue for the patronage networks of the neo-patrimonial rule.

1.2 Security forces and the communal conundrum

One of the key concepts for rehabilitation of the armed forces had been the blending of rank-and-file diversity to enhance a shared national identity, in accordance with the deconfessionalization promised in the Taif Agreement. As early as 1991, in response to high popular expectations and with the support of seasoned top-brass officers trained before the civil war, Emile Lahoud undertook a reshuffling of the army corps with a view to making them more pluralistic. For half a decade, he also imposed rotation among brigades deployed in the five main regions (*muhafazat*) in order to sever local and sectarian connections. The measure was costly, however, became unpopular among officers and was scaled down. Nonetheless, beyond the highly publicized, patriotic rhetoric and apparent unanimity, the issue of sectarian balance within the armed forces remained critical. From 1991 to 2001, military strength rose through recruitment from a low of 12,000 during the civil war, to over 42,000. Fifty-nine per cent of the military was now Muslim – an accurate reflection of Lebanon's global sectarian composition.[37] A problem arose when the armed forces encountered difficulties attracting Christian youth – even from provinces like Akkar, traditional sources of poor Maronite recruits – who became increasingly reluctant to serve under Syrian rule or were leaving the country. Once again the sectarian balance in the security sector was threatened.

While rumour and manipulation might have overplayed the issue, one of the most negative effects was to undermine public confidence in security services. Neither political supporters nor opponents trusted the new state security and judicial institutions, as they were believed to be subordinated to Syrian interests and rife with sectarianism. Through deeper Syrian intervention and also due to growing competition within state constituencies, a decade of troika rule (a Christian president under Syrian tutelage, a Shiite speaker of parliament allied with the Syrian regime, and a Sunni PM struggling for governmental autonomy) was followed by a phase of intense confessional tension, as observed in the Legislative elections of 2000 and 2005.[38] Political leaders and local communities preferred to rely on primordial loyalties. All security agencies and units within military and police agencies became linked to communal and/or private interests through primordialist networks (*'asabiyya*) in return for clientelist material reward. What was at stake beyond claims of justice and fair sectarian balance was the control of strategic state institutions, with the political leverage and financial advantages attached. What was at work beyond claims of secularization within army and police forces was the selective recruitment of agents according to communal identity. For example, the Presidential Guard became the precinct of Christian and Shiite officers trained in Syria and demonstrating loyalty to Emile Lahoud, while a government guard of some 1,000 men – an offshoot of the ISF, meant to ensure the Sunni prime minister's personal security – was said to be recruiting mainly among Sunnis. The result was a growing sectarian imbalance within and between security forces, mainly between the army and the police (ISF).

The competition to attract foreign aid and take responsibility for specific domains such as customs led to the fragmentation and growing privatization of security functions. A stark illustration was the case of the rehabilitation, reshuffling and expansion of the ISF under the premiership of Rafiq Hariri, motivated as it was by his distrust of the regular army which he suspected of being the personal tool of Emile Lahoud. After the ISF were released from Syrian control in 2005, General Ashraf Rifi was put in charge of ensuring domestic security, with the police under the authority of the Prime Minister and the Interior Ministry.[39] Within a few months, police forces grew from 14,000 to 20,000, and were projected to reach 30,000 men. The forces were trained with French cooperation[40] and re-equipped by the United States.[41]

The ISF were frequently accused by Shiite and pro-Syrian opponents of implementing a sectarian agenda in response to massive demonstrations by forces opposed to Siniora's Western-backed government. The ISF's inability to curb the (Sunni) Islamist assault on the Danish consulate in February 2006 and to the Sunni–Shiite riots in downtown Beirut in January 2007 were considered proof of sectarian bias.[42] The ISF also raised criticism from civil society because they were suspected of corruption in their daily control of local populations.

The sectarian strife that plagued the reconstruction of security forces mirrored the rift that was deepening between (government) "loyalists" and the opposition, following deterioration of the national consensus after 2000,[43] and especially after the opening of the institutional crisis in September 2004.[44] This became public knowledge following the stream of assassinations which targeted "sovereignist" (anti-Syrian) political leaders between 2004 and 2007. Each political leader's security seemed to depend on a particular defence unit, more often than not, private and foreign,[45] under the supervision of a senior officer projecting informal power into the region under his control. Like the politicians, local security leaders competed with one another. After the indictment in relation to Rafiq Hariri's assassination of the Commander of the Presidential Guard, the Director of ISF, the Director of *Sûreté Générale* and the head of Army intelligence in August 2005, the lack of cooperation between the army and the ISF, already denounced in the Fitzgerald report, became particularly evident.⁴⁶ At least five rival intelligence units overlapped and obstructed the sharing of information while the Interior Ministry remained incapable of staffing a common operation room as agreed in August 2005.⁴⁷ Overlapping security and mismanagement were apparent also when the (Shiite) Director of the *Sûreté Générale* – allegedly linked to *Hezbollah* – was excluded from a security meeting organized at the Interior Ministry.⁴⁸ Dysfunctional communications proved particularly costly during the fight against *Fatah al-Islam* militants in Tripoli in May–August 2007.⁴⁹ The takeover of West Beirut by *Hezbollah* and their allies in May 2008 confirmed the sectarian division of the security sector: while the ISF retreated into their barracks after failing to protect the Sunni neighbourhoods, the army smoothly took over from *Hezbollah* in the streets where the Party of God had gained ground.

In this respect, the shattering of the Lebanese security sector in parallel to the fragmentation of the political scene reflects regional trends. Robust American intervention in the Middle East before and after 11 September caused a broad reshuffling of regional security systems. All over the Arab East, violence was recast according to identity criteria.⁵⁰ In Syria, military leaders were striking local deals with Kurdish or Islamic opponents to organize social control and predation. In Iraq, the security sector (either governmental or oppositional) was rebuilt along sectarian criteria. The high political stakes of state crisis in each of these countries (mainly the regional conflict with Israel, confrontation with US military intervention and the disastrous state of the economy) were blurred by deafening choruses of identity rhetoric. Yesterday, they opposed Islam to Christendom; now they were obsessed with Sunni–Shiite confrontation. One can hardly deny, however, that regional conflict formation and the ideologization of state power, while rooted in domestic circumstances, are also the product of antagonist Western ideological discourse and intrusive military intervention.⁵¹

2. Security and the Transformation of State Sovereignty

The transformation of state security in the Arab world is mainly the result of globalization. New security stakes related to the conflict between "the West" and "Islamic terrorism" and new security practices involving greater external intervention within the national space have required the adaptation of the state's military and security agencies as fragmentation of the power structure and reliance on informal modes of government have made local regimes more dependent on external influences.[52] The new practices have conveyed the notion of a decline in sovereignty. Most Arab states had enjoyed a remarkable margin of manoeuvre despite their alliance with one of the great powers at the time of the Cold War.[53] At that time, state sovereignty was still based on Westphalian criteria (the world was organized into independent and equal state units) and Weberian criteria (the state was meant to be the only legitimate holder of physical force). Now, globalization and the unipolar domination by the United States has forced a reorganization of the world, and especially of the Arab Middle East, into unequal hierarchical units, crisscrossed by networks of transnational actors.

In order to assess the reorganization of Lebanon's system of power, the functions and operational style of its security sector are considered first. Here, the main hypothesis is that local security forces – including the military – were increasingly confined to internal security and police operations. In return, examination of national defence highlights the contrast between Lebanon's regular armed forces and *Hezbollah* resistance. It draws attention to growing external intervention within the Lebanese security domain by great powers, international organizations and transboundary networks, and questions the very notion of Lebanese sovereignty while portending structural change in the regional balance of power.

2.1 Confusion between army and police tasks

The Western allies denied the Lebanese military the lethal armaments necessary for its rehabilitation as a national defence force.[54] As for Lebanon's Syrian patrons, they pre-empted the Lebanese defence by subordinating Lebanese interests to their own, denying the military command autonomous action. The Taif Agreement itself, along with several Syrian–Lebanese agreements concluded during the 1990s,[55] relegated the military to a support role, even as surrogate for diminished police forces. Lebanese armed forces were thus implicitly considered a local agency in the Syrian regional security system.

For more than a decade, the military, submissive to Syrian command and to president Lahoud, their former Commander-in-Chief, not only assisted the police but took the lead in domestic security operations. They mounted roadblocks, enforced curfews, maintained identity controls and domestic surveillance, breaking up demonstrations and strikes, and tapping telephone lines. They were responsible for extra-judiciary arrests, abductions and imprisonments at army headquarters. At the same time, human rights practices deteriorated.[56] Military repression affected every sort of confessional or social group indiscriminately when they took issue with authoritarianism and with the Syrian domination, including the crowd of *Hezbollah* supporters on 13 September 1993, demonstrating in the Shiite suburbs in support of Palestinians in the Occupied Territories, Lebanese Forces cadres in Christian Kisrawan contesting the legitimacy of the government, pro- and anti-Joumblatt rioters in the Druze Shuf district in 1994. In 1996, the army arrested numerous Sunni militants following the assassination of Sheikh Nizar al-Halabi, a pro-Syrian Sufi cleric. In 1997, they enforced a curfew on demonstrators affiliated with the main workers' union, the Confédération Générale du Travail. They crushed Sheikh Subhi al-Tufayli's "hunger revolution" in Baalbeck in 1998, and were directly involved in arresting sovereignist militants in Christian areas in the summers of 2000 and 2001.[57] Although Lebanon remained far from the Arab *mukhabarat* state, a state whose society was caught between fear of, and complacency toward, its leader, where the public sphere was silenced, the post-Taif state had become much more coercive than the consensus state of the 1960s and 70s.[58] It is no wonder that the political class and some segments of society felt threatened by the new security rules and the repressive methods that used to be blamed on Arab brother regimes. A political cleavage appeared between those supporting the intervention of armed forces on the domestic scene (who more than often happened to be Syrian proxies), and citizens and leaders of various denominations who stood for the independence of their country and the rule of law, assuming at that time that liberation from Syrian rule and full sovereignty would pave the way for a civilian democratic government. Maronite patriarch Nasrallah Sfeir complained of abuses by security forces and illegal arrests. Prime Minister Rafiq Hariri denounced several anti-constitutional measures while Druze leader Walid Joumblatt, in the middle of political tension with Bashar al-Assad, claimed that since President Lahoud's election, Lebanon was "living under military regime".[59]

While the security policy of the postwar Lebanese state served Syrian interests, it remained subject to the security demands of the Western powers. The United States and the EU had established tight guidelines regarding the international fight against (Islamist) terrorism, illegal immigration and unlawful trafficking. These demands were intensified following 11 September. Together with Syrian rule, Western demands caught Lebanese armed forces in a web of sometimes convergent sometimes contradictory cooperation. The Syrian regime would publicize its struggle against smugglers and traffickers (an accusation it directed against its domestic opponents) and cooperate with Western agencies in hunting down Islamist militants, while top Baathist leaders were organizing illegal trafficking networks and the Syrian secret police incited radical Sunni groups to inflame the Lebanese domestic scene. The Lebanese army was subsequently confronted with a mix of criminal rings and ideological groups entrenched in off-limits zones clustered around the Palestinian camps. They were called indiscriminately to deal with robberies, riots and assassinations,[60] while Syrian interference and communal tensions prevented them from moving decisively against armed groups outside and inside the refugee camps.

In the period following the civil war, most LAF operations were engaged against Sunni radical groups as police actions: the campaign against the Sir al-Dinniye stronghold, a northern mountain enclave where two to three hundred Islamic militants had taken refuge in December 1999, the assault on the Palestinian training camp at Wavel (al-Jalil, near Baalbek) in September 2002, the multiple attempts to take control of Tamir, an outlaw area near the Ain al-Helweh (Sidon) refugee camp in 2005, 2006 and again in 2007; and the May to August 2007 siege of the Nahr al-Barid (Tripoli) camp where the Jihadist *Fatah al-Islam* group had entrenched themselves among 30,000 Palestinian refugees. Some of these operations resulted in heavy losses among the rank-and-file and none of them ended with a clear victory for the LAF, showing their lack of preparation and equipment to wage the kind of new war fought by committed insurgents in populated areas. Notwithstanding the ambiguous attitude of the Syrian rulers and the Lebanese Sunni leadership,[61] the LAF along with the ISF had progressively become agents of a globalized struggle between Western powers and Middle Eastern Islamic networks more or less related to *al-Qaʿida*.[62]

After the assassination of Rafiq Hariri in 2005, a divided Lebanese government was unable to clearly identify the source of threat, define a national strategy or provide the LAF with appropriate military means. In the meantime, Western powers were willing to reform and train the LAF but on their own terms and in relation to their own strategic priorities. Indeed, the United Kingdom in 2006 acting by proxy for the US, offered to design and supervise a thorough security sector reform.[63] The US, which had kept military cooperation at a low level since their retreat from Beirut in 1983, unblocked USD 40 million in military aid in 2006. In February 2007, Congress approved aid for Lebanon which included $280 million for security.[64] In May, Western governments wasted no time labelling the *Fatah al-Islam* insurgency in Tripoli a "danger to international security" so that within two weeks, a dozen planes delivered American arms and equipment for LAF use, attesting to the international stakes involved in the fighting at Nahr al-Barid. Such responsiveness contrasted directly with the summer war of 2006, when the population had to wait six weeks for a ceasefire between Israel and *Hezbollah* to be imposed by the Security Council[65] and no defensive arms or civil protection equipment were forthcoming from Western allies. At Nahr al-Barid, the Lebanese military were confronted with militants from various nationalities including Saudis, Europeans and Bangladeshis alongside Palestinians, many of whom had just returned from the Iraqi front. Eliminating or capturing the Islamist combatants – the only alternative presented by Commander-in-Chief Michel Soleiman from the beginning of the siege – was indeed a national issue. For the Lebanese army, it also amounted to acting as a proxy in a regionalized conflict the United States had failed to win in Afghanistan and Iraq.

In spite of the Israeli withdrawal in 2000 and the Syrian retreat in 2005, the state of Lebanon was becoming a police state of a special kind. It was a weak, penetrated and dominated, a surrogate actor in a regional conflict. Taking advantage of its pluralistic society and coalition government, the regional conflict infused its domestic scene, reflected on its political divisions and weakened its legitimacy as a national state. Since the end of the civil war, it had often been argued that the army was the only unified national sector in the government – every other sector having borne witness to state failure. This unity, however, proved fragile since it had been built under heavy Syrian influence and because government actions remained constrained by contradictory domestic and international commitments. With the increasing strife between the Group of the 14 March[66] pro-government groups backed by the West, and the opposition backed by Iran and Syria, the military were repeatedly called upon for police actions, deploying several thousand men in downtown Beirut in December 2006, taking control of Tripoli in May 2007, and local actions against the Palestinian camps at Nahr al-Barid and Ain al-Helweh in June 2007, to say nothing of their new commitment in the South and at the Syrian border. While such security drift overstretched Lebanon's limited military capacity in spite of rapid Western and even Syrian logistic support, it also shot the military command to the political forefront, suggesting that the Commander-in-Chief might be the only leader able to break the political deadlock. Indeed, Michel Soleiman became President in May 2008, but his election took place after nine months of political stalemate and harsh controversy and thanks to external diplomatic intervention, limiting his autonomy of decision in the future.

2.2 Toward a redefinition of state sovereignty
The Nahr al-Barid crisis was not the only time in the post-1990 period that the new Lebanese army was put under pressure. During the 2006 summer war between *Hezbollah* and Israeli Defence Forces (IDF), several army barracks and other security facilities had come under Israeli fire but, except for firing a few anti-aircraft shells, the army abstained from retaliation or even from defending itself. The army's lack of lethal armament, particularly the absence of an air force, explained why it was unable to fight the Israelis. Several other reasons should also be taken into account. Sectarian divisions among the political elite reflected embarrassed and diverse reactions to the war. Some leaders hardly hid their satisfaction at seeing the IDF attacking *Hezbollah*. Siniora's government was not keen to engage the army in support of the "Islamic Resistance" and merely acquiesced in displaying national solidarity in response to the scale of civilian losses.[67]

To be sure, there was another cause for the military's paralysis. Since the civil war, the army was no longer the only Lebanese armed force exerting "legitimate violence" for the preservation of state sovereignty. In fact, the Islamic Resistance stood in competition and had been legitimized by the President and the government on several occasions.[68] Until the Israeli withdrawal in 2000, it had substituted for the army in South Lebanon by organizing and leading a successful guerrilla resistance against the IDF and their local allies. After the Israeli withdrawal in May 2000, the Islamic Resistance took exclusive military control of the "liberated" areas down to the international border, heralding a Middle East trend toward privatization and transnationalization of the security sector.[69] Since 1985, when *Hezbollah* began marginalizing and eliminating rival groups in the resistance to Israeli occupation, it had become *the* military actor confronting Israel in Lebanon. Born under the auspices of the Islamic Republic of Iran,[70] *Hezbollah* was recognized by Syria as the main national resistance group and Shiite party to the May 1988 Damascus agreement ending the (Palestinian) "Camps war". It was exempted from DDR in 1991 because the South remained occupied by Israel after the end of the civil war, notwithstanding the fact that it was a privileged strategic ally for Syria in Lebanon.

After its creation in 1982, *Hezbollah* had developed into a social movement embracing every aspect of the Lebanese Shiites' private and public life. The party had the capacity to mobilize by appeal to religion, history and identity, and was in a position not only to modify the structure, norms and ethics of the Shiite society but to challenge the foundations of the "consensus" state.[71] Thanks to family and sectarian connections and to the skilful blurring of boundaries between military structures, party organization and the Shiite society, *Hezbollah* enjoyed an unlimited army of supporters. Moreover, beside the strong roots which grounded its national legitimacy and effective military infrastructure, *Hezbollah* was able to leverage the powerful transnational network centred in Tehran which provided abundant financial resources and armaments along with political and religious support.[72] As in many other Middle Eastern countries, narrow localism and transregional strategy, clerical domination of society and the cult of armed sacrifice were contributing to eroding the model of the territorialized state, democratic accountability and citizenship.[73]

At the same time, *Hezbollah* became a paragon of the new military structures fighting asymmetric wars in the wake of the "revolution in military affairs".[74] It was a unified, strictly hierarchical, territorialized military institution of a few thousand combatants, with a command structure inspired by the Palestine Liberation Organization (PLO). It was also organized in small, mobile, extremely well-trained, decentralized and autonomous cells combining sophisticated intelligence technologies and high-tech arms with audacious improvisation.[75] These characteristics accounted for its success in the war of attrition waged against Israeli occupation forces prior to 2000 as well as for its remarkable resistance in the summer of 2006.[76]

Hezbollah's military structure was the mirror opposite of the post-civil war Lebanese army. The contrast between their initiatives on the ground was even more striking. *Hezbollah*'s successful resistance against the powerful IDF underscored the absence of the Lebanese army on the Israeli front in the period in which the South was twice invaded (in 1993 and 1996). The absence of Lebanese security forces became even more obvious following the Israeli withdrawal in 2000. President Lahoud gave his consent to a limited deployment in response to pressing international demands only after receiving the green light from Syria.[77] In May 2003, responding to a demand by US Secretary of State Colin Powell that the Lebanese army be deployed south, along the Israeli border, he indicated that he feared such a move would split the army along sectarian lines. And when the Syrian military finally withdrew from Lebanese soil in April 2005 in accordance to UNSC resolution 1595, no attempt was made to send more troops to the Israeli border or to obtain Damascus' official acquiescence in Lebanese sovereignty over the Shebaa Farms territory.[78]

At the same time, a covert strategic relationship between the Islamic Resistance and the army had been fostered under Syrian tutelage. It involved intelligence-sharing as well as tolerance of illegal militia training and the traffic of arms between the Syrian border, the Beqaa and the South. *Hezbollah*'s leadership referred to its relations with the army as "conceptual continuity"[79] and pointed to its role in the April 1996 international arrangement ending the Israeli "Grapes of Wrath" operation, as in the 1998 and 2004 prisoner exchanges with Israel,[80] and to the presence of government officials at several rallies organized by the party. Not only was the duality of defence forces publicly acknowledged, but the issue of the disarmament of the Shiite militia (stressed in several UNSC resolutions from R1559 to R1701) and their integration into the Lebanese army advocated by United Nations envoy Terje Roed-Larsen[81] would have to be negotiated between the Lebanese government and *Hezbollah* on equal terms, taking into consideration regional (Syrian, Palestinian, and possibly Iranian) requirements. Inside the military institution, *Hezbollah*'s public stance became a subject of contention among army officers, feeding sectarian resentment as well as distrust toward Shiite officers.[82] Therefore, the future of *Hezbollah*'s forces remained the stumbling-block of state sovereignty and the state's monopoly on legitimate violence. Even after a compromise was signed in Doha in May 2008 between government and the opposition, and a "unity" government was formed, the security issue remained at the top of the agenda of the 14-member National Dialogue committee.

Notwithstanding the case of Iraq, such a drift toward diminished sovereignty could be compared to what was happening in several other Arab states such as Algeria or Yemen, where territorial and communal segments of the country were gradually escaping state rule. And yet, the question remained: would heavy foreign intervention in support of the government and the military help re-establish Lebanese sovereignty, domestically and within its regional environment?

The Lebanese army did not take any meaningful initiative in the South until after summer 2006 when it received strong logistical and political support from the West acting under UN cover. UNSC resolution 1701 (11 August 2006) ending Israel's war on Lebanon made reference to the government's decision to deploy 15,000 men between the international border and the Litani (7 August). Since then, the coordination between UNIFIL II and the four Lebanese brigades deployed in South Lebanon has improved steadily: The commander of the international force succeeded in involving Lebanese officers in tripartite security meetings with IDF representatives; at the same time, Lebanese officers were mediating between UNIFIL and *Hezbollah* forces in the new security zone.[83] Military cooperation with Western powers even extended to surveillance of Lebanese territorial waters and the national airport, and to control of land borders between Syria and Lebanon, beyond UNIFIL's mission but in conformity to UNSC resolution 1701. While vigorously criticized by Damascus, surveillance of the Syrian border was first organized with German and Belgian cooperation then upgraded through dispatch of an "independent" team by United Nations Secretary General (UNSG).[84] Beside tensions between the various UNIFIL national contingents regarding rules of engagement, what was going on was *de facto* participation of the Lebanese army in a UN operation. Moreover, through their cooperation with the "coalition of the unwilling" members of NATO[85] in UNIFIL II, as well as their military and police operations against Jihadist militants suspected of being linked to *al-Qa'ida*, what was taking place was a covert integration of the Lebanese security sector into the US "war on terror" in the "broader Middle East".[86]

Such a downgrading of the Lebanese military's autonomy came along with the growing intervention of the American (and French) ambassador(s) into Lebanese domestic politics. Still intent on "bringing democratization" to the Middle East, the US government was transferring its great expectations from Iraq to Lebanon.[87] Hence the close linkage between the heavy UNIFIL intervention, the financial support granted by the international community to Lebanon's bankrupt economy,[88] and the political support of the US and France to the Siniora government against its domestic (*Hezbollah*) and external opponents (Syria). After the creation of a UN International Independent Investigation Commission in 2005, the establishment of the International Tribunal to probe Hariri's assassination under chapter 7 of the UN Charter was the ultimate emblematic display of this exceptional support, leading to the externalization of one more attribute of the sovereign state – administering justice.[89] Altogether, integration of its military and externalization of its authority bore testimony to the relegation of Lebanon to a "neo-trusteeship" of a kind reminiscent of the post World War I colonial period.[90]

3. Conclusion

Several dimensions of the international and transnational interventions in the Lebanese security sector suggest that the likely outcome in the future will be similar to that of some entrenched and weakened states in the Arab world. Their destinies are subordinated to external interests – energetic, ideological or strategic.[91] Their polities are partitioned and classified according to primary loyalties and their political spaces are constructed upon rejection of the "other" (the Syrian ruler, the Palestinian outsider, the Israeli enemy). Correlatively, the identity of such states is guaranteed by military means rather than politically. Far from being an exception, the Lebanon of the 2000s should be considered the reverse image of Iraq, and a portent for the delegitimization and militarization of the state in the Arab Middle East.

NOTES

1 While the former option is advocated in Huntington (1991), Stepan (1989) shows that power-sharing arrangements are more common among Latin American authoritarian regimes.
2 This state of affairs was reached by giving the presidency of the state, the parliament and the government to the three major sects. For a critical view on postwar conservative institutional arrangements, cf. Picard 1994.
3 Alongside the remilitarization of domestic security tasks, post-civil war reconstruction is often characterized by the slackening of the judiciary control on police operations. Cf. Call 2002.
4 United Nations Security Council (UNSC) resolutions 425 and 426, April 1978.
5 In January 2007, 9,084 out of 11,512 men. Cf. UNIFIL 2007.
6 Rougier 2007.
7 Leenders 2007b.
8 In post-conflict societies, the reconstruction of the military, police and intelligence forces in order to recover national security, democratic control and public credibility requires the retraining and reorganization of these forces with international support. Cf. Schnabel *et al.* 2006.
9 Especially in term of numbers and social influence as the Lebanese military increased eightfold from 10,000 to 80,000. Cf. Pollack 2002.
10 Rafiq Hariri financed the pay of the armed forces under General Aoun's authority in 1989–90.
11 MacLaurin 1991.
12 Freiha 1980.
13 Emile Lahoud developed such a doctrine in his first presidential address (24 November 1998), in which the words "order", "justice", "citizenship" and "state reform" were leitmotivs.
14 Owen 2004.
15 Law 88, adopted by parliament on 13 June 1991, specified that 6,000 militiamen would be reintegrated in the first phase and a decree dated 19 October allocated an initial expenditure of USD 500,000 for the operation. The army, however, had 10 operational brigades at the time and could not accommodate more than 25,000 to 30,000 men. Cf. Picard 1999.
16 First adopted in June 1974, the decree was never implemented. During a lull in 1979, the government set the term of service at 18 months and, in 1983, under the presidency of Amin Gemayel, the military command succeeded, in a few months, in recruiting around 2,000 men. Law 97 of 21 September 1991 reinstated the general draft.

17 In 1991, after the war ended, 253 officers were retired, of whom 67.9 per cent were Christian. As a result, the percentage of Christians in the officer corps declined to 47.1 per cent; Cf. Barak 2006, p. 85.
18 In contradiction with the Taif Agreement (1989) ending the Lebanese civil war, which stipulated in part II article 1 that all militia groups had to be demilitarized, Syria allowed *Hezbollah* to continue its "resistance" military operations against Israel from the South. Only on that condition would *Hezbollah* accept the Taif Agreement and participate in the second Lebanese republic after 1990.
19 The vocation of the military is to become a total and self-sufficient institution, centred on the notion of compliance, alien to the notion of counter-power, and keeping up minimum lateral relations with the society. Cf. Etzioni 1975.
20 Dagher 2002. Dagher quotes an unpublished report in Arabic by Colonel Jamil al-Sayyid, at the time assistant director of Military Intelligence and adviser to General Lahoud, *Integrating the Lebanese Armed Forces: Transitory Experience or Permanent Politics?*, 1997, note 39.
21 Each draftee earned USD 70 per month and cost the state budget USD 1000 (*L'Orient-Le Jour*, 15 July 2003). Rafiq Hariri began complaining of the excessive cost of military service in 1997 (*L'Orient-Le Jour*, 2 August 1997).
22 Interviews with a Western military attaché, Beirut, 20 April 2006; and with retired Brigadier General Baabda, 29 November 2006.
23 "al-Ma'ahid al-harbiyya takhruj dima' jadid lil-watan", *al-Sharq al-Awsat*, 19 and 20 May 1996; Interview with General Said Hanna, Zouk Mosbeh, 14 November 2006. Approximately 25 officers were regularly on leave for 18-month periods, more than half of them in Syria.
24 Huntington 1959, p. 62.
25 According to Law No. 102 (1983); cf. Khalil 1990.
26 Law 12 (6 September 1990) reorganized the ISF and created the *Majlis al-amn al-dakhili*, the ruling council of the *Sûreté Générale*, composed of the Interior Minister, the State Prosecutor, the Governor of Beirut, the army commander, the head of the ISF, and the Director of the *Sûreté Générale*.
27 Lebanese army strength rose from 21,000 in 1990 to 44,300 in 1995, and 63,570 in 2002, according to The International Institute for Strategic Studies (2002). With the gendarmerie and the *Quwwat al-amn al-dakhili* (ISF), which amounted to 13,000 men in 2001, the total armed forces of Lebanon exceeded 80,000. While the growth of armed forces put an important sector of the new Lebanese state under Syrian influence, it might also have been a covert way of fighting unemployment and promoting specific groups within the society.
28 At 25.9 per cent of the national budget in 1992 and 22.9 per cent in 1993, national defence was the government's largest budget item, before education (13.3 per cent and 10.2 per cent, respectively). In subsequent years (1996 and 1997) the defence budget consumed 11.33 per cent and 12.78 per cent of budget resources, while interest on debt ranked first (40.26 per cent and 42.16 per cent respectively). In 1998, the defence budget rose to nearly 20 per cent, or 28 per cent if we include the social advantages granted to the military, such as retirement pensions (based on interviews with Minister of Defence Khalil Hrawi, *al-Nahar*, 28 February 2001, and economist Kamel Mehanna, *L'Orient-Le Jour*, 8 June 2002). In 2003, defence remained second at 15.83 per cent of the budget without debt service and 9 per cent with debt included. Military spending rose

by USD 140 million in 2007 following the deployment of the army in the South (*The Daily Star*, 23 May 2007).
29 Bahout 1998, p. 68.
30 [Eds' note:] Cf. Droz-Vincent's chapter in this book.
31 *al-Anwar*, 25 October 1993.
32 USD 1,000 per month for officers with the rank of captain and higher.
33 In the sense analysed by Rouquié 1980.
34 In 1999, an unidentified military commando ransacked the office of the Minister of Finance, Fouad Siniora, who had attempted to scrutinize military expenses.
35 Adwan 2004. As a matter of example, according to *al-Nahar*, 30 May 2000, some 3,600 mobile phones had been allocated to public employees, senior military and security personnel and their families since 1995, resulting in an estimated loss of USD 100 million.
36 The *khuwa* was traditionally a protection tax levied by the Bedouins on urban and village populations.
37 This figure was a fair reflection of the demographic balance in post-civil war Lebanon. Due to emigration and different birth rates between urban and rural communities, the official register of voters (citizens over 21) numbered 1,558,000 Muslims (56.55 per cent) and 1,197,000 Christians (43.45 per cent) in 2000. The Muslim/Christian ratio for the total (resident *and* non resident) population is estimated around 60:40.
38 Cf. Kassir 2000; European Union Election Observation Mission n.d.
39 Minister of Interior Hassan al-Sabaa was a career military police officer trained in France. He became Interior Minister in April 2005 but resigned after his failure to control the Islamic demonstrations of February 2006. Since his return to government in November 2006, he has been a strong supporter of the majority government.
40 A complete audit of ISF was implemented in the autumn of 2005. Training is supported by an EU subvention of several million dollars. Commission of the European Communities 2005; Interview with a Western military attaché, Beirut, 20 April 2006.
41 *The Globe and Mail*, 1 December 2006; *AFP*, 26 January 2007; "US backing 'covert war' against Hezbollah", *The Christian Science Monitor*, 11 April 2007; Interview with a Western military attaché in the Middle East, Geneva, 10 May 2007.
42 They had to be assisted by five army regiments; "6,000 Lebanese troops assigned to maintain peace in Beirut"; "Army command adopts stringent approach to enforce law, order", *al-Nahar*, 31 January 2007.
43 Inter-communal consensus in support of the Shiite Islamic Resistance withered after the Israeli withdrawal in May 2000. That same year, Syrian security services launched a crackdown on Christian opponents after the summer Legislative elections.
44 After Syria imposed the prolongation of Emile Lahoud's presidency (2 September) and UNSC adopted resolution 1559 (3 September).
45 French gendarmes in civilian garb were unofficially in charge of the Prime Minister's security after Hariri's assassination. "Beirutis turn to private security firms after wave of bombings", *The Daily Star*, 8 June 2007.

46 UN Programme on Governance in the Arab Region, 2005.
47 *Daily Star*, 11 August 2005, 25 August 2005, 5 October 2005; *al-Nahar*, 19 August 2005; 23 September 2006; *al-Mustaqbal*, 6 November 2005; *al-Safir*, 17 January 2006; *L'Orient-Le Jour*, 3 October 2006.
48 *al-Akhbar*, 4 May 2007.
49 ISF stormed Islamic militants' apartments in Tripoli on May 20 without giving notice to the army. That same day, 27 soldiers were ambushed and killed by *Fatah al-Islam* in retaliation.
50 A stereotype aptly deconstructed by Armatya Sen (2006).
51 Vaÿrynen 1984, p. 352.
52 Cf. Guazzone *et al.* 2007.
53 Picard 1988.
54 In 1999, the Lebanese army had 300 tanks, less than 300 mortars, some 30 helicopters only four of which were armed, and three outdated aircraft. The International Institute for Strategic Studies 2002. In 2007, the Lebanese skies were still dominated by the Israeli air force, while Israel's security and military edge over its neighbours was a tacit Western priority. Interviews with Western military attachés, Beirut, 20 April 2006 and 3 December 2007.
55 Syrian–Lebanese Military Cooperation Treaty, 1 September 1991. Even after Israeli withdrawal in 2000 and the Syrian withdrawal in 2005, Damascus continued to use the issue of pendent Israeli border encroachments (Shebaa, Ghajar) to promote its Golan Heights' strategy.
56 "Members of the security forces used excessive force and tortured and abused some detainees. Prison conditions remained poor. Government abuses also included the arbitrary arrest and detention of persons who opposed government policies. Lengthy pretrial detention and long delays in trials were problems, and the courts were subject to political pressure". US Department of State 2000.
57 "Lebanese army command issues internal 'guidance' on recent arrests", *al-Safir*, 10 August 2001.
58 But not more than some of the militia statelets which *de facto* divided Lebanon in the 1980s.
59 *al-Nahar*, 21 April 2001.
60 Such as the murder of four judges in June 1999, or the December 2002 assassination of three intelligence army officers in Sidon, murders attributed to '*Usbat al-Ansar*, a Jihadist network based in the Ain al-Helweh camp.
61 The search for Sunni support by Rafiq Hariri and, after his assassination, by his son Saad, his sister MP Bahiya and Prime Minister Siniora was punctuated by electoral agreements with Sunni fundamentalist groups during the Legislative elections of August 2000 and June 2005 as well as financial and security deals including the amnesty of Sunni insurgents in relation to the pardon of the Lebanese Forces' leader Samir Geagea in July 2005. Cf. Picard 2001b; Rougier 2007; Hersh S., "The redirection: Is the Administration's new policy benefitting our enemies in the war on terrorism?", *The New Yorker*, March 2007, http://www.newyorker.com/reporting/2007/03/05/070305fa_fact_hersh (retrieved 18 April 2007).
62 Fisk R., "A front-row seat for this Lebanese tragedy", *The Observer*, 22 May 2007.
63 Interviews of two Lebanese security specialists and two Western military attachés, Beirut, November 2006.

64 Since the end of the civil war, US military cooperation had been restricted to the selling of non-lethal and second-hand equipment, to training in the United States between 80 and 100 officers each year and the deployment of experts and language teachers in the Ministry of Defense. Cf. Congressional Research Service, 2001; "U.S. Studies Lebanon's Military", *The Chicago Tribune*, 2 March 2006; US Department of State 2006; *The Daily Star*, 22 March 2007; *al-Nahar* 31 May 2007.

65 UNSC resolution 1701 (2006) put an end to the war on 11 August.

66 In reference to the demonstration in March 2005 in protest against the assassination of Hariri and the Syrian occupation.

67 In this respect, the seven-point truce plan presented by Prime Minister Fouad Siniora in Rome (27 July 2006) was testimony to limited governmental support to the resistance.

68 At the time of Israeli attacks in April 1993 and April 1996, again during the Israeli withdrawal in May 2000 and in the Siniora Government's ministerial declaration of 19 July 2005, at a time when the government included three *Hezbollah* members.

69 Picard 2000.

70 Chehabi 2005.

71 Charara 1999.

72 The *Hezbollah* information department has pointedly abstained from commenting on figures cited by Israeli sources such as Gambill (2002).

73 Cf. Ruggie 1993.

74 Courmont *et al.* 2002.

75 Tomes 2005.

76 Leenders 2006.

77 He promised to send LAF units on 27 May 2000. On Army Day (30 July 2000), he declared: "the role of the army will be defined in relevant time". In return, Bashar al-Assad expressed "Syria's unfailing support" to Lahoud (*al-Nahar*, 14 August 2001). The government finally sent a joint force of 1,000 military and ISF which maintained a limited cooperation with UNIFIL (Interview with an ex-UNIFIL officer, Geneva, 11 May 2007).

78 Remaining border disputes after the May 2000 Israeli withdrawal include the Shebaa Farms land, occupied by Israel in 1967. The UN proposal to take hold of the territory until a final Lebanese–Israeli agreement is signed is blocked by Syria, thus legitimizing ongoing *Hezbollah* attacks against the IDF.

79 Talal Atrissi, director of the Center for Strategic Studies (Beirut) quoted in Wärn 2000.

80 After a successful exchange of prisoners negotiated with Israel, Hassan Nasrallah, Secretary General of *Hezbollah*, declared: "The blood of the martyrs of the army and the martyrs of Hezbollah has been mixed"; *Agence France Presse*, 25 June 1998.

81 Report of the UNSG to the UNSC, 29 April 2005.

82 Young, M., "What's Hizbullah's problem with the army?", *The Daily Star*, 25 May 2007; interview with a Western military attaché, Beirut, 20 April 2006.

83 The Litani valley was under the control of the Lebanese army which regularly attested that no armament was shipped to the South; "Hezbollah: UN troops welcome in South", *The Daily Star*, 30 March 2007; "UNIFIL denies reports of weapons smuggling in South", *The Daily Star*, 4 May 2007.

84 "Germany promises 'modern' project to monitor Syrian border", *The Daily Star*, 6 March 2007; "Independent team to monitor arms movements next week", *al-Nahar*, 26 May 2007.
85 France and Germany did not join the US–UK "coalition of the willing" against Saddam's Iraq; Spain quitted "Operation Iraqi Freedom" in April 2004, and Italy in November 2006.
86 Western powers (namely US Secretary of State Condoleeza Rice and French Foreign Minister Bernard Kouchner) expressed unqualified support for a strong military strike against Nahr al-Barid insurgents; *al-Nahar*, 24 and 25 May 2007.
87 Craner 2006.
88 At the time of the Paris III conference in January 2007, the national debt amounted to USD 41 billion i.e. 180 per cent of the GDP.
89 UNSC Resolution 1757, 30 May 2007.
90 Fearon *et al.* 2004.
91 Bilgin 2004.

11

THE SAUDI SECURITY ENVIRONMENT:
PLUS ÇA CHANGE ...

Paul Aarts and Joris van Duijne

Introduction

In this chapter we will look at the security arrangements of the Kingdom of Saudi Arabia. As opposed to the other Middle Eastern states under review in this book, the Saudi case presents a textbook example of a country which is both a traditionalist (tribalist), monarchical and absolutist system and a long-time ally of "the West". Furthermore, it is a country with vast oil wealth and a relatively small population (in comparison to most countries of the Levant and Iran, but not the smaller Gulf monarchies). This gives rise to a two-way relevance for security affairs: on the one hand, oil makes the Saudis of particular importance for most global powers, not only the West, but increasingly also the East, and on the other hand, the al-Saud dynasty has been able to use the wealth to increase its security in many ways, ranging from buying legitimacy to buying high-tech weapons. In many ways, this suggests an interdependence between Saudi Arabia and the outside world, as opposed to the more dependent situation of the other subjects of this volume.

As such, it is probably extremely insightful to study further the impact of military globalization on the way the Saudis have managed both their internal and external security. From this and by means of comparison to the other cases, we can learn what the impact of the "unique" Saudi position has been on the pressures that changes in world politics since the end of the Cold War have produced *vis-à-vis* regimes in the Middle East.

First, we consider it necessary to place Saudi security in a broader foreign policy context. In this section, we will also at times broaden the historical perspective a little, since this will contribute to understanding present-day choices and relationships. Next, we will focus our attention on the reign of the Al Saud. We will study in particular its durability and the extent to which it has been based on different kinds of legitimacy. Building on these important background questions, we can turn to the actual research question: has the Saudi security sector changed much in recent years? If this is the case, why is it so? And if not, why not?

1. The Saudi Security Environment: Different Levels, Different Threats, Different Roles

Many simplistic evaluations of the external relations of the Kingdom of Saudi Arabia (KSA) tend to view the country as a faithful ally of the United States. It is true that a "special relationship" exists between the two countries, and that is has shown a remarkable resilience. However, for many different reasons, it would be a mistake to conclude that the KSA is merely a follower of US regional and global policy.

A good starting-point for an explanation of the many limitations of this view is to distinguish between different levels in the Saudi security environment. The main reasons for so doing are firstly that the political elite in the KSA has different role perceptions at these different levels, and secondly that different, though often related, threats present themselves. In line with both Gerd Nonneman[1] and F. Gregory Gause,[2] we will distinguish between four different levels: the global, the regional (or wider Middle East), the Gulf and the domestic.

1.1 Global relations

It is true that the Saudis largely (though not solely[3]) depend on the US for their external security and military equipment and training. This does not, however, necessarily mean that it is appropriate to speak of Saudi Arabia as being a "lapdog" to US strategic interest.

Several observations point in a different direction. First and foremost, we must acknowledge that Saudi relations with the US, and also to a large extent Europe, are better characterized by interdependence. A central reason for this is of course Saudi oil wealth, its unique ability to act as a "swing producer" and its consequent importance as a market for Western goods, and its foreign investments in Western economies.[4] Hence, it seems plausible to present the special relationship between the US and the KSA as a tradeoff: oil for security. However, it is also important to add that Saudi support for the US in both wars against Saddam Hussein (openly in the first and tacitly in 2003) was of critical importance to the American war effort.[5]

But as regards the KSA as an actor, there are serious limitations to its positioning as a mere "follower" in the global political arena. History shows that Saudi rulers since Ibn Saud have been masters in balancing powers against one another in order to keep some autonomy. Before World War II, the al-Saud dynasty largely depended on Britain, but at all times kept open communication channels with, for instance, Germany and the Soviet Union, and in the 1930s it signed oil deals not only with the British and Americans, but also with an entrepreneur from New Zealand and with Mussolini. More recently, there have been several instances where the Saudi leadership, though often briefly, diverted their strategic attention to put pressure on the US. For instance, after the Arab–Israeli war of 1967, the KSA only purchased weapons from France and Britain for a period of three years.[6]

More recently, especially after 11 September, some have argued that the special relationship between the US and the KSA has been showing serious cracks.[7] The limits of this assessment will be dealt with elsewhere, but here it is useful to suggest that, while according to this train of thought the growing involvement of China in the KSA[8] can be presented as further evidence of such a rift, the previous analysis suggests a somewhat different view: the Saudi establishment has always balanced different powers, and most probably will continue to do so with the help of Chinese involvement. To suggest that Chinese involvement is *in itself* evidence of a u-turn in Saudi foreign (and especially security) policy would demonstrate a lack of historical understanding.[9]

A final point to note as regards the global Saudi context is that there are indeed many signs of growing global integration and increasing interdependence, as has been noted elsewhere in this book, that have important implications for the Middle East and also for Saudi Arabia. This has translated into the growing integration of the policies and economies of Gulf countries, mainly through the Gulf Cooperation Council (GCC), and many grandiloquent initiatives, such as European Union–GCC cooperation, NATO's Istanbul Cooperation Initiative (ICI) and the like. However, the notable exception to this trend has been the security sector, which has remained largely, if not solely, a bilateral affair. We will further elaborate on this in the final section of this chapter.

1.2 Regional affairs

Saudi security concerns in the Middle East currently tend to focus on two main issues: Iraq and Iran. However, in the literature and among the Saudi elite, there is barely any consensus on what both these issues actually mean and what the threats for Saudi Arabia are. Roughly, the principal divide is between a holistic approach and a threat assessment on a case-by-case basis. The first view sees, for instance, clear linkages between sectarian violence in Iraq, the war in Lebanon, Iranian involvement in Iraq and possible internal problems between Saudi Shiites and Sunnis, while the second sees the growing civil strife in Iraq and Iran's ambitions as two largely separate issues that both require their own kind of Saudi diplomacy. Not to say that the KSA is not wary of Iranian involvement in Iraq, but according to the second view this meddling represents Iranian power politics, not sectarian domination.[10] What is interesting to note is that the broader Saudi public is largely of the all-embracing view, while the policy elite tends to treat these regional issues in rather separate, classical "balancing" terms.[11]

Saudi policy concerning Iraq (and regional affairs in general) has been remarkably silent for quite some time. It seems that the Saudi leadership found itself split: it was wary of Iranian ambitions, but wanted to keep communication channels and the option of cooperation open and, worried about the growing tensions in Iraq, did not want to overly antagonize the Americans. Furthermore, it seems that the Saudi leadership has learned its lesson from Afghanistan in the early 1980s and now knows the risks involved in the sponsorship of militants, which would in the short term be an option if it wished to counter Iran. It goes without saying that developments in Iraq – positive or negative – will have an influence on Saudi Arabia's security situation. At the time of writing, it looks extremely unlikely that things will turn out favourably in Iraq, meaning that the jihadists would leave Iraqi territory, but even if this were to happen, Saudi Arabia would still be adversely affected in that the jihadists would most probably look for safe havens elsewhere in the region, Saudi Arabia included. In the case of a negative outcome, this "jihadist effect" would be multiplied. In the worst-case scenario (the disintegration of Iraq into mini-states with the Americans being pushed out), the jihadists would claim victory, feel emboldened ("after Afghanistan and Iraq now the Peninsula!") and turn their eyes and energy to the US-supported monarchies and emirates in the Gulf region.[12]

After the 2003 Gulf war and the removal of Saddam Hussein, the old regional security paradigm (balancing Iran and Iraq against each other) did not work anymore. In this new configuration, Iran's nuclear programme figures prominently and seems to worry all Arab Gulf States, Saudi Arabia in particular.[13] Saudi Arabia is afraid of being targeted by Iran in retaliation, were the US to strike Iranian nuclear installations.[14] It seems that the Kingdom has been struggling to come to terms with these changes in its regional security environment.

More recently, the KSA, mainly through the work of former Ambassador to the US and current Secretary General of the Saudi National Security Council, Prince Bandar bin Sultan, has geared up its diplomacy and put an end to this silence. In our opinion, this is largely the personal choice of key individuals, such as King Abdullah and Bandar himself, who have recognized the need to re(!)-establish the KSA as an important regional player. Cunningly, this diplomacy has largely avoided the issue of Iraq, because this would mean antagonizing either the US or the Saudi (and broader Middle Eastern) public.[15] Instead, the main focal points have been issues such as Arab–Israeli peace, bridging the rift between *Fatah* and *Hamas*, sponsoring (if not directing) the Organization of the Islamic Conference (OIC) "Mecca Declaration" against sectarian violence, Lebanon and most recently Chad–Sudan relations.[16]

A quick assessment of American reactions to the Saudi diplomatic drive, especially in the case of the future role of *Hamas*, might suggest a rift between the two long-term allies.[17] However, such an analysis fails to take into consideration the long-term Saudi perception of being an important regional player, as well as US recognition of that position. Furthermore, the frequent trips by Prince Bandar – the "Arab Kissinger"[18] – to Washington might even suggest that the "startled" US reactions are a coordinated effort to rally regional support for this Saudi initiative by publicly detaching it from US foreign policy. In any case, such a quick assessment fails to recognize the history of Saudi regional semi-independent foreign policy.

1.3 The Arabian peninsula

If the Saudi position on the global level is largely subordinate, and if regionally it sees itself as *one of the* key powers, by contrast it has a self-perception of hegemony as far as the Peninsula is concerned. Many Saudi elite members in fact see the area as "all Saudi", their legitimate position only disturbed by British intervention in the early twentieth century. To some extent, there is academic difference as to whether this hegemony is accepted by the "satellites". While some commentators focus their attention on frictions with Yemen or Oman, others point to the success of the GCC, *despite* the enormous differences in size and capabilities of its member states, and to the resolution of many sources of conflict between GCC states, most notably a number of highly politicized border issues.[19]

Both arguments hold some truth; it is a mixed relationship with ups and downs. As noted before, however, issues of national security are more difficult to integrate into multilateral frameworks than, say, trade. In short, the success of the GCC in other fields has hardly extended itself to the security sector, again apart from the quite easily delineated issue of counter-terrorism. By contrast, such success probably exacerbates the suspicions of the smaller Gulf monarchies.

1.4 Internal security

Between 12 May 2003 and the end of 2004, there was a wave of attacks in the KSA, which resulted in a comparable explosion in the literature concerning the terrorist threat. Most of these accounts, however, are monolithic in more than one way: they tend to report recent events without explaining the mechanisms behind radicalization[20] and without reference to earlier periods of dissent, radical action and appeasement in Saudi history. Cordesman and Obaid, for instance, provide a 12-page-long chronology of terrorism in the Kingdom, starting from 1970 and thus including, amongst other things, the seizure of the Grand Mosque in Mecca in 1979 and two large-scale bombings on 13 November 1995 and 25 June 1996.[21] Though their subsequent analysis largely considers events since 2003, it does show that violent opposition is not new to Saudi Arabia. One could even trace the pattern back further to include the Brotherhood (*Ikhwan*) rebellion of 1929–30.[22] Whatever historical starting-point one takes, the point to be made is that

> [t]he official ulama who supported the government's position – in 1929, 1979, 1990–4, 2001 and 2003 – were confronted by a minority of younger and lower-ranking ulama together with students, who adopted radical, activist interpretations of the early Wahhabiyya. Cooptation of radical elements promptly caused the emergence of new radical groups.[23]

This historic parallel is further emphasized by the important position that has been "given" to a number of Islamist scholars in recent years, most notably Salman al-Awda and Safar al-Hawali. Previously known as strong supporters of *al-Qa'ida*, both have recently propagated moderation, a sign of the government trying to use their popularity[24] in a dual strategy of cooptation and ruthless repression.[25] Thus the cycle continues, and while the violence of recent years might seem unprecedented to an outsider with a limited understanding of the Saudi domestic scene and the relationship between Islam and the state, the al-Saud family is all too familiar with this mechanism.

This being said, the magnitude of the attacks within the Kingdom in the period 2003–4 still deserves attention. Here, a review of the background of the insurgents can provide useful insights. Roel Meijer and Thomas Hegghammer in particular have carried out extensive research in this regard, and both have argued for the crucial, if not decisive, importance of the "Afghanistan factor". While the Saudi violent Islamists prove remarkably diverse in social, spacial and educational terms, most have had experience in combat against the Russians, or on other battlefields such as Chechnya or Bosnia (or at least have received training in Afghanistan under the Taliban). Furthermore, both authors point out that those who are too young to have had such experience almost always have family links with those who have, such as brothers who fought.[26]

In this light, the *intensity* of domestic terrorism in recent years clearly has its roots in government support of *mujahidin* during the 1980s. Some observers, primarily Saudi officials, like to see the lull in insurgent activity since the end of 2004 as evidence of the government having a firm hand on matters.[27] Others think that the peace may not last, and even see the lull as the calm before the storm.[28] These observers see both the attempted attack on the Abqaiq oil facilities in the Eastern Province of February 2006 – the first major terrorist assault in the Kingdom since December 2004 – and later the shooting of four French civilians near Madain Saleh in February 2007 as significant turning-points.

Hence, the most likely prognosis is that acts of terror will continue inside the Kingdom. However, given that state support for radical elements has been declining sharply since the mid-1990s,[29] it is likely that the crackdown in recent years will prove largely successful, though Iraq possibly poses some challenges to this conclusion.

Much the same applies to Sunni–Shia relations within the KSA. While it is sometimes suggested that the sectarian strife in Iraq might "spill over" into the Kingdom,[30] it is probably manageable for the authorities, given the current state of affairs and the limited number of Saudis in Iraq. Though there is certainly no consensus on the issue, serious research has shown that the Shia of Saudi Arabia have, for the time being, chosen a path of cooperation with the royal family.[31] Thus, as long as the authorities are able to handle the "homecoming" of Sunni radicals, sectarian relations within the Kingdom should be under state control.

Finally, there is the issue of reform: many scholars emphasize the need for profound political, economic and social changes in the KSA. While some also link this directly to internal security,[32] this link is not as straightforward as is often suggested. A more detailed analysis of the relationship between reform and internal security will be presented in the final part of this chapter.

There have indeed been major changes in the Saudi strategic environment since the dawn of the twenty-first century. The "Arab Cold War" of the second half of the last century is now in the past, and the Kingdom is no longer threatened by Nasserist or Marxist ideologies, nor by unwieldy neighbours such as Yemen or Iraq.[33] Instead, there are serious new challenges: an Islamist revival, a volatile Iraq and a wannabe-nuclear Iran. But, despite these enormous changes in the security environment, the previous analysis indicates that there is remarkable consistency in both Saudi Arabia's role conception and its role performance. The Saudi regime sees itself as able to balance powers on the global scene, as a key player and – more often than in the past – a mediator in regional affairs, and finally as a hegemon on the Peninsula.

Next, before turning to the main research question, we will elaborate on the fourth level in the Saudi security environment: the domestic. The fact that the House of Saud, despite changing security environments, has one of the highest "YIPPI-score" (years in power per incumbent) on earth deserves special attention.

2. High and Dry: Explaining the Resilience of the House of Saud

Middle Eastern monarchies (and republics for that matter) appear extremely persistent, the House of Saud being the *primus inter pares*. It has ruled the country since 1932 in an unremittingly authoritarian fashion, notwithstanding the fact that its fall has often been predicted. Clearly, the Kingdom is not quite the dinosaur that "instant experts" seem to think.[34] An interesting discussion has commenced which offers an almost exhaustive list of different explanations for the "resilience" phenomenon, some of course having more exegetic power than others. Most of these explanations, although not lacking in expressiveness, have their own weak spots. Gause has done a good job of summarizing these weaknesses, and his piece will not be repeated here.[35] What is important to bear in mind is that all these attempts to explain resilience, together with what later came to be known as the "rentier-state" perspective, limit themselves to internal causes.[36]

Each explanatory framework that focuses on local actors and factors naturally leads to important insights, but no framework offers a sufficient elucidation of the persistent character of monarchies. Part of the answer we are looking for certainly lies somewhere "outside the box" of domestic politics. It appears to be more conceivable that the crucial difference between the success and failure, or the persistence and fall, of monarchies can be found in the regional and global strategic-economic picture, rather than the local one. At the very least a combination of the two perspectives is necessary to arrive at a reasonable explanation. It would be rather simplistic to attribute the survival of regimes *solely* to external backing, but it would be equally naïve to suppose that such support (or the lack of it) would be of no importance.

In a recent contribution to the debate, Bellin comes close to such a combined-perspective approach. First, she forcefully reacts against conventional explanations ("that suggest a litany of regional failures") – such as the weakness of civil society, state-controlled economies, poverty and high illiteracy rates, the remoteness of the region from the epicentre of democratization, and the cultural factor (Islam in particular). Her conclusion is that none of these explanations is sufficient. In all these respects, neither the Middle East nor North Africa is unique. Other regions, with similar characteristics, have nonetheless managed to make the transition to less authoritarian forms of governance.

> Cross-regional and cross-temporal comparison indicates that democratization is so complex an outcome that no single variable will ever prove to be universally necessary or sufficient. Any notion of a single prerequisite of democracy should be jettisoned.[37]

Interestingly, and of direct relevance for this contribution on Saudi Arabia's security sector, Bellin subsequently suggests that it is mainly the will and capacity of the Middle Eastern states' coercive apparatus to suppress democratic initiatives that have extinguished the possibility of transition to political liberalization. "Herein lies the region's true exceptionalism."[38] The robustness of this coercive apparatus is then explained by referring to four variables, of which one relates to the external environment: successful maintenance of international support networks.[39]

From this focus on the repressive apparatus it should, however, not be concluded that Arab regimes have necessarily had recourse to excessive force. In particular in the case of Saudi Arabia, this has only occasionally been the case (as is also pointed out by Hertog elsewhere in this volume). Although it is obvious that the police, the intelligence services and the various divisions of the armed forces (the National Guard in particular) ensure the immediate survival of the regime, it would be very difficult for it to survive for long on this basis alone. For sure, the regime of the Al Saud possesses both judicial (or negative) and empirical (or positive) sovereignty. Different sources of legitimacy come into play, some stronger or weaker than others.[40] From its earliest days, the regime has been largely successful in using the Wahabi *'ulama'* to manufacture consenting subjects, providing "shared meanings that tied people to a particular configuration".[41] However, with the passage of time, this became increasingly difficult (as was shown clearly by the events which took place in Mecca in 1979). As Madawi al-Rasheed lucidly explains,

> A product of state control and modernity, Saudi religio-political discourse proliferated, fragmented and challenged state authority. Unexpectedly, control under authoritarian rule produced the seeds of mutation. Wahabiya developed interpretations that challenges the discourse of control.[42]

Some of these dissident voices have turned into violent jihadists who do not refrain from confronting the House of Saud head-on. Their emergence was the immediate cause for the "restructuring" of the security sector, to which we now turn.

3. The Saudi Security Sector: Managing the Manageable

The final section of this chapter will pay specific attention to the reactions of the Saudi state to changes in the security requirements of the country. We will argue that, at least for the time being, the security challenges at hand are perceived as being within the limits of day-to-day management: the Saudi regime still feels confident enough to tackle new threats through (rather limited) reallocations of resources, rather than any significant restructuring of its security arrangements, and through tried-and-tested (diplomatic) balancing strategies. First, we will look at "hard security", i.e. the military and other agencies designed to protect the KSA. Afterwards, it will be useful to take a look at some external pressures on the Kingdom to significantly alter its security sector, as well as the limited impact of those pressures. Finally, some observations will be made that broaden the look at Saudi security to include "softer" aspects of its power relations.

The differentiation we will use draws on Christopher Hill's *The Changing Politics of Foreign Policy*. In this work, he presents a "spectrum of means" of asserting power in external affairs. This spectrum ranges from "influence" (or soft power, using means such as culture and diplomacy), through propaganda and subversion, to (hard) power, which includes deterrence, blackmail and, finally, physical coercion. Different means have different benefits but also different costs, and therefore leaders have to constantly weigh them up. Furthermore, it is hardly ever the case in practice that a single strategy is used: agents most likely have a combined strategy of "muscle" and "getting others to want what you want".[43]

3.1 The military and intelligence

Apart from some of Peterson's contributions, study of the Saudi security sector is almost monopolized by Cordesman and his co-authors.[44] Hence, for an elaborate, detailed and comprehensive analysis of the Saudi military and intelligence configuration, it will suffice to refer to Cordesman's extensive, almost endless, list of publications. Here, we will only make some general observations that will contribute to understanding the rest of this section.

Saudi security forces comprise a mix of regular military forces, a separate National Guard and various internal security and intelligence services. Prince Sultan, Minister of Defence and Aviation since 1962, is the actual decision-maker on everything related to the regular armed forces, while King Abdullah has controlled the National Guard since 1963. Most intelligence and internal security services are overseen by Prince Naif, Minister of the Interior since 1975. He is in charge of a wider range of institutions than any one other single person.[45] Finally, there is a specific number of intelligence services which are each controlled by one of the leading princes or the king himself: Military Intelligence, controlled by Prince Sultan; the National Guard Intelligence Directorate, controlled by King Abdullah; and the General Security Service (GSS) or *Mahabith* (the domestic intelligence service), controlled by Prince Naif. To top it all off, there is the General Intelligence Presidency (GIP), controlled by Prince Turki al-Faisal until his replacement by Prince Nawaf bin Abd al-Aziz on 1 September 2001, which focuses on external affairs.

In terms of size and finance, the Saudi military is by far the largest in the Arab part of the Gulf. Though budgets and staff numbers are confidential, it is estimated that the KSA spends some USD 20 billion annually on its different military units (about a third of its budget, though it must be noted that there is no distinction made between pure military expenditure and intelligence/internal security expenditure), and combined personnel numbers are about 200,000.[46] These figures, however, also point towards an inherent weakness: in 1997 (but no differently today), Saudi Arabia ranked 9th in the world in terms of military expenditure, though the size of its armed forces ranked 31st.[47] In this regard, neighbouring Iran has a consistent edge over the KSA by means of its much larger population. By any standard, the Saudi army is small, lacks combat capacity and is understaffed; accordingly it also lacks projection capabilities.[48] Indeed, all GCC armies have to rely partially on foreigners for their manpower, and to maintain an edge in armaments to make up for this.[49] It is also important to note that this military expenditure, which is relatively large even on a global scale, has multiple goals: the purchasing of high-tech weaponry has an element of prestige and is meant to assure the Kingdom of Western support (often all the more so in view of the fact that Gulf leaders buy "package deals", including long-term maintenance contracts and training programmes), as much as such weaponry is used for deterrence and defence purposes.[50] As noted before, extensive cooperation within the GCC on military affairs could be part of a cure for this. But, apart from noteworthy progress on the counter-terrorism front,[51] the military role of the GCC has remained "largely a symbolic one".[52]

In contrast, since the attacks in 2003, the total budgets of the different institutions involved in policing and intelligence in the Kingdom have increased dramatically. In a "truly massive effort", the total internal security budget reached USD 7 billion in 2003 and an estimated USD 8 to 8.5 billion in 2004, with a virtual "open end".[53] However, despite this increase in resources, there have been little or no structural changes to the inherent weaknesses of the Saudi security sector: though some officials are beginning to realize the problems, interaction between different services and branches still relies on personal contacts and briefings, not on systematic analysis, leaving much to be desired in terms of efficiency.[54]

3.2 The internationalization of security arrangements?

Since the mid-1990s, there has been a tendency amongst Western policy-makers and a part of the scholarly elite to make a case for the (partial) internationalization of security in certain key areas of the world. This section will explore the reasons for doing so, the necessary Security Sector Reforms (SSR), experiences with comparable projects in the past and the particularities of the case of the Gulf region. We will take as an example the NATO ICI, but the same analysis can be applied to, for instance, the Partnership for Peace programme (PfP).

In short, the argument is that, especially since 11 September and the war in Iraq and in relation to terrorism targeted both at the West and at the legitimacy of Gulf monarchies, the strategic insecurity in the Persian Gulf "has provided new impetus for Arab Gulf states to reflect on their own security".[55] This fact is seen as an opening for cooperation between the Gulf countries and NATO, which has extensive experience with security building, especially in Eastern Europe. The different Gulf monarchies face closely related, if not similar, threats, and NATO could facilitate inter-operability and confidence building within the GCC so as to "develop integrated military capabilities to prevent, deter and contain [common threats]".[56] This could be done with Western assistance, but (because of the broader framework) without the politically dangerous link to US foreign policy.[57]

However, the document clearly states it is an addition to the PfP programme, the ultimate goal of which is to "promote the development of effective defence institutions that are under civilian control and that are capable of cooperating with NATO forces if the need arises".[58] This is clearly derived from experiences in the former Soviet Union and Eastern Europe, though similar strategies have also been effectively applied in Central America and Africa. Most importantly, however, the success stories of NATO-guided SSR have taken place in post-authoritarian and post-conflict settings, where the need for such reform was felt internally. Some countries even had to build a security sector from scratch.[59] It is highly dubious, to say the least, whether Saudi Arabia feels urgently compelled to put the military under civilian control, or to make budgets more transparent.

Participating Gulf countries tend to see it, unrealistically, only as a diplomatic shift in their external security package. Equally unrealistically, some NATO officials see great potential.[60] Different Gulf countries readily accepted cooperation on the counter-terrorism front, but avoided anything that resembled externally dictated reforms of their security arrangements. Furthermore, there is little confidence in the Gulf that anything significant can be offered by NATO.[61] On the subject of the danger of an Iranian attack, for instance, one senior Kuwaiti official said: "We won't put our fate in the hands of NATO decision-making. By the time they decide, there won't be a Kuwait. NATO is a 'European Arab League'".[62]

In any case, while SSR might be seen as an aim of NATO, rather than a means, for the GCC countries it is rather something to avoid. Rightly, Gulf regimes are quite satisfied with the way they have managed their countries in such a turbulent region over the past decades, and it is highly questionable whether they would benefit from professional standing armies that could challenge, or even threaten, their regime's position.[63] As Droz-Vincent aptly remarks, "The Saudis' overspending in training, equipment, and military bases can thus be interpreted as an investment in a marvellous sandcastle to buy the quiescence of a weak army."[64]

As a final point in this regard, it is important to note that while four GCC countries (Bahrain, Qatar, Kuwait and the United Arab Emirates) have signed up to the ICI, Saudi Arabia has not. This fact alone explains in part why the smaller Gulf States feel comfortable with the initiative. They fear the KSA's size and capabilities, and are wary of entering into security arrangements with it.[65]

3.3 Internal security and reform

In much the same way as security sector reform is presented as a blessing for Gulf rulers, many Western analysts and policy-makers argue for serious political reform in the Middle East. Here too, the argument is that reform will benefit the security of the country in question. Cordesman and Obaid write that "It cannot be stressed too firmly that Saudi security is best preserved by broad progress and reform, and not by reforming the Saudi military or intelligence services. [. . .] True internal security is based upon popular support."[66] There are also many in the West at governmental level who vaunt the merits of reform for the Middle East and Saudi Arabia.[67]

Richard Young's *Democracy and Security in the Middle East*[68] provides a comprehensive insight into the debates between those who extend "democratic peace" studies to the Middle East, and those who are more sceptical. The latter point out, for instance, that a comparison of opinion polls in different countries has shown little correlation between levels of repression and "radicalism", and others even question whether security and political systems are related issues.[69] Research has furthermore pointed out that fundamental changes that have taken place, for instance in Bahrain and Qatar, were primarily a response to "domestic imperatives" and not to outside pressure, and that in practice democracy and security have been contradictory rather than complementary or mutually reinforcing concepts for Middle Eastern states.[70]

Refraining from normative discussions and wild guesses as regards reform in Saudi Arabia, the only conclusion we can reach on the basis of current knowledge is that it is unclear what far-reaching reforms would mean for Saudi internal security. What is more, it is important always to bear in mind whose security is being addressed. For instance, when Dioun writes that "many reforms that are needed to promote long-term stability may cause short-term unrest",[71] he is clearly not referring to the al-Saud family. In fact, one could even say that for the Saudi regime, the opposite is true: many reforms which have had positive effects in the short- to mid-term (for example reform of the educational system and Saudization) might in the longer run undermine the position of the ruling family.

Finally, and for this particular chapter most importantly, it is essential to note that, as a result of its personal character, the Saudi security apparatus is probably the last sector that is likely to be reformed. There are indeed many domestic and international imperatives for change in Saudi Arabia in the social, economic and political fields, as is shown in other chapters in this volume. But perhaps even because of these imperatives, reform of the security sector, which "would require rulers to assert their authority by enhancing their legitimacy through political processes, instead of relying on cooptation, coercion and coup-proofing strategies",[72] is not a policy priority of the al-Saud family. This is especially true given that they are confident, as noted above, that the "same old" will suffice. Indeed, Cordesman and Obaid also conclude that "Saudi Arabia's primary need for reform does not affect its security apparatus".[73]

3.4 Soft (and not so soft) power: the Saudi diplomatic drive

The Saudis are certainly pursuing their own agenda in the Middle East, and increasingly so. In February 2007, they brokered the "Mecca Accord" between *Hamas* and *Fatah*, calling for an end to the US and European boycott of the Palestinian administration.[74] One month later, they reached out to Iran when President Ahmadinejad was hosted by the Saudi king, and during the Arab summit in Riyad in late March the US occupation of Iraq was denounced as "illegitimate" by Abdullah. All this should be considered against the background of Washington's failure to promote Saudi Arabia's regional interests. The US is seen as regionally hamstrung, and its president as domestically neutered. Its invasion and subsequent occupation of Iraq have fuelled new waves of anti-American sentiment in the Middle East, and thus "[t]he House of Saud is forced to make a show of opposing Washington".[75]

Surprisingly, this "anti-Americanism" also finds echoes in Saudi Arabia's attitude *vis-à-vis* Iran's growing confidence and consequent influence in the region. There are not only worries about Tehran's nuclear ambitions, but also about its sway over the Iraqi government and Shiite militias, its alliance with Syria and its support for *Hezbollah* (and *Hamas*). One should, however, not fall into the trap of simplifying this by placing it within the context of the much-discussed Shii–Sunni divide. Although at first glance this sectarian frame of reference may appear convincing, at closer inspection it has many flaws. As many justly point out, conservative Arab leaders are not so much afraid that Iran will export the cultural and theological aspects of Shiism, but are rather much more worried about the prospect of political Shiism spreading around the region. Groups like *Hezbollah* are developing into the torchbearers of a new Arabism – much to the chagrin of the Saudis. Feeling under the pressure of Arab public opinion both inside the country and in the wider region, they are attempting to reassert their role as leaders of the Arab and wider Muslim world.[76] That is why they have to talk tough against Washington.

This, however, is not the end of the story. Very much in keeping with the historical pattern of Saudi pragmatist diplomacy, Riyad simultaneously entered into a series of informal understandings with the Bush administration and Israel in order to contain Iran's growing weight in the region.[77] The key player on the Saudi side was Prince Bandar bin Sultan, the Saudi national security adviser. Together with Vice-President Dick Cheney, deputy national security adviser Elliot Abrams and the outgoing Ambassador to Iraq Zalmay Khalilzad, a multifarious anti-Iranian strategy was conceived. Details of the plan were revealed by David Samuels:

> While the "get tough" crew favored military action against Iran, the administration chose a more subtle mix of diplomatic and economic pressure, large-scale military exercises, psychological warfare, and covert operations. The bill for the covert part of this activity, which has involved funding sectarian political movements and paramilitary groups in Iraq, Iran, Lebanon, and the Palestinian territories, is said to amount to more than USD 300 million. It is being paid by Saudi Arabia and other concerned Gulf states [. . .] The Saudis agreed to cooperate with the United States not because they were enamored by American policy in the region but because they felt they had no choice.[78]

One element of this anti-Iran programme requires further discussion because of its soft-power ramifications, namely the allocation of funds to weaken the government of Syria's President Bashar al-Assad.[79] Here again the Saudis appear to follow a double-track approach. Although the KSA supports opposition groups in Syria, Saudi investment capital – though mainly from the private sector – also flows into the country (and also, in greater quantities, into Lebanon).[80] This is part of a much larger trend of Arab economic integration which is mainly fuelled by large-scale foreign direct investment from GCC countries.[81] Hertog rightly stresses the political externalities of this integration process: "With assets spread across the region, the costs of diplomatic, economic or military conflict increase. This is a good reason for external players to support regional economic integration."[82] Because GCC countries are relatively weak in military terms, they can profit from flexing their economic muscles, though one should not over-estimate capital's ability to "buy" stability in the region. "Still, the 'soft power' of Gulf capital is not an academic point [and] economic power will increasingly come to the fore in defining inter-Arab relations."[83]

A final example of Saudi soft power which is close to the middle of Hill's continuum is the use of oil as a lever by Saudi Arabian American Oil Company (ARAMCO), the Kingdom's "national flagship". The Saudi government has on many occasions used changes in export levels to meet foreign policy goals. When that occurs, geopolitical considerations outweigh the national oil company's commercial interests and corporate efficiency (in this respect the company is similar to many other national oil companies).[84] In its struggle for hegemony with Iran, it has been suggested, more than once, that Saudi Arabia has the ability to lower the price of oil through higher production rates.[85] Iran's economy and leadership is much more vulnerable to downward changes in oil prices, giving the Saudis a means of putting pressure on Tehran.

4. Conclusion

Grandiose terms like "military globalization" do not seem to describe very well the situation that contemporary Saudi Arabia faces. It is rather difficult to see how we can speak of the much-discussed transformation in the security sector including a shift from so-called traditional Clausewitzian inter-state wars to post-industrial warfare. The Saudi armed forces – though the largest in the Arab part of the Gulf region – have never been a real military force, and hence have been dependent on an outside (i.e. American) umbrella. Equally, they hardly have been able and/or willing to fight a traditional Clausewitzian inter-state war.[86]

Compared to the other case studies in this volume, Saudi Arabia might be seen as a peculiar case also as regards the relationship between the military and the civil authorities. The "classical" picture of politicized national armies does not apply to the Saudi case.[87] No more has the Saudi military's role in politics moved from "revolutionary plot to authoritarian state",[88] simply because of the fact that it never functioned as a revolutionary actor. In most Arab states in the Gulf region, control over the military is asserted by rulers through their families and the tribes with which they are allied. The House of Saud has developed this method of familial and tribal control most fully.[89] This does not mean that civil–military relations have always been as cordial as the ruling strata within the al-Saud family might have wished. That is why the National Guard has been set up as a counterweight to the regular armed forces. What we have here is therefore a "military-tribal complex" *par excellence* that fully conforms to the much-discussed notion of patrimonialism (as opposed to institutionalization).[90]

More or less in line with the above, there is at least one more respect in which the Saudi case is "exceptional". In most Arab states not only has a "military society" evolved, but Arab armies have also become business actors in their own right. In Saudi Arabia, though, the notion of an expanding "economic wing" of the military is largely absent. There is a simple reason for this: the Kingdom has been extremely slow in developing its indigenous defence industry, and there is nothing like a "military-industrial complex".[91]

We have argued that there is a quantitative rather than a qualitative change in Saudi Arabia's security policies. The Al Saud have until now felt comfortable enough to rely on the wealth of the country to "buy off" the threats they face. Externally, the Saudi regime relies largely on its "special relationship", while internally threats are in the main considered manageable. Therefore, whether through buying weaponry or increasing police and intelligence budgets, oil money conceals and postpones the "domestic imperative" for serious change in the security sector.

Notes

1. Nonneman 2005/2006.
2. Gause III 2002.
3. For instance, in terms of military equipment, there have currently been deals with Pakistan (Super Mushak training aircrafts and al-Khaled tanks), Britain (for Typhoon Eurofighters) and Dutch Damen for a series of patrol boats. Furthermore, there has been much talk of Saudi deals with Germany, France, Russia and China along the same lines. al-Qallab 2006.
4. Gause III 2002; Aarts 2004; Also cf. Cordesman 2006. The latter also adds that "[t]he 'best case' limit U.S. energy policy can put on our percentage of dependence on oil imports through 2025 is to keep it constant" (p. 34). It should be remarked, however, that spare capacity of the Saudis has been falling in recent years and it is unclear whether they will regain it via production increases or demand decreases.
5. Cf. for instance Gresh 2003.
6. Nonneman 2001.
7. One notable example is Da Lage 2005. He argues that "[the US is] openly wary of the Saudi regime and doesn't seem any longer to consider its survival a strategic priority" (p. 7). Bronson is another example (Bronson 2005/2006).
8. Cf. for instance The Gracia Group 2002; also Aarts *et al.* 2007. Both in fact recognize that the short-term strategic implications are rather limited, but do not rule out serious mid- or long-term consequences of the growing Chinese energy needs. Niblock concludes that "[I]n the long term, Saudi Arabia's interests may well be best served by shifting its international cooperation towards the countries of South Asia and the Far East" (2006, p. 170).
9. The quick and anxious judgement (especially in the media) in this case has, for instance, been convincingly countered by Blatteis 2007.
10. "Iran's attempt to exploit the current instability in Iraq to consolidate and assert its political leverage at the expense of the other parties sends wrong signals. It is not just a direct intervention in the affairs of an Arab country whose political stability and security are directly linked to the Gulf environment as whole, but it is seen as an attempt to destabilize the regional balance of power and sends clear signals that Tehran's foreign policy is still motivated by narrow interests", Sager 2005, http://209.85.135.104/search?q=cache:1Mz7iEVvxlMJ:www.saudi-us-relations. org/newsletter2005/saudi-relations-interest-06–28.html+Iran%E2%80%99s+ attempt+to+exploit+the+current+instability+in+Iraq+sager+2005&hl=it&ct= clnk&cd=1&gl=it (retrieved 28 November 2008).
11. Gause III 2007.
12. Aarts 2007a.
13. Kaye and Wehrey interestingly note, however, that many regional actors do not perceive a direct nuclear attack from Iran to be the greatest threat. They point out it will be the reactions to or the spillover from a nuclear Iran that poses the greatest threat. Even more interesting is what they noted as the smaller states' worry that the Saudis might undertake a "hegemonic overreaction", "[i]n which Riyad would exploit the threat from Tehran to win Washington's recognition of Saudi pre-eminence in the Sunni Arab world" (Kaye *et al.* 2007, p. 112).

14 Several interviews in Riyad, December 2006.
15 One notable exception was a warning that the KSA would back Sunnis in Iraq, should the US decide to leave. However, issues surrounding this statement suggest this is a matter of controversy amongst the Saudi establishment. For details, see Helene Cooper, "Saudis say they might back Sunnis if U.S. leaves Iraq", *The New York Times*, 13 December 2006; al-Rasheed 2006b.
16 For the latter, cf. Sager 2007. Also cf. Aarts 2007a.
17 Clear examples are Andrew Hammond, "Saudi diplomatic drive runs into U.S. Opposition", *Reuters*, 21 February 2007; and "All puffed up and stalling on reform; Saudi Arabia", *The Economist*, 3 March 2007.
18 Ibid.
19 Examples of latter are Gause III 2002, pp. 198–9 and Peterson 2002, pp. 25–6; while more emphasis on the difficulties is put by for instance by Nonneman 2005/2006, p. 332 or Da Lage 2005.
20 Hegghammer 2006. Indeed, "the extremism of Saudi militants is explained by the fact that they are Saudi" (p. 39).
21 Cordesman *et al.* 2005.
22 Steinberg 2005.
23 Ibid., p. 33.
24 Ibid., p. 34 and Jones 2005.
25 Since the insurgency began, an estimated number of 129 suspects have been killed and another 464 arrested. For an instructive timeline with many references cf. "Terrorism in Saudi Arabia" n.d., *Wikipedia*, http://en.wikipedia.org/wiki/Insurgency_in_Saudi_Arabia (retrieved 6 June 2007).
26 Hegghammer 2006 and Meijer 2005.
27 Cordesman and Obaid certainly belong to the category of these 'optimists', though they remain surprisingly critical *vis-à-vis* the regime, pushing for a reform agenda. Cordesman *et al.* 2004; Cordesman 2005. The optimist view was also expressed in several interviews in Riyad, in particular with Abd al-Aziz al-Fahad (15 December 2006): "Jihadism is manageable".
28 Shades of opinion here, varying from cautious pessimism (like *The Economist*, 19 October 2006; and Richard Russell, "Insurgency in Waiting", *Foreign Policy*, November 2005) to outright warnings that the worst still has to come (like Scheuer *et al.* 2006). Some of the interviews in Riyad and Jedda (December 2006) confirm the pessimist view.
29 Hegghammer 2006, p. 54. The change in policy came first, but it took some time, especially to stop financial support from rich, private Saudis.
30 Cf. for instance Solomon 2006 and Daniel L. Byman, "Saudi Arabia's own Iraq nightmare", *Salon.com*, 8 February 2007.
31 International Crisis Group 2005; private conversation (Riyad, December 2006) with a researcher on the Saudi Jafari Shiites, who conducted several interviews in the Eastern Province; Kaye *et al.* 2007 (p. 116). For a recent evaluation of the Saudi regime's uneasy relationship with the Shiites, cf. Jones 2007.
32 Cf. Hegghammer 2006 and Looney 2004, for interesting examples of this school of thought. This view was also expressed, though in different degrees, by some interviewees in Riyad, like Matruk al-Falih, Abdullah al-Hamid and Khalid al-Dakhil.
33 Zuhur 2005, p. 7.

34 Peterson 2002, p. 68.
35 Gause III 2000.
36 A recent volume tries to push the debate further. The authors do not ask *when* democratization might ultimately occur, or *what* the Middle East "lacks". Rather, the research interest there is on *how* political rule in Arab countries is effectuated, organized and executed, see Schlumberger 2007. In there, Aarts 2007b.
37 Bellin 2004b, p. 141. The article later reappeared in a slightly edited form as "Coercive Institutions and Coercive Leaders" in Pripstein Posusney *et al.* 2005, pp. 21–41.
38 Ibid., p. 143.
39 The others are maintenance of fiscal health, the "patrimonial logic" of both the regimes and their coercive apparatuses, and low levels of popular mobilization.
40 A useful survey is given by Niblock 2006, pp. 7–18.
41 al-Rasheed 2006a, p. 256.
42 Ibid., p. 257.
43 Hill 2003.
44 Cordesman's books often read like "*The Military Balance* on steroids", as Peterson rightly remarks in his recent review essay (2006, p. 152). On the earlier period, see of course Safran 1988.
45 Cf. Cordesman *et al.* 2005, Figure 2, p. 26.
46 Cordesman *et al.* 2004, pp. 8–9; more detailed figures in al-Qallab 2006, pp. 219–20.
47 Peterson 2002, p. 40. For the most recent expenditure figures, cf. SIPRI 2007.
48 Droz-Vincent 2007a.
49 Kahwaji 2003.
50 Nonneman 2005/2006, p. 331. Details in al-Qallab 2006, pp. 215–39.
51 Alani 2006; Hussain 2007.
52 Cordesman *et al.* 2004, p. 31.
53 Cordesman *et al.* 2005, p. 22.
54 Ibid., pp. 29–30.
55 Laipson 2006, p. 10. The text is the result of a workshop in which high-ranking officials from NATO, the US military and State Department and the US National Intelligence Council participated, alongside many scholars. (A similar argument has been put forward in Laipson 2007.)
56 Ibid., p. 17.
57 Ibid., p. 12.
58 Legrenzi 2007a, p. 3. For an expanded version of this paper, see Legrenzi 2007b.
59 Laipson 2006, p. 8 and p. 15 for the clear example of Ukraine.
60 Nonneman 2006.
61 Aliboni 2006, pp. 40–4. Also see Amir Taheri's devastating critique, "NATO has little to offer the GCC states", *Arab News*, 16 December 2006.
62 Cited in Kaye *et al.* 2007, p. 113.
63 Legrenzi 2007a, pp. 4–6; 2007b, p. 71.
64 Droz-Vincent 2007a, p. 206.
65 Laipson 2006; Peterson 2002; Kaye *et al.* 2007.
66 Cordesman *et al.* 2004, p. 36.
67 A recent and decent overview of statements and initiatives is provided by Dalacoura 2005.
68 Young 2006.

69 Young 2006, pp. 3–6. For equally sceptical views, cf. Dalacoura 2006 and Gause III 2005. For a similar discussion on security and reform in Saudi Arabia cf. Zuhur 2005, pp. 41–5.
70 Dalacoura 2005, pp. 969–70.
71 Dioun 2005.
72 Laipson 2006, p. 12.
73 Cordesman *et al.* 2004, p. 30.
74 The Mecca Accord was a diplomatic success, if alone for the fact that it largely extricated Hamas from Iran's influence.
75 Mohammad Bazzi, "The Saudi Paradox", *The Nation*, 10 April 2007, www.thenation.com/doc/20070423/bazzi (retrieved on 5 July 2007).
76 Ibid.; Valbjorn *et al.* 2007. Also Fuller 2006 and Gause III 2007.
77 Seymour M. Hersh, "The Redirection", *The New Yorker*, 5 March 2007, www.newyorker.com/reporting/2007/03/05/07030fa_fact_hersh? (retrieved on 22 May 2007). A similar "alliance" was built with Egypt, Jordan and neighbouring Persian Gulf countries.
78 David Samuels, "Grand Illusions", *The Atlantic*, June 2007, pp. 52–3.
79 Hersh, op. cit, p. 5. Hersh mentions that Saudi Arabia lends financial support to amongst others Abdul Halim Khaddam, former Syrian vice-president who defected in 2005 and lives in Paris (p. 8).
80 Hertog 2007a.
81 Ibid.
82 Ibid., p. 66. This is linked to the wider, theoretical discussion about the relation between trade and democracy. E.g. see Mousseau *et al.* 2003 and Layne 1994.
83 Hertog 2007a, p. 68.
84 For an elaboration of three exemplary cases of Saudi ARAMCO serving political goals, cf. Myers Jaffe *et al.* 2007.
85 For more technical details on the "flood the market" approach (and alternatives), cf. Obaid 2000.
86 In the 1960s, during the civil war in Yemen no Saudi troops were sent by King Faisal. Saudi aid was confined to providing subsidies and weapons to the royalist forces. During the second Gulf War (in February 1991), a symbolic contingent of Saudi troops was sent into Kuwait.
87 As Waterbury remarked, in many Arab states "[p]raetorians have dominated the political scene to a degree and with a technological impregnability that 'tin-pot' African dictators or Latin American caudillos could seldom boast" (Waterbury, 1994, p. 26). In the Saudi case, we have a special variety of a "mission-oriented state", not focused on anti-imperialism, liberation or socialism, but on "Islamic justice". That is also why the Saudi monarchs, at least since King Fahd, preferably label themselves as "Custodian of the Two Holy Mosques".
88 This refers to Elizabeth Picard 1988.
89 As a result of this policy, a separate "military society" did not come into existence in Saudi Arabia like it did in most other Arab states, at least not to the extent that it did elsewhere. Cf. Droz-Vincent 2007a, pp. 203–6.
90 As Salamé once aptly remarked, "In short, no ministerial post related to national security is outside the hands of the sons of Ibn Saud, and it has always been this way" (Salamé 1980, pp. 9–10).
91 The only analysis we have seen is Yezid Sayegh (1993).

12

SECURITY POLICY AND DEMOCRATIC REFORM IN MOROCCO: BETWEEN PUBLIC DISCOURSE AND REALITY

Issandr el Amrani

Introduction

Morocco is often seen as a relatively peripheral country in the Arab world. Aside from its involvement through international organizations like the Arab League or the Organization of the Islamic Conference, it has little direct impact on the Arab–Israel conflict or the Persian Gulf, the two areas of greatest strategic interest in the region for Western powers. Nonetheless, largely due to the personal diplomacy of the late King Hassan II, Rabat has occasionally played a greater role than its remote positions from these "traditional" Middle Eastern conflicts would lead one to believe, notably helping to broker Israeli–Arab peace talks in the 1970s or cultivating a long, if secretive, relationship with the Jewish state since the 1960s – one that has at times estranged it from some of the more radical Arab republics.

Likewise, while it is one of the larger Arab states, with a population of 34 million, its political, economic and cultural integration with the rest of the region is limited. Moroccan emigration has built deep and complex links with Western Europe, but only more recently have Moroccans begun to emigrate to the Arab countries in large numbers. Emigration to France and Spain began in the 1920s during the colonial era, and large migrant communities in France, Belgium, the Netherlands, Germany and Italy now total over 2.3 million. In contrast, less than 250,000 Moroccans are believed to work currently in Arab countries out of a total migrant population of over 3 million.[1]

This tendency to look northwards rather than eastward has been exacerbated by Morocco's poor relationship with its immediate neighbour, Algeria, and the resulting failure of regional political and economic efforts such as the Union of the Arab Maghreb. Although the main cause of the failure of Morocco to integrate deeply with the rest of North Africa has been the Western Sahara conflict, Rabat's alignment with the West between the 1960s and 1980s, at the height of the Cold War, and its poor relations with radical republican regimes in Algeria, Libya and Egypt during that period have also been a factor.

A key result of this relative isolation from its eastern neighbours is that the Moroccan economy is more integrated with southwestern Europe than the rest of North Africa. The European Union (EU) is Morocco's first trade partner, accounting for some 60 per cent of its exports. Since Morocco does not produce strategic commodities such as hydrocarbons (even if it is an important producer of phosphates) and does not have a highly developed export-oriented industrial sector, this trade relationship is naturally imbalanced, with Morocco holding little economic leverage over its northern trade partners compared to, for instance, Algeria, a major supplier of natural gas. Morocco–EU trade, indeed, amounts to less than €20 billion, compared to Algeria's €32 billion.[2] Furthermore, Morocco's trade balance is in the EU's favour. Considering that its economy is highly dependent on low-yield agriculture (with a year of bad rainfall reducing Gross Domestic Product growth from 8 per cent to 2–4 per cent), in recent years Morocco has maintained socio-economic stability (notably through fuel subsidies, since it must import all of its hydrocarbons) and upheld the purchasing power of its inhabitants in the face of global inflationary pressures (most notably the rise of oil and cereal prices on international markets) in good part thanks to remittances from EU-based migrants and aid from allied Arab and Western countries.

If these strategic constraints have contributed to Morocco's isolation, it has also been compounded by the monarchy's own discourse, which has fostered an image of Morocco as unique because of its mixture of Arab, Berber and Andalusian heritage and religious practices, which differ from those commonly found in the rest of the Middle East and North Africa. The prevalence of Sufi brotherhoods, the official adherence of the state *'ulama'* to the Malikite rite of Sunni Islam, or the modern creation of a monarchy in which the King has an explicitly religious role, have all been used both to legitimize the monarchy and delegitimize radical Islamist opponents, whether violent or non-violent.[3] Morocco, Kamrava argues, is, like Jordan, a "civic myth monarchy [. . .] where the monarchical state perpetuates a largely artificial sense of historical resonance".[4]

Western policy- and opinion-makers, finally, have often been a prime target of official discourse aiming to strengthen foreign support for the monarchy – what has occasionally been dubbed as "pastilla diplomacy", in reference to the Moroccan culinary delicacy and the regal treatment often accorded to influential visiting dignitaries. As a result, in official discourse and in the media, Westerners often ascribe a different character to Morocco than the rest of the Arab world.[5] Indeed Morocco's recent reputation as a liberalizing if not liberal Arab country is one of its main assets in the international arena, justifying the preferential treatment it has received over the years from close allies such as the United States or France, notably over the Western Sahara conflict, for which Rabat has received either tacit or explicit backing for its autonomy proposal for the disputed area.

The importance of image is particularly striking when it comes to Morocco's security sector and its integration into a wider regional and global security architecture. Arguably, more than any other large Arab country, the Moroccan security sector has dramatically changed its public image in the last decade. There is a near-universal consensus that the era of heavy-handed security intervention in public life is over, particularly the systematic human rights abuses that characterized the *années de plomb* ("years of lead") under King Hassan II from the early 1970s to the mid-1990s. Morocco is the only country in the region to have created a truth commission to look into past abuses, with an Equity and Reconciliation Commission that concluded in 2004 airing the grievances of victims of the security services on national television, a first in any Arab country. The military, frequently a dominant force in national politics elsewhere in the region, does not play a major public role, although it remains a powerful (and untransparent) player in regime politics.

Can we then say that Morocco fits into any dominant model for the security sector in the Arab world? Is Morocco an exception to the general picture of state–security relations in the region? Are its relations with Western powers substantially different from those of its neighbours?

This chapter will argue that, in most fundamental ways, Morocco is not an exception to the general dominance of the security sector over politics in the Arab world and that it has been shaped by many of the same processes seen elsewhere in the region. What differentiates Morocco, especially in comparison to other major Western allies in the region such as Egypt or Saudi Arabia, is that it has relatively little to offer strategically or in terms of resources. Western powers supported King Hassan II throughout his reign because he was a skilled diplomat, building personal ties with foreign leaders and unequivocally allying himself to the West during the Cold War in both the security and commercial spheres.[6] Morocco also was a willing provider of operational and diplomatic help to further Western interests in Africa, the Middle East and elsewhere. For most of its history since independence, therefore, Morocco's security policy was driven above all by the imperative of preserving the monarchy, particularly at a time when several monarchies elsewhere in the region were overthrown and the Soviet Union and much of the non-aligned movement backed the republican left. In the global security architecture of the Cold War, it was first and foremost a diplomatic and security subcontractor, not a major initiator of policies.

If much of Morocco's security policy was driven by relatively stable fundamentals – the monarchy's determination to remain a dominant political player (or ensure its survival), Cold War rivalries, the Western Sahara conflict – how have these been changed by the major political shifts of the last two decades? How has Moroccan security policy responded to the end of the Cold War, the rise of a unipolar world, and the advent of globalized salafist jihadism and the violent radical movements it inspires? Morocco may be a case worth watching because in several respects it has been an innovator and an early adaptor to new regional trends.

1. Historical Background

1.1 Is there a Moroccan specificity?

Any research into Morocco's security sector must take into account the political vocabulary of the country – the symbolic associations made with the political-security establishment and its historic legitimacy. Algeria has *le pouvoir* whose legitimacy is derived from a war of independence, Saudi Arabia a public alliance between the al-Saud family and supporters of Wahabism, Egypt a military regime inherited from the Free Officers who staged the 1952 coup – all handy shortcuts to describe, and sometimes justify, the presence of a political oligarchy and its associated repressive apparatus. These often obscure much more than they reveal.

Morocco, more than most of its neighbours, makes use of such a shortcut to explain away the power structure of the country: the *makhzen*.

The *makhzen* is an old term, as those who use it will attest. Literally, in Arabic it means "storehouse", and more specifically the supply depots (or supply lines) in military operations. The French and English equivalent term, "magazine", was derived from the Arabic word and used in much the same way in English until the mid-eighteenth century, when it was replaced by the still commonly used military term "commissary". Its usage in Morocco refers to the practice, dating from the Arab invasions to the early twentieth century, of a central, urban and usually Arab-led government claiming sovereignty over a particular area of land and collecting taxes and tributes from the frequently rebellious tribes that inhabit them. The urban political centres that claimed sovereignty over these areas were unable to police rebel areas permanently; they would have to launch military incursions periodically to collect taxes and impose peace. Hence the division, commonly referred to in the Moroccan political discourse, to *bilad al-makhzen* ("the land of the storehouse") and *bilad al-siba* ("the land of dissent") – a political centre able to use overwhelming violence to reaffirm the legitimacy of its sovereignty over an area and demand allegiance.

As the historian Daniel Rivet showed, the French protectorate in Morocco ushered in an era of wide-ranging transformation in the nature and structure of the Moroccan state. Colonial officials who governed Morocco between 1912 and 1956 perceived the existence of a traditional "*haut makhzen*" of about 50 officials. This traditional *makhzen* was supplanted by a colonial *makhzen* composed of both French and Moroccan officials. But the French colonial officials did not desire only to supplant a traditional elite: they also had specific ideas about how to reform the Moroccan state and its administration.[7] This took many forms, from the introduction of new bureaucratic methodologies to a "pacification" campaign against those who refused to bow to the new order, killing an estimated 30,000 in the process. Despite its relative brevity, Morocco's colonial era introduced fundamental changes in the idea of state and governance, arguably bringing into being the first coherent Moroccan state. Whatever *makhzen* existed in 1912 when French officials formally took over governing Morocco, it no longer exists today.

Nonetheless, the idea of the *makhzen* is very much alive and underpins much of current discourse on Moroccan politics and the nature of the security sector. Asked to describe the *makhzen*, one prominent journalist said it was "an economic–security nexus", a confluence of interests.[8] It includes the King, the most important political actor, as well as high-level civil servants, large economic and landholding interests, businessmen, politicians, and more. The notable families of Fez that provided the majority of Morocco's major post-independence political actors and still wield considerable influence (and are well represented in parts of the security sector) are often described as a core part of the *makhzen* (although they have also provided leading anti-*makhzen* dissidents, such as the leftist-nationalist leader Mehdi Ben Barka). But then so is the military, which was in the early post-independent years dominated by Berber officials who had been favoured by the French colonial administration. Despite this, however, Morocco's security establishment is neither tribally nor provincially based, as is the case in many of the Gulf States. This is true even if tribalism or provincialism does play a role in military promotion and recruitment, since ultimately "loyalty to the King is the sole criteria for promotion",[9] and counterbalances to ethnic and tribal dominance of the military were put in place by Hassan II after the failed coups of the early 1970s.

The *makhzen*'s borders are vague and permeable; attempts to delimit them are difficult. To complicate matters, we are told that ambiguity is a "makhzenian" strategy; that individuals and institutions can be "makhzenified" or "de-makhzenified"; that the *makhzen* is in a state of perpetual flux and reinvention, with its very members always at risk of exclusion or loss of influence. Finally, the concept of the *makhzen* as "traditional" or rooted in Morocco's history acts as a form of self-justification for existing power structures. This is not to say that a *makhzen* (i.e. a form of power elite, whether religious, military, economic, or political) does not have a historical basis, but rather that the term obfuscates rather than clarifies Moroccan politics.

1.2 Security priorities since independence

Morocco's independence, which came in 1956, was a negotiated political settlement rather than the outcome of a prolonged, brutal war as in neighbouring Algeria. After independence, over 80,000 French troops remained in the country as guests of the newly independent government while French officers continued to play a central role in the training of the

Royal Armed Forces. The negotiated nature of Morocco's independence and continued collaboration with France shaped many of the particularities of Morocco's security outlook, notably its integration into Western security structures and the lack of taboos about collaboration (notably security collaboration) with former colonial powers (unlike much of the rest of the Arab world at the time). It also legitimized a monarch who, despite having been exiled by France because of his refusal to abide by colonial policies, had not been at the forefront of the liberation movement and was not a national political leader in the same sense that, for instance, the historic leader of the *Istiqlal* ("Independence") Party, Allal al-Fassi, had been.

Muhammad V came to power after independence as one of several dominant political players and, unlike his successors, did not have the institutional right to make security policy. By the time of the second government formed by Mbarek Bekkai, Morocco's first Prime Minister, the Ministries of the Interior and Foreign Affairs had both fallen under the control of the dominant *Istiqlal*.[10] This is in stark contrast to later practice lasting to this day, in which the Ministries of the Interior, Foreign Affairs and Defence are labelled as "ministries of sovereignty" and placed under the control of the palace. In terms of setting security policy, the new King – whose legitimacy is partly based on his role in obtaining independence from France – had to contend with a partisan world that rallied around international calls for decolonization as well as the national ambitions of politicians. Initially, he had to allow national politicians inclined to show solidarity with anti-colonial struggles a free hand. But within a few years, and especially by the time of Hassan II's reign, this practice would end. Indeed, Moroccan nationalist leaders who acquired an international profile, such as Mehdi Ben Barka, a strong advocate of Algerian independence and political rival of the King, would be sidelined and eventually exiled and assassinated.[11]

By the 1970s, after a decade of social and political upheaval, political parties such as the *Istiqlal* and its left-leaning offshoot, the *Union National des Forces Populaires* (UNFP), which would later become the *Union Socialiste des Forces Populaires* (USFP), were effectively de-fanged and played a negligible role in influencing foreign and security policy. It was under Muhammad V's short reign that the "securitization" of the monarchy would first be promoted by then Crown Prince Hassan, who was appointed head of the Royal Armed Forces and maintained close links with the head of the nascent security apparatus, General Muhammad Oufkir, who would become his right-hand man and, eventually, attempt a coup against the monarch in 1972. The clampdown against political parties and social movements that characterized much of the 1960s gave way, in the early 1970s, to a more pressing concern for the Palace: that the powerful security establishment, most notably the military, was itself trying to oust Hassan II. The successive coups of Skhrirat in 1971 and Oufkir in 1972 confirmed this in Hassan II's mind and initiated a change in tactic for the monarch, who had hitherto relied chiefly on the armed forces to ensure stability. In the short term, it led to purges in the military and the establishment of intelligence units tasked with the surveillance of the officer corps (as well as other intelligence agencies), resulting in an expansion of the security sector. It also caused the King to pursue a policy of cooptation of the leadership of the armed forces, most notably through the personal enrichment of senior officials and the encouragement of corruption. Most significantly, though, Hassan II saw that the officer corps needed to be kept occupied by external threats rather than domestic concerns. His decision to launch the Green March in 1975 to lay Morocco's claim to the Western Sahara, until then a Spanish colony, served this purpose, as well as that of uniting a discontented population towards a nationalist goal.

Since the second half of the 1970s, the linkage between the monarchy's political legitimacy, the nature of its relationship with the security establishment (notably the armed forces) and continued Moroccan sovereignty over the Western Sahara has been a key factor in Morocco's role in the global security architecture, whether during the Cold War or afterwards. It has also contributed to the unusual role the country has played in regional politics. Not only did Morocco maintain excellent relations with Israel between 1956 and 1967, it continued the relationship covertly after the 1967 Israel–Arab war and developed close intelligence ties with the Israeli intelligence agency Mossad as well as Israeli political leaders.[12] When the Arab–Israeli conflict began to thaw in the 1990s, with a comprehensive peace process considered possible for the first time, Morocco was an enthusiastic backer of normalization with Israel. This support for engagement with Israel – hardly an issue of direct national security relevance for Morocco and one that earned the disapproval of much of the domestic opposition – was closely tied to its lobbying effort on the issue of the Western Sahara, where pro-Israel US congressmen such as Tom Lantos have long been among the most ardent supporters of Morocco's position.[13]

At the same time, Morocco often played a role in supporting US allies in the region and beyond, particularly in the context of the Cold War and American concern about the spread of communism in the developing world. For instance, it took part in an informal intelligence-gathering and military operations network known as the "Safari Club", a late 1970s US-led effort at destabilization of pro-Soviet Sub-Saharan African countries involving France, Egypt, (pre-revolutionary) Iran and Saudi Arabia, created to some extent to enable parts of the American intelligence community to conduct undercover operations without congressional oversight. Morocco's role in that particular initiative was to provide "muscle" for counter-insurgency operations, as it did in 1978 in Kowelzi, a mining city in southern Zaire that had been overtaken by rebels.[14] Morocco would provide similar services to Saudi Arabia in 1979, with Hassan II sending his close aide Moulay Hafid Alaoui and *Gendarmerie Royale* commandos when the Grand Mosque of Mecca was taken over by an Islamist faction seeking the overthrow of the al-Saud family.[15] In the 1980s, like many Arab states, Morocco participated in the US-led support for Afghan rebels after the Soviet invasion, encouraging local Islamists to join Arab *mujahidin* in Afghanistan.[16] As we shall see, Morocco's practice of making itself available as a useful ally and provider of various security services continues to be a cornerstone of its foreign and security policy after the Cold War.

2. Security Reform under Muhammad VI

2.1 Monarchical transition and the security sector

Morocco's domestic politics, foreign policy and security policy all intersect at a single point: the royal palace. The constitution gives the monarch not only the legal power to appoint the Ministers of Justice, Interior and Foreign Affairs but also provides a religious justification for this arrangement, since the King is *amir al mu'minin* ("commander of the faithful") and is symbolically tasked with protecting the country against both internal and external threats. More importantly, the King heads the armed forces and directly appoints most of the senior officials in both the uniformed military and in paramilitary and security agencies. The practice of statecraft is actually more important: Hassan II, under whom the modern system of governance was chiefly developed, delegated decision-making powers to only a few senior officials and advisers and frequently took an active role in the management of security issues.

Muhammad VI has largely perpetuated this tradition, even if the consolidation of his key advisers took time. Of particular concern to the new monarch was carrying out a smooth transition from his father's security team, which had changed little since the early 1980s, to new personalities who had his trust. Considering the highly personalized nature of governance in Morocco and the considerable powers invested in the person of the King, a change in the leading policy-makers and policy-implementers was thus inevitable. It was already known that a circle of advisers, former classmates and friends of Muhammad VI when he was still Crown Prince would come to replace the "old guard" of his father; the question was the pace and extent of this change.

It came as little surprise that the first "old guard" member to go was Idris al-Basri, the powerful Minister of the Interior whose name had become synonymous with repression in the 1980s. Basri, who held the post of Minister of Information as well as the Interior portfolio, was a pure product of Morocco's security apparatus, having been promoted from a minor police position in the 1970s to become one of the key architects and implementers of security policy in the 1980s and 90s.[17] Paradoxically, Basri was also one of the main implementers of the political reconciliation with the opposition that took place in the mid-1990s, often dealing with figures that had been his sworn enemies, such as former Prime Minister and USFP leader Abd al-Rahman Yussufi. Basri was disliked by most of Muhammad VI's entourage and some of the old guard, as well as by the new King himself who is widely believed to have resented Basri's spying on his activities for his father.

This alone may have been a motive to remove him, but the most important one was that Basri was a living symbol of Morocco's repressive past. The decision to sack him came only a few months after Muhammad VI became King and highlighted the new monarch's intention to make a clean break with the past. The new King was eager to distance himself from his father as much as he appropriately could: this was not just a question of temperament, but of political and diplomatic necessity. Hassan II had survived numerous coup attempts and continued to rule absolutely throughout his reign, building a new monarchical institution with complete dominance over the political system. But he did so while ignoring, sometimes deliberately, wider questions such as economic growth, social justice, education, and judicial and agrarian reform. He also personally encouraged corruption among high officials, believing that personal enrichment would distract them from politics, and would reward his supporters lavishly. This was especially true of the security sector, where personnel in the armed forces or security services could count on many advantages and high-ranking officials were given opportunities to benefit massively from "royal gifts" of land, fishing licences, or monopoly positions on the domestic market.[18] This practice is not believed to have ceased entirely, and while the military now plays a less prominent role in domestic politics, the families of officials who were top brass under Hassan II have been assured an important role in the public and private spheres, notably in business.

2.2 Muhammad VI and the marketing of security sector reform

Muhammad VI inherited all the prestige, power and stature that Hassan II had put into the monarchy,[19] but also arrived on the scene keenly aware, as his father had been during his last years, of the urgency of moving away from old patterns of authoritarianism. Perhaps the clearest sign that the new monarchy saw the role of the security services at least in part differently than his father was a speech introducing a "new concept of authority" that sought to redefine the relationship between "agents of authority" (police officers and other representatives of the state) and citizens. Only three months after ascending to the throne, Muhammad VI said this would be "a concept based on the protection of public services, local affairs, individual and collective freedoms, the preservation of security and stability, the [effective] handling of local affairs and the maintenance of social peace".[20]

One (albeit short-lived) experiment to come out of the "new concept of authority" was the idea of a *police de proximité* ("neighbourhood police") intended to act as a more immediate and approachable form of authority, particularly in "difficult" neighbourhoods that had not effectively been policed before. The implementation of the *Groupes Urbains de Securité* (GUS), as the new police were called, between 2004 and 2006 was in part a reaction to the completely unexpected Casablanca bombings of 16 May 2003, whose perpetrators issued mostly from a Casablanca slum where state services, as well as authority, barely existed (and thus had limited intelligence-gathering capabilities). Despite the official boost given to the new units, they were poorly received at the local level and did not survive the removal from his post of their primary backer, General Hamidou Lanigri, a senior security chief.[21]

In spite of the lack of success of the new policing methods, the King's speech signalled, early in his reign, a willingness to move beyond the long-standing, and frequently antagonistic, pattern of relationships between the state and citizens. In many respects, that process of gradual democratization, improvement in the respect of human rights and reform of state institutions would be the signature of Muhammad VI's regime. This was not only the result of the monarch's frequently professed genuine desire for a clean break with his father's authoritarianism, but part and parcel of a strategy for regime adaptation made unavoidable by domestic circumstances, the rise of new threats such as jihadist violence and the linkage between security and democratization made at the geostrategic level.[22]

2.3 Public discourse on reform and governance in an age of globalized norms

The last three decades have seen the discourse of human rights and democratization take an increasingly important place in international affairs. The formula derived at the Helsinki Accords for the monitoring of human rights in Eastern Europe and the Soviet Union – an often lauded model that engendered one of the world's most influential human rights groups, Human Rights Watch and is occasionally credited for contributing to the demise of the Soviet bloc – has more recently been redeployed towards the Middle East, often perceived as one of the last parts of the planet where the "third wave" of democratization has not taken place. In particular, it has been a particularly prominent part of the discourse of the United States, both in justifying military action (as in Iraq) and exerting pressure on allies for political reform (as in Egypt or Saudi Arabia). Even if this policy is now widely seen to have been abandoned in favour of *realpolitik*, it remains an important part of both formal Western discourse and an object of debate in the domestic arenas of both Western and Arab states. Even countries that have a policy of only making muted reference to issues of democratic governance and human rights, like most European countries, must contend with this debate and its possible ramifications in bilateral and multilateral relations. The European Union, for instance, routinely includes articles on human and political rights in its trade agreements with southern Mediterranean countries, even if it rarely enforces those provisions.

In Morocco, these external calls for greater respect of human rights and referencing of democratic norms have also largely been internalized by domestic actors – not only among the opposition, which has long called for better governance and respect of human rights and sees an opportunity in these new normative concerns, but also among regime elites. As argued above, Morocco's experience is that of an "early adopter" of a democratization discourse, for both domestic and international reasons. King Hassan II's decision to begin a partial liberalization of his political system, often linked to the publication of Gilles Perault's *Notre Ami Le Roi* in France in 1990, had international public opinion in mind as well as domestic concerns, most notably preparing the ground for a smooth monarchical succession. This opening saw new royal advisers coming to the fore, the creation of a think-tank within the royal cabinet, the recruitment of technocrats to advise on policy, and of most symbolical importance the courting of former dissidents and opposition forces culminating with the formation of a government by the *Union Socialiste des Forces Populaires* in 1996. The dynamic created in the mid-1990s of a gradual political opening was continued by Muhammad VI after the death of Hassan II, often using the same methods.

In this regard, the role of the security apparatus as a repressive mechanism played a prominent role. A major political success for the young monarch was the successful wooing of several of Morocco's most prominent dissidents, including former militants Abraham Serfaty and Idris Benzekri, both of whom had spent 17 years in jail for their membership of the radical Marxist-Leninist movement *Ila al-amam* ("Forward") before being released and exiled in 1991 due to international pressure. Benzekri went on to play a key role, again both domestically and internationally, in rehabilitating the role of the security services in the public eye by chairing the Equity and Reconciliation Commission (ERC) charged with looking into human rights abuses during Hassan II's reign. In many respects, the ERC was a groundbreaking initiative in the Arab world: no other country had ever had such a public recanting of past abuses, with the testimony of torture victims aired on television for the first time in the region.

It was presented as a royal initiative and as a sign of Muhammad VI's commitment to democratic reforms. As Human Rights Watch noted in its appraisal of the ERC, it was an unprecedented development in the Middle East and North Africa, and Moroccan authorities presented it as proof of the country's commitment to political reform.[23] Yet Moroccan and international human rights groups, while lauding the ERC, remained critical of the limitation of its scope.

Critics regretted the considerable constraints on the ERC. First, the ERC could not publicly name officials whom it found to be responsible for, or implicated in, the commission of grave human rights abuses. This limitation seemed that much harder to accept given that a number of officials suspected of ordering or participating in the commission of grave abuses continue to hold high positions within the government, and certain types of abuses are continuing to occur in Morocco.

There were also concerns about the ERC mandate, which seemed to focus on forced disappearances and arbitrary detention while excluding other forms of grave abuse, such as torture. Critics also asked how the ERC would go about obtaining the cooperation of state agencies, given that it had no statutory powers to compel cooperation or punish non-cooperation.[24]

Despite these limitations, the ERC played a major role in enhancing Morocco's image, both domestically and abroad, and confirming the regime's argument that a serious, if gradual, democratization was underway. Just as importantly, the real decrease in heavy-handedness by the security services and the cessation of previous practices common under Hassan II – such as "disappearances" of political dissidents and the widespread use of torture – suggested that the "years of lead" were truly over. Combined with reforms in the political arena, most notably the integration of Islamist movements into a monarchy-led political consensus (as in the case of the Justice and Development Party), they presented an image of a relatively pluralist Morocco whose regime had the ability to integrate and defuse potentially destabilizing political forces. Domestically, it gave political parties and an increasingly robust and diverse civil society renewed confidence in a government that, even if it has dampened nearly a decade into the Muhammad VI era, is rarely seen elsewhere in the region.

The public commitment to democratization was also important to reassure some of Morocco's main backers in the international arena, which were becoming less tolerant of the kind of authoritarianism that had prevailed in the region during the Cold War, especially Washington, which had a domestic political need for success stories of democratization in the Arab world after the Bush administration's vocal adoption of democracy promotion as a signature policy. Indeed, in the three Western countries for which Morocco's political stability is an important strategic and security issue – the United States, France and Spain – the question of Morocco's human rights record and the degree of political reform were to lesser or greater extents domestic issues, whether because of the espousal of specific normative policies towards the region (the US) and a perceived need for public diplomacy successes (i.e. "hearts and minds" campaigns geared not only to building up pro-US governments, but also publics in the Arab world), or because of domestic constituencies (such as immigrant communities and non-governmental organizations) whose activism resonated in public debate.

In the latter case, the inadequacy of the transition process was to have direct consequences on Morocco's security sector. As we have seen, some key symbolic personalities implicated in the human rights abuses of the Hassan II era were removed early on in Muhammad VI's reign, such as former Minister of the Interior Idris Basri. Others, particularly those close to Basri, were removed from important offices or forced to retire early. But many long-serving personalities of the security sector remained or acquired new positions of importance. In late 2007, the changing legal landscapes of France and Spain would come to affect some key security personnel directly. In October, Patrick Ramael, a French judge investigating the death of Moroccan leftist dissident Mehdi Ben Barka in 1965, issued international arrest warrants for the questioning of five senior Moroccan officials, including the head of the *Gendarmerie Royale*, General Hosni Benslimane, and Inspector General of the Royal Armed Forces, Abd al-Qadir Qadiri – both members of Hassan II's "old guard" and key military figures. Separately, Baltasar Garzon, a Spanish judge investigating atrocities committed in the Western Sahara in the 1970s and 80s at the request of Spanish pro-Polisario activists, asked for 13 international arrest warrants against security officials on 30 October, including Benslimane.

Should the arrest warrants be validated (which would require their confirmation by the ministries of justice of France and Spain), they would prevent the persons concerned from undertaking any international travel. The allegations made against Benslimane are especially damaging considering that he still holds a senior position, controlling Morocco's largest paramilitary institution. Garzon had reportedly also considered summoning Yassin Mansouri, the head of Morocco's intelligence *Direction générale des études et de la documentation* (DGED) and a key counter-terrorism official close to Muhammad VI, but eventually decided against it.[25] Although it appears that, for now, both the French and Spanish governments will protect their ally and prevent the arrest warrants from being enforced, this type of "judicial activism" (as Moroccan authorities have dubbed it) sets a precedent for future pressure on the country and reinforces the notion that transnational norms pose an increasing challenge to the principle of national sovereignty that has long protected domestic elites.

3. Mixed Messages: The "War on Terror" and Democratic Reform

3.1 Counter-terrorism and social policy

The terrorist attacks of 11 September 2001, the emergence of a globalized jihadist effort and the launch by the United States of a "global war on terror" brought changes to the security policies of states throughout the region, and particularly those traditionally allied to Washington. Morocco's own encounter with the violent Islamist phenomenon in its contemporary form dates from the 1970s, but it remained largely shielded from major terrorist attacks or the spread of jihadist ideology among the Islamist opposition, even during neighbouring Algeria's civil war in the 1990s. The post-September 11 strategic environment began to change this, and the country took a definitive turn with the Casablanca bombings of 16 May 2003 which, despite occasional minor attacks in the 1990s and awareness of growing salafist jihadist activism among Moroccans (especially in Europe), had taken the security establishment by surprise. From an environment in which such attacks were unknown and extremist militant groups were believed to have little or no domestic support networks, terrorism emerged as a problem for Morocco as it has elsewhere.

On the domestic front, the Casablanca bombings launched a debate – both public and within the regime – as to whether democratization had been too hasty or had contributed to the rise of homegrown terrorist movements. This debate was widely framed in media accounts and by analysts as one between "*securitaires*" (security types) who wanted to espouse a "Tunisian model" of tightly controlled secular illiberalism and reformists who were keen to preserve and build upon the advances made in the 1990s, including the political integration of moderate Islamists who could be used as a bulwark against salafist jihadism. Indeed, moderate Islamists frequently see themselves as "safety valves" for young Moroccans who might be tempted by the radicalism of *al-Qaʻida* and its affiliates.[26] And while the initial reaction to the 16 May bombings included a backlash against Islamists by some, particularly among the more secular parts of Morocco's socio-economic elite, at the higher levels of government a consensus has remained on the gradual integration of Islamist political forces begun in 1996.

Others had a different analysis still: that the emergence of religious terrorism in Morocco was a result of years of social neglect by the government and that Muhammad VI's new regime had acted too hesitantly to redress the grievances of the poor.[27] For many, that most of the 16 May bombers came from the Casablanca shantytown of Sidi Moumen – a part of the city where makeshift homes built atop a garbage dump are shared by residents, chickens and sheep – gave credence to the idea that terrorism was fuelled by social injustice and poverty. The Moroccan government also seems to have adopted this line of thinking: over the next few years, it invested heavily in a new social housing programme and declared the eradication of shantytowns by 2012 as a major goal – one that would require the construction of 200,000 homes every year.[28] Security officials have made the relationship between counter-terrorism and social disaffection quite explicit. "Morocco does not have extensive homegrown terrorist networks or key ideologues based here", explained one senior counter-terrorism official. "Most key [Moroccan] radical leaders are abroad, in Europe or Afghanistan or elsewhere. Our key problem domestically is rising social inequality".[29]

3.2 The internationalization of Moroccan terrorism

Of course, Morocco's security sector has had to adapt to the spread – and evolution – of Islamist radicalism after 11 September and the Casablanca bombings. Officials said new personnel had to be brought in, including from outside the traditional security establishment (including universities) to face the rising threat of attacks and gain a better understanding of the phenomenon, as well as the bureaucratic-security procedures overhauled.

The nature of the threat has also evolved considerably since the Casablanca bombing, most notably with the expansion of *al-Qa'ida*'s global activity after 11 September. The 11 March 2004 Madrid bombings, with the significant role played by Moroccan jihadists in the operation, highlighted the fact the Moroccans now play, at the militant if not the ideologue level, an important part in the international salafist jihadist movement. Indeed, the central role of Moroccans in European networks, their access to more experienced radicals in Afghanistan and elsewhere, has become a major threat to both Europe and Morocco. Groups such as the *Groupe Islamique Combatant Marocain* (GICM), believed to be responsible for the Casablanca and Madrid bombings, have proved successful in evading both Moroccan and European authorities, and rely on multinational networks and sleeper cells drawn from among Moroccan immigrants abroad, *mujahidin* in Afghanistan and local cells. The emergence of the group as the major jihadist group targeting Morocco, aiming to overthrow the monarchy and establish an Islamic state, was a blow to Morocco's self-image as a nation of moderate Islamic practice and island of stability in a troubled region. Most of all, it showed the need for greater coordination between European and Moroccan security services.[30]

The Madrid bombings, pointing to worrying radicalization among the immigrant Moroccan community in Europe, has engendered an era of interdependence between European (particularly Belgian, French, German and Spanish) intelligence agencies and those of Morocco. Most of the threat warnings indicating possible attacks in Morocco have come from Europe – for instance, the high state of alert announced in June 2006 was the result of information delivered by German intelligence based on investigations of Moroccan immigrants based there.[31]

3.3 Counter-terrorism subcontracting and the limits of security reform

More controversially, Morocco now also plays a significant role in the United States' counter-terrorism effort as one of the main countries involved in the CIA's rendition programme, and has built a detention and interrogation centre near Temara, just outside of the capital Rabat, for that purpose.[32] According to officials and lawyers for detainees who have been released, the centre also serves as a major routing point for suspects held at the US detention centre in Guantanamo, Cuba, where Moroccan interrogators have also been invited to carry out questioning. Beyond the controversy over its legality under the laws of the countries involved, the rendition programme also presents the paradox of using a country that has carried out a historic public examination of the past use of torture and pledged to move beyond the practice as a "torture subcontractor" for international counter-terrorism investigations.

That irony has not been lost on Morocco's human rights activists, who claim that the programme perpetuates the use of torture and other human rights abuses they have long campaigned against and denounce the United States' contradictory discourse of democracy promotion.[33] The programme has also had the role of limiting US pressure on Morocco for certain democratic reforms: one security official involved in the rendition programme, complaining of US pressure on other fronts to reform procedural legislation used to detain suspects, exclaimed confusedly: "I don't understand what they want from us. We are giving them everything they want [on security cooperation]. What do they want from us!?"[34] Contradictory pressures by external actors such as the US or EU have benefited the status quo since they have done little, despite rhetoric promoting democratization, to encourage more thorough security sector reform. The use of Morocco's security services as interrogation and torture subcontractors has now further added to the mixed messages Morocco's Western patrons are sending.

As a result, what reforms the security services have gone through have largely ignored issues such as the promotion of the rule of law in favour of technical support and a more technocratic approach to controlling the salafist jihadist phenomenon, notably strengthening regional counter-terrorism collaboration with an unlikely partner, Algeria. Despite long-running diplomatic tensions between the two countries over the Western Sahara, and poor personal relations between Algerian president Abd al-Aziz Bouteflika and King Muhammad VI, in recent years counter-terrorism has been significantly enhanced. The formation in 2005 of *al-Qa'ida* in the Islamic Maghreb (AQIM), an outgrowth of Algeria's *Groupe Salafiste pour le Combat et La Predication* (GSPC), and its attempts to recruit other North African jihadist groups under the *al-Qa'ida* banner has presented a common new threat for the "brother enemies". This common threat increased significantly in 2007 as AQIM claimed responsibility for a series of attacks in Algeria and key *al-Qa'ida* leader Ayman al-Zawahiri, in several statements, urged fellow jihadists to take up arms against regimes allied with the United States and personally targeted King Muhammad VI and President Bouteflika.[35]

Moroccan officials say that since mid-2007 Algerian officials have shown a "surprising" willingness to coordinate counter-terrorism efforts.[36] Recent joint operations have focused on the border town of Oujda, a major transit point for contraband between the two countries. In early November 2007, for instance, three men believed to be members of AQIM were arrested at the border.[37] Operations have focused on the contraband routes between the two countries – used to smuggle subsidized Algerian goods into Morocco and Moroccan hashish into Algeria – not only because of worries that jihadists could use the smugglers' routes to bring in people and explosives, but also because smuggling itself is suspected of being a source of income for radical groups that combine jihadist activities with organized crime. For Morocco, a main aim of the operation is preventing Moroccan jihadists from travelling to Southern Algeria or Mali, where AQIM is believed to operate training bases.

4. Conclusion

The idea, popularized in recent years, that democratization and security are inextricably linked and that there is a direct relationship between the rise of radical ideologies and authoritarian governance in the Arab world has yet to be fully tested. It could be that the two bear little relation, and that causes for the rise in radical ideology and non-state violence have other roots. Morocco offers a singular opportunity to test such linkages, yet the matter has remained largely unexplored. As we have seen, Morocco in the early 1990s was among the first countries in the region to respond to new globalized norms of democratic governance in the Arab world, and took important symbolic steps in the last decade to acknowledge the role that bad governance (whether economic, political or social) can play in encouraging radicalism. Yet, despite a discourse of democratization adopted by both Morocco and its main Western allies, in practice the Cold War bargain of unconditional support for regimes in exchange for strategic security alliances has continued – and arguably taken new, more pernicious, forms with the practice of extraordinary rendition.

What could an alternative policy – one that fully takes into account the shared risks presented by globalized terrorism but also the "soft security" issues of migration control, drug and contraband traffic[38] and food security issues,[39] among others – look like?

To begin with, for Western countries, it could link the preservation of mutually beneficial regional security structures with the need for socio-economic reforms that take into account the fragility of these societies. This has largely been done in rhetoric since the beginning of the Barcelona Process in the 1990s, but has had little impact in practice due to the lack of serious interest among Western states and, at times, strong resistance from Arab governments. In the region, Morocco presents the advantage that the debate on these issues among the political elite and society at large is more advanced than in virtually any other Arab country. For Moroccan policy-makers, resistance to change may be overcome by the prospect of long-term partnerships on a more equal footing that offer the opportunity to promote stability without yielding to the status quo. The US, which has pledged significant funds for Morocco's economic development[40] and adopted the rhetoric of democracy promotion, could with other countries play this role but has limited its influence by subcontracting its own anti-democratic counter-terrorism practices to Morocco. The EU, as its policy towards the Arab world undergoes a third transformation with the Union for the Mediterranean, appears to be further shying away from political pressure despite the fact that it is the biggest donor of aid to Morocco, preferring to focus on commercial relations and soft security issues such as migration.

More crucial than external factors, though, will be how the long-standing debate on constitutional reform will be resolved. For several decades, Moroccan political forces on both left and right have demanded that the current constitution, which gives virtually all important powers to the King, be amended to establish a better balance between elected officials and the Palace. Issues such as judicial independence, parliamentary oversight of the Ministries of the Interior and Defence, are key. Thus, though not negligible, most of the Moroccan regime's reforms of the security sector have been superficial, and have inherently placed a modernizing monarch at their centre. As Kamrava argues about both Jordan and Morocco:

> [the monarch] has made himself indispensable to the controlled liberalization process that is currently underway and is highly unlikely to be swept away by a tide of popular excitement of the kind that cost East European autocrats their powers. Liberalization has turned into both regimes' newest source of popular legitimacy, having become a safety valve for pent-up pressures. Yet control over foreign and defence policies resides firmly with the king, and he remains the nominal as well as the real commander of the armed forces. Beneath the surface of the new democratic era, therefore, old political formulas for maintaining power continue to prevail.[41]

Although much enthusiasm for enacting these changes exists, notably among newer leftist parties and elements of several Islamist movements,[42] these are not currently in power.

King Muhammad VI himself has shown little initiative in leading the way on constitutional reform, although he has occasionally raised the issue in public. The irony is that such reforms, while they would radically change the nature of the Moroccan monarchy, could be the most effective way to reduce the fundamental insecurity of monarchies in the Arab world: the possibility of being overthrown by the very same security services and armed forces they must rely on.

Notes

1 Migration Information Source 2005.
2 European Commission 2008.
3 A thorough historical discussion of the religious self-justification of the Moroccan monarchy can be found in Tozy 1999.
4 Kamrava 2000, p. 87.
5 For example, when announcing a US–Morocco Free Trade Agreement in 2004, US Trade Representative Robert B. Zoellick said the agreement would boost "deeper economic and political partnership with Morocco, a bright light of reform and moderation in the Islamic world" (cited in "USA under Bush loses trust of Arabs; but new American trade & aid ideas are interesting", *APS Diplomat News Service*, 21 June 2004). In his message to Congress asking for the ratification of the trade agreement, President George W. Bush said "Leaders in Morocco support a reformist and tolerant vision that includes free parliamentary elections, the sale of state-owned businesses, the encouragement of foreign investment that can be connected to broad-based development, and better protection of the rights of women and workers. It is strongly in the interests of the United States to embrace these reforms and do what we can to encourage them", cited in White House statement archives, 15 July 2004, http://www.whitehouse.gov/news/releases/2004/07/20040715–12.html (retrieved 29 October 2008). In France, coverage of Morocco in high-circulation magazines such as *Le Point* or *L'Express* frequently give fawning coverage of Moroccan politics or of the monarchy.
6 In the case of France in particular, Hassan II built up personal relationships with scores of French politicians both right and left, notably a close friendship with Jacques Chirac that became part of the legacy he bestowed Muhammad VI. Cf. Perrault 1990. Also Tuquoi 2006.
7 Rivet 2004 (see chapter 4 in particular).
8 Interview with Ali Amar, editor of *Le Journal Hebdomadaire*, Casablanca, July 2007.
9 Ibid.
10 The second Bekkai government lasted between October 1956 and May 1958.
11 Ben Barka is widely believed to have been assassinated by Hassan II's right-hand man, General Muhammad Oufkir, in Paris in 1965, with the cooperation of French authorities.
12 A recently published book has shed new light on the extent of this relationship, most notably Hassan II's role in mediating between Egypt and Israeli in the prelude to Egyptian president Anwar al-Sadat's historic trip to Jerusalem in 1977. Cf. "Ben Barka enterré a Paris", *Agence France Presse*, 25 January 2008. The book in question, published in Hebrew, is Segev 2007.
13 In June 2007, for instance, Lantos (who was until his death in February 2008 chairman of the House Committee on International Relations) wholly adopted Morocco's autonomy proposal for the Western Sahara, saying that he hoped "Polisario is wise enough to accept the reasonable and realistic offer currently on the table". Lantos is one of several ardent supporters of Israel who have consistently backed Rabat's position on the Western Sahara. The Bush administration's endorsement of the Moroccan autonomy proposal has also in large part been attributed to the influence of Elliott Abrams, a key Middle East

14 Tasked with the Moroccan part of that effort (France and Belgium were also involved) was Hamidou Lanigri, who became head of the *Direction de la Sureté du Territoire* (DST) when Muhammad VI ascended to the throne. He has since been removed from that position (Interview with retired Moroccan security official, August 2007). Lanigri was detached to head the United Arab Emirates' Sheikh Zayed bin Sultan al-Nahyan's security services through much of the 1990s, another example of Moroccan security aid to allied countries.

15 New documentation on this episode was unearthed in Trofimov 2007.

16 Interestingly, Moroccans have also played the same role of foot soldiers in *al-Qa'ida*'s hierarchy, where they have rarely had leadership positions but constitute a sizeable group.

17 Of modest origins, Idriss al-Basri was recruited in 1974 by General Ahmad Dlimi, the military strongman of the regime after the death of General Muhammad Oufkir. Basri served as Minister of Interior between 1979 and 1999, as well as Minister of Information between 1985 and 1995, and at the height of his influence was widely considered to be the *de facto* Prime Minister. He is credited for having micromanaged Morocco's political landscape, notably through the creation of "administrative parties", run day-to-day security issues and played a major role in the handling of the Western Sahara question. Until his death on 27 August 2007, Basri oscillated between conciliatory and threatening attitudes towards the new political elite, notably threatening to reveal state secrets (he never did, much to the chagrin of activists). He spent the last years of his life in Paris, in an imposed exile.

18 Mahmoud Tobji, a former army officer who commanded the royal guard and was an *aide-de-camp* to former military strongman General Ahmad Dlimi, retells in his exposé on the Moroccan military a well-known anecdote: after the 1972 coup attempt by General Muhammad Oufkir, Hassan II gathered top officials and senior officials and told them to "make money, not politics" (Tobji 2006).

19 As Maghraoui notes, Hassan II's funeral – attended by many prominent world leaders and the scene of genuine, spontaneous grieving for thousands of Moroccans – was paradoxical considering his authoritarian record and lack of achievements in developing Morocco. This "paradox of the popular (but unjust) prince", Maghraoui argues, was a "popular validation of institutional monarchical authority, not of personal royal power" (Maghraoui 2001, p. 74).

20 Speech at the royal palace in Casablanca, 12 October 1999, http://www.map.ma/mapfr/discours/casa1210.htm (retrieved 28 November 2008).

21 The creation of the GUS was accompanied by a public relations effort to improve the image of the police among ordinary Moroccans through various efforts including television advertisements and the publication of *Police Magazine*, which sought to give a (rather rosy) insider's view of law enforcement. This effort had limited success, in part due to reports of protection rackets run by police officers. Cf. "Police: Bye bye les GUS!", *Tel Quel*, 19 November 2006.

22 The link between regime adaptation, security reforms and pressure for democratic reform in Morocco and elsewhere is explored by Heydemann 2007. Heydemann argues that "Even in Morocco, often cited as an examplar of Arab reform, the political openings engineered by King Muhammad VI are now recognized as steps

towards reconfiguring authoritarianism rather than a process of democratization that would constrain the power of the monarchy. Repression and human rights abuses remain commonplace in Morocco, even if they are less severe or widespread than in many other Arab states" (p. 3).

23   Human Rights Watch 2005b.
24   Ibid.
25   Cf. "Affaire Ben Barka: un juge français lance cinq mandats d'arrêt internationaux", *Le Monde*, 23 October 2007; and "Garzón abre diligencias por un delito de genocidio de Marruecos contra el Sáhara Occidental", *El País*, 30 October 2007.
26   Such an opinion was voiced by both Lahcen Daoudi of the legal Justice and Development Party and Nadia Yassin of the banned Justice and Charity (*al-'Adl wa'l-ihsan*) movement – Morocco's largest Islamist group – in interviews with the author.
27   One such analysis came from a palace insider, Moulay Hisham al-Alawi, the King's estranged cousin, who wrote in a 27 October 2001 opinion article in *Le Monde*, "Mortel attentisme au Maroc" ("Deadly waiting game in Morocco"), warning of a "persistent inadequate situation that showcases the exhaustion of the old political structures and highlights the disaffection of a growing number of citizens who cannot find their place, hope or future in this status quo. This growing feeling of impotence, translated as withdrawal on oneself, cynicism and barely contained anger, carries with it the heavy threat of the most extremist uprisings". Cf. also Selma 2004.
28   One of the first new social housing developments was built in Sidi Moumen itself, highlighting the explicit linkage the government has made between radicalism and social disaffection. Also, cf. "Au Maroc, un promoteur bâtit son succès sur le logement social", *Le Monde*, 9 October 2007. The French word for shantytown, "bidonville", was itself first coined in a report on Morocco in the French newspaper *Le Monde* in 1953.
29   Interview with senior counter-terrorism official, Rabat, September 2007.
30   "Morocco connection is emerging as sleeper threat in terror war", *New York Times*, 16 May 2004.
31   Interview with senior counter-terrorism official, Rabat, September 2007.
32   The extraordinary rendition programme, by which suspected jihadist operatives are kidnapped by US operatives and taken to a number of collaborative countries for interrogation, was designed to allow US security officials to bypass laws restricting the use of torture on US soil or by US officials. See Grey 2006. Both international and Moroccan media have covered the alleged use of security facilities in Temara, near Rabat, to detain and question suspected *al-Qa'ida* members "rendited" from across the world. Cf. "Des 'black sites' au Maroc?", *Le Journal Hebdomadaire*, 16 December 2006.
33   Interview with human rights activist and torture victim lawyer Abd al-Aziz Nouaydi, whose organization *'Adala* campaigns on judicial reform issues, Rabat, August 2007.
34   Interview with senior counter-terrorism official, Rabat, September 2007. Incidentally, EU countries have their own examples of contradictory policies towards Morocco and other Maghreb countries. On the issue of migration control – probably the top bilateral issues between Morocco and Southern European countries – they have advocated that Morocco operate detention centres to

process and deport the growing number of Sub-Saharan African migrants using Morocco as a transit country. Morocco – which has a poor record of treatment of Sub-Saharan African migrants – has refused to allow migration control to be "subcontracted" to it, although migration control and border patrolling have been enhanced, in part through EU funding.

35 *al-Qa'ida* singled out the Maghreb countries as a next major operation theatre after Iraq in taped statements made in September and November 2007. The latter statement, interestingly, specifically highlighted Morocco's international security partners – France, Spain and the United States – and denounced Muhammad VI and other North African leaders as "the Westerners' slaves". See "al-Qaida appelle les musulmans du Maghreb au djihad", *Le Figaro*, 3 November 2007.

36 "Maghreb: Le Maroc et l'Algérie décident, au plus haut niveau, de renforcer leur coopération contre le terrorisme", *Aujourd'hui Le Maroc*, 6 August 2007. It is probable that European pressure played a role in the rapprochement on counter-terrorism between Algeria and Morocco, with notably Spanish Foreign Minister Miguel Angel Moratinos conducting shuttle diplomacy between the two countries in summer 2007.

37 "Terrorisme: Arrestation de trois suspects à Oujda", *Aujourd'hui Le Maroc*, 2 November 2007. According to the report, one of the men had been detained after the 2003 Casablanca bombing and had spent time in Afghanistan.

38 Particular as Morocco currently provides about 80 per cent of the European Union's consumption of hashish and has emerged in recent years as a major transit country for Colombian cocaine through West African networks. Cf. United Nations Office on Drugs and Crime (UNOC) 2006.

39 In September 2007 a major demonstration in the town of Sefrou provoked by an increase in the cost of subsidized bread turned violent, reminding many observers of the brutally repressed bread riots of the 1980s.

40 On 31 August 2007 the Millenium Challenge Corporation, a US government developmental organization, gave Morocco a USD 697.5 million grant "to Spur Economic Growth, and Increase Employment Opportunities". The grant was seen by many as a reward for Rabat's strategic cooperation with Washington in the "war on terror". See http://www.mcc.gov/countries/morocco/index.php.

41 Kamrava 2000, p. 90.

42 Among Islamists, the call for a constitutional overhaul is a fundamental issue for the banned *al-'Adl wa'l-ihsan* movement and among segments of the Justice and Development Party. Among leftist parties, it has long been a key demand of the radical left and is now being raised more consistently by new moderate parties such as the Unified Socialist Party.

13

THE ARAB STATE AND NEO-LIBERAL GLOBALIZATION

Karen Aggestam, Laura Guazzone, Helena Lindholm Schulz,
M. Cristina Paciello, Daniela Pioppi

This concluding chapter reconsiders the key research issues and hypotheses presented in the introduction in the light of the empirical findings of the country case studies collected in this volume. The chapter is divided into four sections[1]: the first three review the findings in the three sectors of politics (Daniela Pioppi), economics (Maria Paciello) and security (Karin Aggestam and Helena Schulz); the final section (Laura Guazzone) considers some of the common and diverging patterns that have emerged in the new Arab regimes with the restructuring of state power as a result of neo-liberal globalization.

1. The Changing Patterns of Political Mobilization and Participation

The case studies of this volume confirm that the nearly three decades of neo-liberal globalization have seen the consolidation in the Arab World of neo-conservative and neo-authoritarian political regimes characterized by a "deepening authoritarian rule masked by limited and reversible liberalization".[2]

From a strictly political point of view, global dynamics have contributed in many ways to this neo-authoritarian restructuring: not only through direct external interference in the domestic politics of Arab states (e.g. support/opposition for specific groups, as in the case of Lebanon, geostrategic rent for friendly regimes, as in the case of Egypt, and so on), but also, from a structural point of view, by providing new techniques and languages of power. Today's "liberal internationalism"[3] provides a state model (the neo-liberal state) and a pattern of political (de-)mobilization that can be followed successfully by dependent states at the periphery of the global system. This process is very similar, although the opposite of what happened in the two decades after independence, when nationalist and anti-colonial regimes all over the Third World were inspired by the socialist Soviet model.

Following this reasoning, current neo-conservative Arab regimes display a number of political patterns that are by no means *unique* to their region, although they certainly have their own regional and country specific dynamics. The first pattern is the apparent lack – or lack of importance – of a state ideological project. I say apparent because in the end all regimes embrace democratic reformism and the neo-liberal model as the discursive-ideological and policy framework of reference.[4] This is, of course, most evident in countries that used to have a strong ideological basis and strong welfare policies in the two decades after independence, such as Egypt, Algeria or Syria, but it can be said of every regime in the region: more than on their leaders' charisma or wide distributive policies, Arab regimes today rely on the masses' political demobilization enforced by varying degrees of naked coercive force.[5]

A second feature of Arab states today, lying more at the heart of the power system, is their almost exclusive reliance on a neo-patrimonial or clientelist system of governance. This neo-patrimonial/clientelist mode of government can also be reinforced – depending on the country – by confessional politics and/or communitarian affiliation/cooptation, whether tribal, ethnic or religious. This is the case in Lebanon and Saudi Arabia (as seen in this volume), but also in Iraq, Jordan and even, outside the Arab world, Israel. The neo-patrimonial system of governance which, again, is by no means a feature of the Arab world alone, goes together with a globally enthused decentralization of the state and the strengthening of local identities and local centres of power. This is certainly the case in Morocco, where the traditional politics of the Palace rely on a complex arbitration with local notables, but also in a traditionally centralized state like Egypt, where the rolling back of the agrarian reform is reconstituting the power of local landowners.[6]

There are obvious consequences in this neo-patrimonial system of governance: the substantial absence of the rule of law, since citizens rights are bestowed or withdrawn according to one's loyalty to the regime; the increasing difficulty in distinguishing between the public and private spheres and the consequent fictitious nature of reforms aimed at the privatization of goods and services which are not truly public to begin with; and also fragmentation of the political order, in terms of both the multiplication of centres of power and the increased difficulty in organizing a unified, nationally based opposition.

A third and final feature to which we would like to draw the reader's attention is the ability shown by neo-authoritarian regimes to coopt elites and even "create" them. To this purpose, personal patronage is still the most efficient tool, but important attempts have also been made to build more institutional forms of patronage where they did not exist before (as in Saudi Arabia) or to restructure former corporatist institutions. In general, there is a decline in corporatist-populist institutions in former populist regimes (for example, the state party and the state trade union in Egypt). But, at the same time, as society becomes more complex, there is also a need to accommodate different elite factions through formal channels or, in some cases, to create new interest groups from scratch (e.g. importers-exporters), which are then granted a representational monopoly by the state and are organized along functional, non-competing lines.[7] This is the case of the ad hoc creation of business organizations such as chambers of commerce in Morocco[8] and Egypt or, on a different level, of the national dialogues organized by Arab regimes at the end of the 1980s. But, more importantly, the same can be said for political liberalization reforms, which in most cases simply involve the artificial creation by the regime of formal channels of elite representation. Ironically, as noted by Hertog in this volume, these formal channels of representation are not particularly appealing in a clientelist society: elites prefer more secure and established informal clientelist relations. That is why representational institutions such as parties are so often empty shells and suffer from a chronic lack of significance.

So far, we have listed the common political patterns of regimes that used to be in two opposing battlefields during the Cold War – with all the well-known ideological and institutional consequences. As noted by Hertog in the concluding remarks of his chapter, today there is a convergence between post-populist regimes (e.g. Egypt) and traditional monarchies (e.g. Saudi Arabia or Morocco), as the former are dismantling populist institutions that the latter never had, and the latter have moved from personal patronage towards more institutional forms of patronage. Formerly progressive (socialist) populist regimes (such as Egypt, Algeria, Syria and Iraq) had to move from hegemonic, inclusive regimes to more competitive and elitist oligarchies and, in general, had more difficulty in adapting to neo-liberal globalization (e.g. internal and external legitimacy crises, etc.). By contrast, conservative (oil and non-oil) monarchies were more in line with the prerequisites of the neo-liberal global state and are more comfortable with the current forms of neo-clientelist authoritarianism. In general, the latter show more continuity than change. This is especially the case in Morocco and Jordan, but also in Saudi Arabia and the small oil monarchies of the Arabian Peninsula that have been more efficient in maintaining the inclusive, distributional agenda (thanks to the recent oil boom) even though this agenda was never tied to political mobilization as in populist regimes. To these examples, we can add the case of Lebanon which has, since independence, had a system of government more in line with the contemporary global model of a more decentralized, less ideological state.

1.1 Elites and opposition politics
In the previous paragraph, we mentioned elite cooptation as one of the common features of today's neo-conservative Arab regimes. But who make up the important Arab elites today? Are Arab elites more varied than they were after independence?

As shown by the contributors to this volume, but also by the growing literature on neo-authoritarian Arab regimes, almost three decades of *infitah* policies have led to the emergence of a crony private business sector. Good examples are reformist Egyptian businessmen, grouped around the son of President Mubarak and playing an increasingly important role in the regime's party, the National Democratic Party (NDP); as well as the Saudi business sector, probably the only organized social group in the country. But good illustrations of the *infitahi* private sector can be found everywhere in the Arab world. As widely demonstrated by recent studies, this rising Arab bourgeoisie is by no means a class in itself. On the contrary, it is more like the *compradora* bourgeoisie of old colonial times. Together with the new *infitahi* elites, "old" post-independence elites still hold the reins of power. The "state bourgeoisie" or upper echelons of the public administration and security sector elites (army, security forces)[9] are still very important in the power structure, as are old community leaders (for example, in Lebanon) and local notables.

Consequently, the increased elite variety and complexity seem to be mainly the result of a more complex society, rather than the product of new, independent, emerging classes. Most of all, as corroborated by the case studies in this volume, this relative increase in elite variety does not imply politicized competition between elite factions, nor greater efforts on the part of the elite to politicize social conflict or to politically mobilize large part of society. As shown very well in Hertog's chapter, in clientelist/neo-patrimonial political systems, elites are dependent and apolitical. We might add that they could still have an interest in building large personal constituencies to hold more sway with their respective patrons, but in a clientelist fashion and not on a political basis. Furthermore, the general fragmentation of society inherent in clientelist systems (e.g. clientelism in Egypt and Saudi Arabia, politics of the *Zuama'* in Lebanon) makes it difficult to build horizontal-national anti-systemic coalitions.

The cooptation of elites and state corporatist restructuring is specifically meant to face the increased complexity of society and the increase in elite diversity and has an impact on the way elites mobilize. This volume's findings question (or at least do not confirm) the widespread idea that elites are the key actors of political change. Why should the (*compradora*) bourgeoisie in these countries work for regime change if the current power structure is favourable to their interests? The industrial bourgeoisie may be more entrepreneurial and independent than businessmen or contractors, but the two sectors often overlap, given the conglomerate structure of many Saudi – but also Egyptian – family businesses.[10] Without organized social pressures from below, elites will not form the vanguard of change as they did in other historical contexts.

The only organized and efficient form of opposition in the Arab world is Islamism, with both its systemic and majority reformist component and its anti-systemic splinter groups. Mass-based Islamism has flourished since the 1970s, thanks also to the global decline in secular leftist ideologies. Reformist Islamism, of which the Muslim Brotherhood is the prototype, has concentrated on building an efficient network of social institutions. Where possible, it has become involved in the electoral processes, sometimes creating new political parties as in the case of Morocco and Jordan and, in general, has succeeded in becoming by far the strongest opposition bloc. However, as explained by Beinin in this volume, mainstream Islamism is currently "split in two souls": while some would like to pursue it, forceful opposition to the regime has turned out to be too risky and could lead to the loss of all the political and economic power gained in the last 30 to 40 years. Thus there exists an unresolved contradiction between the traditional discourse of Islamist populism, on one side, and *infitahi* Islamist business interests, on the other. Not solving this contradiction helps to maintain the primary face of political Islam as a social movement opposed to neo-liberal policies. However, the recent trajectories of the Justice and Development Party in Morocco, or outside of the Arab World, of the Turkish Islamist party, suggest that, ultimately, Islamists' business (elite) interests are likely to prevail in a country like Egypt as well.

On the other side, the activism of anti-systemic, often violent forms of Islamism, has provided the regimes with the excuse to repress any form of political dissent and shift towards neo-conservatism and political stagnation (this was the case of Egypt in the 1990s, but also of Morocco and Tunisia, just to mention a few). In this repressive strategy, regimes have been supported by their external "patrons" who after 2001 asked them for full cooperation in the "war against terror", disregarding the effects of this war on the respect for human and political rights.

Counterbalancing the success of Islamism is the crisis of secular parties and ideologies and the failure of "liberal" elites' opposition strategies. In Egypt, the *Tajammu'* lost much of its popular base in the 1990s, partly because of its choice to support the regime against the Islamists but also because of the global crisis of the left.[11] The traditional socialist opposition in Morocco was successfully coopted when it formed its first coalition government at the end of the 1990s. But also in a country like Lebanon, where communitarian politics has always prevailed, there is a crisis in post-independence secular ideologies. In this sense, *Hezbollah* can be seen as a sort of anomaly, something in between a party grounded in an old ideology (nationalism, anti-imperialism) and a sectarian movement, with this last trait reinforced by current national and international circumstances after the 2006 war.

In general, secular/liberal parties are being substituted everywhere – without exception – by extra-parliamentary opposition represented mainly by NGOs. However, associations do not have the capacity or the mission to mobilize popular opposition to a regime. On the contrary, they may act as inhibitors of wider political mobilization. Civilian activism is often internationally funded and encouraged and concentrates on internationally inspired themes (e.g. human rights, elections and/or constitutional reforms, civil liberties). As described by Karam in this volume, "civil mobilization" in Lebanon has been characterized by the urban and middle-class milieu of the people involved and by the fact that political campaigns focus on specific questions (electoral law, war refugees, women, etc.) rather than on more systemic issues. Such mobilization – as is also the case of *Kifaya* in Egypt – remain marginal to the political game and cannot, in the absence of a broader popular mobilization, seriously throw the power structure into question. Furthermore, they can actually be counter-productive in that they can give the impression of a "democratic" atmosphere without seriously challenging the system.

1.2 The lack of organized political mobilization from below

The findings of this volume show that there is almost no organized political mobilization from below in the Arab world. Today's political opposition to regimes is not only elitist in character, but also weak and/or coopted; in the worst cases, it is completely absent. As argued before, Islamist elites do not have a strong interest in questioning the status quo for fear of losing their elite status. Anti-systemic Islamists and/or spontaneous violent protests are always possible (and increasingly likely due to the worsening living conditions), but are also easily repressed and not sustainable in the absence of organized mass mobilization.

Some important examples of working-class protests have been seen in Egypt, but also Lebanon and Morocco, but they have failed so far to spark a larger protest movement, as a result of both unfavourable global conditions (e.g. the global power balance between capital and labour; the dismantling of large industrial complexes and the growing importance of the informal manufacturing sector) and local circumstances (the efficacy of coercion everywhere; the lack of coordination between urban upper middle-class mobilization and working-class protests, for example, in Egypt).

Besides the global crisis of the working-class movement, global and regional changes in the forms of political mobilization are not favourable to mass mobilization from below for a number of reasons. The first is the ideological deresponsibilization of the state already mentioned. Popular demands are, in fact, increasingly channelled towards the private sector (charities, local notables and/or landowners, etc.), making it harder to find a unified target for popular grievances. In this sense, it is interesting to note that Islamist networks of charities providing social services to the population participate in the regime's project of delegating state functions to private actors according to neo-liberal tenets.[12] Of course, this is less the case in countries such as Saudi Arabia, where the oil price boom has made it possible to maintain welfare policies, but it is not unheard of even in such contexts of abundance.

To this must be added the dismantling of populist institutions. Of course, populist institutions are an example of popular mobilization from above or "passive" mobilization, but they were still symbols of the regime's reliance on low- and middle-class consensus, whereas the processes of political liberalization of the 1980s and 90s coincided with an elitization of political confrontation and the demobilization of the lower classes. We have seen how the increased importance of NGOs is part of this global phenomenon. Finally, the efficacy of the coercive means and neo-patrimonial strategies or the communitarian affiliation of regimes are clearly an important obstacle to organized political mobilization.

This is not to deny the potential for popular mobilization in the Arab World as the mass demonstrations in Lebanon or recent bread riots in Egypt reveal. Instead, what is lacking in the Arab World and elsewhere is a political *relais* willing and capable of providing the ideology and structure for organized popular mobilization. Only in the presence of such organized mass mobilization from below will the grasp on societies of neo-conservative and neo-authoritarian regimes be challenged.

2. The Changing Patterns of Wealth Accumulation and Distribution under Economic Reform

2.1 Key internal and international dynamics of state restructuring

Since the mid-1980s, with rising economic difficulties associated with serious foreign debt problems and falling oil prices, all Arab countries – without exception – have implemented some form of economic liberalization. While countries like Morocco and Egypt agreed to externally imposed macro-economic stabilization programmes with formal assistance from the International Monetary Fund (IMF) and the World Bank in return for international financial flows, in Lebanon and Saudi Arabia, market-oriented reforms were carried out without a formal arrangement with the IMF, but still inspired by the recipes advocated by the Bretton Woods institutions.

Although the concrete implementation of economic reforms has varied from one country to another, the reforms have not delivered the predicted results in terms of long-term economic growth, increased investment, strong productivity and competitiveness. In other words, the economies of Arab countries continue to be hardly diversified, vulnerable to natural and external shocks, and highly dependent on external rents. However, as the findings of this volume show, by providing new opportunities for wealth accumulation and distribution, the reforms have been used by ruling elites to reorganize and consolidate the regime's power system, both internally and externally. Moreover, while economic reforms have not implied the termination of control and domination of the economy on the part of the Arab regimes, the channels and modes of state intervention and influence are being reshaped. As argued by Catusse in this volume, market-oriented reforms seem paradoxically to have paved the way for stronger state interference in the economic and social arenas.

Privatization programmes are a case in point. In Egypt, Morocco and Lebanon, they have been part of the regime's strategy to redistribute privileges to select businessmen in order to buy domestic support and coopt new economic actors. As a result, privatization programmes have largely implied a shift in patronage networks from the public to the private sector, making it possible for the existing regimes to persist and crony capitalism to take shape. Economic reforms have therefore reinforced clientelist social relations and community networks. Crony capitalism, however, is not the only mode of state regulation. As shown in this volume, new modalities and tools of state control have emerged in Morocco. For example, while central government has, in accordance with pressure from Western countries and international organizations, devolved the administration of investment and development to local governments, it nonetheless continues to be the main supervisor of economic activities. So, decentralization reforms have neither challenged existing power structures nor increased local governments' autonomy from central authority. In the name of economic efficiency, the regime has also chosen to depoliticize economic policy by promoting the "technocratization" of policies and politics. But in fact, by marginalizing the role of politics from the economic arena, the regime has actually reinforced its control over society.

In Arab countries, the state has also been reorganizing the provision of welfare. From the 1950s through the 1970s, governments in many Arab countries pursued generous social policies, albeit to different extents, progressively redistributing income from the upper to the lower strata through land reforms, universal food subsidies and free access to education. The ruling elites used the welfare state as an instrument of power to create national unity and a social support base among the formal working class and middle class. Egypt and Saudi Arabia are cases in point. In Lebanon, also, where the welfare state model has been historically less developed, social spending in the postwar reconstruction period was enormous and served to redistribute resources and power along sectarian lines, thus circumscribing religious conflict. However, since the 1990s, the social policies of the past have been challenged by declining rents and the neo-liberal agenda. Arab countries are increasingly unable to finance or sustain their previous levels of health, education and welfare services. In Lebanon, after the period of expansionary fiscal policy up to 1998, the growth of debt, debt servicing and the state's fiscal crisis caused a diversion of resources away from reconstruction and social expenditures.[13] Moreover, although declining social spending is now a less relevant issue for oil-rich countries in the context of rising oil prices, fiscal policy continues to be vulnerable to oil fluctuations. In addition, as the case of Saudi Arabia suggests, spending on social welfare needs to increase in order to ensure more employment for Saudis and greater equity, as well as to make Saudi labour as productive as migrant labour.[14]

Morocco provides an interesting case study of how the state is reorganizing in the context of decreasing public resources. While retreating from some functions because of budget constraints, public powers have found new tools of control and power in the field of social policy. For example, privatization has reshaped the social contract insofar as the state is no longer the main employer and, therefore, the role of public sector employment as a tool of state power has declined. However, in a context of declining public resources, the state is reorganizing by increasingly decentralizing social policies and delegating its social welfare functions to private or semi private-public actors, both local and international. The appearance of various institutions such as the Muhammad V and Hassan II Funds established by key political figures to organize aid to the needy provided by private and public sources can be seen as an example of the ongoing process of state restructuring that implies increasing reliance on indirect/private modes of government, but not necessarily a decline in the capacity of the state, understood as a system of power. The two institutions are indeed publicly funded agencies that are independent of the government, but they are under the patronage of the King. Their ambiguous nature allows the King to ingratiate himself with the public, while unburdening the state of responsibility for citizens' social rights.[15] Moreover, despite the proliferation of non-governmental associations in Morocco, many of them continue to be coopted and too weak to influence economic and social policies since the state retains the power to regulate the boundaries of acceptable practice. This can be observed in most Arab countries. In addition, many of the social initiatives inaugurated by the Moroccan regime may be more cosmetic than real. In parallel with the spread of public initiatives to address poverty and unemployment, financial resources are declining. In the face of resource shortages, Morocco is increasingly dependent on international aid to finance a substantial part of its social spending, but this means that, in the long run, particularly following trade liberalization, social policies are likely to turn out to be unsustainable.

Under the pressure of economic reforms and globalization, state labour relations have also been changing. Before the end of the oil boom, governments in the Arab countries pursued generous employment policies in the public sector, albeit to different degrees, that helped provide job opportunities for a growing part of the population in the region. Under market-oriented reforms largely introduced to reduce budget deficits, public employment is no longer used by ruling elites as a tool for redistribution and power. Moreover, as illustrated for Morocco and Saudi Arabia in this volume, the obligation to liberalize trade and reduce customs duties resulting from membership in international fora such as the World Trade Organization (WTO) and the EU–Mediterranean partnership may expose local industries to unequal competition and pose problems with regard to employment. Most Arab countries, including Egypt, Morocco and Lebanon, have begun to take anti-labour measures and to revise their labour laws to introduce more labour market flexibility and allow their countries to be competitive on international markets.

In the face of such trends, Arab governments fear that full-scale economic reforms could entail social dislocations and politically destabilize their countries. This may explain why they have shown a preference for gradual economic reform. In Saudi Arabia, for example, the negotiation for entry into the WTO was handled skilfully: the market was opened up, but the government retained instruments to protect Saudi business, seeking to limit the impact on labour of globalization.[16] In order to minimize social conflict at a time when unemployment and social tensions are on the increase, the states are also reconfiguring labour relations, with the result that trade unions are losing ground everywhere in the Arab region. In Morocco, while the state appears to be retreating from the sphere of labour relations, it is actually reinforcing its control over labour confrontations: social conflicts are depoliticized and privatized.[17] With the involvement of a new actor – the employer – the process of social negotiation becomes a private affair between him and the worker, outside of the political arena.

Finally, as shown by contributors to this volume, most of the trends discussed above have not been in opposition to outside pressure, rather they have been legitimized and reinforced by global factors, albeit to different degrees in different countries. First, both international actors and external developments have contributed to consolidating the state power system in various ways. For instance, as Egypt and Lebanon illustrate, although donors may lose the leverage to pressure Arab governments to implement reform programmes if they write off debt without conditionality, this can nonetheless contribute to reinforcing the internal power system by providing ruling elites with a way out of a fiscal crisis and new opportunities for rent-seeking activities. In this regard, Lebanon shows how exogenous factors such as capital inflows, remittances and international aid in the postwar period contributed to creating a non-productive rentier economy. Yet, after 11 September 2001, the Saudi government opted to treat the issue of the WTO accession more urgently because it refused to implement the political reforms which the Western world was pressing on the country. This, as explained by Niblock in this volume, allowed the country to postpone political change, while regaining international acceptance.

Second, globalization has not helped Arab countries diversify their productive structure, thus leaving incentives for rent seeking and other unproductive activities unchanged. Although Arab countries have signed numerous international trade agreements, foreign direct investment (FDI) has neither increased nor stimulated local production capacity and supply as expected. Third, the findings of this volume show that ruling elites in Arab countries tend to comply with outside pressure when this is desirable for their own interests. For example, as noted before, adherence to the WTO was above all an instrument used by Saudi businessmen and the government to promote their own agenda for change. However, as highlighted in the next section, global pressures may also contribute to bringing on unintended consequences.

2.2 Consequences of the reorganization of the Arab state

The findings of this volume suggest that the social effects of the ongoing process of state restructuring in Arab countries have been negative. The reorganization of the Arab state has contributed to increasing inequality within countries and has backed a new distribution of resources which is more favourable to the upper class. Economic reforms have been unable to create enough jobs to keep apace with the steady increase in the workforce. Unemployment remains high, the cost of living is on the increase and social indicators have worsened. Moreover, economic policies have generally favoured the economic interests of the elite, while marginalizing the rest of the population. As shown in this volume, redistribution in Lebanon during the post-reconstruction period promoted confessional or sectarian interests, generating serious inequalities in wealth and revenues.

In all countries, privatization has redistributed former state-owned assets to only a limited number of well-connected and privileged groups. Fiscal policy reform has been generally regressive insofar as corporate taxes have remained negligible or have been reduced (as for instance in Egypt and postwar Lebanon). The gains from trade liberalization are likely to be unequally redistributed among the population, with large, well-connected businesses benefiting more with respect to smaller businesses which suffer more from increased global competition (this is the case in Egypt and Saudi Arabia, for example). Also, as the case of Saudi Arabia suggests, trade liberalization seems unlikely to solve the unemployment problem in Arab countries unless the questions of quality and labour costs are addressed.

In addition, the declining role of the state in providing social welfare services has further contributed to the growing marginalization of large parts of the Arab population. Everywhere, the current social protection system is increasingly inadequate and hardly sufficient to serve all entitled people. Even in Morocco, where social initiatives are growing, the current social and employment policies seem to be rather ineffective in dealing with unemployment and poverty. Decentralization and privatization of social services, for example, do not seem to have led to the delivery of more effective basic services to people.

Finally, state economic restructuring is having and will continue to have an impact on internal political and social dynamics. On the one hand, as the case studies in this volume show, while the reform process has led to the emergence of a new class of businessmen, the ruling elite is still powerful with respect to the private sector. As noted by Wurzel, "as long as the new business class continues to lack a political project and to depend on its privileged and strong links to the regime, it is unlikely to promote a real process of economic reform".[18]

On the other hand, although the regime still maintains control of the process of wealth accumulation and distribution, this does not mean that it could not get out of control and create its own dynamics of growing opposition. First, as shown by Egypt and Morocco, since the business elites are a heterogeneous group, complying with the different factions' demands in terms of privilege and opportunities for doing business could become less and less feasible for the regimes. Second, with the worsening of people's standard of living and the termination of the old social contract, economic reforms have already begun to meet with resistance and to erode the legitimacy of the regimes everywhere except the richer oil countries, as confirmed by the case studies in this volume. By reshaping the social contract, the privatization of public utilities in Morocco has generated opposition and protest from citizens who have been transformed into clients. In Egypt, the massive strikes of 2006–7 illustrate the growing discontent, while in Lebanon, after 1997, with the worsening of public finances, sectarian conflicts over redistribution have increased, leading to political conflict that has intensified since 2000. In Saudi Arabia, those who have joined the radical Islamist cause abroad are mainly young men who have been unable to find satisfactory employment in their country. This suggests that the Arab regimes can no longer ignore the social effects that follow from high unemployment and the rising cost of living. In brief, we can conclude that, while the opportunities for substantial change are still limited in Arab countries, the possibility that new dynamics of opposition can contribute to triggering real socio-economic change and overcoming the established system of power in coming years cannot be excluded.

3. Change and Continuity of National Security in the Arab World

In the history of Arab state formation and nation-building, the military and security apparatus have in many instances served a crucial function. Despite the diversity in the security policies of Arab states, there are some salient shared features, which affect the haste and depth of change and continuity in the national security discourses. To further knowledge about continuity and change in the security sector, it is particularly important to consider two factors, namely military globalization and the intimate nexus between the state and the military.

3.1 Globalization of security

Globalization challenges the security system of Arab states in a variety of ways, ranging from dependency to the erosion of sovereignty. Globalization of security means fragmentation of the principle of sovereignty through the interference of international actors in state affairs as well as the proliferation of armed forces, which challenges state sovereignty and legitimacy in many parts of the world. In the Middle East, profound challenges toward state sovereignty have been felt through international interventions in Iraq, first after the first Gulf War in 1991 and then through the US-led intervention in 2003, which thoroughly reshuffled the regional security landscape. The renewed international interventionism under the pretext of fighting global terrorism has implied new external threats challenging state sovereignty for Arab regimes. At the same time, what Western regimes define as global terrorism or jihadism, organized in globalized networks and alliances, is what Arab regimes see as domestic opposition. Islamist terror groups act globally as transnational communities, distributing messages and information via extensive networks. Territory and geography therefore mean less in terms of serving as the prime object of security, which has direct bearing on sovereignty. External and internal threats become blurred, as jihadists threaten, first and foremost, regimes and state structures in the Arab world.

The American "war on terror" consequently poses a considerable challenge both to states and regimes. Picard's analysis of Lebanon in this volume identifies a renewed Western political and military penetration of the area resembling the colonial era. Heavy Western involvement in Lebanese security politics has extended from the French mandate, through US involvement in the civil war in 1958, to the United Nations interim force in Lebanon (UNIFIL) I and II. The contemporary era is in fact characterized merely by an acceleration of Western intervention in Lebanese affairs, involving a more visible European presence than during the Cold War. Western influence is also occurring through training and assistance in reforming the security sector. This should be seen in addition to the presence and influence in Lebanon first and foremost of Syria, but also of Iran and Saudi Arabia.

Lebanon is also becoming the scene of militarized globalized networks, such as *al-Qa'ida*-influenced groups. These networks take advantage of the presence of transnational communities that are already established in the country, such as the Palestinian refugee population, as was the case with the *Fatah al-Islam* group, which used a Palestinian refugee camp as its base for action. In this way, the sovereignty of Lebanon and the state's control of its security and territory are increasingly challenged and the degree of involvement of foreign and sub-state actors in Lebanon's security affairs question the essence of the state in Lebanon.

3.2 American hegemony
The American intervention in Iraq in 2003 was a response to the globalization of security. The second international intervention in Iraq in less than 15 years raised profound issues of sovereignty as well as the reorganization of security in the Arab world. Iraqi sovereignty has still not been restored more than five years after the invasion. To Arab regimes, the intervention serves as an illustration of the risks entailed in American hegemony. For Saudi Arabia, it has meant a strong shift in the power balance in the region in favour of Iran. Previously, the Saudi regime was able to use the power struggle between Iraq and Iran to its advantage, but the chaotic situation in Iraq has pushed Saudi Arabia to nurture increasingly closer relations with Iran. The war in Iraq has fuelled anti-American sentiments in Saudi Arabia as well, making the regime orient itself increasingly away from American dominance. At the

same time, Saudi Arabia is trying to promote itself as an important regional player by taking diplomatic initiatives, which range from promoting a peace plan for the resolution of the Arab–Israeli conflict, bridging the *Fatah–Hamas* divide, to preventing sectarian violence in Lebanon.

Global military and security networks have also been defined by US security interests. Egypt's reliance on American technology, training and financing has resulted in what Droz-Vincent calls "dependent security". Yet he underlines that the "special relationship with the US" differs from that of other client states in the region in that Egypt shares a number of the United States' strategic security objectives, such as settling the Israeli–Palestinian conflict and broadening regional stability and security. Egypt's role as an American partner is therefore perceived to enhance its position as a regional leader. Yet, such a strategic alliance is risky and controversial, as dependence on the US is opposed by strong domestic forces, particularly after the US involvement in Iraq.

However, Arab security alliances with the US are not necessarily heading in the direction of outright dependency. Given the strategic importance of Saudi Arabia for access to oil, Paul Aarts and Joris van Duijne describe the relationship between the US and Saudi Arabia as one of interdependence: the West's dependence on Saudi oil implies a "tradeoff: oil for security". Moreover, the House of Saud has shown a strong capacity for balancing powers against each other. Currently, Chinese interests in Saudi Arabia are signs of Saudi Arabia's potential for keeping different interests in balance.

3.3 State–military relations

One of the most salient features of Middle East politics is the intimate nexus between the state and the armed forces.[19] The army and the other security institutions have served a crucial role in state formation and nation-building in the Arab world. In the post-colonial period, national liberation was often orchestrated by highly ideological discourses and national armies were politicized in the realm of anti-imperialism. Regimes relied heavily on armies in processes of mobilization of populations in a new era when colonial institutions were taken over and transformed into state-governing structures. This was frequently related to the absence of a single unifying vision around which to rally and held back the emergence of a corporate unified sense of identity among the officers.[20]

The role of armies in modelling the Arab state system was strongly interrelated to conflicts and wars, although this occurred in a variety of ways, as the case studies in this volume illustrate. Perceptions of threat and military insecurity paved the way for militarized states to legitimize themselves through "missions", such as the struggle against imperialism, for Arab unity, or for the liberation of Palestine, rather than through the rule of the people. The army also served as a modernizing institution in post-colonial states, given its reliance on modern technology and its strict mode of organization. As armies played the role of nation-building and state construction "rather than state protection",[21] they view themselves as the core function of the state.

Arab armies have frequently been organized along ethnic, tribal or other identity lines. In the case of Saudi Arabia, entire branches of the military and security structure are "family business". Hence, the Saudi military has never functioned, as Aarts and Duinje underline, as a symbol of a modernizing institution-building actor, but rather as "military-tribal complex".

An important consequence of organizing armies along ethnic and tribal lines has, in some cases, been to hinder them from taking political action. The various militias of Lebanon can be seen as a prime example of the fragmentation of security and as a forerunner of the civil wars plaguing our times. Picard shows how the reconstruction efforts of the Lebanese army following the Taif Agreement were based on the idea of national integration through the army and the intention of creating a neutral army. This ambition was not, however successful, partly due to Syrian influence and the reluctance of some groups to join the army. The security sector has therefore once again receded into factionalism and tribalism. In Lebanon, the restructuring of state–military relations has resulted in a decrease in the use of direct regime violence against oppositional forces, but also in an increase in the use of what Picard calls symbolic violence.

3.4 Regime survival

The enduring authoritarianism of Arab states is partly the result of the patrimonial form of the militaries and the capacity of the security apparatus to repress dissent. Bellin underlines the link between the exceptional strength of the security apparatus and the limited degree of popular mobilization for democratic reforms in the Arab world. Low levels of popular mobilization for democratic reforms mean low costs of repression, which subsequently increases the likelihood that the security establishment will resort to force to impede reform initiatives.[22] Security forces are used continuously to curb unrest, which in Egypt could be defined as anything ranging from civil manifestations to local and national elections. Droz-Vincent argues that the newly found stability of the Egyptian regime can be traced back to the restructuring of the security institutions, whereby the paramilitary forces under the Ministry of the Interior were given an increasingly important role in addressing internal security, involving, among other things, political demonstrations, social unrest and Islamist militancy. The restructuring of the security sector has been legitimized through a national security discourse built around the image of Egypt as an insecure "strong" nation-state.

Moreover, the patrimonial linkage between the regime and the security institutions means that democratization can only be carried out successfully when the state's security apparatus refrains from acting against such a process. However, if the military remains coherent and effective, it can face down popular dissatisfaction and survive significant illegitimacy.[23] Western support for non-democratic and coercive regimes also explains the robustness of authoritarian regimes in the Arab world. This support includes significant foreign military aid and strategic rent. "Western governments have contented themselves with purchasing Saudi oil and soliciting Saudi contracts while maintaining a shameful silence toward Saudi abuses." Similarly, "Egypt has secured from the US government massive aid and tacit acceptance of its human rights violations."[24] The dependence of some Arab regimes on technology and assistance from the West has no doubt increased since the end of the Cold War. At the same time, as long as Islamist movements are perceived as anti-Western, many Arab leaders will continue to enjoy relative freedom from external pressures for change and, doing away with authoritarianism, they will use repression as a remedy against even "Islamist-flavoured" opposition. As Droz-Vincent underlines, Arab leaders have an inclination to securitize and frame many political issues as existential threats in order to secure their positions within the state. In the case of the Egyptian regime, it has made extensive use of the myth of Egypt as a secular state besieged by violent Islamists.

However, the security sector is under increasing pressure from transnational networks that take advantage of weak state institutions and weak sovereignty to further their interests and their anti-Western politico/military campaign. One vivid illustration of this is the way in which the Lebanese armed forces were prevented from entering the Nahr al-Barid refugee camp to fight the rebellious *Fatah al-Islam* group. An agreement between the Lebanese regime and the Palestine Liberation Organization (PLO) dating back to 1969 declares that the refugee camps are no-go zones for the Lebanese Army. Hence, the fragmentation of Lebanese sovereignty. Another example of this fragmentation is the strong challenge to the legitimate control of the Lebanese armed forces in the security sector presented by *Hezbollah*, now acting as a "state within the state", as the PLO once did.

Saudi Arabia has witnessed strong internal opposition and a multitude of terrorist attacks after 2000. These internal threats have resulted in a boost in expenditure for internal security. In Egypt, the armed forces have, in the last decades, expanded their role to non-military areas, such as water management, agriculture and electricity generation. In the post-colonial period, the military acted as development agents. Today officers are more involved in commercial activities, in line with the global trend of military involvement in the accumulation of capital. Hence, several countries are characterized by a "merchant/military complex", in which the security apparatus has extensive networks of clientelism, patronage and corruption.[25] The privileged position of military officers remains an important feature of state–military relations in Egypt and, as a result, the military is deeply entrenched in the authoritarian status quo. In Lebanon, through the reformation of the armed forces and the attempt to create a "national" security sector, officers have attained a privileged position and now act as an interest group defending their positions. In fact, in her contribution to this volume, Picard shows how the reformation of the armed forces has strengthened neo-patrimonial relations between the regime and the military.

Yet there is some ambivalence in the relationship between regimes and the security institutions. In Egypt, for example, while professionalization is employed to reduce the potential political influence of the armed forces, on the one hand, on the other, regime dependence on the military serves to strengthen the armed forces. In Lebanon, the current period is, in fact, one of increased coerciveness of the security institutions *vis-à-vis* the domestic scene.

To conclude, the challenges posed by military globalization and changing state–military relations have resulted in a transformation of the security sector in several Arab states. This transformation involves changes in threat perceptions, security institutions, security politics, as well as in the relationships between the military and the civilian spheres. Sovereignty and therefore state control is challenged from "above" as well as from "below" the state level. Yet, the role of the military and the security sector in Arab politics remain salient. The political role of the security institutions may be seen as one of the critical factors behind the remarkable strength of the Arab state in the era of globalization. In fact, we seem to be witnessing an "in-between" situation in which armies remain large, maintaining their special position among state institutions and the keeping of their missionary legacy in mind, but in which political change could also lead to a more limited role for the army.

4. Globalized Arab Neo-authoritarianism: Regional Frameworks and National Paths

The analysis of the research findings presented in the previous sections shows that the processes of state restructuring in the Arab world due to neo-liberal globalization are subject to the same global trends affecting the rest of the world,[26] but also that they have evolved at a different pace and with different dynamics in the various national contexts considered.

This observation calls into question the assumption that the Arab world can still be considered a coherent regional subsystem providing a significant framework of analysis for social sciences. As some argued at a certain point in the discussion in our research group, it may very well be that in the context of globalization this is no longer the case, and that more significant comparisons can be drawn with country case studies from outside of the Arab region – for instance, between Egypt and Brazil. However, analysis of the research findings confirms the relevance of the Arab regional framework of reference because comparing the different types of state power systems existing before and after the present phase, i.e. at the time of the consolidation of post-independence Arab regimes and after their restructuring induced by neo-liberal policies, allows for a more precise analysis of the change that has occurred. This regional framework makes it possible, for instance, to emphasize how processes such as depoliticization and demobilization have affected mainly the former populist republics (e.g. Algeria, Egypt) rather than the modernizing monarchies (Morocco, Jordan).

Using a regional framework of analysis helps also to see how, paradoxically, the end results of the different national trajectories of change have made Arab political regimes more alike than ever. So much so that, for instance, the privatized and apolitical modes of governance of Egyptian politics are more similar than ever to those of the reformed Arab monarchies, in spite of the sometimes very different dynamics of specific national contexts. In this perspective, the main result of the restructuring of Arab states as a result of globalization has been the emergence and consolidation of a new model of authoritarian Arab state, in which the pre-existing functional differences between different types of power systems – for instance between the radical republics and the conservative monarchies – are increasingly blurred.

Finally, using a regional framework helps to situate the analysis in a historical perspective, drawing attention to the analogies that the current situation bears with the epoch of the so-called first globalization, i.e. the period of European colonial expansion in the Middle East. This historical similarity emerges in the pattern of the interaction between the international system and the internal dynamics of the region, now and then largely determined by the capacity of local actors to adapt or react to external pressures for reform.

Talk of a "model" of neo-authoritarian Arab state is substantiated by the identification of some common patterns that emerge – above and beyond national differences – through comparison at the regional level. As already mentioned in the introduction, the neo-authoritarian Arab state is characterized by fragmentation of the power structure and by an increase in informal modes of government (neo-patrimonialism, corruption), with the parallel political and economic marginalization of large social sectors. Contrary to our starting hypotheses, however, this less centralized and more elitist neo-authoritarian Arab state does not seem to be markedly more dependent and vulnerable than its predecessors to external pressures and foreign influence. In effect, as noted in the analyses of the economic and political sectors, implementation of the reforms that have restructured the power system has been in line with and encouraged by international actors and developments, not simply imposed from the outside. During the same period, a much deeper external penetration has taken place in the security sphere; the activities of terrorist networks and those of the states sponsoring or opposing them have multiplied direct interventions on the soil or in the jurisdiction of many Arab states. These interventions have become so frequent and extended to impose serious limits on the very meaning of 'national' security. Overall, however, the dependency of the Arab regimes has never translated into direct obedience to the requests of external actors: a good example is the strategic relationship between Egypt and the US as analysed by Droz-Vincent in this volume. Another example of this relativization of dependency can be seen in the "morphing" of Western democracy promotion policies into the regimes' strategies of demobilization and elitization, thanks to the ability of the regimes directly to participate in and/or to pose restriction on the actual implementation of US and EU policies of empowerment of NGOs and civil society at large.[27] Once again, it has to be stressed that this is not due to any exceptional resilience of Arab regimes but, on the contrary, simply to their ability to participate in the globalized international system, albeit in a subordinate position.

A final observation about the "model" of the neo-authoritarian Arab state is its apparent stability. Against all odds and expectations, most of today's Arab regimes are stable, but their stability resides in the patrimonial management of a power structure fragmented among different segments of the business elite and/or the different ethnic and confessional communities. This fragmentation of the power system is coupled, as said before, to the atomization of society and to the political and economic exclusion of large social sectors. Therefore, the stability is only apparent and neo-authoritarian Arab regimes can survive only as long as they are able – and they are less and less able – to respond to the diversified and increasingly contradictory demands of international partners, competing elites and popular movements. The apparent stability of the present regimes could falter, for instance, because, as argued in sections 1–2 above, the business elites are such a heterogeneous group that it could become impossible to comply with the different factions' demands in terms of privilege and opportunities especially in the face of worsening public finances engendered, for instance, by a sudden decrease in oil prices, something that would affect all rentier states.

Thinking about the possible causes of change in the present status quo of Arab neo-authoritarianism it appears that the faltering ability of some of the incumbent regimes to cope with the demands of the components of the increasingly varied and complex elites – described in section 1 above – emerges as the most likely cause of new dynamics of change – or even crises – that may be able to restructure today's power system further. In effect, analysis of the different national paths toward the common Arab model underlines, *inter alia*, profound differences in the ability of the neo-authoritarian regimes to ensure stability by managing these increasingly diversified demands. In Saudi Arabia, the keys to stability continue to be neo-patrimonial, which seem to remain within the reach of the incumbent regime through the practices of new corporatism analysed in Hertog's contribution to this volume. Also in Morocco, stability remains within the reach of the incumbent regime because, in spite of a possibly looming social crisis, the monarchy is still able to manage a legitimating political discourse based on democratization and globalization, as argued here by el Amrani. In Egypt, on the contrary, meeting contradictory demands seems to be over-stretching the capabilities of a ruling elite unable to elaborate any legitimizing "vision" and increasingly reliant on the security sector for its survival in the face of an impoverished and weakened society, increasingly fractured along class and confessional lines. Finally, in Lebanon, stability remains as elusive as ever: the restructuring of the state is following the trends common to the other neo-authoritarian Arab states, but here the composition of the ruling elites – and thus the functioning of the political regime – is being restructured by the process of resectarianization, which is still ongoing after the apparent failure of efforts to foster horizontal – i.e. non sectarian – political mobilization and alliances.[28]

In addition to this potential for inner instability in the regimes themselves, transformation of the present neo-authoritarian model could come from various other sources. Further change could, for instance, be put into motion by new or renewed political and social actors, as well as by a substantial alteration of what we defined in the introduction as the context of globalization under the aegis of neo-liberalism. The analysis of the different national paths toward the common Arab model developed in sections 1–3 above shows that there are indeed some national political actors that could, in their respective countries, act as catalyzers of significant transformations in the present status quo of Arab neo-authoritarianism.

Social movements in the lower strata remain, in principle, among the most important potential actors of change, but empirical findings show that even sustained working-class protests – like those that took place in Egypt between 2004 and 2007 – have failed so far to spark a larger protest movement because of their lack of a national strategy and/or of a full-fledged oppositional project. The same can be said of the various waves of citizens' mobilization for civil rights or specific objectives (e.g. the campaigns for the reform of the personal code in Lebanon and Morocco or the 2003 campaign against the war in Iraq in many Arab countries).

As noted several times in this volume, Islamists remain the only effective – that is organized, efficient and broadly based – oppositional actor in the Arab world. As also noted, the Arab Islamist movements contain a majority component that aims at reforming the power system and splinter groups that aim at overthrowing the system by radical means including violence. Analysis of the case studies confirms that Islamist radical groups do not represent a credible alternative to the present regime in any of the countries considered, nor are they able to ignite revolutionary processes that can alter the status quo; quite to the contrary, their very existence provides an excuse for the securitization of the public policies that legitimize neo-authoritarianism domestically and internationally (the "war on terror"). As for the mainstream reformist Islamist movements, it remains to be seen whether they represent a structural alternative to the present neo-authoritarian power system. There is no doubt that in Egypt, Morocco and Lebanon, as well as in other Arab countries not directly examined in this volume, such as Syria, Jordan or Tunisia, the conservative Islamist bourgeoisie – with its different components, ranging from the new business entrepreneurs to traditional large families – aspires above all to accessing the ruling circles and is ready to enter various tactical alliances to this end with other opposition and ruling elites. Actually, the moderation of the Egyptian Brotherhood is often seen as tactical politics, aimed at damage limitation *vis-à-vis* the regime's repression. But the example of the Moroccan Justice and Development Party's "integrationist" strategy points to a different explanation, one that sees conservative Islamism as a *de facto* component of the present power system, playing the role of a hidden junior partner in the ruling coalition.

Summing up what emerges from the analysis of the different sectors and the national case studies considered in this volume, it does not seem that further transformation of Arab neo-authoritarianism can be brought about by any single actor on the present domestic political scene – the regimes, the counter-elites or the lower strata. Instead, the transformation of Arab neo-authoritarianism can be engendered by a renewed interaction of domestic and international factors that could emerge, for instance, as a consequence of the present global financial crisis, the ongoing critical reappraisal of neo-liberal policies or the looming change of strategy of major international powers – from China to the US. In other words, further structural change can only be the consequence of the Arab countries' continued participation in the globalized international system.

NOTES

1. Each section has been elaborated autonomously by the respective author(s).
2. Beinin in this volume.
3. Roland Paris quoted in Jung 2006, p. 4.
4. See also Paciello's paragraph in this concluding chapter.
5. Beinin in this volume. Saudi Arabia is a partial exception.
6. Bush 2002.
7. Cf. Hertog in this volume.
8. Cf. Catusse in this volume.
9. See Droz-Vincent in this volume.
10. Hertog in this volume.
11. Beinin in this volume.
12. Pioppi 2007.
13. Dibeh 2005.
14. Niblock 2006.
15. See Pioppi's section in this concluding chapter.
16. Niblock in this volume.
17. Catusse in this volume.
18. Wurzel in this volume.
19. Kamrava 2000.
20. Ibid., p. 77.
21. Kroonings *et al.* 2002.
22. Bellin 2005, pp. 21, 35.
23. Ibid., p. 26.
24. Human Rights Watch, quoted in Brownlee 2005, p. 59.
25. Krause 2004, p. 114.
26. This commonality is analysed also in chapter 1.
27. On the case of Morocco, cf. Catusse and el Amrani in this volume.
28. Picard and Karam in this volume.

Bibliography

AARTS, Paul (2004), "The Internal and the External: The House of Saud's Resilience Explained", *EUI Working Paper*, Florence, RSCAS, No. 33.

AARTS, Paul (2007a), "Saudi Arabia Walks the Tightrope", *The International Spectator*, Vol. 42, No. 4, December.

AARTS, Paul (2007b), "The Longevity of the House of Saud: Looking Outside the Box", in O. Schlumberger (ed.), *Arab Authoritarianism: Debating the Dynamics and Durability of Nondemocratic Regimes*, Palo Alto, CA, Stanford University Press.

AARTS, Paul and Machteld VAN RIJSINGEN (2007), "Beijing's Rising Star in the Gulf Region: The Near and the Distant Future", in E. Woertz (ed.), *Gulf Geo-Economics*, Dubai, Gulf Research Center.

ABDELRAHMAN, Maha (2004), *Civil Society Exposed: The Politics of NGOs in Egypt*, London, I.B. Tauris.

ABIR, Mordechai (1988), *Saudi Arabia in the Oil Era: Regimes and Elites*, London, Croom Helm.

ABDEL-KHALEK, Ghouda (2000), "Domestic Public Debt in Egypt: Magnitude, Structure and Consequences", in G. Abdel-Khalek, K. Korayem, *Fiscal Policy Measures in Egypt: Public Debt and Food Subsidy*, Cairo Papers in Social Science, Cairo, AUC Press.

ADMINISTRATION CENTRALE DE LA STATISTIQUE (1998), *Conditions de vie des ménages*, Beirut, Lebanon.

ADWAN, Charles (2004), *Corruption in Reconstruction: The Cost of National Consensus on Post-war Lebanon*, Washington, DC, Center for International Private Enterprise (CIPE), 1 December, www.cipe.org/pdf/publications/fs/adwan.pdf.

AKESBI, Azeddine (2003), "Ajustement structurel et segmentation du marché du travail", *Annales marocaines d'économie*, No. 7, Hivers.

ALANI, Mustafa (2006), "Internal Security Developments and Terrorism", *Gulf Year Book 2005–2006*, Dubai, Gulf Research Center.

ALBRECHT, Holger and Oliver SCHLUMBERGER (2004), "Waiting for Godot: Regime Change without Democratization", *International Political Science Review*, Vol. 25, No. 4.

ALIBONI, Roberto (2006), "Europe's Role in the Gulf: A Transatlantic Perspective", *The International Spectator*, Vol. 41, No. 2, April–June.

ALLAIN MANSOURI, Béatrice (2005), "La délégation du service privé de la gestion de l'eau potable au Maroc. Le cas de Rabat-Salé", in C. De Miras (ed.), *Intégration à la ville et services urbains au Maroc*, Paris, Rabat, INAU/IRD.

al-AMIN, ADNAN (1997/1998), "Le Politique dans lc Comportement des Jeunes Libanais pendant la Crise d'Avril 1996", *Bahithat*, Beyrouth, Lebanese Association of Women Researchers, No. 4.

AMIN, Galal (1995), *Egypt's Economic Predicament: A Study in the Interaction of External Pressure, Political Folly and Social Tension in Egypt 1960–1990*, New York-Köln-Leiden, Brill.

ANDERSON, Lisa (1991), "Absolutism and the Resilience of Monarchy in the Middle East", *Political Science Quarterly*, Vol. 106, No. 1.

ANDERSON, Lisa (2000), "Dynasts and Nationalists: Why Monarchies Survive", in J. Kostiner (ed.), *Middle East Monarchies, The Challenge of Modernity*, Boulder, CO, Lynne Rienner.

ATTAC Maroc (2005), *Privatisations: stoppons l'hémorragie*, Groupes d'Agadir et de Rabat, Rabat.

AYOOB, Mohammed (1995), *The Third World Security Predicament*, Boulder, CO, Lynne Rienner.

AYUBI, Nazih (1995), *Over-stating the Arab State*, London, I.B. Tauris.

BAFOIL, François (2006), "Economies politiques des privatisations", *Critique Internationale*, No. 32, Juil–Sept.

BAHOUT, Joseph (1998), "Le Liban et le couple syro-libanais dans le processus de paix. Horizons incertains", in M. Chartouni (ed.), *Le Couple syro-libanais dans le processus de paix*, Paris, IFRI.

BAHOUT, Joseph (1999), "Du Pacte de 1943 à l'Accord de Taëf. La réconciliation nationale en question au Liban", in J. Hannoyer (ed.), *Guerres civiles. Économies de la violence, dimensions de la civilité*, Beyrouth-Paris, CERMOC-Karthala.

BAHOUT, Joseph (2005), "Liban/Syrie: une alliance objective franco-américaine ?", *L'Orient Le Jour*, 15 Octobre.

BARAK, Oren (2006), "Toward a Representative Military?", *Middle East Journal*, Vol. 60, No. 1, Winter.

BARKAWI, Tarak and Marc LAFFEY (1999), "The Imperial Peace. Democracy, Force and Globalisation", *European Journal of International Relations*, Vol. 5, No. 4.

BAYART, Jean-François (1993), *The State in Africa: The Politics of the Belly*, London and New York, Longman.
BAYART, Jean-François (ed.) (1994), *La Réinvention du capitalisme*, Paris, Karthala.
BAYART, Jean-François (2004), *Le gouvernement du monde. Une critique politique de la globalisation*, Paris, Fayard.
BEININ, Joel (1993), "Will the Real Egyptian Working Class Please Stand Up?", in Z. Lockman (ed.), *Workers and Working Classes in the Middle East: Struggles, Histories, Historiographies*, Albany, NY, State University of New York Press.
BEININ, Joel (2007), "The Militancy of Mahalla al-Kubra", *Middle East Report Online*, 29 September, http://www.merip.org/mero/mero092907.html.
BEININ, Joel and Hossam el-HAMALAWY (2007), "Egyptian Textile Workers Confront the New Economic Order", *Middle East Report Online*, 25 March, http://www.merip.org/mero/mero032507.html.
BEININ, Joel and Zachary LOCKMAN (1987), *Workers on the Nile: Nationalism, Communism, Islam and the Egyptian Working Class, 1882–1954*, Princeton, NJ, Princeton University Press.
BEYHUM, Nabil (1991), "Introduction. Les paris sur le possible", in N. Beyhum (ed.), *Reconstruire Beyrouth. Les paris sur le possible*, Lyon, Collection Études sur le Monde Arabe, No. 5.
BELLIN, Eva (2004a), *Stalled Democracy: Capital, Labour, and the Paradox of State-Sponsored Development*, Ithaca, Cornell University Press.
BELLIN, Eva (2004b), "The Robustness of Authoritarianism in the Middle East: Exceptionalism in Comparative Perspective", *Comparative Politics*, Vol. 36, No. 2.
BELLIN, Eva (2005), "Coercive Institutions and Coercive Leaders", in M. Pripstein Posusney and M. Penner Angrist (eds), *Authoritarianism in the Middle East: Regimes and Resistance*, Boulder, CO and London, Lynne Rienner.
BEN NÉFISSA, Sarah, Nabil ABD AL-FATTAH, Sari HANAFI and Carlos MILANI (eds) (2005), *NGOs and Governance in the Arab World*, Cairo, American University in Cairo Press.
BENNANI CHRAÏBI, Mounia (1995), *Soumis et rebelles: les jeunes au Maroc*, Casablanca, Le Fennec.
BERTHÉLEMY, Jean-Claude, Sébastien DESSUS and Charbel NAHAS (2007), "Exploring Lebanon's Growth Prospects", *World Bank Policy*

Research Working Paper, No. 4332, August, Washington, DC, World Bank.

BICCHI, Federica, Laura GUAZZONE and Daniela PIOPPI (eds) (2004), *La Questione della Democrazia nel Mondo Arabo. Stati, Società, Conflitti*, Monza, Polimetrica.

BILGIN, Pinar (2004), "Whose 'Middle East'? Geopolitical Inventions and Practices of Security", *International Relations*, Vol. 18, No. 1.

BINDER, Leonard (1978), *In a Moment of Enthusiasm*, Chicago, Chicago University Press.

al-BISHRI, Tariq (2002), *The Arabs Confront Aggression*, Cairo, Dar al-Shuruq [in Arabic].

BLATTEIS, Samuel (2007), "The GCC Strengthens Geo-Economic Ties to the US, Moves Away from China", European University Institute, Robert Schuman Centre, March.

BOLTANSKI, Luc (1979), "Taxinomie sociale et lutte des classes. Mobilisation de la 'classe moyenne' et 'l'invention des 'cadres'", *Actes de la Recherche en Sciences Sociales*, No. 29.

BOUACHIK, Ahmed (1993), *Les Privatisations au Maroc*, Casablanca.

BOUCEK, Christopher (2007), "Extremist Reeducation and Rehabilitation in Saudi Arabia", *Terrorism Monitor*, Vol. 5, No. 16, August.

BRAND, Laurie (2006), *Citizens Abroad: Emigration and the State in Middle East and North Africa*, New York, Cambridge University Press.

BRONSON, Rachel (2005/2006), "Understanding US–Saudi Relations", in P. Aarts and G. Nonneman (eds), *Saudi Arabia in the Balance*, New York, New York University Press.

BROWNLEE, Jason (2005), "Political Crisis and Restabilization: Iraq, Libya, Syria and Tunisia" in M. Pripstein Posusney and M. Penner Angrist (eds), *Authoritarianism in the Middle East: Regimes and Resistance*, Boulder and London, Lynne Rienner.

BRUMBERG, Daniel (2002), "Democratization in the Arab World? The Trap of Liberalized Autocracy", *Journal of Democracy*, Vol. 13, No. 1.

BRYNEN, Rex, Bahgat KORANY and Paul NOBLE (eds) (1998), *Political Liberalization and Democratization in the Arab World*, Boulder, Lynne Rienner.

BURGAT, François (2005), "Les mobilisations politiques à référent islamique", in E. Picard (ed.), *La Politique dans le monde arabe*, Paris, Armand Colin.

BUSH, Ray (ed.) (2002), *Counter-Revolution in Egypt's Countryside: Land and Farmers in the Era of Economic Reform*, London and New York, Zed Books.

BUSH, Ray (2007), "Mubarak's Legacy for Egypt's Rural Poor. Returning Land to the Landlords", in A.H. Akram-Lodhi, S.M. Borras Jr and C. Kay (eds), *Land, Poverty and Livelihoods in the Era of Globalization: Perspectives from Developing and Transition Countries*, London, Routledge.

BUZAN, Barry (1991), *People, States and Fear*, Harlow, England, Longman.

BUZAN, Barry and Ole WAEVER (2003), *Regions and Powers: The Structure of International Security*, Cambridge, Cambridge University Press.

BUZAN, Barry, Ole WAEVER and Jaap DE WILDE (1997), *Security: A New Framework for Analysis*, Boulder, CO, Lynne Rienner.

CALL, Charles T. (2002), "War Transitions and the New Civilian Security in Latin America", *Comparative Politics*, Vol. 35, No. 1.

CAMAU, Michel (1997), "D'une République à l'autre. Refondation politique et aléas de la transition libérale", *Maghreb-Machrek*, No. 157, Juillet–Septembre.

CAMAU, Michel and Vincent GEISSER (2003), *Le Syndrome autoritaire: politique en Tunisie de Bourguiba à Ben Ali*, Paris, Presses de Science Po.

CAMMETT, Melani (2004), "Challenge to Networks of Privilege in Morocco: Implications for Networks Analysis", in S. Heydemann (ed.), *Networks of Privilege in the Middle East: The Politics of Economic Reform Revisited*, New York, Palgrave Macmillan.

CARAPICO, Sheila (2002), "Foreign Aid for Promoting Democracy in the Arab World", *Middle East Journal*, Vol. 56, No. 3.

CARNEGIE, Dale (1936), *How to Win Friends and Influence People*, New York, Simon & Schuster.

CARNEGIE ENDOWMENT FOR INTERNATIONAL PEACE (2005), "Interview with George Ishak, Founding Member of the Egyptian Movement for Change (*Kifaya*)", *Arab Reform Bulletin*, Vol. 3, No. 6, July, http://www.carnegieendowment.org/files/Interview1.pdf.

CAROTHERS, Thomas (2002), "The End of the Transition Paradigm", *Journal of Democracy*, Vol. 13, No. 1.

CASSARINO, Jean Pierre (1999), "The European Association Agreement and the Impact of the Programme de Mise à Niveau on Political and Economic Developments in Tunisia", *The Middle East Journal*, Vol. 3, No. 1.

CASTEL, Rober (1995), *Les Métamorphoses de la question sociale. Une chronique du salariat*, Paris, Gallimard.

CATTEDRA, Raffaele (2001), *La Mosquée et la Cité. La reconversion symbolique du projet urbain à Casablanca (Maroc)*, Thèse en géographie, Université de Tours.

CATUSSE, Myriam (2001), "Les Métamorphoses de la question syndicale au Maroc", *Critique Économique*, Rabat, No. 5, Juin.

CATUSSE, Myriam (2005), "La réinvention du social dans le Maroc ajusté", in E. Longuenesse, B. Destremau and M. Catusse (eds), *Le Travail et la question sociale au Maghreb et au Moyen Orient*, REMMM, No. 105–6.

CATUSSE, Myriam (2006), "Ordonner, classer, penser la société: les pays arabes au prisme de l'économique politique", in E. Picard (ed.), *La Politique dans le monde arabe*, Paris, Armand Colin.

CATUSSE, Myriam (2007), *Maroc: les politiques de l'entrepreneur. Action publique et mobilisations dans la libéralisation*, Paris, Maisonneuve et Larose.

CATUSSE, Myriam, Raffaele CATTEDRA and Mohamed IDRISSI-JANATI (2005), "Municipaliser les villes? Le gouvernement des villes marocaines à l'épreuve du politique et du territoire", in C. De Miras (ed.), *Intégration à la ville et services urbains au Maroc*.

CENTER FOR TRADE UNION AND WORKERS SERVICES (2007), *Facts about the Trade Union Elections for the Term, 2006–2011*, Cairo/Helwan, Center for Trade Union and Workers Services.

CENTRAL ADMINISTRATION OF STATISTICS (2006), *Living Conditions*, Lebanon.

CHAMESS ED-DINE, Mohamed H. (1997), "L'épreuve 'Raisins de la colère' quand les Libanais ne se divisent pas autour de leur sang", *al-Mirqab*, Liban, Université Balamand, No. 1, Automne.

CHARARA, Walid (1998), *Dawlat Hizb Allah. Lubnan mujtama'a islamiyya*, Beirut, Dar al-Nahar.

CHAUDHRY, Kiren Aziz (1997), *The Price of Wealth: Economies and Institutions in the Middle East*, Ithaca, Cornell University Press.

CHEHABI, Houchang (2005), "Iran and Lebanon in the Revolutionary Decade", in H. Chehabi (ed.), *Distant Relations: Iran and Lebanon in the Last 500 Years*, London, I.B. Tauris.

CHEYNIS, Éric (2005), "L'altermondialisme au prisme marocain", *Critique Internationale*, No. 27, Avril–Juin.

CLARK, Ian (1999), *Globalization and International Relations Theory*, Oxford, Oxford University Press.

CLARK, Janine A. (2004), *Islam, Charity, and Activism: Middle-Class Networks and Social Welfare in Egypt, Jordan, and Yemen*, Bloomington, Indiana University Press.

CLEMENT, Henry Moore (1990), "Islamic Banks and Competitive Politics in the Arab World and Turkey", *Middle East Journal*, Vol. 44, No. 2.

COLLA, Elliott (2006), "Solidarity in the Time of Anti-normalization", in J. Beinin and R.L. Stein (eds), *The Struggle for Sovereignty: Palestine and Israel, 1993–2005*, Stanford, CA, Stanford University Press.

COMMISSION OF THE EUROPEAN COMMUNITIES (2005), *Annex to European Neighbourhood Policy: Country Report Lebanon*, Sec 289/3, Brussels, 2 March.

CONGRESSIONAL RESEARCH SERVICE (2001), "U.S. Assistance to Lebanon", *Issue Brief for Congress*, 11 December.

CORDESMAN, Anthony (2005), "Saudi Arabia and the Struggle Against Terrorism", Washington, DC, Center for Strategic and International Studies, April.

CORDESMAN, Anthony (2006), "Saudi Arabia: Friend or Foe in the War on Terror?", *Middle East Policy*, Vol. XIII, No. 1, Spring.

CORDESMAN, Anthony and Nawaf OBAID (2004), "Saudi Military Forces and Development: Changes & Reforms", Washington, DC, Center for Strategic and International Studies, 30 May, working draft.

CORDESMAN, Anthony and Nawaf OBAID (2005), "Saudi Counter Terrorism Effort: The Changing Paramilitary and Domestic Security Apparatus", Washington, DC, Center for Strategic and International Studies, 2 February, working draft.

CORM, Georges (2003), *Le Liban contemporain. Histoire et société*, Paris, La Découverte.

COUNCIL FOR DEVELOPMENT AND RECONSTRUCTION (2006), *Development Program 2006–2009*, CNBureau, Dar al-Handash and IAURIF, http://www.cdr.gov.lb/Plan/main.htm.

COURMONT, Barthélémy and Darko RIBNIKAR (2002), *Les Guerres asymétriques: conflits d'hier et d'aujourd'hui, terrorisme et nouvelles menaces*, Paris, PUF.

COVEY, Stephen R.W. (1989), *The Seven Habits of Highly Effective People*, New York, Simon & Schuster.

CRANER, Lorne (2006), "Democracy in the Middle East: Will U.S. Democratization Policy Work?", *Middle East Quarterly*, Vol. 13, No. 3.

DAGHER, Carole (2002), *Le défi du Liban d'après guerre*, Paris, l'Harmattan.

DALACOURA, Katerina (2005), "US Democracy Promotion in the Arab Middle East since 11 September 2001: A Critique", *International Affairs*, Vol. 81, No. 5.

DALACOURA, Katerina (2006), "Islamist Terrorism and the Middle East Democratic Deficit: Political Exclusion, Repression and the Causes of Extremism", *Democratization*, Vol. 13, No. 3, June.

DA LAGE, Olivier (2005), "Saudi Arabia and the Smaller Gulf States: The Vassals Take their Revenge", International Conference: The Gulf Monarchies in Transition (colloquium), CERI, January.

DEBIÉ, Franck and Danuta PIETER (2003), *La Paix et la crise: le Liban reconstruit?*, Paris, PUF.

DELACROIX, Jacques (1980), "The Distributive State in the World System", *Studies in Comparative International Development*, Vol. 15, No. 1, Fall.

DENIS, Éric (1994), "La Mise en scène des 'ashwaiyyat. Premier acte: Imbaba, Décembre 1992", *Egypte/Monde Arabe*, Vol. 20, 4e Trimèstre.

DENOEUX, Guilain (2002), "Le mouvement associatif marocain face à l'État: autonomie, partenariat, ou instrumentalisation ?", in S. Ben Nefissa (ed.), *Pouvoirs et associations dans le monde arabe*, Paris, CNRS Editions.

DESTA, Melaku Geboye (2003), "OPEC, the WTO, Regionalism and Unilateralism", *Journal of World Trade*, Vol. 37, No. 3.

DESTREMAU, Blandine (2004), "Les enjeux de la protection sociale dans les pays de la méditerranée méridionale et orientale", *Premier congrès de l'AFS*, 24–27 February.

DIAMOND, Larry (2002), "Elections without Democracy: Thinking about Hybrid Regimes", *Journal of Democracy*, Vol. 13, No. 1.

DIBEH, Ghassan (2005), "The Political Economy of Postwar Reconstruction in Lebanon", *WIDER Research Paper* 44, July, WIDER.

DIDRY, Claude (2001), "Symposium sur les métamorphoses de la question sociale", *Sociologie du Travail*, No. 43.

DILLMAN, Bradford (2001), "Facing the Market in North Africa", *Middle East Journal*, Vol. 55, No. 2.

DIOUN, Cyrus (2005), "Democracy within Boundaries: Managing Risks While Promoting Liberalization in Saudi Arabia", *Policy Background and Options Paper Series*, Nathan Hale Foreign Policy Society/Middle East Program, February.

DIOURI, Moumen (1992), *A qui appartient le Maroc?*, Paris, l'Harmattan.

DIRECTION DE LA STATISTIQUE (2000), *Enquête nationale sur le niveau de vie des ménages 1998–1999*, Rabat, Royaume du Maroc.

DIRECTION DE LA STATISTIQUE (2003), *Enquête nationale sur le secteur informel non agricole 1999/2000*, Rabat, Royaume du Maroc.

DONZELOT, Jacques (1994), *L'Invention du social*, Paris, Seuil.

DROZ-VINCENT, Philippe (2004), "Quel avenir pour l'autoritarisme dans le monde arabe?", *Revue Française de Science Politique*, Vol. 54, No. 6, December.

DROZ-VINCENT, Philippe (2007a), "From Political to Economic Actors, the Transforming Role of Middle Eastern Armies", in O. Schlumberger (ed.), *Debating Arab Authoritarianism: Dynamics and Durability in Nondemocratic Regimes*, Stanford, CA, Stanford University Press.

DROZ-VINCENT, Philippe (2007b), *Vertiges de la puissance, Le moment américain au Moyen-Orient*, Paris, La Découverte.

DUFFIELD, Mark (2001), *Global Governance and the New Wars: The Merging of Development and Security*, London, Zed Books.

EFG HERMES BANK (2007), *Saudi Arabia Economics: Building on the Boom*, EFG Hermes, Riyad, 28 October.

EHTESHAMI, Anoushiravan (2007), *Globalization and Geopolitics in the Middle East: Old Games, New Rules*, New York, Routledge.

EISENSTADT, Samuel N. and Rene LEMARCHAND (eds) (1981), *Political Clientelism, Patronage and Development*, London, Sage Publications.

EISENSTADT, Samuel N. and Luis RONIGER (1984), *Patrons, Clients and Friends: Interpersonal Relations and the Structure of Trust in Society*, Cambridge, Cambridge University Press.

EL-AOUFI, Nourredine (1998), "L'Hypothèse salariale au Maroc", *Annales Marocaines d'Économie*, No. 22–3.

EL-AOUFI, Nourredine (2000), "L'Impératif social au Maroc: de l'Ajustement à la régulation", *Critiques Économiques*, Rabat, No. 3.

EL-AOUFI, Nourredine and Mohammed BEN SAÏD (2005/2006), "Chômage et employabilité des jeunes au Maroc", *Employment Strategy Paper*, Geneva, ILO.

EL-FARRA, Taha (1973), *The Effects of Detribalizing the Bedouins on the Internal Cohesion of the Saudi State*, PhD thesis, University of Pittsburgh.

EL-KHAZEN, Farid (2003), "The Postwar Political Process: Authoritarianism by Diffusion", in T. Hanf and S. Nawaf (eds), *Lebanon in Limbo: Postwar Society and State in an Uncertain Regional Environment*, Baden-Baden, Nomos Verlagsgesellschaft.

EL-MALKI, Habib (1989), *Trente Ans d'économie marocaine. 1960–1990*, Paris, éditions du CNRS.

EL-MALKI, Habib and Abdelali DOUMOU (1990), "L'interventionnisme de l'État marocain à l'épreuve de l'ajustement", in J.C. Santucci and H. el-Malki (eds), *Etat et développement dans le monde arabe. Crises et mutations au Maghreb*, Paris, éditions du CNRS.

EL SHAFEI, Omar (1995), "Workers, Trade Unions, and the State in Egypt: 1984–1989", *Cairo Papers in Social Science*, Vol. 18, No. 2, Summer.

ELSENHANS, Hans (1981), *Abhängiger Kapitalismus oder bürokratische Entwicklungsgesellschaft. Versuch über den Staat in der Dritten Welt*, New York and Frankfurt, Campus.

EMPERADOR BADIMON, Montserrat (2005), *Le Mouvement des diplômés chômeurs au Maroc: l'Idéologisation comme source d'éclatement et de pérennisation d'un mouvement social*, Aix-en-Provence, IEP, Mémoire de Master.

ETZIONI, Amitai (1975), *A Comparative Analysis of Complex Organizations: On Power, Involvement, and Their Correlates*, New York, Free Press.

EUROPEAN COMMISSION (2008), *Morocco: Bilateral Trade Relations*, July, http://ec.europa.eu/trade/issues/bilateral/countries/morocco/index_en.htm.

EUROPEAN UNION ELECTION OBSERVATION MISSION (n.d.), *Parliamentary Elections Lebanon 2005: Final Report*, http://ec.europa.eu/external_relations/human_rights/eu_election_ass_observ/lebanon/final_report.pdf.
al-FAHAD, Abdulaziz H. (2005), "Ornamental Constitutionalism: The Saudi Basic Law of Governance", *Yale Journal of International Law*, Vol. 30, No. 2.
FAHMY, Ninette S. (2002), *The Politics of Egypt: State–Society Relationship*, London, Routledge Curzon.
FANDY, Mamoud (1999), *Saudi Arabia and the Politics of Dissent*, New York, St Martin's Press.
FAVIER, Agnès (2006), "La spirale de la crise dans le Liban libéré (2004–2006)", *Perspective MOM*, Juin.
FEARON, James and David LAITIN (2004), "Neotrusteeship and the Problem of Weak States", *International Security*, Vol. 28, No. 4, Spring.
FERGUSON, James (1990), *The Anti-Politics Machine: Depoliticization and Bureaucratic Power in Lesotho*, Cambridge, Cambridge University Press.
FERRIÉ, Jean-Noël and Alain ROUSSILLON (2004), "Réforme et politique au Maroc de l'alternance: apolitisation consensuelle du politique", *Naqd*, No. 19/20.
FRANK, Thomas (2004), *What's the Matter with Kansas? How Conservatives Won the Hearts of America*, New York, Henry Holt and Co.
FRANCKFORT, Isabelle, Florence OSTY, Renaud SAINSAULIEU and Marc UHALDE (1995), *Les Mondes sociaux de l'entreprise*, Paris, Desclée de Brouwer.
FREIHA, Adel (1980), *L'Armée et l'État au Liban: 1945–1980*, Paris, LGDJ.
FUKUYAMA, Francis (1989), "The End of History", *The National Interest* (web edition), Summer.
FULLER, Graham (2006), "The Hizbullah–Iran Connection: Model for Sunni Resistance", *Washington Quarterly*, Vol. 30, No. 1.
GAMBILL, Gary C. (2002), "Hezbollah's Strategic Rocket Arsenal", *Middle East Intelligence Bulletin*, Vol. 4, No. 11, November/December, http://www.meib.org/articles/0211_l2.htm.
GAUSE III, F. Gregory (2000), "The Persistence of Monarchy in the Arabian Peninsula: A Comparative Analysis", in J. Kostiner (ed.),

Middle East Monarchies: The Challenge of Modernity, Boulder and London, Westview Press.
GAUSE III, F. Gregory (2002), "The Foreign Policy of Saudi Arabia", in R. Hinnebusch and A. Ehteshami (eds), *The Foreign Policies of Middle East States*, Boulder and London, Lynne Rienner Publishers.
GAUSE III, F. Gregory (2005), "Can Democracy Stop Terrorism", *Foreign Affairs*, September/October, www.foreignaffairs.org.
GAUSE III, F. Gregory (2007), "Saudi Arabia: Iraq, Iran, the Regional Power Balance, and the Sectarian Question", *Strategic Insights*, Vol. VI, No. 2, March.
GEISSER, Vincent, Karam KARAM and Frédéric VAIREL (2006), "Espaces du politique. Mobilisations et protestations dans le monde arabe", in E. Picard (ed.), *La politique dans monde arabe*, Paris, Armand Colin.
al-GHOBASHY, Mona (2003), "Egypt's Summer of Discontent", *Middle East Report Online*, 18 September, http://www.merip.org/mero/mero091803.html.
al-GHOBASHY, Mona (2005), "Egypt Looks Ahead to Portentous Year", *Middle East Report Online*, 2 February, http://www.merip.org/mero/mero020205.html.
GIDDENS, Anthony (2000), *The Third Way and its Critics*, Cambridge, Polity Press.
GILMAN, Neil (2007), *Mandarins of the Future: Modernization Theory in Cold War America*, Washington, DC, The Johns Hopkins University Press.
The GRACIA GROUP (2002), *The Sino–Saudi Energy Rapprochement: Implications for US National Security*, 8 January, http://www.rice.edu/energy/publications/docs/SinoSaudiStudyFinal.pdf.
GRESH, Alain (2003), "After the Winning of the War. Saudi Arabia: Radical Islam or Reform?", *Le Monde Diplomatique*, June, http://mondediplo.com.
GREY, Stephen (2006), *Ghost Plane: The True Story of the CIA Rendition and Torture Program*, New York, St Martin's Press.
GRIMMETT, Richard F. (2005), *Conventional Arms Transfers to Developing Nations 1997–2004*, CRS Report for Congress, 29 August.
GUAZZONE, Laura (2004), "Il dibattito occidentale sulla democrazia nel mondo arabo: tra interessi strategici e paradigmi dominanti", in F. Bicchi, L. Guazzone and D. Pioppi (eds), *La questione della*

democrazia nel mondo arabo. Stati, società e conflitti, Modena, Polimetrica.

GUAZZONE, Laura and Daniela PIOPPI (2007), "Globalisation and the Restructuring of State Power in the Arab World", *The International Spectator*, Vol. 42, No. 4.

HAENNI, Patrick (2005a), *L'ordre des caïds: conjurer la dissidence urbaine au Caire*, Paris, Karthala.

HAENNI, Patrick (2005b), *L'Islam de marché*, Paris, Editions du Seuil et la République des Idées.

HAKIMIAN, Hassan and Ziba MOSHAVER (eds) (2001), *The State and Global Change: The Political Economy of Transition in the Middle East and North Africa*, Richmond, Surrey, Curzon.

HARRIS, William (1997), *Faces of Lebanon: Sects, Wars, and Global Extensions*, Princeton, NJ, Markus Wiener Publishers.

HAUT COMMISSARIAT AU PLAN (2007), *Enquête nationale sur l'emploi*, Maroc, Direction de la Statistique.

HEGGHAMMER, Thomas (2006), "Terrorist Recruitment and Radicalisation in Saudi Arabia", *Middle East Policy*, Vol. 13, No. 4, Winter.

HEGGHAMMER, Thomas (2007), *Violent Islamism in Saudi Arabia: The Origins of al-Qaida on the Arabian Peninsula*, PhD thesis, Paris, Sciences Po.

HEGGHAMMER, Thomas and Stephane LACROIX (2007), "Rejectionist Islamism in Saudi Arabia: The Story of Juhayman al-Utaybi Revisited", *International Journal of Middle East Studies*, Vol. 39, No. 1.

HENRY, Clement M. and Robert SPRINGBORG (2001), *Globalization and the Politics of Development in the Middle East*, Cambridge, Cambridge University Press.

HERB, Michael (1999), *All in the Family: Absolutism, Revolution, and Democracy in the Middle East*, Albany, SUNY Press.

HERTOG, Steffen (2006a), "Modernizing without Democratizing? The Introduction of Formal Politics in Saudi Arabia", *International Politics and Society*, No. 3.

HERTOG, Steffen (2006b), "The New Corporatism in Saudi Arabia: Limits of Formal Politics", in A. Khalaf and G. Luciani (eds), *Constitutional Reform and Political Participation in the Gulf*, Dubai, Gulf Research Center.

HERTOG, Steffen (2007a), "The GCC and Arab Economic Integration: A New Paradigm", *Middle East Policy*, Vol. 14, No. 1.

HERTOG, Steffen (2007b), "Shaping the Saudi State: Human Agency's Shifting Role in Rentier State Formation", *International Journal of Middle East Studies*, Vol. 39, No. 4, November.

HERTOG, Steffen (forthcoming), *Segmented Clientelism: The Politics of Economic Reform in Saudi Arabia*, Ithaca, Cornell University Press.

HEYDEMANN, Steven (1993), "Taxation without Representation: Authoritarianism and Economic Liberalization in Syria", in E. Goldberg, R. Kasaba and J.S. Miqdal (eds), *Rules and Rights in the Middle East*, Seattle, University of Washington Press.

HEYDEMANN, Steven (2002), "La question de la démocratie dans les travaux sur le monde arabe", *Critique Internationale*, Vol. 17, Octobre.

HEYDEMANN, Steven (2004), *Networks of Privilege in the Middle East: The Politics of Economic Reform Revisited*, New York, Palgrave Macmillan.

HEYDEMANN, Steven (2007), "Upgrading Authoritarianism in the Arab World", *Saban Center Analysis Paper*, October.

HIBOU, Béatrice (1998), "Economie politique du discours de la banque mondiale en Afrique sub-saharienne. Du catéchisme économique au fait (et méfait) missionnaire", *Les Etudes du CERI*, No. 39, Mars.

HIBOU, Béatrice (1999), "De la privatisation des économies à la privatisation des Etats. Une analyse de la formation continue de l'Etat", in B. Hibou (ed.), *La Privatisation des Etats*, Paris, Karthala.

HIBOU, Béatrice (ed.) (2004), *Privatising the State*, London, Hurst & Company.

HIBOU, Béatrice (2006), *La force de l'obéissance. Économie politique de la répression en Tunisie*, Paris, La Découverte.

HIBOU, Béatrice and Mohammed TOZY (2002), "De la friture sur la ligne des réformes. La libéralisation des télécommunications au Maroc", *Critique Internationale*, No. 14.

HILL, Christopher (2003), *The Changing Politics of Foreign Policy*, London, Palgrave Macmillan.

HIRSCHMAN, Albert O. (1991), *Deux Siècles de rhétorique réactionnaire*, Paris, Fayard.

HUDSON, Michael (1977), *Arab Politics: The Search for Legitimacy*, New Haven, Yale University Press.

HUMAN RIGHTS WATCH (2001), *Egypt: Human Rights Background*, Human Rights Watch, October.

HUMAN RIGHTS WATCH (2003), *Egypt's New Chill on Rights Groups*, 21 June, http://hrw.org/english/docs/2003/06/21/egypt6167.htm.

HUMAN RIGHTS WATCH (2005a), *Egypt, Margins of Repression*, Human Rights Watch, 4 July.

HUMAN RIGHTS WATCH (2005b), *Morocco's Truth Commission: Honoring Past Victims during an Uncertain Present*, Human Rights Watch, November.

HUMAN RIGHTS WATCH (2007), *Anatomy of a State Security Case*, Human Rights Watch, 11 December.

HUNTINGTON, Samuel (1959), *The Soldier and the State: The Theory and Politics of Civil–Military Relations*, Cambridge, MA, Belknap Press of Harvard University Press.

HUNTINGTON, Samuel (1991), *The Third Wave: Democratization in the Late Twentieth Century*, Norman, University of Oklahoma Press.

HUSSAIN, Syed Rifaat (2007), "Responding to Terrorist Threats: Perspectives from Saudi Arabia and Pakistan", *Gulf Year Book 2006–2007*, Dubai, Gulf Research Center.

IBRAHIM, Fouad (2006), *The Shi'is of Saudi Arabia*, London, Saqi Books.

IBRAHIM, Saad Eddin (1996), "The Changing Face of Egypt's Islamic Activism", in R. Aliboni, G. Joffé and T. Niblock (eds), *Security Challenges in the Mediterranean Region*, London, Frank Cass.

INDEX MUNDI (n.d.), *Egypt Inflation Rate*, http://www.indexmundi.com/egypt/inflation_rate_(consumer_prices).html.

INTERNATIONAL CRISIS GROUP (2005), "The Shiite Question in Saudi Arabia", *Middle East Report*, No. 45, 19 September.

INTERNATIONAL INSTITUTE FOR STRATEGIC STUDIES (2002), *The Military Balance 2002/2003*, London, IISS.

INTERNATIONAL INSTITUTE FOR STRATEGIC STUDIES (2004), *The Military Balance 2004/2005*, London, IISS.

INTERNATIONAL LABOUR ORGANIZATION (ILO) (n.d.), *Natlex database*, http://www.ilo.org/dyn/natlex/natlex_browse.home.

INTERNATIONAL MONETARY FUND (2005), *Public Information Notice*, No. 05/72, 7 June, http://www.imf.org/external/np/sec/pn/2005/pn0572.htm.

INTERNATIONAL MONETARY FUND (1996), Arab Republic of Egypt, *Staff Report for the 1996 Article IV Consultation and Request for Stand-by Arrangement*, Cairo.

ISMAIL, Salwa (2000), "The Popular Movement Dimensions of Contemporary Militant Islamism: Socio-Spatial Determinants in the Cairo Urban Setting", *Comparative Studies in Society and History*, Vol. 42, No. 1, January.

JADWA INVESTMENT (2007), *The GCC Economies and the Global Context*, 4 September, www.jadwa.com.

JONES, Toby C. (2005), "The Clerics, the Sahwa and the Saudi State", *Strategic Insights*, Vol. 4, No. 3, March.

JONES, Toby C. (2007), "Saudi Arabia's Not So New Anti-Shi'ism", *Middle East Report*, No. 242, Spring.

JUNG, Dietrich (ed.) (2006), *Democratization and Development: New Political Strategies for the Middle East*, New York and Basingstoke, Palgrave Macmillan.

KAHWAJI, Riad (2003), "Gulf Cooperation Council Threat Perceptions and Deterrence Objectives", *Comparative Strategy*, Vol. 22, No. 5.

KALDOR, Mary (2006), *New and Old Wars: Organized Violence in a Global Era*, Cambridge, Polity Press.

KAMRAVA, Mehran (2000), "Military Professionalization and Civil–Military Relations in the Middle East", *Political Science Quarterly*, Vol. 115, No. 1, Spring.

KARAM, Karam (2006), *Le mouvement civil au Liban. Revendications, protestations et mobilisations associatives dans l'après-guerre*, Paris, Karthala.

KARSHENAS, Massoud and Valentine MOGHADAM (2006), *Social Policy in the Middle East: Economic, Political and Gender Dynamics*, Basingstoke, Palgrave Macmillan.

KASPARIAN, Choghig (2003), *L'entrée des jeunes libanais dans la vie active et l'émigration*, Beirut, St Joseph University.

KASSEM, Maye (2004), *Egyptian Politics: The Dynamics of Authoritarian Rule*, Boulder, CO, Lynne Rienner Publishers.

KASSIR, Samir (2000), "Dix ans après, comment ne pas réconcilier une société divisée?", *Maghreb-Machrek*, No. 169, Juillet-Septembre.

KAYE, Dalia Dassa and Fredric M. WEHREY (2007), "A Nuclear Iran: The Reactions of Neighbors", *Survival*, Vol. 49, No. 2.

KEPEL, Gilles (2004), *Jihad: The Trail of Political Islam*, London, I.B. Tauris.

KERNEN, Antoine (2004), *La Chine vers l'économie de marché. Les privatisations à Shenyang*, Paris, Karthala.

KHALIL, Ibrahim (1990), "Qanun al-difa'. Qiyada jam'iyya am shalal fil-qiyada?", *al-Difa' al-watani*.

KIENLE, Eberhard (2000), *A Grand Delusion: Democracy and Economic Reform in Egypt*, London, I.B. Tauris.

KINGDOM OF MOROCCO (2006), *Report on Human Development 2006*, Rabat, Morocco.

KINGDOM OF SAUDI ARABIA (2005), Central Department of Statistics, *Social Statistics, Labour Force Survey*, www.planning.gov.sa/statistic/sindxxe.htm.

KINGDOM OF SAUDI ARABIA (2006), *Achievements of the Development Plans: 1970–2005*, Riyad, Ministry of Economy and Planning.

KINGDOM OF SAUDI ARABIA (2007), "Statement on the 2008 Budget", *Press Release*, Ministry of Finance, 11 December.

KNAUERHASE, Ramon (1977), *The Saudi Arabian Economy*, New York and London, Praeger.

KNAUPE, Henk and Ulrich G. WURZEL (1995), *Aufbruch in der Wüste. Die Neuen Städte in Ägypten*, Frankfurt/M., Peter Lang.

KORANY, Bahgat, Paul NOBLE and Rex BRYNEN (eds) (1993), *The Many Faces of National Security in the Arab World*, London, MacMillan.

KRAUSE, Keith (2004), "State-Making and Region-Building: The Interplay of Domestic and Regional Security in the Middle East", in Z. Maoz, E.B. Landau and T. Malz, *Building Regional Security in the Middle East: International, Regional and Domestic Influences*, London, Frank Cass.

KROONINGS, Kees and Dirk KRUIJT (2002), *Political Armies: The Military and Nation Building in the Age of Democracy*, London and New York, Zed Books.

KUBBA, Laith (2000), "Arabs and Democracy: The Awakening of Civil Society", *Journal of Democracy*, Vol. 11, No. 3.

LACEY, Robert (1981), *The Kingdom*, New York and London, Harcourt Brace Yovanovich.

LACROIX, Stéphane (2004), "Between Islamists and Liberals: Saudi Arabia's New Islamo-Liberal Reformist Trend", *Middle East Journal*, Vol. 58, No. 3, Summer.

LACROIX, Stéphane (2007), *The Political Sociology of Islamism in Saudi Arabia*, PhD thesis, Paris/Sciences Po.

LACROIX, Stéphane (2008), "L'apport de Muhammad Nasir al-Din al-Albani au salafisme contemporain: de la régénération critique du wahhabisme à l'invention d'un apolitisme militant", in B. Rougier (ed.), *Qu'est-ce que le Salafisme?*, Paris, PUF.

LAÏDI, Zaki (1993), "Sens et puissance dans le système international", in Z. Laïdi (ed.), *L'Ordre mondial relâché. Sens et puissance après la guerre froide*, Paris, Presses de la FNSP.

LAIPSON, Ellen (ed.) (2006), *Security Sector Reform in the Gulf*, The Henry L. Stimson Center, May, www.stimson.org.

LAIPSON, Ellen (2007), "Prospects for Middle East Security-sector Reform", *Survival*, Vol. 49, No. 2, June.

LAKE, Anthony (1994), "Confronting Backlash States", *Foreign Affairs*, March–April.

LANGOHR, Vickie (2005), "Too Much Civil Society, Too Little Politics: The Case of Egypt and the Arab Liberalizers", in M. Pripstein Posusney and M. Penner Angrist (eds), *Authoritarianism in the Middle East: Regimes and Resistance*, Boulder, CO and London, Lynne Reiner.

LAYNE, Christopher (1994), "Kant or Cant: The Myth of the Democratic Peace", *International Security*, Vol. 19, No. 2, Autumn.

LECA, Jean (1990), "Social Structures and Political Stability: Comparative Evidence from the Algerian, Syrian and Iraqi Cases", in G. Luciani (ed.), *The Arab State*, London, Routledge.

LEENDERS, Reinoud (2006), "How the Rebel Regained His Cause: Hizbullah & the Sixth Arab–Israeli War", *MIT Electronic Journal of Middle East Studies*, Vol. 6, Summer, http://web.mit.edu/CIS/www/mitejmes.

LEENDERS, Reinoud (2007a), "Au-delà du « Pays des deux fleuves »: une configuration conflictuelle régionale?", *Critique Internationale*, No. 34, Janvier–Mars.

LEENDERS, Reinoud (2007b), "Regional Conflict Formations: Is the Middle East Next?", *Third World Quarterly*, Vol. 8, No. 5, July.

LEGRENZI, Matteo (2007a), "Nato Istanbul Cooperation Initiative in the Gulf: Who is Doing a Favor to Whom?", Florence, European University Institute, Robert Schuman Centre, March.

LEGRENZI, Matteo (2007b), "NATO in the Gulf: Who is Doing Whom a Favor?", *Middle East Policy*, Vol. 14, No. 1, Spring 2007.

LERNER, Daniel (1958), *The Passing of Traditional Society: Modernizing the Middle East*, Glencoe, IL, The Free Press.

LE SAOUT, Didier and Marguerite ROLLINDE (eds) (1999), *Emeutes et mouvements sociaux au Maghreb. Perspective comparée*, Paris, Karthala.

LINZ, Juan (1975), "Totalitarian and Authoritarian Regimes", in F.I. Greenstein and N.W. Polsby (eds), *The Handbook of Political Science: Macropolitical Theory*, Vol. 3, Reading, MA, Addison Wesley Publications.

LIPJHART, Arend (1997), "Changement et continuité dans la théorie consociative", *Revue Internationale de Politique Comparée*, Vol. 4, No. 3.

LIPSET, Seymor (1959), "Some Social Requisites of Democracy: Economic Development and Political Legitimacy", *American Political Science Review*, Vol. 53, No. 1.

LOONEY, Robert (2004), "Combating Terrorism through Reforms: Implications of the Bremer-Kasandra Model for Saudi Arabia", *Strategic Insights*, Vol. 3, No. 4, April.

LUCIANI, Giacomo (1990), "Allocation vs. Production States: A Theoretical Framework", in G. Luciani (ed.), *The Arab State*, London, Routledge.

LUCIANI, Giacomo (2005), "Saudi Arabian Business: From Private Sector to National Bourgeoisie", in P. Aarts and G. Nonneman (eds), *Saudi Arabia in the Balance: Political Economy, Society, Foreign Affairs*, London, Hurst.

MACLAURIN, Ronald D. (1991), "From Professional to Political: The Redecline of the Lebanese Army", *Armed Forces & Society*, Vol. 17, No. 4, Summer.

MAGHRAOUI, Abdesalam M. (2001), "Monarchy and Political Reform in Morocco", *Journal of Democracy*, Vol. 12, No. 1, January.

MAÏLA, Joseph (1989/90), "Document d'entente nationale. Un commentaire", Les cahiers de l'Orient, No. 16–17.

MBEMBE, Achille (1999), "Du gouvernement privé in direct", *Politique Africaine*, No. 73.

MEIJER, Roel (2005), "The 'Cycle of Contention' and the Limits of Terrorism in Saudi Arabia", in P. Aarts and G. Nonneman (eds),

Saudi Arabia in the Balance: Political Economy, Society, Foreign Affairs, London, Hurst.

MENOUNI, Abdeltif (1979), *Le Syndicalisme ouvrier au Maroc*, Casablanca, Éditions Maghrébines.

MERMIER, Franck and Elizabeth PICARD (2007), *Liban – Une guerre de 33 jours*, Paris, La Decourverte.

MIGRATION INFORMATION SOURCE (2005), *Morocco: From Emigration Country to Africa's Migration Passage to Europe*, October, http://www.migrationinformation.org/Profiles/display.cfm?ID=339.

MINISTÈRE DES FINANCES ET DES PRIVATISATIONS (n.d.), "Oualalou s'exprime sur l'ALE Maroc/Etats-Unis", Maroc, http://www.finances.gov.ma/portal/page?_pageid=33,4502299&_dad=portal&_schema=PORTAL.

MINISTÈRE DE L'ECONOMIE ET DES FINANCES (1995), *Bilan du Programme d'Ajustement Structurel*, Direction des Etudes et des Prévisions Financières, Royaume du Maroc, Octobre.

MINISTRY OF FINANCE (n.d.), *Data and Statistics*, Lebanon, www.finance.gov.lb.

MITCHELL, Richard P. (1969), *The Society of the Muslim Brothers*, Oxford, Oxford University Press.

MITCHELL, Timothy (1991), "The Limits of the State: Beyond Statist Approaches and their Critics", *American Political Science Review*, Vol. 85.

MITCHELL, Timothy (2002), *Rule of Expert, Egypt, Techno-Politics, Modernity*, Berkeley, LA and London, University of California Press.

MOENSCH, Richard U. (1988), "Oil, Ideology and State Autonomy in Egypt", *Arab Studies Quarterly*, Vol. 10, No. 2, Spring.

MONTAGU, C. (2006), *Civil Society, the Al Saud and the Voluntary Sector*, M.Sc. thesis, London/School of Oriental and African Studies.

MOUKHEIBER, Ghassan (2000), "La justice, instrument du pouvoir politique", *Maghreb-Machrek*, No. 169, juillet–septembre.

MOULINE, Mohammed Tawfik (2005), "Etude comparative, en termes de développement humain, du Maroc et d'un échantillon de quatorze pays pour la période 1955–2004", in Royaume du Maroc, *Cinquante ans de développement humain*, Rabat.

MOUSSEAU, Michael, Hegre HAVARD and John R. O'NEAL (2003), "How the Wealth of Nations Conditions the Liberal Peace", *European Journal of International Relations*, Vol. 9, No. 2.

MYERS JAFFE, Amy and Jareer ELASS (2007), *Saudi Aramco: National Flagship with Global Responsibilties*, The James A. Baker III Institute for Public Policy, Rice University.

NAHAS, Charbel (2003), *Chances to Avoid Crisis and Conditions to Overcome it: Account of an Attempt to Reform*, Dar al-Nahar, August [in Arabic].

NATIONAL COMMERCIAL BANK (2004), *Saudi Arabia: Business and Economic Developments*, www.saudiecnomicsurvey.com/html/reports.html.

NIBLOCK, Tim (2006), *Saudi Arabia: Power, Legitimacy and Survival*, London, Routledge.

NIBLOCK, Tim and Monica MALIK (2007), *The Political Economy of Saudi Arabia*, London, Routledge.

NONNEMAN, Gerd (2001), "Saudi–European Relations 1902–2001: A Pragmatic Quest for Relative Autonomy", *International Affairs*, Vol. 77, No. 3.

NONNEMAN, Gerd (2005/2006), "Determinants and Patterns of Saudi Foreign Policy: 'Omnibalancing' and 'Relative Autonomy' in Multiple Environments", in P. Aarts and G. Nonneman (eds), *Saudi Arabia in the Balance*, New York, New York University Press.

NONNEMAN, Gerd (2006), "EU–GCC Relations: Dynamics, Perspectives, and the Issue of Political Reform", *Journal of Social Affairs*, Vol. 23, No. 92, Winter.

NORTON, Augustus Richard (ed.) (1996), *Civil Society in the Middle East*, Leiden, E.J. Brill.

OBAID, Nawaf (2000), *The Oil Kingdom at 100: Petroleum, Policymaking in Saudi Arabia*, Washington, DC, Washington Institute for Near East Policy.

O'DONNELL, Guillermo (1973), *Modernization and Bureaucratic Authoritarianism*, Berkeley, CA, IIS.

O'DONNELL, Guillermo, Philippe SCHMITTER and Laurence WHITEHEAD (eds) (1986), *Transitions from Authoritarian Rule: Comparative Perspectives*, Baltimore and London, The Johns Hopkins University Press.

OFFERLÉ, Michel (1994), *Sociologie des groupes d'intérêt*, Paris, Montchrétien.

OWEN, Roger (2004), *State, Power and Politics in the Making of the Modern Middle East*, London, Routledge.

PACIELLO, M. Cristina (2006), "The Changing Patterns of Wealth Accumulation and Distribution under Economic Reform in the Arab World", *Documenti IAI*, No. 0625, Rome, Istituto affari internazionali.

PEET, Richard (2003), *Unholy Trinity: The IFM, World Bank and WTO*, New York, Palgrave Macmillan.

PERRAULT, Gilles (1990), *Notre Ami Le Roi*, Paris, Gallimard.

PERTHES, Volker (2004), *Arab Elites: Negotiating the Politics of Change*, Boulder, CO and London, Lynne Rienner.

PETERSON, John E. (2002), *Saudi Arabia and the Illusion of Security*, London, International Institute for Strategic Studies.

PETERSON, John E. (2006), "The Kingdom of Enigma", *Survival*, Vol. 48, No. 2, Summer.

PFEIFER, Karen (1999), "How Tunisia, Morocco, Jordan and Even Egypt became IMF 'Success Stories' in the 1990s", *Middle East Report*, No. 210, Spring.

PICARD, Elizabeth (1988), "Arab Military in Politics: From Revolutionary Plot to Authoritarian State", in A. Dawisha and I. Willam Zartman (eds), *Beyond Coercion: The Durability of the Arab State*, Rome and London, Instituto Affari Internazionali/Croom Helm.

PICARD, Elizabeth (1994), "Les habits neufs du communautarisme libanais", *Cultures & Conflits*, No. 15/16.

PICARD, Elizabeth (1997), "Le communautarisme politique et la question de la démocratie au Liban", *Revue Internationale de Politique Comparée*, Vol. 4, No. 3.

PICARD, Elizabeth (1999), *The Demobilization of the Lebanese Militias*, Oxford, Centre for Lebanese Studies.

PICARD, Elizabeth (2000), "Autorité et souveraineté de l'État à l'épreuve du Liban sud", *Maghreb-Machrek*, No. 169, Juillet-Septembre.

PICARD, Elizabeth (2001a), "Le système consociatif est-il réformable?", *The Lebanese System: A Critical Reassessment*, Beyrouth, AUB, 18–19 May.

PICARD, Elizabeth (2001b), "Élections libanaises: un peu d'air à circulé ..", *Critique Internationale*, No. 10, 1.

PIOPPI, Daniela (2007), "The Privatization of Social Services as a Regime Strategy: Islamic Endowments (Awqaf) in Egypt", in O. Schlumberger (ed.), *Debating Arab Authoritarianism: Dynamics and Durability in Nondemocratic Regimes*, Stanford, CA, Stanford University Press.

PIPES, Daniel (1983), *In the Path of God: Islam and Political Power*, New York, Basic Books.

PISCATORI, James (1983), "Ideological Politics in Saudi Arabia", in J. Piscatori (ed.), *Islam in the Political Process*, Cambridge, Cambridge University Press.

POLLACK, Kenneth (2002), *Arabs at War: Military Effectiveness, 1948–1991*, Lincoln, University of Nebraska Press.

PRIPSTEIN POSUSNEY, Marsha (1993), "Collective Action and Workers' Consciousness in Contemporary Egypt", in Z. Lockman (ed.), *Workers and Working Classes in the Middle East: Struggles, Histories, Historiographies*, Albany, NY, State University of New York Press.

PRIPSTEIN POSUSNEY, Marsha and Michele PENNER ANGRIST (eds) (2005), *Authoritarianism in the Middle East: Regimes and Resistance*, Boulder, CO and London, Lynne Rienner.

al-QALLAB, Brig. Musa (2006), "Defence Affairs", *Gulf Yearbook 2005–2006*, Dubai, Gulf Research Center.

QUANDT, William (ed.) (1988), *The Middle East Ten Years after Camp David*, Washington, DC, Brookings Institution Press.

QUANDT, William (1990), *The United States and Egypt*, Washington, DC, Brookings Institution Press.

RABBATH, Edmond (1986), *La Formation historique du Liban politique et constitutionnel*, Beyrouth, Librairie Orientale.

al-RASHEED, Madawai (2006a), *Contesting the Saudi State: Islamic Voices from a New Generation*, Cambridge, Cambridge University Press.

al-RASHEED, Madawai (2006b), "Saudi Arabia: The Challenge of the US Invasion of Iraq", in R. Fawn and R. Hinnebusch (eds), *The Iraq War: Causes and Consequences*, Boulder, CO and London, Lynne Rienner.

RIST, Gilbert (2001), *Le développement, Histoire d'une croyance occidentale*, Paris, Presses de Sciences Po.

RIVET, Daniel (2004), *Le Maroc de Lyautey a Mohammed V: Le double visage du protectorat*, Casablanca, Editions Porte d'Anfa.

RONIGER, Luis (2002), "Clientelism and Civil Sciety in Historical Perspective", Paper for the workshop Demokratie und Sozialkapital – Die Rolle zivilgesellschaftlicher Akteure, Berlin, German Political Science Association, June.

ROSS, Michael (2001), "Does Oil Hinder Democracy?", *World Politics*, Vol. 53, No. 3, April.

ROUGIER, Bernard (2005), "Le Grand Moyen Orient: un moment d'utopie internationale?", *Critique Internationale*, No. 26.

ROUGIER, Bernard (2007), *Everyday Jihad: The Rise of Militant Islam among Palestinians in Lebanon*, Cambridge, MA, Harvard University Press.

ROUQUIÉ, Alain (1980), *Les Partis militaires au Brésil*, Paris, PFNSP.

ROUSSILLON, Alain (1988), *Sociétés islamiques de placement de fonds et ouverture economique*, Cairo, CEDEJ.

ROUSSILLON, Alain (1996), *L'Égypte et l'Algérie au péril de la libéralisation*, Cairo, CEDEJ.

ROY, Olivier (2004), *Globalized Islam: The Search for a New Ummah*, Columbia University Press.

RUGGIE, John Gerard (1993), "Territoriality and Beyond: Problematizing Modernity in International Relations", *International Organization*, Vol. 47, No. 1.

RUGH, William A. (1973), "Emergence of a New Middle Class in Saudi Arabia", *Middle East Journal*, Vol. 27, No. 1, Winter.

SADOWSKI, Yahia (1991), *Political Vegetables? Businessmen and Bureaucrats in the Development of Egyptian Agriculture*, Washington, DC, Brookings Institutions.

SADOWSKI, Yahia (1993), *Scuds or Butter?*, Washington, DC, Brookings Institution Press.

SAFRAN, Nadav (1988), *Saudi Arabia: The Ceaseless Quest for Security*, Ithaca and London, Cornell University Press.

SAGER, Abdulaziz (2005), "Saudi Arabia, Iran and the Search for Security", Gulf Research Center, www.grc.ae.

SAGER, Abdulaziz (2007), "Sudan-Chad Deal another Saudi Diplomatic Win", Gulf Research Center, www.grc.ae.

SAÏD SAADI, Mohamed (2006), "Secteur privé et développement humain au Maroc, 1956–2005", in Royaume du Maroc, *Cinquante ans de développement humain*, Rabat.

SAINSAULIEU, Renaud (ed.) (1990), *L'Entreprise: une Affaire de Société*, Paris, Presses de la FNSP.
SAKR, Naomi (2001), *Satellite Realms: Transnational Television, Globalization and the Middle East*, London, I.B. Tauris.
SALAMÉ, Ghassan (1980), "Political Power and the Saudi State", *MERIP Reports*, No. 91, October.
SALAMÉ, Ghassan (ed.) (1994), *Democracy without Democrats? The Renewal of Politics in the Muslim World*, London, I.B. Tauris.
SALAMÉ, Ghassan (1996), "Le nationalisme arabe, mort ou mutation?", in J. Rupnick (ed.), *Le déchirement des nations*, Paris, Seuil.
SALEM, Elie A. (1992), "A Decade of Challenges: Lebanon 1982–1992", *The Beirut Review*, No. 5, Spring.
SALEM, Paul E. (1993), "Superpowers and Small States: An Overview of American–Lebanon Relations", *The Beirut Review*, No. 5, Spring.
SALHEEN, M. Abdel-Karim (2007), "Kairo im 20. Jahrhundert", in Institut für Auslandsbeziehungen, *Kairo. Bauen und Planen für Übermorgen*, Dettingen.
SAUDI AMERICAN BANK (2002), *Saudi Arabia's Employment Profile*, Riyad, SAMBA.
SAUDI AMERICAN BANK (2006), *Saudi Arabia and the WTO*, Riyad, SAMBA.
SAUDI ARABIAN GENERAL INVESTMENT AUTHORITY (n.d.), *The Economic Cities: Thinking Big*, Riyad, SAGIA, www.sagia.gov.sa/english/index.php?page=ecs-overview.
SAUDI ARABIAN MONETARY AGENCY (various issues), *Annual Report*, Riyad, SAMA, www.sama.gov.sa.
SAUDI ARABIAN MONETARY AGENCY (2006), *42rd Annual Survey*, Riyad, SAMA.
SAUDI ARABIAN MONETARY AGENCY (2007), *43rd Annual Report*, Riyad, SAMA.
SAUDI BRITISH BANK (2007), *Saudi Arabia: Thinking Big*, Riyad, SABB.
SAYEGH, Yezid (1993), "Arab Military Industrialization: Security Incentives and Economic Impact", in B. Korany, P. Noble and R. Brynen (eds), *The Many Faces of National Security in the Arab World*, Houndmills, London, Macmillan.

SCHAMIS, Hector (1991), "Reconceptualizing Latin American Authoritarianism in the 1970s: From Bureaucratic Authoritarianism to Neo-Conservatism", *Comparative Politics*, Vol. 23, No. 2.

SCHEUER, Michael, Stephen ULPH and John C.K. DALY (2006), "Saudi Arabian Oil Facilities: The Achilles' Heel of the Western Economy", The Jamestown Foundation, May.

SCHLUMBERGER, Oliver (ed.) (2007), *Debating Arab Authoritarianism: Dynamics and Durability in Nondemocratic Regimes*, Stanford, CA, Stanford University Press.

SCHMIDT, Steffen W., Laura GUASTI, Carl H. LANDE and James C. SCOTT (eds) (1977), *Friends, Followers, and Factions: A Reader in Political Clientelism*, Berkeley, University of California Press.

SCHMITTER, Philippe C. (1974), "Still the Century of Corporatism?", *Review of Politics*, Vol. 36, No. 1, January.

SCHNABEL, Albrecht and Hans-Georg EHRHART (eds) (2006), *Security Sector Reform and Post-Conflict Peacebuilding*, Tokyo, United Nations University Press.

SCHOLTE, Jan Aart (2005a), "The Sources of Neoliberal Globalization", *Overarching Concerns Programme Paper*, No. 8, Geneva, UNRISD.

SCHOLTE, Jan Aart (2005b), *Globalization: A Critical Introduction* (2nd edn), Basingstoke and New York: Palgrave Macmillan.

al-SEFLAN, A.M. (1980), *The Essence of Tribal Leaders' Participation, Responsibilities, and Decisions in Some Local Government Activities in Saudi Arabia*, PhD thesis, Claremont Graduate School.

SEGEV, Shmuel (2007), *The Moroccan Connection*, Tel Aviv, Matar Press [in Hebrew].

SELMA, Belaala (2004), "Morocco: Slums Breed Jihad", *Le Monde Diplomatique*, November.

SEN, Amartya (2006), *Identity and Violence: The Illusion of Destiny*, New York, W.W. Norton & Co.

SEZNEC, Jean-François (2002), "Stirrings in Saudi Arabia", *Journal of Democracy*, Vol. 13, October.

SGARD, Jérôme (1997), *Europe de l'Est. La transition économique*, Paris, Flammarion.

SHAMBAYATI, Hootan (1994), "The Rentier State, Interest Groups, and the Paradox of Autonomy: State and Business in Turkey and Iran", *Comparative Politics*, Vol. 26, No. 3, April.

SIGNOLES, Aude (2006), "Réforme de l'Etat et transformation de l'action publique", in E. Picard (ed.), *La Politique dans le monde arabe*, Paris, Armand Colin.

SINES, R. (1998), "Towards an Investor-Friendly Policy Environment", in IBTCI, USAID, *Privatization Project, Evaluation Services Contract, Quarterly Review, for the Period 1 January to 31 March 1998*, Cairo.

SIPRI (2007), *SIPRI Yearbook 2007: Armaments, Disarmament and International Security*, Stockolm, http://yearbook2007.sipri.org/.

SOLIMAN, Samir (2006), *al-Musharaka al-siyyasiyya fi intikhabat al-niyabiyya 2005: al-'Awa'iq wa'l-mutatalabat*, Cairo, al-Jam'iyya al-misriyya lil-nuhud bi'l-musharaka al-mujtama'iyya.

SOLOMON, John (2006), "Saudi Arabia's Shiites and their Effect on the Kingdom's Stability", *Terrorism Monitor*, Vol. 4, No. 15, July.

SPRINGBORG, Robert (1989), *Mubarak's Egypt: Fragmentation of the Political Order*, London and Boulder, CO, Westview Press.

STARK, David (1996), "Recombinant Property in Eastern European Capitalism", *American Journal of Sociology*, No. 4.

STEINBERG, Guido (2005), "The Wahhabi Ulama and the Saudi State", in P. Aarts and G. Nonneman (eds), *Saudi Arabia in the Balance*, New York, New York University Press.

STEPAN, Alfred (1989), *Democratizing Brazil: Problems of Transition and Consolidation*, New York, Oxford University Press.

STRANGE, Susan (1996), *The Retreat of the State, The Diffusion of Power in the World Economy*, Cambridge Studies in International Relations, Cambridge University Press.

SULEIMAN, Ezra N. and John WATERBURY (eds) (1990), *The Political Economy of Public Sector Reform and Privatization*, Boulder, CO and Oxford, Westview Press.

TAMMAM, Husam (2006), *Tahawwulat al-ikhwan al-muslimun: tafakkuk al-idiyulujiya wa-nihayat al-tanzim*, Cairo, Maktabat Madbuli.

TAMMAM, Husam and Patrick HAENNI (2003), "Egypt's Air-conditioned Islam", *Le Monde Diplomatique*, September.

TEITELBAUM, Joshua (2000), *Holier than Thou: Saudi Arabia's Islamist Radicals*, Washington, DC, Washington Institute for Near East Policy.

TILLY, Charles (1985), "War Making and State Making as Organized Crime", in P. Evans, D. Rueschemeyer and T. Skocpol (eds), *Bringing the State Back in*, Cambridge, Cambridge University Press.

TILLY, Charles (1990), *Coercion, Capital and European States: AD 990–1990*, Cambridge, MA, Basic Blackwell.
TOBJI, Mahmoud (2006), *Les Officiers de Sa Majesté: Les derives des generaux Marocains 1956–2006*, Paris, Fayard.
TOMES, Robert R. (2005), "Schlock and Blah: Counter-Insurgency Realities in a Rapid Dominance Era", *Small Wars and Insurgencies*, Vol. 16, No. 1, March.
TOZY, Mohamed (1999), *Monarchie et Islam Politique au Maroc*, Paris, Presses de la FNSP.
TRAÏNI, Christophe (2003), "L'épicentre d'un séisme électoral. Le vote Front national en région PACA", in C. Traïni (ed.), *Vote en PACA: les élections 2002 en Provence-Alpes-Côte d'Azur*, Paris, Karthala.
TROFIMOV, Yaroslav (2007), *The Siege of Mecca*, New York, Random House.
TUQUOI, Jean-Pierre (2006), *"Majesté, Je Dois Beaucoup A Votre Pere": France-Maroc, Une Affaire De Famille*, Paris, Albin Michel.
UNDP (2003), *Morocco Millennium Development Goals Report*, Morocco, Morocco United Nations Country Team, http://www.undg.org/index.cfm?P=87&f=M.
UNDP (2006), *Human Development Report 2006/2007*, UNDP, http://hdrstats.undp.org.
UNIFIL (2007), *Lebanon Facts and Figures*, www.un.org/Depts/dpko/missions/unifil/facts.html.
UNOC (2006), *2006 World Drug Report*, Vienna, United Nations.
UN PROGRAMME ON GOVERNANCE IN THE ARAB REGION (2005), *Report to the UNSG of the Fact-finding Mission to Lebanon Inquiring into the Causes, Circumstances and Consequences of the Assassination of Former Prime Minister Rafic Hariri*, 24 March, http://www.pogar.org/publications/unresolutions/lebanon/hariri-report-e.pdf.
US DEPARTMENT OF STATE (2000), *Country Reports on Human Rights Practices: Lebanon 1999*, 23 February, http://www.state.gov/g/drl/rls/hrrpt/1999/420.htm.
US DEPARTMENT OF STATE (2006), *US Support for Lebanon Remains Firm*, 26 December, http://www.state.gov/r/pa/ei/coffee/78162.htm.
US GAO (2006), *Security Assistance: State and DOD Need to Assess How the Foreign Military Financing Program for Egypt Achieves US Foreign Policy and Security Goals*, Report to the Committee

on International Relations, House of Representatives, April, http://www.gao.gov/highlights/d06437high.pdf.

VAIREL, Frédéric (2005), *Espace protestataire et autoritarisme. Nouveaux contextes de mise à l'épreuve de la notion de fluidité politique: l'analyse des conjonctures de basculement dans le cas du Maroc*, Thèse de science politique, Aix-en-Provence, IEP.

VALBJORN, Morten and André BANK (2007), "Signs of a New Arab Cold War. The 2006 Lebanon War and the Sunni–Shi'i Divide", *Middle East Report*, No. 242, Spring.

VANDEWALLE, Dirk (1998), *Libya since Independence: Oil and State Building*, Ithaca, NY, Cornell University Press.

VAŸRYNEN, Raimo (1984), "Regional Conflict Formations: An Intractable Problem of International Relations", *Journal of Peace Research*, Vol. 21, No. 4.

VITALIS, Robert (2006), *America's Kingdom: Mythmaking on the Saudi Oil Frontier*, Stanford, CA, Stanford University Press.

WAHBA, Mourad (1994), *The Role of the State in the Egyptian Economy: 1945–81*, Reading, Garnet Publishing.

WÄRN, Mats (1997), "The Voice of Resistance: The Point of View of Hizballah", *al-Mashriq*, May, http://almashriq.hiof.no/lebanon/300/320/324/324.2/hizballah/warn/index.html.

WATERBURY, John (1983), *The Egypt of Nasser and Sadat*, Princeton, NJ, Princeton University Press.

WATERBURY, John (1994), "Democracy without Democrats? The Potential for Political Liberalization in the Middle East", in G. Salamé (ed.), *Democracy without Democrats? The Renewal of Politics in the Muslim World*, London, I.B. Tauris.

WEISS, Dieter and Ulrich WURZEL (1998), *The Economics and Politics of Transition to an Open Market Economy: Egypt*, Paris, OECD Development Centre.

WICKHAM, Carrie Rosefsky (2002), *Mobilizing Islam: Religion, Activism, and Political Change in Egypt*, New York, Columbia University Press.

WILLIAMSON, John (ed.) (1990), *Latin American Adjustment: How Much Has Happened?*, Washington, DC, Institute for International Economics.

WORLD BANK (1992), *Arab Republic of Egypt: The Private Sector Regulatory Environment*, Washington, DC, World Bank.

WORLD BANK (1997), *The State in a Changing World: The World Development Report*, Oxford, Oxford University Press.

WORLD BANK (1999), *Mise à jour de l'évaluation du secteur privé. Le secteur privé: moteur de la croissance économique marocaine*, Report No. 19975–MOR, Morocco.

WORLD BANK (2005), *Regaining Fiscal Sustainability in Lebanon: A Public Expenditure Review*, MNSED.

WORLD BANK, IFC (n.d.), *Doing Business: Economic Rankings*, www.doingbusiness.org/economyrankings/.

WORLD BANK, IFC (2006), *Doing Business 2007: How to Reform*, Washington, DC, World Bank.

WURZEL, Ulrich G. (2000), *Ägyptische Privatisierungspolitik 1990 bis 1998. Geber-Nehmer-Konflikte, ökonomische Strukturreformen, geostrategische Renten und politische Herrschaftssicherung*, Hamburg/Münster, Lit-Verlag.

WURZEL, Ulrich G. (2004), "Patterns of Resistance: Economic Actors and Fiscal Policy Reform in Egypt in the 1990s", in S. Heydemann (ed.), *Networks of Privilege in the Middle East: The Politics of Economic Reform Revisited*, New York, Palgrave Macmillan.

al-YASSINI, Ayman (1985), *Religion and State in the Kingdom of Saudi Arabia*, Boulder, CO, Westview Press.

YIZRAELI, Sarah (1997), *The Remaking of Saudi Arabia: The Struggle between King Sa'ud and Crown Prince Faysal, 1953–1962*, Tel Aviv, Moshe Dayan Center for Middle Eastern and African Studies.

YOUNG, Richard (2006), "Democracy and Security in the Middle East", *FRIDE Working Paper*, No. 21, Madrid, March.

ZAKARIYYA, Fu'ad (1986), *al-Haqiqa wa'l-wahm fi al-haraka al-islamiyya al-mu'asira*, Cairo, Dar al-Fikr.

ZAKI, Lamia (2005), *Pratiques politiques au bidonville*, Casablanca (2000–2005), thèse pour le doctorat de science politique, Paris, Institut d'Études Politiques de Paris.

ZAKI, Moheb (1999), *Egyptian Business Elites: Their Visions and Investment Behaviour*, Cairo, Konrad-Adenauer Foundation, Ibn Khaldoun Center.

ZUHUR, Shefira (2005), *Saudi Arabia: Islamic Threat, Political Reform, and the Global War on Terror*, Strategic Studies Institute (SSI), March, http://www.carlisle.army.mil/ssi.

INDEX

Abbas, Kamal   24–5
Abd al-Kafi, Umar   35–6
Abdullah, King   83–4, 88–9, 163–5, 171, 279, 286, 290
Abqaiq oil facilities   281
Abrams, Elliot   291
Abu al-Futuh, Abd al-Munim   21–2
Abu al-Futuh, Sabr   39
Abuk-Suud, Safa   35
Afghanistan   14, 23, 33, 278, 281, 307
Ahmadinejad, Mahmoud   290
aid programmes   20, 231, 241, 262, 319, 334–5, 343
Ain al-Tineh meeting (Lebanon)   64
Al-Ahali (weekly newspaper, Egypt)   28
al-Ahram Strategic Center   26
al-Amana Association   204
Alaoui, Moulay Hafid   307
Alexandria Brothers   39
Algeria   12, 20, 68, 201, 266, 299–302, 317, 326, 346
al-Jazeera Television   235
Amal movement   61, 67, 137, 145, 151
American Chamber of Commerce (AmCham), Egypt   107, 118
Amr, Magda   36–7
Aoun, Michel   55–6, 65, 143–4, 251
Arab-Israeli War (1967)   19–20, 277
Arab League   52, 288, 299
Arab Socialist Union (Egypt)   25
Arab Women's Solidarity Association (AWSA) (Egypt)   27
al-'Arabi (weekly newspaper, Egypt)   28
ARAMCO (Saudi Arabian American Oil Company)   77, 163, 169, 177, 292
armed forces, political role of   341–2, 345
Asaad, Kamel al-   136
'ashwa'iyyat (Egypt)   32
Assad, Bashar al-   47, 53, 260, 291
Assad, Hafez al-   53, 62

Assaf, Ibrahim al-   163
Association for the Defence of Rights and Freedoms (Lebanon)   58
Association pour la Taxation des Transactions pour l'Aide aux Citoyens (Morocco)   191
Attar, Muhammad al-   40
authoritarianism
  in Egypt   21, 99–100, 105, 117, 121, 227–9, 243
  image of   219
  in Lebanon   254–5
  in Morocco   309–10, 313
  new model of   7–8, 19, 90, 318, 328, 346–50
  persistence of   237, 243, 325, 343–4
  in Saudi Arabia   283–4, 293
  and security issues   234, 247–8, 260
Awda, Salman al-   281

Baathist regime   47, 51
al-Badil (newspaper, Egypt)   28
Bahrain   289
Baker, James   233
balance of payments (Lebanon)   127
Bandar bin Sultan, Prince   279, 291
"bandwaggoning"   231
Bankers' Association of Lebanon   145
banking   102–3, 139, 194
Banque Populaire Foundation (Morocco)   204
Basri, D.   199
Basri, Idris al-   308, 313
Bekkai, Mbarek   305
Ben Barka, Mehdi   304–5, 313
Benjedid, Chadli   52
Benjelloun family   196
Benslimane, Hosni   313–14
Benzekri, Idris   311
Berri, Nabih   64, 136–7, 143
Bouteflika, Abd al-Aziz   318

Bretton Woods Agreement   20, 333
"Bright Star" exercise (Egypt)   231
Bristol Group (Lebanon)   63–4
Britain *see* United Kingdom
build-operate-transfer (BOT) schemes   152–3
build-own-operate-transfer (BOOT) schemes   108
bureaucracy (Egypt)   101–2
Bush, George senior   233
Bush, George W.   117, 164–5, 235–6, 241–2, 290–1, 313

Cairo Stock Exchange   103
Camp David Accords (1978 and 2002)   20, 220, 232–5
capital flows (Lebanon)   140
capitalism   99, 114, 116, 189, 208
see also crony capitalism
Casablanca bombings (2003)   309–10, 314–16
Casino du Liban (Lebanon)   143
census data (Lebanon)   142, 148
Center for Trade Union and Workers' Services, Egypt   41, 74
Central Inelligence Agency (CIA) (United States)   317
chambers of commerce   85, 107, 327
Chami, H.   197
charitable institutions   201, 332
Chemical Tariff Harmonization Agreement   170
Cheney, Dick   291
China   39, 116, 277, 341, 350
Chirac, Jacques   155
civil associations (Lebanon)   59–60
civil society   27, 54, 57, 67, 70, 257, 312, 347
clientelism   31, 77, 84–90, 121, 148, 151, 199, 255, 326–9, 333
Clinton, Bill   234
Cold War   302, 307, 313, 319, 327
Communist Party (Egypt)   24, 39
Communist Party (Lebanon)   66
communitarianism   142–3, 330, 332
comparative advantage   159–60, 176–9, 182

Confédération Générale des Entreprises du Maroc (CGEM) (Morocco)   197, 209
Confédération Générale du Travail (Lebanon)   260
conscription   224, 226, 252–3
corporatism   84–6, 90, 229, 255, 327, 329, 348
corruption   101–2, 113, 139, 228, 257, 306, 309
Council for the South (Lebanon)   136–7
crony capitalism   11–12, 193, 221, 333
cultural exceptionalism   3

Darwish, Yusuf   24
debt and debt relief   98, 117, 125, 149–50, 154–5, 171, 199, 334
decentralization   187–8, 333, 338
decision-making power   106
defence expenditure   220, 225, 254, 286–8
democratization
 and civil movements   27, 60, 63, 247
 gradual process of   310–15
 and security issues   318–19, 343
 theories of   1–3
 US policy of   117, 234, 241–2, 267
demonstrations   27–8, 41, 61, 64, 67, 239, 332
"dependent security" concept   232–5, 341
depreciation of currencies   190
developing countries   122
Displaced Fund (Lebanon)   136
Doha Agreement (2008)   66, 69, 266
"Dutch disease"   127

education (Morocco)   201–2
Egypt   5–14, 19–43, 88, 97–122, 219–44, 300, 326–7, 330–8, 341–9
Egyptian Organization for Human Rights (EOHR)   27
Egyptian Trade Union Federation (ETUF)   23
election procedures and results   25–6, 142, 239, 242

elites   10, 64, 70, 76, 84, 87, 89, 144, 319, 327–31, 337–8, 347–8
emigration (from Morocco)   202–3
entrepreneurship (Morocco)   188, 192, 209–10
Equity and Reconciliation Commission (Morocco)   311–12
European Union (EU)   14, 190, 300, 311, 317, 319, 347
  Mediterranean partnership agreements   12, 335
Ezz, Ahmad   31–2

Fahd, King   52, 80–3
failed states   13–14
Faisal, King   76
Fassi, Alal al-   305
Fatah   279, 290, 341
Fatah al-Islam   68, 261–2, 340, 344
Fédération des Industries Textiles et de l'Habillement (Morocco)   196–7
financial services (Egypt)   102
foreign direct investment (FDI)   110, 200, 292, 336–7
France   61–2, 69, 313–14
Free Patriotic Movement (FPM) (Lebanon)   65, 145
free-trade zones   12
freedom of the press   28, 237
Fuda, Faraj   22
Future Movement (Lebanon)   65–6

Ganzouri, Kamal   98
Garzon, Baltasar   313–14
Gaza   243
Geagea, Samir   55–6, 65, 142–4
Gemayel, Amin   65, 251
General Agreement on Tariffs and Trade (GATT)   161–2, 190
al-Ghad ("Tomorrow") Party (Egypt)   28–9
Ghali, Yusuf Boutros   98, 117–18
globalization   1–13, 121, 160–1, 164, 182–3, 185, 226, 229, 236–7, 247, 258–9, 275, 325, 328, 336, 339–40, 345–50

Gore, Al   234
"Grapes of Wrath" (Israeli military operation)   265
Green Forum (*Minbar al-akhdar*) (Lebanon)   58
Green Line (Lebanon)   58
"Group of 8 March" and "Group of 14 March" (Lebanon)   64–7, 263
Groupe Islamique Combatant Marocain (GICM) (Morocco)   316
Groupe Salafiste pour le Combat et la Predication (GSPC) (Algeria)   318
Gulf Cooperation Council (GCC)   277, 280, 286–9
Gulf War (1991)   51, 231, 339

Halabi, Nizar al-   260
Hamas   242–3, 279, 290–1, 341
hard power   285
Hariri, Rafiq   47, 55–6, 59, 65, 136, 140, 143, 145, 151, 154–5, 250, 254, 257, 260, 262, 267
Hariri, Saad   65
Hassan II, King of Morocco   52, 299–313
Hassan II Fund for Economic and Social Development   195, 204–7, 334–5
Hawali, Safar al-   281
Haykal, Muhammad Hasanayn   28, 236
Helsinki Accords   310
Helwan (Egypt)   23–4, 41
Hezbollah   14, 54–5, 61, 65–7, 242, 248, 252, 258–66, 291, 330, 344
Hilali, Nabil al-   24
Hobeiqa, Elie   144
Hoss, Salim   154
Hrawi, Elias   53
human capital   116
Human Development Index   201
human rights   59, 85, 119, 260, 301, 310–13, 317, 330, 343
Human Rights Watch   310, 312
Husayni, Abd al-Aziz al-   39
Hussein, Saddam   277, 279

Ibn Khaldun Center for Development Studies (Egypt)   27

Ibn Saud   277
Ibrahim, Saad Eddin   27, 241
Ila al-amam ("Forward") (Marxist-Leninist movement, Morocco)   311
import retrictions (Egypt)   112
import-substitution-industrialization   32
Intifada (Palestinian)   233–6
intifada al-istiqlal (Lebanon)   63
infitah policies   328, 330
inflation   113, 174
interest groups (Saudi Arabia)   84
International Council of Chemical Associations   170
International Finance Corporation   180
International Monetary Fund (IMF)   20–1, 33, 97–8, 189, 233, 332
Intra Holding Company   143
investmemt expenditure   148
  see also foreign direct investment
Iran   227, 234, 278–9, 290–2, 340
Iraq   13–14, 51, 62, 117–18, 234, 258, 278–9, 282, 326, 339–41
"Islamic investment companies"   34–5
Islamic Republic of Imbaba (Egypt)   33
Islamic society   3
Islamism   19–25, 40–2, 74, 81, 84–5, 89, 118, 222–3, 227–8, 235, 240–2, 248–50, 281, 300, 312–16, 329–32, 338–9, 349
  political economy of   32–7
Israel   14, 20, 30, 42, 48, 51, 57, 62, 136, 227, 230–6, 243, 263, 265, 299, 306, 326
Istiqlal ("Independence") Party (Morocco)   305
Italy   6

al-Jama'a al-islamiyya (The Islamic Group) (Egypt)   22, 222, 228
jihad and jihadism   14, 22, 35, 84–9, 261, 267, 278–9, 285, 302, 314–18, 339
Jordan   11–12, 20, 320, 326–9, 346, 349
Juhayman (group/movement, Saudi Arabia)   80
Jumblatt, Walid   62, 65, 136, 143, 145, 260–1

Justice and Charity Association (*al-'Adl wa'ihsan*) (Morocco)   203
Justice and Development Party (Morocco)   11, 41, 203, 312, 330, 349

Kafr al-Dawwar (Egypt)   23, 38–9
Kamal, Ibrahim   31
Kamil, Salih   35
Khaled, Amr   36–7
Khalilzad, Zalmay   291
Khan, Zahid   174
Khoury, Bishara al-   50
Kifaya movement (Egypt)   11, 28–9, 239, 331

labour costs (Saudi Arabia)   172–3
labour force participation rates (Saudi Arabia)   175
labour legislation   12, 200, 208–9, 335
Labour Party (Egypt)   21
Lahoud, Emile   47, 53, 59, 140, 154–5, 251, 254–7, 260–1, 265
Lanigri, Hamidou   310
Lantos, Tom   306–7
Lebanese Association for Democratic Elections   58
Lebanese Association for Human Rights   59
Lebanese Forces   56, 58, 65–6, 145, 252, 260
Lebanese Women's Council   59
Lebanon   8–14, 47–70, 89, 125–56, 242, 247–68, 292, 326–45, 348–9
liberalization
  economic   11, 90, 100–1, 104, 185–6, 190, 196–200, 332, 337
  political   40, 87–8, 284, 327, 332
  see also neo-liberalism
Libya   300

Mabahith Amn al-Dawla (State Security Investigations) (Egypt)   222
Madrid bombings (2004)   316
Maghreb   191, 200, 230, 299, 318
Mahalla al-Kubra (Egypt)   23–4, 38, 41–2

Majlis al-shura   83–6
makhzen concept   303–4
Mansouri, Yassin   314
market-oriented reforms   333
Mashreq   9
Mecca Accord (2007)   290
Medani, Iyad   163
Mezouar, S.E.   197
Middle East Airlines   143
military-industrial complex   109, 342
Military Intelligence (Egypt)   222
"military society"   224–5, 293
minimum wage provisions (Morocco)   197
al-Misri al-yawm (daily newpaper, Egypt)   28
mobile phone services   112, 152–4, 331–2, 343, 349
modernization theory   2
Mohieldin, Mahmoud   31, 98
monopoly   101, 112, 152, 196, 225
Morocco   5–14, 20, 42, 185–213, 240, 299–320, 326–38, 346–9
Movement for Human Rights (Lebanon)   58
Mubarak, Ahmad Ali   41
Mubarak, Ala   31
Mubarak, Gamal   29–31, 40, 42, 107, 117–18, 222, 243, 328
Mubarak, Hosni   19–25, 28–31, 40–2, 97, 106, 114, 117, 221–4, 229, 234, 238–9, 242–4
Mudawana (Morocco)   11
Muhammad V, King of Morocco   305
Muhammad V Solidarity Foundation (Morocco)   206–7
Muhammad VI, King of Morocco   205, 308–15, 318, 320
Muhammad VI Fund (Morocco)   334–5
mujahidin   281, 307, 316
Mukhabarat (General Intelligence)   222, 238, 260
Muslim Brotherhood   11, 21–6, 29, 33–42, 89, 236–9, 242, 329
Mussolini, Benito   277

Nahr al-Barid (Lebanon)   48, 68, 250, 261–3, 344

Naif, Prince   286
Najun min al-nar ("Saved from Hellfire") (Egypt)   32
Nasser, Gamal Abd al-   19, 21, 35, 227
National Democratic Party (Egypt)   19, 41, 221, 236, 238, 265, 328
National Guard (Saudi Arabia)   76, 284, 286, 293
National Initiative for Human Development (NIHD) (Morocco)   201
nationalism   10, 19, 32, 42, 63, 227, 306, 326
Nawaf bin Abd-al-Aziz, Prince   286
Nazif, Ahmad   30, 38, 40, 98, 117
neoclassical economic theory   203
neo-liberalism   1–13, 20–1, 40, 43, 185–9, 208, 325–6, 328, 332–4, 345–50
"new communities" in Egypt   108, 113
New Woman Foundation (NWF) (Egypt)   27
new world order   3
non-governmental organizations (NGOs)   27, 152–3, 237, 313, 330, 332, 347
North Atlantic Treaty Organization (NATO)   287–8
nuclear weapons   232, 235, 279
Nur, Ayman   29–30, 117, 241

off-shoring   197
Office Chérifien des Phosphates (Morocco)   186
oil prices   20–3, 32–3, 88, 111, 117, 135, 292, 332, 334, 347
oil trade   162, 170–1, 276–7
Omnium Nord Africain   194
Organization of the Islamic Conference   279, 299
Oslo peace process   233
Otaibi, Juhayman al-   80
Othman, Amal Abd al-Rahim   34
Oufkir, Muhammad   305–6
outsourcing   11

Palestine   13–14, 30, 243

Palestine Liberation Organization (PLO) 265, 344
paramilitary forces (Egypt) 222
Partnership for Peace (PfP) programme 287–8
paternalism (Saudi Arabia) 88–9
patrimonialism 293, 326, 329, 332, 342–4, 347–8
patronage 75–9, 90, 255, 327, 333
petrochemical industry 160–6, 169, 176–9, 182
petrodollars 32
Phalangists (Lebanon) 65–6
police forces 239, 257
populism 327–32
Portugal 20
"post-Islamist" developments 36
poverty (Morocco) 202, 204
Powell, Colin 265
power relations 74, 285, 291–2
  see also decision-making power
power-sharing 55, 247–8
Presidential Guard (Egypt) 222
privatization 11, 14, 30–1, 90, 100, 103–6, 109, 119, 152, 154, 185–8, 191–9, 211, 226–9, 237, 264, 326–7, 333–4, 337–8
Progressive Socialist Party (PSP) (Lebanon) 65
protest movements 331, 349
public expenditure (Lebanon) 127, 149
  see also defence expenditure
public-private partnerships (Saudi Arabia) 171
public services (Lebanon) 146–9, 152

Qadiri, Abd al-Qadir 313
al-Qa'ida 13, 228, 261–2, 267, 281, 315–18, 340
  in the Islamic Maghreb (AQIM) 318
Qandil, Abd al-Halim 28
Qasim, Hisham 28
Qatar 248, 289
Qornet Shehwan group (Lebanon) 63
Quartet group 243
Qusaibi, Ghazi al- 163
Qusaibi, Khaled al- 163

Ramael, Patrick 313
"realization model" 229
redistributive measures 107, 111–12, 119–21, 132–46, 150–1, 186
Régie des Tabacs (Lebanon) 137
regional framework of analysis 345–6
regional investment centres (Morocco) 198
rendition 317, 319
rentier system 99–100, 105, 110–11, 118, 120, 186
"revolution in military affairs" 13, 231, 264
Rice, Condoleezza 30, 241–2
Rifi, Ashraf 257
Rivet, Daniel 303
"road map" plan for the Middle East 242
Roed-Larsen, Terje 265
rogue states 234
Russia 161–2

Sadat, Anwar al- 19, 21, 25, 97, 103, 108, 111–12, 221, 223, 233, 240
Sadr, Musa al- 136
"Safari Club" (Morocco) 307
Sahwa movement (Saudi Arabia) 81–4
Said, Rifat 24
Saud dynasty 74, 77–81, 88–9, 275–7, 281–5, 289–90, 293, 302, 307, 341
  resilience of 283–5
Saudi Arabia 8–9, 14, 34, 52, 73–90, 159–83, 230–1, 275–93, 307, 326–8, 332–44, 348
Sayyid, Jamil al- 254
sectarianism 250, 252, 256–8, 263–5, 282, 338, 341, 348
securitization 5, 13–14, 227, 229, 247–8, 305, 343, 349
"security dilemmas" 232
security sector 8, 13–15, 219–23, 226, 238–40, 243–4, 247, 250, 256, 267, 278, 287, 292–3, 301–4, 309, 313, 316, 343–5
September 11th 2001 attacks 84, 90, 117–18, 155, 164, 261, 314
Serfaty, Abraham 311

Index

Sfeir, Nasrallah 260
shar'ia 36
Sharon, Ariel 243
Shatir, Muhammad Khayrat al- 33–4
Shazli, Kamal al- 31
Shebaa Farms (Lebanon) 265
Shihab, Fouad 251
Shiism 143, 282, 291
Shubra al-Khayma (Egypt) 23–4
SIGER 194
Siniora, Fouad 263, 267
Sleimane, Michel 54, 66
small and medium-sized enterprises (SMEs) 101–2, 121, 211
social contract theory 32, 120, 334, 338
social dumping (Morocco) 200
social exclusion (Morocco) 203–5
social policies 334–8
social security 150–1, 189, 201–3, 206
socialism 19
soft power (Saudi Arabia) 285, 291–2
Soleiman, Michel 262–3
Soleiman, Omar 242
Solh, Riad al- 50
Solidere (company, Lebanon) 55–6, 152
Somalia 14
South Korea 116
sovereignty 259, 339, 345
Soviet Union 51–2, 310
Spain 313–14
stability of Arab regimes 347–8
state-owned enterprises (SOEs) (Egypt) 103, 105, 108–9
states
 "over-developed" 89
 role and power of 5–9, 12–14, 121, 336–7
stock markets (Egypt) 103, 112
strike action 24, 37–42, 121, 338
structural adjustment programmes 12, 20, 32, 97–8, 185, 190–2, 198–9, 211
student movements 58
subsidies 132–3, 137, 166, 199, 226
Sudan 14, 227
Suweirki, Ragab al- 35
Syria 47, 51–65, 70, 88, 135, 138, 248–66, 291–2, 326, 340, 342, 349

Syrian National Party (Lebanon) 62

Tadawul (Saudi stock exchange) 174
Taif Agreement (1989) 49–54, 60–3, 69, 248, 251–2, 255, 259, 342
Taiwan 116
Tajammu' (National Progressive Unionist Party) (Egypt) 24, 28, 330
Tawhid movement (Lebanon) 35, 144
taxation 113, 154–5, 149–50, 167, 337
terrorism and counter-terrorism 13, 222–3, 228, 235–8, 280–2, 314–18, 339–40, 344
torture 238, 312, 317
tourism 110, 186
trade unions 12, 23–4, 39, 58, 144–5, 336
transition theories 2–5
Tufayli, Subhi al- 260
Tunisia 12, 20, 185, 201, 207, 330, 349
Turkey 42, 68, 330
Turki al-Faisal, Prince 286
26/26 Fund 207

'ulama' 76, 85, 281, 284, 300
unemployment 33, 173–4, 191, 199, 337
Union of Lebanese Disabled Persons 59
Union du Maghreb Arabe 230
Union National des Forces Populaires (UNFP) (Morocco) 305
Union Socialiste des Forces Populaires (USFP) (Morocco) 200, 311
United Kingdom 20, 262
United Nations
 Charter 69, 267
 Development Programme (UNDP) 147, 201
 Interim Forces in Lebanon (UNIFIL) (1978 and 2008) 248, 250, 266–7, 340
 Security Council 69, 262
  Resolution 1559 47, 62, 265
  Resolution 1701 48, 69, 265–6
United States (US) 6, 14, 20, 52, 54, 61, 69, 90, 117, 119, 164, 190,

230–6, 241–2, 261–2, 276–8, 290, 310, 313–14, 317, 339–41, 347, 350
Agency for International Development (USAID)   24, 241
university education   33

value added tax (VAT)   155

Wafd (Egypt)   21
Wahabism   89, 284, 302
Walid, Prince   35
wars, "post-modern" or "new"   13
al-Wasat al-jadid (New Center Party) (Egypt)   37
Washington consensus   185
welfare state provision   334

Western Sahara   306–7, 313, 317
Westphalian state system   259
Wolfenson, James   155
World Bank   20–1, 97–8, 180, 189, 191, 205, 332
World Trade Organization (WTO)   12, 161–72, 176–83, 189–90, 335–7

Yamani, Hashim Abdullah   163
Yemen   14, 86–7, 266, 282
Yussufi, Abd al-Rahman   308
Yusuf, Sami   36

Zainal, Abdullah   163
zakat   35, 167
Zakoura Foundation   204
Zawahiri, Ayman al-   318